CAMPS

Their planning and management

CAMPS

Their planning and management

ROBERT E. WILKINSON, Ph.D.

Professor, Department of Physical Education,
McGill University, Montreal, Canada

with 52 illustrations

The C. V. Mosby Company

ST. LOUIS • TORONTO • LONDON   1981

MOSBY

1906 **75** 1981
YEARS

A TRADITION OF PUBLISHING EXCELLENCE

Cover photo by Peter Van Wagner, Camp Nominique, Quebec, Canada.

Copyright © 1981 by The C. V. Mosby Company

Printed in the United States of America

The C. V. Mosby Company
11830 Westline Industrial Drive, St. Louis, Missouri 63141

Library of Congress Cataloging in Publication Data

Wilkinson, Robert Edwin, 1924-
Camps, their planning and management.

    Bibliography: p.
    Includes index.
    1. Camps—North America—Management. I. Title.
GV198.M35W54   796.54′068   80-26127
ISBN 0-8016-5550-1

C/VH/VH 9 8 7 6 5 4 3 2 1   01/D/043

To

A pioneer in the camping field

for over 50 years

F. M. Van Wagner

Montreal, Canada

Preface

As camps are forced to compete with many other agencies for the general public's recreation dollar, parents are examining the summer camp experience with increasing concern. Whether or not organized camping flourishes in the coming decades will depend, in large measure, on the quality of administrative leadership that organized camps provide.

Both administrative theory and practice are emphasized in this book. The first three chapters describe the present scope of organized camping in North America and underscore the importance of democratizing administration while preserving the basic leadership role of the camp administrator.

The middle chapters focus on management of the human and physical resources available to camp administrators. Because it is people who most significantly shape the camp experience, considerable attention is devoted to staff recruitment, selection, and on-the-job training of camp personnel. Chapter 5 then examines a number of administrative questions regarding the selection, acquisition, development, and maintenance of the physical site.

While no attempt is made in this book to describe specific camp programs, the reader's attention is directed to factors that affect program selection as well as the administrative considerations that influence the implementation of camp programs.

The latter half of the book examines supporting administrative camp services such as camper health and safety, food services, business and fiscal management, and public relations. Because of the growing concern among camp directors and owners regarding the plethora of lawsuits involving camps, particular emphasis is placed on legal responsibility and the importance of adequate preventive measures. In addition, the chapter on food service management treats sanitation and the hazards of foodborne illness in considerable detail.

The final chapter provides a full examination of the question of evaluation. It includes assessment of campers, the staff, the camp program, and the administration, including the director.

A continuing theme that is emphasized throughout the entire text is the need for systematic planning if the quality of camp administration is to be improved. Too often, the summer camp is perceived as a part-time ten-week operation. When planning does not begin until late spring, the administrative function is often superficial and casual. It is to be hoped that this book will help the reader appreciate the importance of careful, ongoing planning in order that camp management may contribute to a more productive and challenging camp experience.

I wish to express my appreciation to a large number of persons who assisted in the preparation of this book. Thanks to more than 60 camp directors whose camps were visited prior to this project; it is hoped that the many innovative ideas they suggested have found their way into this manuscript. Gratitude is expressed to the publishers' reviewers, Dr. Mildred Little at Texas A. & M. University and Dr. Ronald Havard at Kent State University, for their helpful suggestions during the manuscript preparation. To Nadine Chudobey and Chris Zilberman, who provided such able clerical service, and to Filomene Tedone, who prepared the line drawings, a sincere word of thanks. Special appreciation is reserved for my wife, Mary, who not only typed the initial draft of each chapter but, more importantly, provided unlimited support and encouragement during the entire preparation of this book.

Robert E. Wilkinson

Contents

CAMPS

Their planning and management

CHAPTER ONE

Scope and status of camping

I wish to hear the silence of the night, for the silence is something positive
and to be heard. I cannot walk with my ears covered. I must stand still and
listen with open ears, far from the noises of the village, that night may
make its impression on me, a fertile and eloquent silence.
THOREAU

How many of today's children have had
the opportunity to listen to "the silence of
the night" to which the eminent naturalist,
Henry David Thoreau, refers? The answer
is probably "very few." With the industrial-
ization and urbanization of North American
society, human beings have been largely deprived of their association with the natural
world. Only a few decades ago, children
grew up in rural areas or in small villages
and towns. Nature was all around them, and
space in which to move was boundless.
Cities, for the most part, were not designed
with children in mind. Open, rolling hills,
lakes, streams, and wooded areas, which
once comprised a child's playground, have
all too often been replaced by small, con-
gested ashphalt and concrete "play" areas.

As long as an individual was a member of
an agrarian community, daily life was filled
with meaningful activity and work was regarded as essential for survival. But, as people moved to the city, they became pawns
of mechanization and mass production. In
many cases, work became dull, repetitious,
and meaningless, and the individual was regarded as little more than a cog in the machinery of big industry. With this loss in job

satisfaction came loss of dignity and self-
worth. Mechanization in our industrialized
society eventually led to a depersonalization
and dehumanization of individuals to the
point where they became alienated and
even openly rebellious. The noise, confusion, and frustration of urban life became
unbearable for many, and it was at this point
that a back-to-nature movement began. This
heralded the beginnings of organized camping.

CAMPING DEFINED
Informal camping

Today, millions of North Americans take
to the road annually in their quest to "get
away from it all." A camping group is typically comprised of the family, but it may be
two friends or a party of as many as a dozen
or more persons with similar interests. They
may walk, hitchhike, use bicycles or auto-
mobiles, or resort to more novel modes of
transportation such as horseback, canoe, and
snowmobile.

In the early days of informal camping, it
was possible to travel about the country
with considerable freedom and make shelter
almost anywhere one chose to stop. Today,

1

Table 1-1. Acres of land per inhabitant in the U.S.A.*

Date	Acres of land
1850	8216.0
1900	25.5
1950	12.8
1976	8.4
2000	5.4

*From Report of the Outdoor Recreation Resources Review Commission, Outdoor Recreation for America, Washington, D.C., 1962, p. 41.

Table 1-2. Acres of water surface per person in the U.S.A.*

Date	Acres of water surface
1850	1.4
1900	.4
1950	.2
1976	.12
2000	3600 square feet per person

*From Report of the Outdoor Recreation Resources Review Commission, Outdoor Recreation for America, Washington, D.C., 1962, p.41.

this is no longer possible, and campers must now limit themselves to national parks and forests, state and provincial parks, or private camping areas that have been commercially developed to meet the rapidly growing demand for space.

This need for space is becoming one of the most pressing problems for the total camping movement. It may seem inconceivable that in countries such as the United States and Canada, we could possibly be in danger of running short of physical space. However, where there once was an almost unlimited supply of space, land is fast becoming difficult to locate. Per capita physical space is shrinking at an alarming rate (Table 1-1). The availability of water for aquatic recreation is no less disturbing (Table 1-2). The implications of these projections must be obvious. Individuals, organizations, and agencies concerned with use of large tracts of land must work cooperatively to ensure the multipurpose use of existing physical space.

Organized camping

Although increasing numbers of North Americans are engaging in the type of informal camping described above, the main focus of this text is on organized camps. Organized camping differs from informal

camping mainly in size and degree of structure. This structure, as well as it's organization and management, is the basis of this book.

Whereas those persons who engage in family camping or other forms of informal camping, plan such factors as cost, itinerary, safety, menu planning, and program, this planning is usually done on an informal basis. Organized camping implies that detailed planning *must* occur, with appropriate administrative structures to ensure that all will run smoothly for a clientele who is paying for a service.

Organized camping is distinct from schools, clubs, or athletic or recreation programs in that it (1) is located in a natural outdoors environment, (2) utilizes these natural surroundings in program development, (3) provides an intensive experience in cooperative group living, and (4) provides leaders who are specifically trained for this unique experience. Having identified these elements, we can now define camping. The most widely quoted definition is that of the American Camping Association, which states:

Camping provides a creative educational experience in cooperative group living in the out-of-doors. It utilizes the resources of the natural surroundings to contribute significantly to mental,

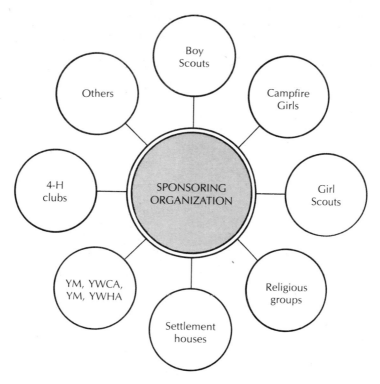

Fig. 1-1. Types of organization camps.

TYPES OF CAMPS

Many different types of organized camps exist today. Because of their heterogeneous nature, they may be classified in a number of different ways including grouping by financial sponsorship, clientele served, length of camp season, sponsoring organization, and program specialization.

Financial sponsorship

Camps are financed in one of three ways: (1) privately funded enterprise, (2) para-physical, social and spiritual growth. It is a sustained experience under the supervision of trained leadership.[1]

public organization that seeks some form of financial support, or (3) public, tax-supported body.

Private, independent camps are owned and operated by an individual, small group, or corporation as a taxable business venture. Many private camps are incorporated. Some are small in size with only a few dozen campers. They do not usually provide the owner with a primary source of income, but are operated on a part-time basis as an avocation or hobby. Teachers and university professors have traditionally operated such camps. Larger camps naturally require a greater time commitment and thus become a full-time occupation. Independent camps, by their very definition, enjoy a degree of freedom in planning and operation that the other two groups do not.

---

1. American Camping Association: Standards for accrediting camps. (Bradford Woods, Martinsville, Ind.: American Camping Association 1965) p. VII.

Parapublic camps include many organization and agency camps that rely on some form of financial support. This assistance may come from donations, public fund raising, or government aid at the local, provincial, state, or federal level. These organizations are, therefore, tax exempt and nonprofit. The list of sponsoring organizations is long; some of the best known are found in Fig. 1-1.

Public (tax-supported) camps are sponsored by all levels of government in both the United States and Canada. Included in this category are the increasing number of outdoor education camps operated by both elementary and secondary public schools. Very few school boards actually own camp sites; the common practice is to rent existing facilities from private or organization camps. With the diminishing availability of land and the immense costs involved, the schools are content to lease sites that have already been developed. Private and agency camp owners find it an effective arrangement because they realize income beyond that of their short summer operation.

Clientele served

Another method of classifying camps is by the group of campers served. By far the greatest number of camps operating in the United States and Canada cater to boys and girls between 7 and 16 years of age. In many cases, separate camps for each sex are conducted because it is considered easier to plan programs to meet the special needs of each group. There are also coeducational camps for this age group. Within coeducational camps, the extent to which children are brought together for program activites varies from those camps that offer independent activities on the same site to a totally integrated program for boys and girls.

The number of day camps for preschool age children is increasing while, at the other end of the continuum, many agency camps provide for the needs of senior citizens. In fact, camps designed to meet the needs of all age groups exist throughout North America (Fig. 1-2).

Organizations that provide for the distinctive needs of a handicapped group are called "special" camps. Current educational philosophy indicates that those persons with some form of handicap or limitation should be included within the "normal" stream whenever possible. However, their condition occasionally so inhibits participation that it is advisable to set up special programs to meet their particular needs. There are "special" camps for mentally retarded, emotionally disturbed, and socially maladjusted persons. Many camps provide for the special needs of physically handicapped persons. When physical handicaps are severe, adaptation of the physical site may be required such as including ramps for campers in wheelchairs or touch lines for blind campers. Modification of diet may also be required as in the case of diabetic campers.

Length of camp session

The length of time a person spends at camp is another means of classification. Camps that children attend daily and return home each afternoon are called *day camps;* camps at which children remain for varying lengths of time are called *residence camps*.

Residence camps are those at which the camper lives and sleeps on the site. Most residence camps operate for 8 weeks in the summer; however, there is a trend toward a 6-week session. A few agency camps operate for as long as 10 to 12 weeks. These semipublic camps frequently receive applications that far exceed their capacity. To meet this demand, the camp season is divided into short periods in which the clientele stay for only 2 weeks (in some cases, 5 to 7 days). The camp may designate specific groups for

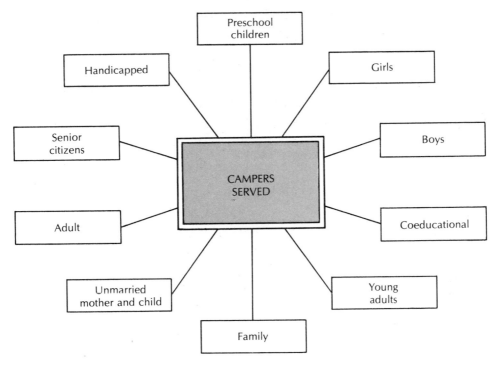

Fig. 1-2. Classification of campers served.

different 2-week periods, that is, first session: girls 6 to 16 years of age; second session: mothers and preschool children; third session: senior citizens; and fourth session: families.

Private residence camps tend to divide the summer into 2-, 3-, or 4-week sessions. Some require campers to be enrolled for the full 6 or 8 weeks. These are referred to as *long-term residence camps* in contrast to the 1- and 2-week, short-term camps described above.

Some camps operate from a base campsite and travel for varying lengths of time by foot, watercraft, animal, or mechanized vehicle. These are called *travel* or *trip camps*.

Day camps are a fairly recent phenomenon within the camping movement and appear to be gaining in popularity. Day camps tend to provide their service for young children, 4 to 8 years of age, the assumption being that this age group should return to their homes each evening. The vast majority of day camps operate Monday through Friday from about 9:00A.M. to about 4:00P.M. Professional camping associations recommend, through their Standards Committees, that day camps be located within an hour's drive of each child's home. Unfortunately, some of these day camps are located in the heart of large cities and are hard-pressed to satisfy any reasonable definition of a camp. This problem has confronted district camping associations for years. Many authorities believe that these operations should not qualify for membership within a camping association since they are little more than an extension of regular year-round programs. Others argue that, since they call themselves a camp, the public looks on them as

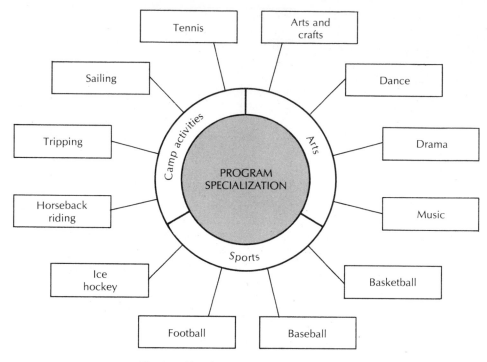

Fig. 1-3. Classification of camps by program.

Table 1-3. Classification of camps by length of season

Type of camp	Length of session
Day	Five days per week (for up to 8 weeks)
Resident, short-term	Five to 14 days
Resident, long-term	Two to 8 weeks or more

such and the entire camping association will suffer if they do not maintain the standards of the association. Some leaders who favor including them in the association suggest that they be placed in a special category called "City Day Camps" under a modified definition of the word "camp."

Day camps may be short-term or long-term. Independent day camps usually offer sessions of 3, 4, 6, or 8 weeks, while many agency day camps have multiples of 1- or 2-week sessions. Table 1-3 illustrates the three main classifications of camps by length of camp season.

Program specialization

A typical camp offers a broad program of activities in the belief that the program must be diversified enough to satisfy the varied needs and interests of its clientele. The vast majority of camps, whether private, semi-public, or public, adopt this approach to program development. However, a growing number of "special interest" camps concentrate on one or two program areas.

Special interest camps devote from 50% to 80% of the total program time to their particular concentration and supplement this with secondary activities such as swimming, boating, and camp fires. The range of program specialization is great. Some have focused on the arts and aesthetic areas, some feature sports camps, and some promote those activities traditionally associated with camping and the outdoors. A sample of typical specialized programs is shown in Fig. 1-3.

CAMPING'S UNIQUE CHARACTERISTICS

Too often, educational and recreational agencies have been guilty of espousing claims for development of human potential that are difficult, if not impossible, to substantiate. Classroom teachers claim to inculcate tolerance and respect for others. Sunday school teachers seek to imbue high standards of integrity in their students. Athletic coaches claim that their players learn sportsmanship and fair play through sports. Social workers defend their ability to change values regarding respect for the law.

Camping personnel have been no less optimistic regarding their claims for a summer at camp. Administrators have been too inclined to make grandiose assertions regarding the unique contributions of the camp experience. The word *unique* implies that the contribution is unequalled or at least rare. In other words, no other agency or institution is capable of realizing that same outcome as effectively as the camp. Camps cannot be all things to all people.

What then can be said about the special characteristics of the camp experience? Rather than talk in terms of *unique contributions*, it is perhaps more realistic to speak of the *unique characteristics* of the camp experience that, if thoughtfully utilized, provide a singular opportunity to effect certain changes in individuals during their stay at camp. Three of these characteristics will be examined briefly.

Outdoor setting

The one thing that sets camping apart from all other institutions is its physical setting. Camps are usually situated on generous tracts of land with a balance between open recreation areas and somewhat primitive wooded areas. Most camps have waterfront property on sea, lake, or river. This natural environment provides the fundamental quality that characterizes a camp. Within this unparalleled setting, campers move freely during all their waking hours. At night, they may sleep under the stars, under canvas, or in a bunk where the sounds, smells, and sights of nature surround them. The conditions of such a physical setting are optimal for instilling within the individual an appreciation of nature's beauty. Even the most blasé youngster will be awed by the experience of sleeping under a stand of giant redwoods or stately pines. Every child is capable of appreciating the exquisite beauty of a cobweb laced with pearls of early morning dew. The true meanings of soil erosion, forest conservation, and air and water pollution are objectively demonstrated as the theory of the classroom and textbook becomes reality before one's very eyes. Nature provides the backdrop against which many experiences are possible. Whether the camp capitalizes on the opportunity to utilize these fabulous resources is another matter.

Total immersion in community living

A second unique characteristic of the camp experience is that the individual is totally involved for every waking hour of every day. In addition, within this immersion, virtually every facet of community involvement is brought into play. All the ingredients of group living are present in a controlled environment. Most children are subject to much adult authority and decision making in the city, whether at home, school, or on the playground. For the first time, they now have the opportunity to associate continuously with their peers. Under wise leadership, children become directly involved in decision making and setting rules for their own conduct. In addition, they should have opportunities to develop self-reliance and self-discipline as they are released from their dependence on family and other adult figures.

Freedom with supervision

The well-conceived camp environment should seek to preserve a delicate balance between freedom and supervision. Camp leaders should actively strive to promote an informal structure with a minimum of external demands and traditional authority. Concurrently, the camp staff must provide the direction necessary to ensure not only a healthful and safe environment but one conducive to optimal development of the camper. Because of the unique physical setting and nature of camp programs, the camper-staff ratio may be as high as three or four to one. The camper-leader relationship is thus a very unique one in which the counsellor is, at times, parent, at other times teacher, but mostly a friend. The counsellor's relative youth, as compared with the traditional adult figure, helps to make this special relationship possible. The real challenge for camp administrators is to mask planning and management behind an air of relaxation and informality. Although permissiveness has become a nasty word in our schools and homes, the camp must seek to provide a permissive atmosphere that is positive and provides the child with freedom to grow. Campers should not feel surrounded by constant, frantic activity and regimentation. If quiet contemplation and reflection are valid exercises for adults, should they not have equal meaning for children?

If these characteristics are the unique advantages of camping what, if any, are the limitations of the camp experience? Two deserve mention. The first is obvious: the length of the camp session. In spite of the special advantages that camps enjoy, it may be difficult to effect significant growth when the length of the experience is as short as 1 or 2 weeks and only 2 months at best.

A second limitation is the dramatic difference between regular urban experiences and camp life. The period of adjustment is obviously greater for some campers than for others. The problem is particularly acute if a child experiences difficulty in "settling in" and is only registered for a short-term session. Everything we know about transfer of learning suggests that the more that two situations, as perceived by the learner, are similar, the greater the chance of effective transfer. If life in the camp community is dramatically different from that of the other 10 months of the year, the possibility of any significant transfer is remote.

SETTING OBJECTIVES

People are the most valued commodity on earth. In the final analysis, every camp organization must measure its ultimate worth by how it influences people. Human growth and betterment become the raison d'etre for the entire camping movement. Individuals everywhere have dreams and goals that they set for themselves. These goals represent human objectives, and groups of people seek fulfillment of these objectives through association with different organizations. Camps comprise but one of these institutions.

Camp administrators are confronted with two fundamental questions: "What is it we should be attempting to accomplish?" and "Have we defined in clear and specific terms what we want to achieve?" Every camp director who wishes to be successful must set goals. Objectives represent the signposts that give the camp direction and purpose toward these goals. A camp without clearly stated objectives is like a ship without a rudder; it drifts pointlessly, lacking a clearly charted route and destination.

Once having established goals for the camp, the administrator must then attempt to articulate, in very precise terms, the objectives to be sought. Such objectives must represent obtainable ends that can be clearly communicated to both parents and campers. Objectives must also serve as standards or measures against which the success or failure of the camp will be evaluated.

Another important approach in developing objectives is to ask the recipient of the organization's services what they seek as outcomes from the program. Some work has been done within the professional camping associations to sample camper and parental objectives.

Parental expectations of camp

Altman[2] conducted an extensive survey in 1975 in an attempt to determine why parents send their children to resident summer camps. The study was sponsored by the National Jewish Welfare Board and involved 16 nonprofit, Jewish camps under Jewish communal auspices in the United States and Canada. The results of the study provided 31 different reasons why parents send their children to summer camp. The most important are:

1. Personal development of child (for example, increased independence and self-discipline)—16%
2. Social development of the child (for example, making friends and living with peers)—13%
3. The camp program—11%

4. Living in a country environment—8%
5. Having fun—7%
6. Friends also attending camp—5%
7. Working parents—3%
8. Educational values—3%
9. Enrichment of Jewish heritage, culture, education, and so forth—3%
10. Being with other Jewish children—3%
11. Getting away from siblings—3%
12. Others—25%

These findings show that parents view the resident camp experience as one that plays an important role in the personal and social development of their children. This is consistent with the views of active professionals in the camping field.

When Altman asked those parents who did not send their children to camp for the reasons, the findings were as follows:

1. Child did not want to go to camp—25%
2. Child was too old for camp—20%
3. Child was too young for camp—10%
4. Cost of camp—12%
5. Family had other vacation plans—8%
6. Child's friend was not attending camp—7%

Of those children who did not attend camp, 54% indicated that they had previously attended a resident camp. The majority of those children cited age as the reason for not returning.

Camper expectations of camp

Very little research has been done to determine why children want to attend a resident summer camp. One study by Corbett[3] involved 220 girls, 10 to 17 years of age. They listed the following as the primary reasons for attending camp:

1. Wanted to learn new skills

2. Altman, S. M.: The impact of family leisure—time patterns on Jewish resident camping. (New York: National Jewish Welfare Board, 1975).

3. Corbett, M.: Survey reveals camper interests, Camping Magazine **47**:2, Nov./Dec., 1974.

2. Wanted opportunity to try new activities such as sailing
3. Wanted to use newly learned skills in the camp program

Kruger[4], a camp director for over 40 years, observes that as children grow older, their program interests tend to narrow and become quite specific. They seek more intensive experiences in aquatics, crafts, outtripping, and so forth. This suggests the possible need for greater specialization of program content, especially for older campers.

General camp objectives

Objectives range from the general to the specific. Explicit objectives may be developed for each activity offered in the camp program. Even within a given activity, the objectives for different age groups will vary. Objectives will naturally differ from one camp to another as they reflect the particular philosophy of that organization.

Although objectives may be highly specific, many professional groups and individuals have developed general goals that are designed to meet the needs of most camps. Such lists of general objectives reflect a high degree of consistency and uniformity. Perhaps the most widely publicized set of general objectives are those prepared by the American Camping Association (ACA).

1. To provide each camper with the opportunity for wholesome fun and adventure in a safe and supervised outdoor program.

Unless individuals thoroughly enjoy the camp experience, there is little hope of them gaining the benefits sought. Too often, public education "turns children off" because it is regarded as too formal and too structured. Because so many camp leaders are teachers during 10 months of the year,

there has been a tendency to transfer the formality and authoritarianism of school to the camp environment. Camp administrators must be alert to this danger and continually seek to achieve what might be termed *structured freedom* within camps.

Another quality inherent in this objective is adventure. One of the things that human beings have forfeited with urbanization has been natural adventure. Some would argue that there is plenty of adventure in our cities: the challenge of the increasing use of tobacco, alcohol, and nonmedical drugs, the challenge of successfully navigating a busy downtown intersection, and the challenge of sheer survival on our busy highways. Such experiences should be construed, not as adventure, but as hazards that society should seek to redress. True adventure implies a stirring or thrilling experience and may involve some degree of daring, but never risk. Camp offers an ideal setting in which opportunities for exciting adventure abound. For some persons, it will mean the completion of an exceptionally difficult portage while travelling by canoe. For another person, it will be marked by a challenging traverse while scaling a mountain. For the youngest campers, it may be the thrill of netting tadpoles in a muddy pond.

The final ingredient in this first objective is the provision of supervision under competent leadership to ensure that this outdoor experience is fun filled and adventurous without the element of risk.

2. To help develop a concept of safe and healthful living by stressing wholesome daily health habits; by stressing safety in camp skills; by offering a chance for increasing strength, vitality, and endurance; and by fostering freedom from mental tensions.

Four components are found in this objective; safe and healthful living habits, safety in program participation, physical well-being, and freedom from stress.

---

4. Kruger, J.: Director, Camp Mah-Kee-Nac, Interview, November, 1975. In Altman, S. M.: Assessing reasons for attending camp, Research Camping and Environmental Education. (University Park, Pa., Pennsylvania State University, 1976).

One of the great advantages of the camp experience is that it involves total community living. But even more important is the fact that almost all facets of the environment can be manipulated by the camp staff. Rest, sleep, diet, and personal cleanliness all may be controlled in such a way that children learn much about personal health and safety.

At the same time, campers have an opportunity to learn how to participate safely in a wide range of activities. They learn that they should never swim without a "buddy," should not stand up in a canoe, should never water ski without wearing a flotation belt, should never whittle while using their knee as a work table, and should always carry an axe at the throat of the handle with the blade turned away from their body. Some camp activities are inherently more dangerous than others, and safety education is an integral part of participation. Such activities include archery, use of a knife, axe, and power tools, canoeing, sailing, mountaineering, riding, riflery, out-tripping, and most water sports.

Many activities that are indigenous to the camp setting involve strenuous physical activity. It is, therefore, not surprising that one of the objectives of camps is to contribute to the physical fitness of the individual. It should not be inferred that only those activities requiring strength, flexibility, and endurance should be included in the program. It *is* implied that there will be adequate provision for such activities.

Much has been written about the threat of urbanization and mechanization to mental well-being. If it is true that the hustle, noise, and frantic pace of present-day city life has a deleterious effect on human beings, surely it follows that to retreat back to nature with its quiet, order, and solitude will indeed have a cathartic effect. A word of caution, however; unless planned otherwise, the camp routine may simply trans-plant the noise, rush, and chaos of the city to the campsite.

3. To contribute to the development of "at-home-ness" in the natural world by imparting an understanding of and appreciation for the world of nature, by fostering an understanding of man's dependency on nature and a sense of responsibility for conservation of natural resources, and by increasing the ability to use basic camping skills.

This objective points up the need to recognize the difference between the world of human beings and the world of nature. With the acceptance of this difference should come a deeper appreciation of our North American heritage as we emulate the ways of the early Indians and pioneers.

With each passing decade, we continue to ravage our natural resources. Camping must play a leading role in sensitizing people to the need for immediate and forceful action. Conservation is a multi-faceted problem that includes soil erosion; timberland management; disappearing wetlands; water, air, land, and wildlife pollution; and contempt for outdoor recreation areas.

City dwellers must learn many skills if they are to enjoy nature without taking all their modern gadgets and conveniences with them. Without a Coleman stove, is it possible to cook meals over an open fire? What tinder should be used on a rainy day? What wood fuel will give a hot, fast fire for coffee, or a slow fire for pancakes or toast? Hundreds of such tips and skills must be learned to cope comfortably in the outdoors.

4. To increase a camper's concept of spiritual meanings and values through encouraging the development of a kinship with the security in an orderly universe, and through gaining an understanding of and appreciation for persons of other religions, cultures, nationalities and races.

Many individuals who are exposed to simple, rustic surroundings and who are encouraged to observe the wonders of nature develop an awareness regarding the order and interdependency of nature. The balance in nature is made apparent, resulting in a respect for the universe and man's place in it. With this awareness comes an appreciation of the beauty to be found in nature. For many people, such an appreciation does not just happen; it must be carefully nurtured. How old must a child be to glimpse the silvery arrows of sunlight coming through a giant stand of Douglas fir to the forest floor, to feel the majestic grandeur of the Rocky Mountains, or to truly see the riot of color of an alpine meadow after an early morning shower?

As individuals "develop kinship with the security in an orderly universe," they become aware of their limited role in the total scheme of things. As this role is brought into much sharper perspective, they should develop a more acute understanding of themselves and their relationship toward others. Tolerance and respect for those who may be different should be strengthened. But again, it must be emphasized that these modifications do not just happen with a change of physical environment: enlightened leadership is required to serve as the catalyst. Without it, growth cannot be expected.

5. *To encourage the development of skills and knowledges that may contribute to wholesome recreation during later years.*

With each passing decade, the workweek grows shorter. It has been conservatively estimated that after subtracting working hours, time for sleep, travel time to and from work, and time for the normal daily routines (including eating, dressing, and so forth), there remains between 40 and 55 hours per week for persons to do with as they wish. Unfortunately, many individuals lack the skills to productively enjoy their leisure. A wholesome camping experience should provide some skills that may contribute to a more satisfactory use of free time, including those abilities necessary to camp

with confidence and relative ease, as well as recreational skills that are normally indigenous to camp, including archery, orienteering, mountaineering, and ability to handle small watercraft such as a canoe or sailboat.

6. *To contribute to the development of the individual through adjustment to group living in a democratic setting by instilling in him a sense of worth of each individual, by helping him to function effectively in a democratic society, and by helping him to develop a sense of social understanding and responsibility.*

This final objective implies that several things can happen to individuals as they truly become active participants in group living, including a first-hand appreciation of democratic decision making as it involves leader and follower and subjugating one's personal desires to the will of the majority. As campers are encouraged to stand on their own two feet and make some decisions for themselves, they gain self-confidence and a personal sense of worth. Finally, they should be led to accept the viewpoint of those who are different from themselves, and this in turn should bring about increased tolerance and open-mindedness toward others.

PROFESSIONAL CAMPING ASSOCIATIONS

Early in the development of camping in both the United States and Canada, those involved in camping recognized the need of formally organizing themselves into a professional association. Such an organization provides a strong and unified voice for those in the camping field.

Today the American Camping Association (ACA) has a membership of approximately 6500 camp directors, camp owners, and camp staff members, and over 2400 accredited camps within the organization. These camps represent about one million acres of prime recreation land and a property investment of over one billion dollars. Whereas there are some 2,000,000 persons attending *accredited* camps, it is estimated that the number of youth who annually participate in organized camping exceeds 8,000,000 persons in over 10,000 organized camps.[5]

The ACA is divided into five geographic regions, and each region is further subdivided into 34 sections, each with its own executive officers and program. The avowed purpose of the ACA is to "assure the highest professional practices and administration and extension of the unique experience of organized camping." To achieve this purpose, the ACA has three primary goals:

1. To maintain contact with contemporary societal forces as related to camping and to develop appropriate response and action
2. To enhance the quality of organized camping experience
3. To interpret the value of organized camping to the public[6]

In Canada, the Canadian Camping Association is based in Toronto, and each province, except Prince Edward Island, has its own association.

Both national organizations publish much relevant material to assist their members, including a regular journal or newsletter and directory of accredited camps in each association. The ACA prepares an annual reference and buying guide for its members as well as a parents' guide for prospective camp families.

Code of ethics

One criterion of a professional association is that it develop a set of principles that serve as guidelines for the ethical and business practices of its members. With the increased attention and concern of the public toward organized camps, it is vital that camp directors give sincere attention to ethical conduct in relation to campers, parents, staff, and the general public. The ACA membership reaffirmed the following ethical practices in March, 1978.[7]

EXEMPLARY ETHICAL PRACTICES FOR CAMP DIRECTORS*

The members of the American Camping Association recognize and support the concept that custody of others' lives and welfare as well as the earth and its living things, calls for reverence for such life, in dedication and commitment to a higher good. Whatever form such a dedication and commitment may take, it must be essentially moral in nature.

The members further:

a. recognize and support the concept of an ecological conscience that a thing is right when it tends to preserve the integrity, stability and beauty of the biotic community
b. recognize and support the concept that a camp is necessarily a total community within the society, with significant impact upon its inhabitants' capacity to learn, grow, develop, assimilate values, create and relate to other persons and the earth
c. accept, respect and will be responsive to the rich diversity of our society

The Association recognizes the Camp Director as the primary professional person assuming the greatest responsibility for actual camping practices. Therefore, the Association shall ask the person assuming this responsibility to subscribe to the following, to the extent permitted by law.

5. Editorial: What the ACA means to your child, Parents' Guide to Accredited Camps, Camping Magazine, pp. 4-5, 1978.
6. American Camping Association: Camp standards and interpretations for the accreditation of organized camps, (Bradford Woods, Martinsville, Ind.: American Camping Association, 1978) p. 1.

7. American Camping Association: Camp standards and interpretations for the accreditation of organized camps, (Bradford Woods, Martinsville, Ind.: American Camping Association, 1978) back cover.
*Reprinted courtesy of the American Camping Association. Printed copies are available from the American Camping Association Publications Service, Bradford Woods, Martinsville, Ind. 46151. Contact them for current price information.

I shall maintain a camp membership enrollment policy without regard to religious affiliations (unless my camp is operated either by or in behalf of an established church for bona fide religious purposes), national origin, or race.

I shall hire, assign, promote and establish other conditions of employment for staff (professional, semi-professional or clerical) without regard to religious affiliation (unless my camp is operated either by or in behalf of an established church or for bona fide religious purposes), national origin, or race.

I shall be truthful and fair in representing my camp and other camps by whatever medium of communication.

I shall be truthful and fair in securing and dealing with campers and staff.

I shall strive to conduct my camp in such a way as to build good will not only for my camp but also for the camping movement.

I shall strive to be responsible and sensitive to the local community influenced by the presence of my camp.

I shall provide a written enrollment policy for all applicants including fees, payment schedules, discounts, dates of arrival and departure, together with a clearly stated refund policy.

I shall provide for each staff member a written job description and contract including period of employment, compensation, benefits and exceptions.

I shall tell parents my procedure for promptly notifying them in the event their child is hospitalized or suffers accident or illness.

I shall maintain in professional confidence camper and staff information, observation, or evaluation.

I shall promptly consult with parents or guardians as to the advisability of removing a child from camp should it be clear that the child is not benefiting from the camp experience.

I shall refrain from actively recruiting any camper or staff member known by me to be currently enrolled or employed at another camp.

I shall honor my financial commitments to parents, staff, vendors and others.

I shall use the proper membership classification and camp registration category as may be defined by the National Board and shall use the ACA seal of accreditation in conformance with policies of the Standards Program.

I shall abide by ACA requirements and respect ACA guidelines for my profession.

The Canadian Camping Association (CCA)* has developed a similar ethical code. The following is the National Code of Ethics for that Association:

1. Our energies are directed to furthering the growth and quality of life of youth and adults through education and recreation in the camping field.
2. We undertake to conduct ourselves in such a manner so as to gain the esteem and confidence of other camping personnel, as well as to respect the dignity of our associates.
3. We will familiarize ourselves with and comply with all government laws and regulations governing the operation of camps.
4. We shall adhere to the Constitution and By-laws of the Canadian Camping Association.
5. We will strive to maintain and improve upon the standards for camping developed by the Association.
6. We shall concern ourselves with the welfare of our national environment and encourage others to do likewise.
7. Our advertising and publicity shall avoid misleading statements and superlatives.
8. We shall refer to the Executive Committee any unethical practices which could be detrimental to the integrity and dignity of the Association.
9. We will help to make the public aware of the Association and its constant striving towards professionalism in the organized camping movement throughout Canada.

Camp standards

In all parts of the United States and Canada, camps are subject to local, state, prov-

---

*From the Canadian Camping Association, Toronto, Ontario, Canada.

incial, and federal laws and regulations. These regulations are primarily concerned with aspects of health and safety. The Center for Disease Control, Public Health Service, has maintained for the United States a Compendium of current laws by state and topic.

In addition to governmental regulations, any professional organization must also be dedicated to maintaining and improving the standard of service that it provides. The ACA and the CCA have developed standards accreditation programs. In each national organization, committees are responsible for developing desirable practices and standards for organized camps.

The ACA has worked to develop acceptable camping standards for nearly 50 years. This accreditation process involves examination of four basic areas—campsite, administration, personnel, and program.

Standards do not remain fixed or static; they are under continuous review and revision. Nor do standards seek to require rigid standardization. On the contrary, they are developed so that many camps with differing philosophies, objectives, and program emphases can be embraced within the Association. In the words of van der Smissen, president of ACA:

In no way, do the Standards attempt to establish sameness in camp program among those camps meeting accreditation criteria: there are as many types of programs and approaches to programming as there are camps—but there is a discernible thread of common concern for meaningfulness of the camp experience.[8]

While the ACA recognizes the importance of high standards in all camps and makes its standards manual available to anyone, only ACA members may have their camps visited and accredited. Two certified

"visitors" make an on-site visit to determine the extent to which a camp is able to comply with the standards.

SELECTED BIBLIOGRAPHY

American Camping Association: Camping is education. (Bradford Woods, Martinsville, Ind.: American Camping Association, 1960).

American Camping Association Monograph: Camp, the child's world. Bradford Woods, Martinsville, Ind.: American Camping Association, 1962).

Ball, A.: A hard look at camping—today and tomorrow, Camping Magazine, 45(4):12-13, 20, May, 1973.

Carlson, R. E.: The values of camping. (Bradford Woods, Martinsville, Ind.: American Camping Association, 1975).

Clarke, G. A., and Eells, E. P.: Early findings on values of camping now available, Camping Magazine, 47(2):8-9, Nov./Dec., 1974.

Dimock, H. S., editor: Administration of the modern camp. (New York: Associated Press, 1948).

Donaldson, G. W., and Goering, O. editors: Perspectives on outdoor education readings. (Dubuque, Iowa: William C. Brown Co., Publishers, 1972).

Hanson, R. F., and Carlson, R. E.: Organizations for children and youth. (Englewood Cliffs, N.J.: Prentice-Hall, Inc., 1972).

Hasell, J.: Standards for camp, Canadian Camping, 27(2):20-22, January, 1975.

Johnson, W. C.: The unique mission of the summer camp. (Bradford Woods, Martinsville, Ind.: American Camping Association, 1973).

Jubenville, A.: Outdoor recreation planning. (Philadelphia: W. B. Saunders Co., 1976).

Mason J. A.: Uncertain outposts: the future of camping and the challenge of its past, Camping Magazine, 51(1):16-20, 25-31, Sept./Oct., 1978.

Melzer, A. O.: Camping—where do we go from here? Camping Magazine 44(1):8-9, January, 1972.

Mitchell, A. V. et al.: Camp counseling. (Philadelphia: W. B. Saunders Co., 1970).

Pearse, J.: If I were to send my child to camp, Canadian camping, 27(2)5-8, Jan. 1975.

Rodney, L. S., and Ford, P. M.: Camp administration. (New York: John Wiley & Sons, Inc., 1971).

Schmidt, E. F.: How parents select a camp, Camping Magazine, 46(5):4, Mar. 1975.

Shivers, J. S.: Camping: administration, counseling, programming. (Englewood Cliffs, N.J.: Prentice-Hall, Inc., 1971).

Webb, K. editor: Camping for American youth, a declaration for action. (Bradford Woods, Martinsville Ind.: American Camping Association, 1962).

---

8. Editorial: What the ACA means to your child, Parents Guide to Accredited Camps, Camping Magazine, p. 5, 1978.

CHAPTER TWO

Elements of administration

A leader is best when people barely know he exists, Not so good when people obey and acclaim him, Worst when people despise him.

Fail to honor people, they fail to honor you. When his work is done, his aim fulfilled, They will say, "We did it ourselves."
LAO-TSE

The goals and objectives of camping were discussed at some length in Chapter one. To realize these desired outcomes, it is necessary to establish an administrative framework that fully utilizes the human and material resources available within a given camp. Only as these resources are carefully organized can the camp's stated objectives be achieved. This is the essence of administration. Stated in its simplest terms, administration is concerned with getting the job done in the most efficient manner possible.

THE MEANING OF ADMINISTRATION

In the early days of organized camping, little consideration was given to a systematic approach to camp administration. Rather, the attempt was to avoid the formality and structure that typified organizations found in the city. A trial and error method was adopted with little concern for administrative principles. As long as camps remained small and intimate, the director could get by with this type of "hit or miss" approach. Today, administrative principles and practices are considered essential to the efficient running of any organization. Administration is the machinery that makes the camp run

smoothly toward the attainment of its stated objectives.

Administration serves people. It is not an end in itself, but rather the means by which people, through various organizations, attain more meaningful, productive lives. It has been demonstrated many times that organizations do not automatically operate smoothly and effectively: they require skilled leadership and direction. This is called *administration*.

Halpin[1] states that there are four components of administration. The first of these is the *task*. Task refers to the purpose or mission of the organization. The purposes of the camping movement were developed at some length in the previous chapter. Second, there must be a *formal organization*, in this case, the camp. There must also be a *work group* comprised of individuals who have been selected to fill specific positions within the camp structure. Finally, there is a *leader* who is selected from among the members of the organization and has the ultimate responsibility for seeing that the *task*

---

1. Halpin, A. W.: Theory and research in administration. (New York: The Macmillan Co., 1966) p. 30.

of the *organization* is accomplished. This does not preclude the possibility of a group of individuals accepting the leadership role, as will be pointed out in the next chapter. With these four factors in mind, it is possible to now define administration.

Administration is conceived as the necessary activities of those individuals (executives) in an organization who are charged with ordering, forwarding and facilitating the associated efforts of a group of individuals brought together to realize certain defined purposes.[2]

Careful scrutiny of many current definitions shows no significant change in the meaning of the term *administration* over the past 30 years. Such an examination makes it abundantly clear that administration is fundamentally concerned with interpersonal relations and the management of human behavior. The key, therefore, to effective camp management is the quality of the leadership.

ADMINISTRATIVE LEADERSHIP

Early studies that examined the question of what differentiates a leader from others focused heavily on personality traits and other characteristics. This approach did not prove very fruitful and Gouldner, as early as 1950, wrote: "At this time there is no reliable evidence concerning the existence of universal leadership traits."[3]

There is growing evidence to indicate that administrative skill is very much learned and is the product of "on-the-job" experience. An individual may function effectively in one administrative role but be quite useless in another. Recent findings would suggest that the qualities and skills required of the administrator are largely determined by the demands of a particular situation.

In spite of the foregoing statements, it is generally accepted that there are some basic attributes that virtually all administrators should possess. These are perhaps best summed up by Tead[4] who stresses the need for:

1. Sheer physical and nervous vitality and drive
2. Ability to think logically, rationally, with problem-solving skill that "gets to the point" more quickly than average
3. Willingness to take the burdens of responsibility for executive decisions and actions
4. Ability to get along with people in a sincerely friendly, affable, yet firm way
5. Ability to communicate by voice or pen in effective ways

The five qualities described by Tead more than 20 years ago are precisely the attributes that a good camp administrator should possess for effective leadership.

I have asked students in my university administration course to list the one outstanding quality that personified the best camp director they had ever known. The following list is a representative sample of those qualities cited most frequently:

1. Established clearly defined objectives for the camp
2. Set high standards for self and staff
3. Placed the right person in the right position
4. Knew the staff, their expectations and limitations
5. Instilled confidence and trust
6. Welcomed and respected the opinion of others
7. Was always available and was a good listener
8. Was considerate and consistent

2. Tead, O.: The art of administration. (New York: McGraw-Hill Book Co., 1951) p. 3.
3. Gouldner, A. W., editor: Studies in leadership. (New York: Harper & Row, Publishers, 1950) p. 34.

4. Tead, O.: Administration: its purpose and performance. (New York: Harper & Row, Publishers, 1959) p. 59.

9. Treated all facets of the camp operation fairly, did not play favorites
10. Delegated authority and responsibility effectively
11. Criticized constructively
12. Praised in public, but reprimanded in private
13. Could say "no" without leaving staff deflated
14. Made staff believe they had something to contribute
15. Could admit own mistakes
16. Possessed ability to come right to the heart of a problem
17. Conveyed a willingness to adapt and be flexible
18. Always provided a good example
19. Took a personal interest in each staff member
20. Evaluated continuously

Administrative skills

Katz has identified three distinct types of administrative skills considered essential for any successful leader:

1. *Technical skill.* This involves an understanding of, and proficiency in, a specific kind of activity, particularly one involving methods, procedures, or techniques. Technical skill involves specialized knowledge, analytical ability within that specialty, and facility in the use of tools and techniques of a specific discipline.
2. *Human skill.* The executive's ability to work effectively as a group member and to build cooperative effort within the team he leads.
3. *Conceptual skill.* The ability to see the enterprise as a whole; it includes recognizing how the various functions of the organization depend on one another, and how changes in any one part affect all the others.[5]

Technical skills for the camp administrator may include a tremendous range of knowledge such as budgeting, office management, equipment purchase, site maintenance, menu planning, food purchase and storage, and program planning for a wide range of activities. Recent evidence indicates that technical knowledge seems to be less important than the other two in distinguishing between successful and unsuccessful administrators.

Human skills, or the ability to work effectively with others, is critical in the camp setting. Every level of camp life involves human interaction from the director's relationships with management personnel to daily association with the campers.

The size of a camp has a profound bearing on the importance of each group of skills. The larger the camp, the greater the *conceptual skills* required to integrate one facet of the operation with all the others. It is one thing to plan half a dozen out-trips for campers during a camp session; it is quite another to coordinate a trip program in a large camp that involves one third of the campers and staff being away from the campsite at any one time. Conversely, the smaller the camp, the greater the need for the director to possess a wide range of technical skills. Because the staff of a small camp cannot employ as many specialists, members of the management team need to be more versatile.

Griffiths,[6] after examining the differences between successful and unsuccessful *school* administrators, concludes that success in administration is related to the degree of human and conceptual skills that the individual possesses. There seems good reason to believe that the same conclusion can be drawn from a comparison of *camp* administrators. Boles and Davenport[7] support Griffith's con-

---

5. Reprinted by permission of the Harvard Business Review. Excerpt from "Skills of an Effective Administrator" by Robert L. Katz (September-October 1974). Copyright © 1974 by the President and Fellows of Harvard College; all rights reseved.

6. Griffiths, D.: Human relations in school administration. (New York: Appleton-Century Crofts, 1956) p. 12.
7. Boles, H. W., and Davenport, J. A.: Introduction to educational leadership. (New York: Harper & Row Publishers, 1975) p. 301.

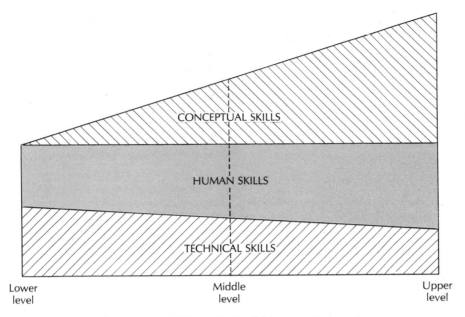

Fig. 2-1. Mix of skills needed by leaders at various levels.

clusion regarding the desired mix of these three types of skills as shown in Fig. 2-1.

Types of administrators

Maintaining a successful camp organization depends primarily on acquiring a team of qualified personnel and coordinating the various sections of the camp toward fulfillment of its objectives. Implicit within this social structure is the recognition by all its memebers that certain individuals have the unquestioned right to make some decisions and take some actions that affect all those within the organization. This is recognition of authority or power and is essential to effective administration.

In political structures, authority ranges from dictatorship to anarchy. In the same way, many different types of leadership exist within camps. Administrators have been conveniently classified into five groups with regard to how they handle the decision-making process. The extremes are administrators who use their authority to manipulate people in a totally autocratic manner and administrators who display complete apathy and allow the group to usurp all authority.

Autocrat. These individuals begin with an assumption that they are the most knowledgeable person among the staff and by virtue of their administrative position are responsible for making all decisions. They run a "very tight ship," which is characteristic of the typical officer—enlisted man relationship in the armed forces. Autocrats leave no room for suggestions or ideas from the group and have total disregard for interpersonal relations since they are the final authority in all matters.

Benevolent dictator. Like the autocrat, these types of administrators believe they are the wisest persons in the group and, therefore, are responsible for all decision making. On the other hand, they invite staff members to come to them with their problems. They are friendly and approachable but rarely act on the ideas and suggestions of others unless they coincide with their own. Their relationship with the staff is similar to that of a father and his young son. This leader requires very submissive staff members who want someone to make all decisions for them. When the benevolent dictator is surrounded by such a staff, morale may be quite high.*

Laissez-faire administrator. This type of administrator is characterized by a policy of noninterference. Laissez-faire administra-

*For further discussion of the benevolent dictator, refer to: Sharenow, A. A camp should be a benevolent dictatorship, Camping magazine, **42**(4):16, April, 1970.

tors frequently delude themselves into believing that by avoiding active participation in decision making, they exemplify democratic leadership when, in fact, they are demonstrating no leadership at all. Such a person encourages the status quo. Occasionally, such an insipid administrator is welcomed, particularly when other members of the senior management team wish to exert authority and relish a situation in which the "boss" does not interfere.

Anarchist. Whereas the laissez-faire administrator is content to preserve existing policies and rules, anarchists support a system in which no policies or rules exist. In the absence of these guides for decision

Table 2-1. Types of administrators

Autocratic	Benevolent	Laissez-faire	Anarchist	Democratic
Characteristic				
Relies on prestige of position	Friendly, approachable	Lacks leadership	Absence of rules	Makes full use of leadership role
Tight and inflexible control	Encourages staff to bring problems for solution	Will not take a stand	Believes *voluntary cooperative action* will solve all issues	Respects subordinates
Not interested in others' opinions	Since the leader is wiser, establishes own policies	Maintains status quo	Misconstrues lack of decision making as democratic	Relates with staff
Ignores human factor		Frequently unsure of self		Involves others in decision making
Employs close, rigid supervision	Does not rely on others' ideas	Abdicates authority and decision making		Good human relations
Makes all decisions				Effective communication
Consequences				
Efficient decision making	Efficient decision making	Attitude of hopelessness	Confusion and disorder	Enriches thinking and initiative
Produces results	Morale usually high	No direction	Everyone waits for others to initiate *voluntary cooperative action*	Promotes active contribution
Low morale and resentment	Greater productivity	Low morale and high frustration		Lessens tension
Loss of staff initiative	Loss of initiative and creativity			Strong leader-staff relations
Decisions lack originality	Ultimately, staff members become disenchanted			Good espirit de corps
Covert hostility and resentment				
High staff turnover				

making, they believe that voluntary cooperative action will come forward when required. With no leadership provided by the designated authority, it is essential that this leadership emerge from the group, otherwise the organization is doomed to vacillation and indecision.

Democratic administrator. These leaders strive for effective communication, and good interpersonal relations are paramount. They invite the opinions of others and actively solicit their participation in the decision-making process at all levels. At the same time, they do not abrogate their authority as the designated leader. They use their leadership role to form the staff into a cohesive group that works collectively toward the goals of the organization. Democratic leadership will be discussed in more detail in the following section.

The five types of administrative leaders are summarized in Table 2-1. The upper section of each column lists the predominant characteristics, and the bottom section outlines some of the possible consequences of the various types of leadership.

Although it is convenient to place each of these administrative styles in discrete classifications for purposes of discussion and comparison, it would be rare to meet a camp director who personified in every detail one of the types described. Leadership style tends to shift from one style to another depending on the particular circumstances. For example, camp directors who feel threatened are likely to exhibit strong autocratic behavior. If, on the other hand, the director is secure and comfortable with the leadership role, it is easier to demonstrate the true qualities of the democratic leader. What is important is that camp directors understand the advantages and limitations of each style and then find the style, or styles, with which they are comfortable and can work most effectively.

DEMOCRATIC ADMINISTRATION
Values of democratic administration

An examination of Table 2-1 should make it apparent that the positive values of democratic leadership far outweigh those of other types. Whenever possible, administrators should seek to utilize cooperative social action in arriving at decisions. Some advantages of democratic administration are described below.

1. *Individuals accept decisions they have helped to formulate.* Camp personnel are more likely to work to their capacity when they share in determining the purposes of their work and are made to believe that what they are doing is indispensable to a successful camp session. Only as counsellors and other camp staff members are treated as responsible people with ideas that are of real worth to the camp will they view their roles in a positive light and thus be able to work effectively with campers. It is particularly important that the staff actively share in determining those policies which affect them directly. For example, it is difficult to conceive of a camp drawing up personnel policy statements, which affect the daily life of each counsellor, without having strong counsellor representation to assist in the formulation of these policies.

2. *Two heads are better than one.* It is a widely accepted axiom that the aggregate thinking of several minds will lead to more productive ideas than will the deliberations of a single person.

3. *Self-actualization is promoted through the democratic process.* Just as the organization benefits when staff members are encouraged to participate in decision making so, too, the individual grows. As staff members believe that they are making signficant contributions to the camp, their sense of self-fulfillment is greatly enhanced.

4. *Group participation in decision making reduces tensions.* One quality that fre-

quently characterizes autocratic administration is a high degree of hostility toward the leader and, eventually, even among the members of the group itself. When individuals are encouraged to work cooperatively toward group objectives, they learn to understand and accept others' points of view so that suspicions and misunderstandings are dissipated.

5. *Staff morale is improved.* When people are encouraged to participate freely in policy and decision making, they see themselves as an integral part of a team. A sense of belonging develops, and a cohesiveness pervades the entire staff. Numerous studies indicate that when members of a group share in the planning and policy making, a greater esprit de corps results. With this improved morale comes greater productivity.

It is important to point out an inconsistency that is frequently observed in camps—the failure to implement democratic decision making at all levels of the camp operation. A camp director may espouse the importance of having campers share in all decisions that affect them and to this end, counsellors are advised to use the group process at every opportunity to democratize the camp experience. Yet, in the same camp, the director often fails to use this principle of involving counsellors in decisions made at the staff level. In other camps, the opposite may be true—the director successfully applies the group process method when arriving at decisions concerning the staff but reverts to autocratic decision making on all matters relating to campers, presumably using the argument that campers are too immature to be consulted even regarding matters that directly affect them.

Limitations of democratic administration

The democratic decision-making process is not without its limitations and to suggest that this form of administration is infallible would be naive. However, several criticisms that have been ascribed to democratic deliberations are not a criticism of the process itself but the manner in which it has been implemented.

1. *The democratic process is slow and inefficient.* Whenever discussion and debate involve a large number of people, it takes time. The essence of the group process is involvement of those who are participating. It is equally true that occasionally delaying a decision may have disastrous results. For example, a child is reported missing at camp. There is no clear indication as to whether he is lost or has run away. This is not a time for a long, protracted meeting in which all staff are invited to make suggestions as to a course of action since, with each passing minute, the child may be wandering deeper into the surrounding woods.

Democratic administration is predicated on a group of individuals recognizing a problem that requires some action. Once the problem is identified, there should be deliberation leading to a decision and the necessary action required to implement the decision. Whenever possible, the deliberation should involve those who will be affected by the decision. However, emergencies sometime require exceptional treatment so that an appropriate decision is reached. In the case of the lost camper, deliberation may mean that the director quickly calls together several key staff members who reach a speedy decision, or the director alone may deliberate as to the best course of action and then advise the staff of the plan. When the administrator or a small group of management personnel makes this type of unilateral decision, it should be clear to all why such expedient action was necessary. If there is any fear in the administrator's mind that the staff will think the actions were autocratic, the administrator must be prepared to explain the reasons for the one-sided decision. It can also be argued that it is sometimes advantageous to deliberate at some length before a decision is reached. When time is not a critical factor, a more leisurely judgment may lead to a better decision.

2. *Majority decision versus consensus.* Democratic decision making implies involvement of the group. But how is the final decision rendered? Is it by simple majority vote? Or is it by consensus? Is a majority decision always right?

Ideally, decisions should be made on the basis of unanimity—all members of the group are in agreement as to the course of action. It is the role of the leader to attempt to bring members of the group to consensus whenever possible. Unfortunately, such total agreement is rare and consensus under these conditions means that individuals with viewpoints that are at either extreme must compromise toward some middle ground. It has been argued that consensus means that nobody is satisfied with the eventual decision. This appears to be a gross overstatement of the case. A position on which the majority can agree is usually toward the middle of the spectrum so that had majority vote been utilized, the decision would have been essentially the same.

Some critics of the simple majority vote process contend that important decisions should not be determined by such a slim margin as a single vote. It can be argued, however, that a majority decision, even an extremely close one, is infinitely, better than that made by *one* autocratic administrator.

As to the question of whether or not the majority ever makes a poor decision, the answer clearly is "yes"—majority votes do occasionally result in bad decisions. But if we accept the premise that many minds are better than one, over the long run, the majority will make fewer mistakes than administrators who believe they have all the answers to all the problems that confront the group.

3. *The democratic process lacks authority.* It is sometimes said that democratic administration is weak administration because it is indecisive. This criticism may be valid if the group process fails to culminate in a firm course of action. Procrastination, when a decision is required, is unacceptable. It is the administrator's responsibility to guide and lead the group to some judgment that is consistent with the established objectives of the organization. This decision must be based on fact and made only after reasonable deliberation. It should lead to clear-cut, effective action.

Throughout this discussion, it has been maintained that a democratic organization vests its staff with responsibility for determining policy that directly affects them and encourages active participation in decision making. At the same time, however, once decisions have been made, it is then the sole responsibility of administrators to see that the decisions are carried out.

Clear lines of demarcation exist between policy-making or legislative roles and executive roles; the democratic process is involved primarily in the former. This is not to say that administrators may not *delegate* their executive role to others. One mark of good executives is their ability to delegate responsibility and authority to those around them. Once this responsibility and authority has been delegated, the administrator's role is a very delicate one. Camp directors must not appear to trespass or oversupervise to the point that it implies lack of confidence in their colleague's ability to handle the job. On the other hand, they do have ultimate responsibility for the action of all members of their staff team. Administrators, therefore, must provide enough direction to satisfy themselves that staff members do not think that they have been burdened with too much responsibility before they are ready for it. The administrator should provide all the help and guidance the colleague desires without appearing to meddle.

BASIC ADMINISTRATIVE PROCESSES

To successfully discharge the many tasks and activities required of a leader, the camp director must carry out certain *administrative processes*. These processes are common to all administrators regardless of the organization or area in which they work. They comprise the methods or means by which objectives are realized in the most effective manner.

Many writers have identified and described the various processes that the administrator follows. Although there are variations in the lists of processes suggested, there is also much similarity. It is largely a matter of how inclusive the author wishes to be. In some cases, it is a matter of using different terminology for the same function. In the following section, five basic processes are described as they relate to camp administration. They are planning, organizing, coordinating, directing, and evaluating.

Planning

The first process involves looking ahead and developing a carefully organized course of action. It includes an overall plan for the entire camp embracing every facet of its operation.

Planning begins with the formation of objectives. As has already been pointed out, no camp can be productive without a set of clearly defined goals. These objectives give each individual, and the camp as a whole, a direction and purpose. They also provide the backdrop against which all planning is undertaken.

Gorton, in referring to the administration of schools, has suggested that planning is concerned with answering four questions:

1. What kinds of activity or actions must occur in order to achieve the goal or decision?
2. What kind of resources—personnel, facilities, supplies—must be utilized to achieve the objective or decision?
3. How should activities be sequenced to best advantage, and resources most efficiently coordinated, to achieve the goal or decision?
4. What kind of time schedule should be followed in implementing the plan of action?[8]

Unless these questions are answered before problems occur, the camp is almost certainly destined to move from one crisis to another. The result is embarrassing delays, shortsighted decisions, and inefficient use of staff resources.

Effective planning does not simply mean capable handling of difficulties as they arise; it means active problem identification on the part of the camp director. The normal course of action for many camp directors is to refrain from seeking out problems. To such individuals, it seems far easier to proceed through the camp session with fingers crossed in hopes that no serious crises will arise. "After all," they argue, "I have my hands full dealing with existing problems without looking for potential areas of difficulty." However, adequate planning enables the director to circumvent many of the day-to-day problems that confront them so that they have more time to devote to preventive planning. The following example may help to demonstrate the efficacy of effective planning.

A large camp, with an expansive waterfront on a lake, is located in an area in which severe electrical storms are common. The camp director has had some concern regarding the installation of the swimming and boating docks. He contemplates replacing the old cables that have been used for many years to stabilize the anchors, but once the

---

8. Gorton, R. A.: School administration: challenge and opportunity for leadership. (Dubuque, Iowa: William C. Brown Co., Publishers, 1976) p. 51.

campers arrive, he is preoccupied with other more pressing matters. When a sudden storm hits, the complete dock installation is carried down to the far end of the lake. Damage is extensive, and it takes his entire staff 4 days to put the boating and swimming areas back into service. Several hours of preventive planning and execution could have prevented the loss of many work hours as well as suspension of two vital camp activities.

Whereas camp directors are ultimately responsible for planning, they should also involve members of their staff in this process. They may delegate certain tasks to individuals or to groups. In many cases, staff members initiate some aspects of planning themselves. When this occurs, administrators should be informed of all planning that is under way. They should also remember to give credit to those members of the organization who initiate and complete some phase of camp planning.

Whereas planning, by definition, takes place in advance of what is to be done, it is nevertheless a continuous process. Because circumstances change, plans must change. Plans are often classified as short, intermediate, or long-range. Short-term plans usually involve decisions that cover a matter of only weeks, whereas intermediate plans may be made as far ahead as 1 year. Long-range plans are usually the most difficult to effect. It is not easy to engender enthusiasm in a transient staff to plan for something that may not produce tangible results for several years. This does not, however, minimize the importance of long-range planning because, without it, years may slip by with no significant growth taking place. It must be remembered that major camp innovations, because of their very scope, usually take some time to implement.

Administrative policies. Too often, problems arise with little warning, and sometimes they are so acute that they create a real crisis situation. How can effective planning prevent this situation? The answer is the formulation of administrative policies in anticipation of areas of concern.

All camps, wishing to function efficiently and consistently, must prepare sound administrative policies to cover a vast range of problem areas. Simply defined, a *policy* is a statement of a prudent course of action that guides the camp administrator and the staff when making decisions on behalf of the organization. Policies are characterized by a degree of flexibility that enables them to be applied in a variety of circumstances. At the same time, they must serve as guidelines that ensure consistency in their application. Policies must not be confused with rules and regulations, which are more restrictive and specific. An example will help to differentiate between policy and rule.

POLICY: Campers should be encouraged to bring personal sporting equipment to camp to more fully enjoy program participation.

RULE: Campers are required to store personal bows and arrows in the archery equipment room on arrival at camp.

Experience has shown that it is wise to put all policies, once approved, in written form and then circulate them to all persons concerned. Policies should be reviewed at regular intervals. As conditions change, policy modification should reflect these changes. Many organizations prepare a color-coded, loose-leaf policy booklet. Color coding permits easy identification, and the binder permits easy revision.

Policy formation takes time, but when conscientiously undertaken, it does much to eliminate chaos and confusion. Resick, Leidel, and Mason provide an excellent summary of the values of administrative policies:

1. A set of policies reveals the ends or goals of the department. A review of a set of policies brings to light the philosophy of the department as expressed in operational terms.

2. A set of policies permits the staff to translate alternatives into action. This ensures some degree of expediency, since ground covered need not be crossed again in like problems.
3. A set of policies prevents inconsistency in solutions which might occur if problems were solved without regard to past performances.
4. A set of policies permits a degree of flexibility in the solution of local problems not possible under iron-clad rules and regulations. This allows a group with divergent views to operate within the framework of the policies.
5. A set of policies performs the function of good public relations, since others are made aware of the bases of decisions which are not compatible with their own views.
6. A set of policies helps the staff realize that decisions which affect them adversely are not made on a personal basis.[9]

Organizing

"The administrative process of organizing an enterprise, or any of its parts, consists of (1) dividing and grouping the work that should be done (including administration) into individual jobs and (2) defining the established relationships between individuals filling these jobs."[10] Newman provides us with the two essential components of organizing: breaking down and classifying the work to be done and clarifying the relationships between people who assume these various tasks.

Organizing within a camp involves arranging units and groups in some logical and systematic manner to carry out the work of the camp efficiently. Because of the complexity of camp life, a variety of divisions and clas-

sifications are usually found. One grouping is based on living units and involves such variables as age, sex, or a combination of both. Another classification may be based on program specialization. The most inclusive distribution of assignments is based on job specialization and is the equivalent of departmentalization as it is found in industry and education. Chapter 3 deals with the question of camp structure and organization in considerable detail.

Delegation. Except in the case of very small camps, directors are incapable of effectively performing the great range of administrative tasks within a camp. They are unable to do so for two reasons: (1) there are not enough hours in the day to competently perform these duties, and (2) they rarely possess the expertise to handle some of these functions as capably as their colleagues. When either or both of these conditions are present, the camp administrator should delegate some tasks to other members of the staff. To fail to do so is one of the most detrimental administrative weaknesses. When directors are overloaded, their efficiency falters and a "snowballing effect" occurs. The result is that the entire camp operation suffers.

In spite of the dangers inherent in failing to delegate, it is a common weakness found in many camp directors. It may be explained by the fact that most camps start with a very small enterprise, and initially it is within the scope of the director to handle all administrative functions. As the camp grows in size, the director is reluctant to relinquish responsibility for these many varied tasks, in the belief that he or she will be as able to cope as in the past. Eventually, there comes a point when smooth, efficient administration is jeopardized.

Heyel identifies the reasons for the administrator's reluctance to delegate responsibility as follows.

9. Resick, M. C., Leidel, B. L., and Mason, J. G.: Modern administrative practices in physical education and athletics, © 1979, ed. 3. (Reading, Mass.: Addison-Wesley Publishing Co., Inc.), Chapter 3, p. 67, "The Purposes of Administrative Policies." Reprinted with permission.
10. Newman, W. H.: Administrative action: the techniques of organization and management. (Englewood Cliffs, N.J.: Prentice-Hall, Inc., 1963) p. 51.

1. He has strong need to be involved in every aspect of administration and cannot bear to delegate any of his responsibilities to others.
2. He is concerned that others may begin to wonder if he is really capable of handling the job if he attempts to delegate some of the responsibilities to other people.
3. He is not confident that others will do a good job if he delegates certain responsibilities or at least doubts whether they could do as good a job as he would in carrying out a task.
4. He has a strong need to be recognized as the leader in the organization, and he is concerned with the possibility that delegation of some of the responsibilities will necessitate the sharing of leadership recognition.
5. He is concerned that by delegating responsibility to someone else, he may be facilitating the advancement of that individual to the point at which the situation could become competitive.[11]

Delegation is so crucial to effective administration that camp directors should regularly engage in some very objective self-analysis to determine whether they are being influenced by any of the considerations described above.

Some camp directors are uncertain as to

---

11. Excerpted from Heyel, C.: Organizing your job in management. (New York: American Management Association, Inc., 1960) pp. 126-135.

when responsibility should be delegated. Fig. 2-2 should be of assistance to the administrator in answering this question.

Another important consideration in delegating authority is to carefully determine exactly what information should be passed on to the staff person who will assume the new duties. The director should ask: "What would I want to know if someone were delegating this responsibility to me?" Such information includes clear definition of the nature and scope of the task, the amount of authority required to see the job through, the extent to which supervisory responsibilities accompany the assignment, and the types of communication necessary to meet the new role. Failure to delegate clearly defined responsibilities usually leads to confusion and ultimately results in inferior performance.

Care must also be taken to ensure that no staff member is responsible to more than one supervisor at one time. When staff members are responsible to different supervisors, there is always the danger that they will be pulled in two different directions at the same time. This type of problem can be minimized through regular meetings of the management team so that there is complete understanding of the work load and schedule imposed on each staff member.

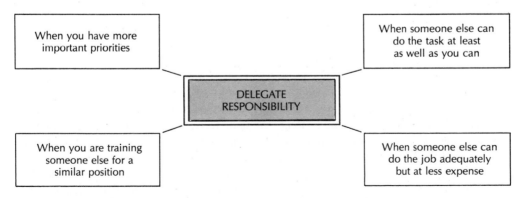

Fig. 2-2. The camp director delegates responsibility and authority.

When responsibility for a function is delegated, it must be matched with the necessary authority to perform that function. This is a fundamental principle of administration that, when violated, invariably leads to frustration on the part of the staff involved. Authority to see the task through must be commensurate with the responsibility. For example, if staff members are given responsibility to plan and organize a "woodsman's competition" at camp, they must be given authority to recruit staff, utilize facilities, and acquire the materials necessary to stage the event. If the camp director has enough confidence in the staff members to ask them to organize such a program, the director must also be prepared to provide them with the necessary materials and human resources to see the job through.

At the same time, it must be made clear that even when administrators delegate responsibility and authority to a colleague, they remain accountable for the actions of all their staff members. If the "woodsman's competition" is unsuccessful because of the incompetence of the staff member in charge, the administrator must accept at least part of the responsibility. Accountability is not removed by delegation.

Coordinating

Closely related to the process of organizing is that of coordinating. Coordination within the camp means unifying and integrating the numerous facets of the organization into a smooth working entity. As has been noted, a camp is comprised of a number of diverse units or departments, including program, health, food, business, maintenance, and administrative services. Each department may be broken into further subunits. The program unit, for example, may include subdivisions such as waterfront activities, arts and crafts, competitive games, and out-tripping. It is quite normal for some

members of the staff to give priority to their unit or subdivision rather than allegience to the total camp operation. Whereas the administration should encourage pride in, and even healthy competition between, different segments of the camp, it is vitally important that such local loyalties do not threaten the teamwork of the entire staff as it concerns the overall goals of the camp.

The need for effective coordination increases in direct proportion to the size and complexity of the camp. Even two people need to coordinate their efforts when carrying a heavy object. When the number of people is multipled many times, the interrelationship of people, tasks, resources, and time schedules requires highly sophisticated coordination so that each unit works harmoniously with all others. Two examples will serve to emphasize this point.

A counsellor is preparing to take a group of campers on a 5-day out-trip. A number of other groups plan to leave at the same time. Each trip counsellor is given a schedule in which the time is listed for her group to come to the trip store and pack. Unfortunately a copy of the packing schedule is not given to the staff member who is responsible for scheduling waterfront duty, and one trip counsellor finds that she has been assigned lifeguard duty at the time when her group is expected to pack.

An out-trip is scheduled to leave camp Monday morning after breakfast. The party is to be transported by camp van to an embarcation point about 10 miles from the main campsite. Again, the staff member in charge of the out-trip schedule neglects to check with the business office regarding the availability of the bus and learns on Monday morning that the vehicle has just departed on a 6-hour trip to the city for camp supplies.

It should be clear from these two relatively simple examples that failure to coordinate may lead to embarrassment, hard feelings between staff members, and a poor public image of the camp.

Poor coordination usually reflects weakness in other processes of administration, namely, planning and organizing. This point is supported by the following statement:

In management, coordination deals with synchronizing and unifying the action of a group of people. Basically, coordination should flow or result from effective planning, organizing, directing and controlling. Continued need for special coordinating devices may, in fact, be an indication of poor planning and organization. It is certain that far too much time will be consumed in coordinating efforts if the other functions of management are not well performed.[12]

Several steps should be undertaken to strengthen the coordinating process within a camp.

1. *Check effectiveness of communication systems within the camp.* Lack of communication, or communication breakdown, is the most prevalent cause of coordination failure. Each individual staff member, as well as each subunit and unit, must be fully cognizant of what the other groups are doing. Any change of plans, procedures, or time schedules must be communicated to *all* persons concerned. Depending on the size of the organization, the transmission of this information may take place verbally or in written form. In the case of the latter, this means written memos, an informal note, or use of strategically located bulletin boards. The camp director should also encourage regular informal contacts among staff members, particularly between different departments of the camp. The medical staff should be encouraged to share a coffee break with the program staff, and business office personnel might sun and swim with the kitchen staff.

12. United States Department of Agriculture: Essentials of good management. (Washington, D.C., 1956) p. 25.

Such regular, informal contacts do much to promote improved coordination.

2. *Organizational charts and printed job descriptions serve to strengthen coordination.* Any printed material that clarifies relationships and duties of staff members will help resolve "gray areas" in which an individual is not clear as to (a) exactly who is responsible for what, (b) who reports to whom, and (c) which supervisor takes precedence when the counselor is responsible to more than one.

3. *Regular supervision will uncover potential problems of coordination.* The administrator must make a point of maintaining close personal contact with all facets of the camp operation. If directors spend most of their time in the office or devote an inordinately large amount of their time to one area of the camp to the exclusion of others, they lose touch. Directors who are continuously in contact with all personnel are able to resolve areas of misunderstanding and clarify responsibilities before major problems develop. Camp directors can only obtain optimal performance from staff members when each person is clear as to what their particular role is in relation to the rest of the staff team.

Directing

Once objectives have been formulated, problems identified, policies established, and decisions reached, the time has come for some type of action. The process of initiating action is referred to as *directing*. Once the planning is completed, the administrator must translate the plan into specific activity. At this point, when execution of the plan takes over, administration becomes less democratic and more autocratic in nature. Directing involves the leader and the follower. It is the leader who is vested with authority to see the plan through to its successful completion.

Camp administrators must initiate action on the part of other people, and they may do this with a variety of approaches. They may command, direct, instruct, request, or suggest. Whichever approach is taken, they must motivate people to action. The particular technique used will probably be the product of a number of factors. How secure does the director feel about his or her authority to direct? How does the director see the staff responding to this authority? To what extent is time a factor in completing the task? Did the staff share in the formulation of the plan for task solution?

If staff members are persuaded as to the merits of a given plan, they will almost certainly bring a greater commitment to the completion of the task. If, on the other hand, they are responding only to the camp director's authority, their involvement is likely to be something less than enthusiastic. The key to successful administrative direction is strong interpersonal relations. The leader's personality and character, plus his or her intimate knowledge and understanding of each individual staff member, are vital factors in successfully motivating staff members toward the enthusiastic resolution of the task.

Whenever possible, directing should be done verbally. Verbal directions have the obvious advantage of allowing the personality and enthusiasm of the camp director to strengthen the communication. It must be kept in mind, however, that directors who lack the personal qualities to motivate their staff may elicit a negative reaction through a face-to-face encounter.

Written directions may be indicated when a large number of staff members are involved in a complex project. In this case, a written statement reduces the chance of ambiguity or misunderstanding. Written guidelines may also be filed and used as a reference at a later date.

Camp administrators should lead by example. Here indeed "actions speak louder than words." Directors should never place themselves in a position in which they require certain actions or behavior from members of the staff that they themselves are not prepared to demonstrate. Camp directors who lead by example command the respect of their staff and almost certainly engender greater support from them.

Evaluating

The process of evaluating represents one of the most important responsibilities of the camp administrator, and yet investigation reveals that it is a process that is all too often ignored. It has been suggested that the main reason for camps failing to use evaluation is lack of evaluation skills and the knowledge of how to use them. Clearly this may serve as a deterrent to some camp directors, but perhaps the greatest obstacle to extensive evaluation is that such a process is potentially threatening to the administrator.

It is interesting to note that when some form of evaluation is conducted by the camp administration, a disproportionate amount of time and energy is spent assessing the camp staff and very little time is utilized to evaluate administrators. Very few camps engage in regular, in-depth assessment of the total camp experience, including the program. These observations lend credence to the suspicion that camp directors tend to be very defensive regarding a thorough examination of the total camp operation, including administrative leadership.

The subject of evaluation is discussed at greater length in the final chapter of this book. Suffice it to say at this time that camp administrators are not doing a complete job until they examine, as objectively as possible, each individual and group, each aspect of the camp program, and each supporting camp service to determine its strengths and weaknesses. Whenever weaknesses are found, effective steps must be taken to ameliorate problem areas.

THE CAMP DIRECTOR AS ADMINISTRATOR

Up to this point, this chapter has examined the meaning of administration, types of administrative leadership, and processes in which administrators generally should engage. We will now turn our full attention to the director of the camp and scrutinize the primary administrative role in the camp.

Qualifications of the camp director

As one examines the literature in the field of administration in an attempt to determine which qualities are necessary to fulfill this role, one is struck by the long list of desirable characteristics. Clearly, the administrator must be someone who is only slightly less than a saint. The following characteristics are important attributes of camp directors regarding their role as senior administrative officer. It is not reasonable to expect that all these qualities will be found in a single individual. However, they do provide a model against which camp directors and aspiring administrators may judge themselves.

Clear recognition of the goals of the camp. Directors must not only have a sharp perception of the objectives that the camp seeks to realize, but they must also be persons of vision and courage to plan boldly and wisely for the future.

Health and fitness for the job. This implies that camp directors possess the physical stamina to sustain them through a short but very intensive camp session. In addition, a high degree of emotional stability must be demonstrated.

Intellectual capacity. Whereas a strong formal education is desirable, it is not mandatory. Of greater importance is the capacity

to exercise sound judgment and make wise decisions.

Personality for leadership. Camp directors should possess those personal qualities that inspire confidence and support. The most important of these is the ability to effectively relate to others.

Adaptability. Camp directors must be flexible and able to adjust to social change to be capable of functioning in many different situations.

Integrity. The director's honesty must be above reproach in dealing with staff, campers, parents, and other groups.

Ability to make decisions. Any administrator must be capable of making decisions, many on short notice, with little opportunity for consultation.

Communication skills. Camp directors must possess superior skill in oral communication as well as the ability to write well.

Command of administrative skills. Camp directors are required to possess technical knowledge of a vast range of areas to effectively administer a camp.

Camp administrative responsibilities

Another method of assessing the camp director's role is to examine the administrative assignments that must be performed. These responsibilities can be divided into eight major areas of concern: (1) staff personnel relations, (2) camper personnel relations, (3) program development, (4) health services, (5) finance and business management, (6) site and facilities maintenance, (7) food services, and (8) public relations. Several specific tasks are included in each of these areas. Fig. 2-3 provides some idea of the vast range of assignments for which the camp director is ultimately responsible. Except in the case of a very small camp, the director cannot be solely responsible for all these duties. Many tasks must be delegated to other members of the staff. The camp di-

STAFF PERSONNEL

1. Formulate staff personnel policies
2. Recruit camp personnel
3. Assign staff responsibilities
4. Outline camp objectives to staff
5. Orient staff to camp
6. Supervise and direct staff
7. Help resolve staff problems
8. Coordinate work of entire staff
9. Maximize staff potential
10. Promote staff morale
11. Evaluate staff

CAMPER PERSONNEL

1. Formulate policies for camper conduct
2. Orient campers to camp
3. Ensure camper health and safety
4. Supervise camper discipline
5. Arrange for camper assessment

PROGRAM DEVELOPMENT

1. Formulate program objectives
2. Help select program content
3. Coordinate program, personnel, and facilities
4. Provide necessary material resources
5. Supervise program
6. Provide in-service training of program staff
7. Evaluate program regularly

HEALTH SERVICES

1. Formulate safety policies for all personnel
2. Develop sound health practices
3. Ensure adequate medical service
4. Provide broad insurance coverage
5. Guarantee safe, efficient transportation of campers

BUSINESS MANAGEMENT

1. Prepare budget
2. Establish system of accounting
3. Administer camp purchases
4. Organize efficient office management

SITE AND FACILITIES

1. Develop master plan for site
2. Implement orderly growth of facilities
3. Develop efficient operation of site
4. Ensure maintenance of site and facilities
5. Supervise custodial staff

FOOD SERVICES

1. Ensure nutritious menu
2. Budget food purchases carefully
3. Ensure sanitary kitchen and dining room
4. Provide for adequate refrigeration and garbage disposal

PUBLIC RELATIONS

1. Plan camper recruitment
2. Coordinate public relations
3. Facilitate two-way communication
4. Cooperate with other community organizations
5. Maintain active membership in camping association

Fig. 2-3. Scope of camp director's administrative tasks.

rector is responsible, however, for ensuring that all tasks, whether handled personally or delegated to others, are successfully completed.

Roles of the camp director

Another way to discuss the senior administrative position in a camp is to examine some of the roles the director is expected to play, five of which are described briefly below. Not all roles require equal amounts of time and energy, but each should receive some attention. At times, directors will delegate one or more roles to their colleagues either because they do not have sufficient time to accomplish all the roles, or because they are confident that a staff member can fill the role at least as well as, and in some cases better than, themselves.

Manager. In their role as manager, directors are "the ones who keep things running smoothly." They are expected to acquire, organize, and coordinate the human and material resources of the camp to effectively achieve the objectives of the organization. In this capacity, directors are concerned with all matters leading to the efficient operation of the camp. Some camp directors dislike the term *manager* because they believe that it carries a negative connotation. To some, it lacks glamour and implies concern with the mundane. Organizing schedules, coordinating programs, helping to formulate policy, and helping others to accomplish tasks and goals is anything but routine and ordinary. Perhaps it is the term *manager* that needs to be changed.

Program facilitator. Of all the roles that directors are asked to play, that of planning the program brings them closest to campers. Because of this, it is usually regarded as the most important by parents and campers.

There has been a tendency, in recent years, for camp directors to hire more and more program specialists for aquatics, sail-

ing, water skiing, arts and crafts, nature, out-tripping, archery, riding and so on. This move toward specialists has done much to enrich each individual program but, at the same time, has created new problems of scheduling and coordinating the total program when all specialists see their own area as the most important. As increasing numbers of specialists are hired, the tendency has been for the camp director to withdraw from program planning, leaving this role to the "experts." It is vital that someone coordinate the total program of activities. Since this is the heart of the total camp experience, the camp director should be expected to play the crucial role in integrating program development.

Innovator. In recent years, the camping profession has increasingly sought new and creative types of camp experience. This has come in response to the growing awareness that man is a social being, living in a society that is marked by dramatic change. The writings of Toffler[13] and others have made it apparent that those persons responsible for administering social organizations must be acutely sensitive to man's changing needs. In this capacity as change agent, camp directors must be able to (1) diagnose the need for change, (2) propose an acceptable innovative plan, and (3) orient and sell the target group on the new idea.

It must be emphasized that change for the sake of change is insufficient as a reason for innovation. Change is only justified if the new idea has potential for improving the camp experience.

Communicator. Camp directors are continually playing the role of communicator. The very nature of this position requires that they relate to a variety of people, including campers, staff, parents, fellow administra-

---

13. Toffler, A.: Future shock. (New York: Bantam Books, 1970).

tors, and other community groups. With the possible exception of decision making, camp directors probably spend more time in this role than any other. This is a difficult, and often neglected, administrative skill. It requires that some *message* be delivered clearly and unambiguously so that no misunderstandings occur. Problems arise when the director believes that communication ends with the actual transmission of the message. Communication is not complete unless the message registers with the receiver and leads to some desired action. For example, a camp director is concerned about the length of time that it takes for campers to settle down after "lights out." After investigating the problem, he concludes that counsellors are leaving their units too soon after the lights are turned out instead of remaining until all campers are quiet. The message, then, is that counsellors should remain in their cabins until they are satisfied that all campers are settled for the night. The director now has a choice of several different media for communication. He can write a memo, announce his decision over the camp public address system, post notices, place it on the agenda of a staff meeting, or have the section heads "pass the word" to all cabin counsellors. Each of these means of transmission may have advantages and disadvantages, and it is important that the director select the medium that is best suited for that particular message.

Whether the counsellors take action on the problem of noise after "lights out" will depend on a number of things. If the message is not clearly stated, they may misinterpret it to mean that responsibility rests with the night patrol to handle the problem. Or the staff may clearly understand what the director wants, but they do not accept the decision. A further possibility is that they understand the message and agree with the director's request but because no one follows through and checks on whether counsellors are remaining in their cabins, they quickly revert to their original pattern and leave their cabins right at "lights out." In each of the examples above, appropriate action did not result and so the director has failed to communicate.

Many factors can cause breakdowns in the lines of communication. The following list represents some of the pitfalls to effective human relations.

1. The biggest barrier to communication is the failure to keep people informed.
2. The director's personal example is a powerful means of communication.
3. *How* we communicate may be as important as *what* we communicate.
4. Whenever administrators "loose their cool," communication tends to break down.
5. Failure to empathize with the other person's point of view impedes communication.
6. Whenever information is deliberately or unconsciously distorted, communication is jeopardized.
7. Jumping to conclusions without sufficient evidence may endanger communication.
8. Communication deteriorates when administrators blame others for their mistakes.
9. Failure to encourage staff suggestions and ideas leads to poor communication.
10. The administrator who does not praise in public and reprimand in private reduces effective communication.

Disciplinarian. Many camp directors would deny that one of their roles is that of disciplinarian. They argue that the nature of the camp setting is such that there is rarely the necessity for someone to be disciplined. If the term *disciplinarian* implies that someone *punishes* some other person, they may be justified in refuting this role. But the fact remains that when many campers are involved, there must be rules of conduct and behavior to guide them. In spite of strong denials, camper conduct constitutes a major problem in many camps today. Unfortunately, too many directors spend much time handling administrative "busy work" that could better be assigned to a subordinate. As a result, that they are not fully cognizant of what is going on in the "front lines."

Mediator. Closely related to the role of disciplinarian is that of *mediator*. As mediator, the director is frequently required to adjust differences. Such differences may arise between campers, campers and counsellor, counsellor and counsellor, counsellor and administration, or camp personnel and parent. In this role, the director must secure all the facts of the dispute and determine how each side perceives the problem. Resolution of the crisis invariably involves some "give and take" on the part of the two parties before the conflict can be resolved.

THE VALUE OF ADMINISTRATIVE GUIDELINES

During the course of a normal day, the camp administrator is called on to make many decisions, some of which may have far-reaching impact on the entire camp operation. On what should these decisions be based? Is it satisfactory for those in management positions to make ad hoc judgments based on little more than intuition, the mood of the moment, or personal bias and prejudice? If there is danger in making impetuous or "gut reaction" decisions, it is equally unacceptable to formulate hard and fast rules and regulations that make no provision for flexibility and interpretation because of the special circumstances surrounding a particular problem.

Those persons responsible for decision making require administrative principles or guidelines based on knowledge, experience, wisdom, and judgment. Such guidelines should be specific enough to provide clear directions for decision making and, at the same time, be general enough to permit interpretation. That is not to say that principles cannot change. It is possible that what was once considered fact can no longer be verified in the light of new evidence and so a principle must be restated. Persons in administrative positions need such a set of guiding principles on which to base judgments and make correct decisions.

A list of administrative guidelines is presented at the end of each chapter throughout the rest of this book. They should prove helpful to students of camp administration and also serve to summarize the main points that have been discussed in each chapter.

ADMINISTRATIVE GUIDELINES

1. Administration is designed to facilitate the camp operation and get the job done in the most efficient and self-effacing manner possible.
2. Camp administrators should possess the right "mix" of three types of skills: technical, human, and conceptual.
3. Administrative style varies greatly with regard to how authority is used. Camp administration should be characterized by a high degree of democratic decision making whenever possible.
4. The administrative process is comprised of five basic steps: planning, organizing, coordinating, directing, and evaluating. Camp administrators should utilize these steps in dealing with all major camp problems.
5. The formulation of camp policies is an important administrative device for management personnel. Such policies should be recorded and made available to all personnel who are affected by them.
6. Comprehensive, long-range planning is the

starting point for the entire administrative process. Camp management personnel must be prepared to devote considerable time to this important process.

7. Strong camp administration provides for delegation of responsibility and authority commensurate with a staff member's ability to accept it.

8. Coordination between the various departments, or functional units, of any camp is vital. Coordination failure results most frequently from breakdowns in communication. All facets of the total camp operation should be aware of what other groups are planning.

9. Sound administration depends on strong human relations. Camp administrators must strive to develop the interpersonal skills required to work effectively with colleagues.

10. The final step in the administrative process is ongoing evaluation. Camp administrators must be prepared to appraise critically the entire camp operation, including the administrative function.

11. Camp directors must possess many important qualities to effectively discharge their managerial role. It is important that those contemplating this important function acquaint themselves with the list of criteria that are deemed desirable for this responsibility.

12. Camp directors have a wide range of supervisory responsibilities that can be classified into eight major areas of concern: staff relations, camper relations, program development, health services, finance and business management, site and facilities maintenance, food services, and public relations.

13. The camp director plays a variety of roles, including manager, program facilitator, innovator, communicator, disciplinarian, and mediator.

SELECTED BIBLIOGRAPHY

American Camping Association: Camping administration course outline for colleges and universities. (Bradford Woods, Martinsville, Ind.: American Camping Association, 1961).

Breuer, S. E.: Program goals or administrative needs? Camping Magazine, 43(5):23-24, May, 1971.

Gorton, R. A.: School administration: challenge and opportunity for leadership. (Dubuque, Iowa: William C. Brown Co., Publishers, 1976). Chapters 3, 4, 5, and 6.

Griffith, F.: Six mistaken meanings of democratic administration, Education Digest, 32:15-17, Jan., 1967.

Grossman, A. H.: Lead, don't boss, your staff, Camping Magazine, 47(8):9-11, June, 1975.

Hall, J. T., et al.: Administration: principles, theory and practice. (Pacific Palisades, Calif.: Goodyear Publishing Co., Inc., 1973). Chapter 1, 2, and 3.

Herman, J.: A new look at organizing administrative functions, The Clearing House, 47:273-276, January, 1973.

Johnson, J. J.: Why administrators fail, The Clearing House, 48(1):3-6, Sept., 1973.

Johnstone, R.: Camping policies and practices, Conference Report of Ontario Camping Association, 1975, pp. 168-170.

Ledlie, J. A., editor: Managing the Y.M.C.A. camp. (New York: Association Press, 1961).

Meyer, H. P.: The director: key man in setting camp "tone," Camping Magazine 47(8):15-16, June, 1975.

Resick, M. C., et al.: Modern administrative practices in physical education and athletics. Reading, Mass.: Addison-Wesley Publishing Co., Inc., 1979). Chapters 1 and 2.

Rodney L. S., and Ford, P. M.: Camp administration. (New York: John Wiley & Sons, Inc., 1971). Chapter 2.

Talley, E. J.: To what extent should staff be involved in camp operations? Camping Magazine, 43(3):22-24, April, 1973.

CHAPTER THREE

Organizational patterns

The organization should only exist in order to carry out some specific purposes implicit in the forecast and the plan. Every piece of it should make a definite and authorized contribution to that purpose.[1]

A camp must be structured in such a way that the organization plan facilitates the attainment of its objectives. Organization, then, is a means to an end. It must never become so inviolable that the plan is more important than the program it is designed to serve. The camp administrator must organize people, tasks, and services to facilitate the efficient and effective conduct of the total camp program. As the camp increases in size, programs become more diversified, larger numbers of staff are required, tasks become more complicated, and the organizational plan grows in complexity and specificity. But, primarily, camp structure is formulated around human relationships. The organization has meaning only to the extent that human expectations are satisfied in harmony with camp expectations.

THE HUMAN ELEMENT
Personal Expectations

Camp organization is concerned with more than defining positions and juggling relationships on an organizational flowchart. Since it is *people* who fill each of the boxes in the organizational plan, the plan is unlikely to function effectively if the needs and expectations of individuals are ignored.

The administrator's goal is to develop an organizational structure that enables the camp to meet its objectives and, at the same time, satisfy staff expectations. It is difficult to visualize a situation in which camp and staff expectations are totally incompatible. The director, however, must strive to bring the two into as much congruence as possible. To achieve this harmony between personal needs and camp goals, directors must familiarize themselves with the expectations of their staff. Such information will be of great help as they identify roles and establish relationships between the various components of the camp organizational structure.

It should not be concluded from the preceding discussion that staff expectations take precedence over organizational goals. What *is* implied is that the camp director must not overlook the human element when developing the organizational design. To attempt to build the plan exclusively around the needs and competencies of personnel may be very shortsighted. This opinion is shared by Pfiffner and Presthus who write:

It is helpful in analyzing organizations to think of positions or roles rather than of individuals in

1. Urwick, L.: The elements of administration. (New York, Harper & Row, Publishers, 1943) p. 42.

them. In the main, function, prestige, and authority inhere in the role itself rather than in the person who may occupy it at any given time. This attribute gives the organization continuity and reduces to some extent its dependence upon any given individual. At the same time, it is important to recognize that any role is affected to some extent by the people in it.[2]

Informal organization

If the camp director ignores human expectations entirely, there is every probability that the staff will develop their own *informal organization* to fulfill their personal needs. Informal organization comprises all the forms of casual interpersonal relationships in which staff members engage. These informal associations may occur between those persons who share common work assignments and problems, or they may involve individuals from different units of the camp. Examples of such informal groups are many. They may comprise the office staff who share their coffee break each day and spend part of the time talking shop, the group of kitchen staff who swim together daily, or counsellors who review the day's happenings over a hamburger in the village during evening hours.

Such informal groups are going to form, and the staff "grapevine" will occasionally misinterpret actions and events that have taken place, regardless of any steps the administration may take to prevent it. The important thing for the camp director to understand is that informal organization is not necessarily negative and deleterious. It may be a therapeutic and highly desirable form of communication. When informal organization is the breeding ground for dissatisfaction and thwarts camp policy, it is obviously symptomatic of larger communication problems. Vigilant directors take advantage of

the positive elements of informal association and, at the same time, are alert to its potential negative aspects so that they may seek the proper ameliorative action at once.

FORMAL ORGANIZATION

We now turn our attention to the main focus of this chapter—the formal structuring of the camp. Formal organizations, and most camps are no exception, tend to develop pyramidal or hierarchical structures (Fig. 3-1). Camps place most of the authority or power in the hands of very few persons at the apex of the pyramid. Ultimate authority inevitably rests with one individual, usually the camp director. As a camp becomes larger and more complex, it also tends to become more hierarchical, that is more job classifications develop in which each group is responsible to the group above in the pyramid. Another characteristic of a large camp is that it invariably becomes more bureaucratic, resulting in increased departmentalization as task assignment is broken down into workable units.

Departmentalization

One of the most formidable tasks the camp director faces is that of organizing people, resources, programs, and services into specialized units that are capable of effectively realizing camp goals.

In the field of administration, these units are most frequently referred to as departments. Peterson and co-workers[3] have identified four types of departmentalization: (1) territorial (place), (2) commodities (products), (3) customer (clientele), and (4) functional (process). For purposes of this discussion, only two of these will be considered relevant to camp organization: customer and functional. *Customer* (or camper) *depart-*

2. Pfiffner, J. M., and Presthus, R.: Public administration. (New York, The Ronald Press Co. 1967) p. 7.

3. Peterson, E., Plowman, G. E., and Trickett, J. M.: Business organization and management. (Homewood, Ill.: Richard D. Irwin, Inc. 1962) p. 149.

mentalization is found in most camps and will be discussed later in this chapter under camper organization.

Functional departmentalization exists in almost all camps today in which size justifies some separation of activities or responsibilities. Camps rarely refer to these units as departments, but they qualify under this administrative definition. Functional departmentalization occurs whenever a camp grows to the point that it subdivides some of its basic functions by task. The tasks that qualify for departmentalization usually have a homogeneous quality and are somewhat specialized from other tasks. It may also be necessary to consider grouping of activities by close association rather than because they are identical or even similar in nature. This is what makes this particular assign-

ment so difficult for the camp director and yet so important: there is undoubtedly one best combination or grouping of administrative units. Careful attention to this aspect of organizational planning pays rich dividends.

Functional units

Few camps use the term *department* when referring to their functional units, perhaps because camp directors do not wish to adopt the formal structures of business and educational organizations. Many camp authorities, seeking to emphasize the relaxed informality of camp life, are hesitant to transpose the terminology of school or industry to the rural outdoor setting in the belief that it profanes the unique quality of camping. I prefer the term *functional unit*.

Because camps vary in size and complex-

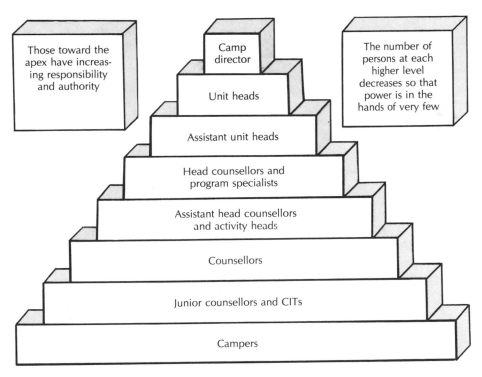

Fig. 3-1. Typical pyramidal camp structure.

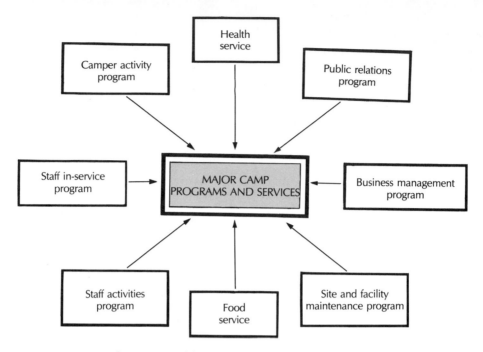

Fig. 3-2. Typical functional units found in a large camp.

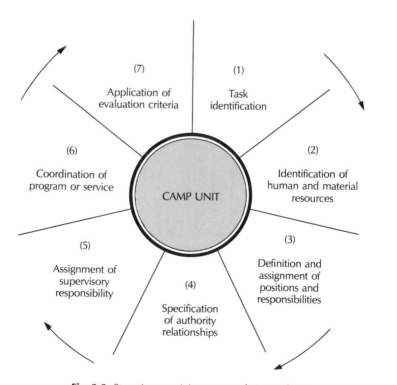

Fig. 3-3. Steps in organizing a camp functional unit.

ity, as well as program emphasis, it is impossible to identify a group of organizational units that are appropriate to all camps. A small camp may group all tasks or programs under two general areas, program functions and administrative functions. Fig. 3-2 identifies eight major functional areas that are usually found in a large camp. Each program and service listed is representative of a group of functions that are undertaken by most camps, and each has a degree of autonomy that sets it apart from the other units.

Although the nature of the specific tasks undertaken by individual units may be quite different, the manner in which each functional unit is organized is essentially the same. Fig. 3-3 outlines in sequential order seven steps the director might take to organize a camp functional unit.

Principles of organization

Although it is impossible to prescribe an organizational plan that would be suitable for the wide diversity of camps in existence today, it is feasible to enumerate organizational principles that can serve as guidelines when developing any camp organizational structure. Such principles allow for variations in the particular way in which they are applied to a given organization. The following guidelines should assist directors as they attempt to determine what structure best meets the special needs of their camp.

1. *The organizational plan must be based on a clear statement of purpose.* This point has already been discussed at some length. Objectives form the foundation on which the camp is built. Organizational structure is designed to serve these goals.

2. *Units in the organizational plan must be selected on the basis of functionalism.* Because the camp is created to meet avowed purposes, only those functional units that contribute directly toward the attainment of these objectives should be considered. Too often, there is a tendency to develop camp programs around the skills and talents of a few individuals. In many cases, these abilities serve very limited, ancillary, or even ulterior purposes. For example, camp staffs often include many persons with strong backgrounds in baseball, basketball, volleyball, and other competitive team games that form the core of many school athletic programs. To develop a program around these special talents, simply because they are available, may seriously compromise the camp program objectives.

3. *Functional units should be selected on the basis of need.* Before a functional unit is selected, analysis of its need and relationship to other units should be carefully examined. Some seemingly apparent programs or services may, on closer examination, be better relegated to a subordinate position or eliminated completely from the organizational plan. Such peripheral services should only be eliminated when they actually interfere with or hinder the realization of important camp objectives. The programs and services shown in Fig. 3-2 do not include a camp store although this is a major project in many camps. The sale of camp souvenirs is promoted, and much staff time and energy is spent on this endeavor. A camp director might find it difficult to justify such an enterprise on the basis of stated camp objectives. It is not suggested that camps should not operate a camp store, but perhaps such a venture should be considered incidental in the total organizational plan.

4. *The human element should be considered paramount when developing an organizational plan.* Consideration of human expectations has been discussed earlier in this chapter.

5. *Delegation of responsibility and authority should be commensurate with ability.* The camp director should seek to challenge all staff members to the extent of their

abilities. This implies careful assessment of the competency of individuals to accept responsibility. Along with the assigning of responsibility must go the authority to carry out the task. Once assignments are allocated, staff members must have a clear understanding of duties and the person, or persons, to whom they are accountable.

6. *Executive control should be delegated as far down the organization as possible.* This statement is closely related to the preceding principle. Camp directors should pass responsibility as far down the camp hierarchy as possible, but, at the same time, they must be assured that in every case the task can be successfully discharged. There are several reasons for this principle:

   a. It reduces administrative costs.
   b. It encourages growth and responsibility among staff members.
   c. It encourages wider experimentation and creativity.
   d. It permits adaptation to the local conditions within a specific unit of the camp.
   e. It is a time-saver.

7. *Lines of administrative responsibility should be direct.* It has already been pointed out that the "chain of command" descends from the top of the pyramid to the various levels within the hierarchy. Staff members are responsible to a supervisor at the immediate level above and rarely to a colleague of equal rank. A few camps would like to operate on the premise that there are no ranks and that all staff are of equal status and authority. This is a distortion of the democratization of administration. Everyone should have an opportunity to share in policy making, but executive responsibility rests, in varying degrees, with selected individuals.

8. *Authority should be centralized at both the organization and unit level.* The senior administrative official of the camp, usu-

ally the camp director, has ultimate authority for all decisions within the camp. At the same time, once the subdivisions or functional units of the camp are clearly defined, the director should in no way attempt to perform all the duties within each unit but should delegate tasks and authority to ensure that they are successfully completed. Some authority, then, is centralized within each functional unit so that it may operate with a degree of independence. A delicate balance must be achieved between unit autonomy and unit supervision. Freedom from control and effective coordination of all functional units requires a confident, experienced camp administrator.

9. *Division of responsibility must be carefully coordinated.* The foregoing principle stresses the importance of one executive authority. However, staff members may occasionally be asked to perform duties that clearly lie in different functional units. In this case, they may be responsible to two or more superiors. For example, it is not uncommon in some small camps to ask the camp nurse to assist in some aspects of the general camp program. In the majority of camps, counsellors are responsible to the head of a living group and are also required to conduct part of the camp program. The same counsellor may also be responsible to the waterfront director at certain times in the day. To avoid overlapping assignments, it is important that those responsible for the various functional units meet regularly and clearly specify lines of communication and responsibility.

10. *Care should be taken to fill executive positions with persons who complement each other.* There is sometimes a tendency for a camp director to employ, in senior executive positions, individuals who bring the same personal qualities and abilities to the job. An inexperienced director may feel more secure in hiring young, compliant staff who

invariably support the director. Another director will select older, conservative persons who are reluctant to make changes and inclined to preserve the status quo. There are real advantages in bringing together an executive team comprised of individuals who are of very different temperaments and abilities. It is desirable to have an "idea" person who possesses imagination, creativity, and much enthusiasm. At the same time, such a person may need to be counterbalanced by a level-headed businessperson with a sense of economic values. It is also desirable to have a good "mix" of age and maturity to reflect different needs and values.

11. *Division of responsibilities should be based on clear-cut differences in tasks performed.* Duties that are similar in nature should be grouped together and assigned to one executive head; duties that are dissimilar should not be assigned to the same person. However, in a small camp, it is not always possible to apply this principle, because of limited numbers of senior staff members.

It is equally important that executive persons not be asked to take on more duties than they are able to handle effectively. Careful attention must be given to this principle when developing job descriptions. It would be unwise to invite a senior section head to supervise sailing if he or she possessed little background or experience in that activity. It would be equally unrealistic to ask that person to accept sole responsibility for the close personal supervision of staff and campers in the senior section of the camp if it comprised 200 campers and over 40 staff members.

12. *The organizational plan must be based on flexibility.* The activities within each functional unit should change to meet new needs. In other cases, a new and innovative suggestion may appear to be functional and worthy of a trial period. Personnel within a unit certainly change from year to year, and this change requires adapting the particular skills of the new staff to the tasks required. There may, in fact, need to be an annual redistribution of some duties within each unit. In general, it is less disrupting to the overall organizational plan if the director asks persons at the lower levels of the hierarchy to adapt and assume new duties than to redistribute assignments at the upper levels. Reallocation of duties of senior staff members tends to cause turmoil for more people and effect the continuity of a larger segment of the camp.

Organizational plans

Just as camper populations vary in age, sex, and religious and socioeconomic background, so too, are great differences found in program emphasis. Camps also differ greatly in size, from those with several dozen campers to those that accommodate 500 or more persons during a single session. The administrative structures of camps reflect these great divergencies so that no one organizational plan may be singled out as appropriate to all situations. The best that can be done is to outline several hypothetical models that will give the reader some awareness of the diversity of organizational structures.

Small camp. In a small camp (less than 75 campers), camp directors often accept responsibility for supervising. all operations within the camp (Fig. 3-4). They personally handle all aspects of public relations, staff hiring, purchasing, and other details of business management that take place prior to the opening of camp. Once camp is in session, they participate in planning all phases of the program, as well as directing the kitchen, health center, and maintenance and business office details. If the scope of the camp operations is too large to enable them to undertake all these responsibilities, the

Fig. 3-4. Model of small private camp of less than 75 campers.

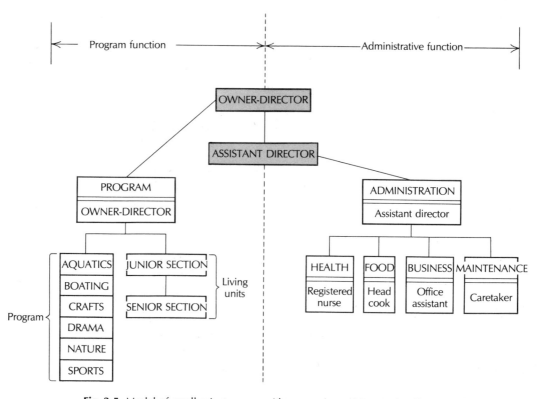

Fig. 3-5. Model of small private camp with one senior assistant to the director.

director may hire one senior assistant with whom the work is shared. Assistants might be given one of several titles depending on the division of duties. If they accept primary responsibility for program, they may be designated as head counsellors or program directors. However, if the camp director is more inclined toward the program side of camp operations, an assistant should be hired who is able to handle the tasks normally assigned to a business manager. Again, it is vital that directors hire someone for this position who complements their own personal skills and experience so that the many duties may be dispatched efficiently. Fig. 3-5 provides an organizational model for a small camp in which the director has an assistant. It shows the assistant director assuming responsibility for all the supportive services, sometimes referred to as the administrative functions. The owner-director, in this example, is directly responsible for all aspects of the program. It would be quite possible for them to switch roles if their individual expertise suggested such an alignment or the responsibilities could be distributed in an entirely different configuration. For example, the owner-director might choose to handle all program responsibilities and, in addition, undertake direct supervision of the infirmary and the general health and safety of the camp community, leaving all other tasks to the assistant.

Large private camp. The organizational chart in Fig. 3-6 is typical of a large camp. In this plan, five functional units are identified, and each is headed by one person who has considerable administrative responsibility. The units vary greatly in size. For example, the director of health services has only a small staff who answer to him, whereas the program director may have over 50 counsellors and intermediate staff members who are responsible for the con-

duct of the camp program. This plan calls for the same program personnel to supervise all campers in their living units. These two seemingly disparate areas of responsibility are combined under one administrative head because there is almost complete duplication of personnel who work in these two areas. Counsellors who conduct the program also serve as cabin or tent counsellors. For this reason, it is considered wise to combine these tasks within one functional unit. Because it is such a large unit, involving the majority of the staff, the program director has a number of program specialists and unit heads who are given responsibility for some part of the total camp program (Fig. 3-7). Fig. 3-8 shows a similar administrative distribution of responsibilities within the living units.

Referring back to the organizational plan in Fig. 3-6, it should be noted that the dietitian in this camp actually takes on the role of director of food services and has responsibility for three separate groups within this functional unit— the food preparation staff, the dining hall staff, and the dishwashers. Some camps place chefs or head cooks directly below the dietitian and make all dining hall and dishwasher staff accountable to them. This is recommended only when the chef has strong managerial skills. It is more common to place the dishwashers under the cook so that there is a division of labor between the kitchen and dining hall. In this pattern, dishwashers may be responsible for minor food preparation before the meal. Another scheme provides for the dishwashers to double as waiters. Under this plan, their responsibilities are as follows: set and wait on tables, clear tables, wash dishes, and do preliminary setting of tables for the next meal.

The plan in Fig. 3-6 provides for a camp advisory board, under the owner, to whom the camp director is responsible. This board is a

Text continued on p. 50.

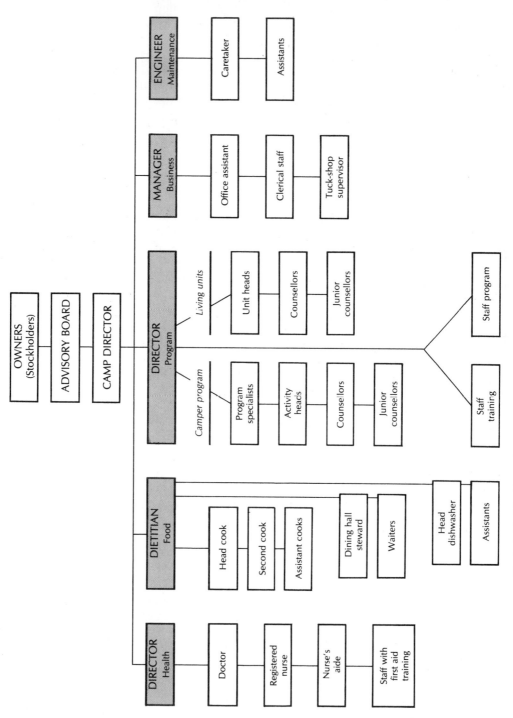

Fig. 3-6. Model of large private camp (over 300 campers) with five primary functional units.

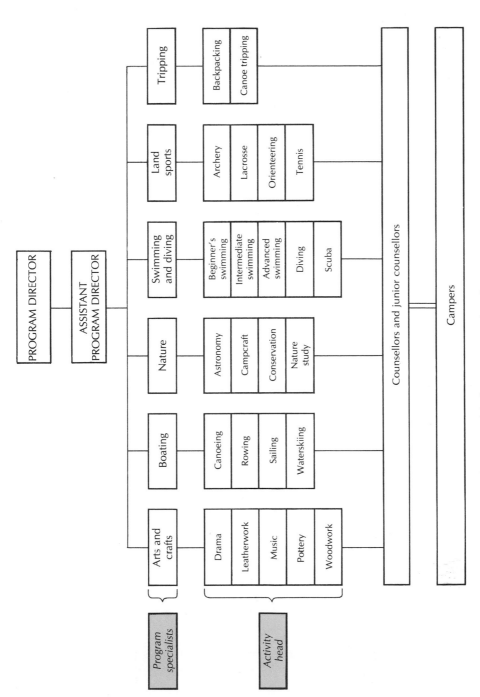

Fig. 3-7. Model of a program unit for a large camp.

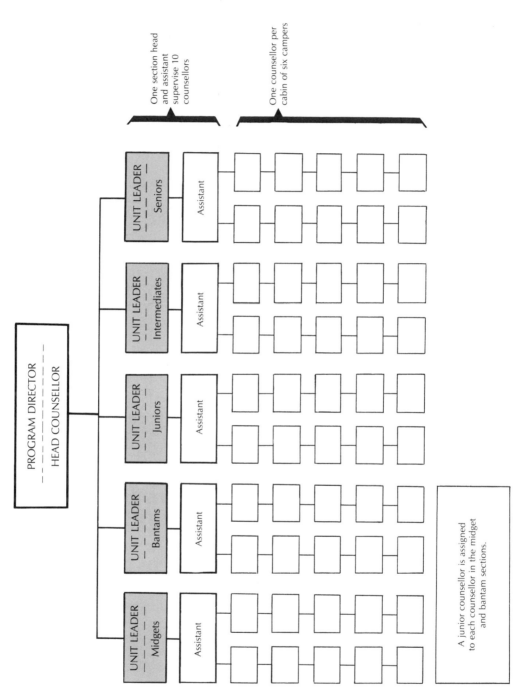

One section head and assistant supervise 10 counsellors

One counsellor per cabin of six campers

PROGRAM DIRECTOR
HEAD COUNSELLOR

UNIT LEADER Midgets — Assistant

UNIT LEADER Bantams — Assistant

UNIT LEADER Juniors — Assistant

UNIT LEADER Intermediates — Assistant

UNIT LEADER Seniors — Assistant

A junior counsellor is assigned to each counsellor in the midget and bantam sections.

Fig. 3-8. Model showing division of responsibility by living unit for approximately 300 campers.

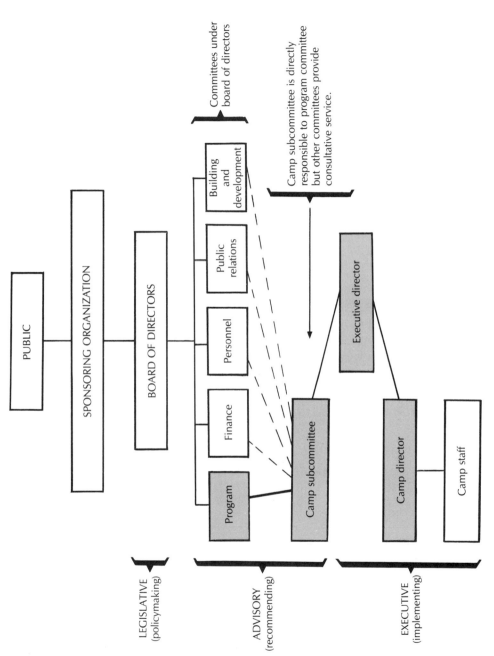

Fig. 3-9. Model of board and committee structure of a large organization camp.

policy-making body, and its function is discussed in greater detail later in this chapter.

Large organizational camp. Several features characterize the large, semipublic, or public camp. The first is that they receive much, if not all, of their support from public funds. As a result, the organization that sponsors the camp is accountable to the public from which it derives its support. A second characteristic of the agency camp is that it invariably appoints, or elects, an advisory board or board of directors who serve as watch dog for the community. As such, the board usually comprises a group that is representative of the public it serves. Fig. 3-9 outlines a hypothetical organizational chart for a large agency camp, with the board of directors assuming a legislative or policy-making role.

It is also customary that a number of advisory committees do much of the detailed work in the name of the board of directors. The example in Fig. 3-9 places camping under a subcommittee that reports to the general program committee of the larger organization. Sometimes camping or outdoor education is accorded full committee status and is placed on the same level as the program committee. This occurs when outdoor education is a major part of the total program emphasis of that particular organization. In such cases, it is not uncommon to find several camps operating under the auspices of the organization. For example, a Y.M.C.A. might run a boy's residence camp, a residence camp for girls, and a coeducational day camp all under one camping or outdoor education committee.

Evaluating the organizational plan

Frequently the weaknesses within a poor organizational plan are not readily apparent to the camp director. There may also be reticence on the part of camp personnel, who have identified the source of the problem,

to pass on the information so that changes may be made. A plan may appear to be excellent on paper, but unless it works, it will lead to confusion and dissatisfaction among the staff.

The following questions should assist camp administrators in assessing the strengths and weaknesses of their organizational plan and determine whether some revision is required.

1. Are the objectives of the camp clearly stated, and is the organizational plan designed to facilitate the achievement of these objectives?
2. Is the plan efficient in its structure so that it provides optimal utilization of human resources?
3. Does the plan adequately account for the personal needs of those persons who will carry out the plan?
4. Is the plan acceptable to the majority of campers and staff?
5. Are the responsibilities of each position in the plan clearly stated and understood by all those involved?
6. As persons assume a new position in the plan, are they fully briefed with regard to their particular role?
7. Does each member understand the lines of authority within the plan?
8. Are all lines of communication open (vertical as well as horizontal)? Are all lines reciprocal, that is, not only from superior to subordinate but from subordinate to superior?
9. Is the total organizational plan adequately coordinated so that there is no duplication of effort or omission of duties?
10. Are facilities, equipment, supplies, and support staff adequate to effectively implement the plan?
11. Are means provided for evaluation and revision of the organizational plan?

CAMPER ORGANIZATION

Just as the staff and their duties are subdivided into functional units, campers are organized into *living units*. As camps increase in size and complexity, it has been noted that frequently much of the intimacy and sense of community is lost. To counteract this tendency toward "bigness," many camps are divided into a series of smaller units that have varying degrees of autonomy.* This process is called *decentralization*. The living units are usually geographically separate from one another and are comprised of as few as four to six sleeping units (cabins, bunks, tents, and the like) and as many as eight to ten.

The degree of autonomy enjoyed by each living unit varies greatly. Boy and girl scout camps, for example, are usually highly decentralized. Each unit has its own site that is separate from other units by a sizable tract of wooded area. Each unit may have its own kitchen, lodge, and washing and toilet facilities, and many will have their own program areas. A few even have separate swimming and boating facilities along the waterfront.

A more common practice is to provide an element of privacy for each living unit with some common facilities in a centralized location that service all living units (Fig. 3-10). In this layout, the living unit, in addition to enjoying some seclusion from other units, has its own toilet and washroom, campfire area, and in some cases, limited recreational facilities within the living unit area such as horseshoe pits and tetherball courts.

---

*Camps adopt a variety of terminology referring to these decentralized units. Some use the term *camp* (for example, junior camp, intermediate camp). Others refer to them as sections, while still others call them tadpoles, chipmunks, beavers, and so forth to differentiate sections. To avoid any ambiguity, this text refers to a tent or cabin group as a *sleeping unit* and a homogeneous group of several sleeping units as a *living unit*.

The campers themselves may be housed in tents, cabins, or small dormitories, the most common being small cabins that accommodate four to eight campers. Since the cabin group replaces the camper's family, it is extremely important that considerable care be exercised in determining its composition. Several criteria may be used. The most obvious, and sometimes the only consideration, is that of age. Other camps group clientele on the basis of grade in school. The use of grade level implies that the school has already done some screening to provide a more homogeneous population. Many camps welcome requests from campers to be with friends. Although this has certain advantages, in that children already know each other and may be assumed to be compatible, it should only be one of a number of considerations. If this becomes the major criterion in determining cabin mates what does the director do when Johnny requests that he be placed with Tom but the desire is not reciprocal? What if the cabins only accommodate five campers, and six children request to be together?

Another consideration is the physical maturity of the camper. When much of the program is oriented toward physical skills, tall, strong, and well-coordinated children may be far happier if placed with campers who are at least a year older. Of perhaps even greater importance is the social and emotional maturity of the child, or what Shalinsky[4] speaks of as *interpersonal behavior* of the individual. By this he refers to the "camper's behavior *toward* others and their ability to cope with behavior *from* others." This includes such characteristic behavior as shyness, aggressiveness, degree of self-control, reaction to shy or aggressive behavior of others, and willingness to submit to control by others.

---

4. Shalinsky, W.: Criteria used in cabin composition, Camping Magazine, **40**(5):15 May, 1968.

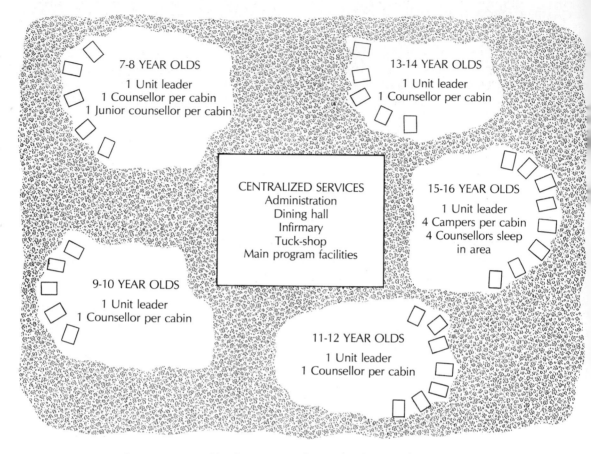

Fig. 3-10. Layout of five living units with centralized services for 175 campers.

The problem with attempting to use interpersonal behavior as a criterion for cabin selection is one of measurement. How does the camp assess these qualities? When a child is returning to camp for another session, the problem is less acute: staff members should have formed some definite opinions regarding the camper's behavior from previous sessions. But when a youngster is coming to camp for the first time, it may be necessary to rely on the personal interview with the camper and parental assessment of a child's social and emotional makeup.

Assuming that it has been possible to gain some insight into an individual's interpersonal relationships, what does the camp do with the information? Research in the field of sociology suggests that compatible groups function more effectively than incompatible groups. Such grouping may work very well for those with high or average skills but there can be real danger in placing a group of persons with low social skills together in a cabin. The writer's experience suggests that such individuals should be spread throughout a number of groups. Perhaps the more important consideration, with these individuals, is to carefully pair them with an experienced counsellor who is patient and able to empathize with such youngsters.

Some camps attract campers from other countries, in which case language, cultural, and religious differences impose additional problems. Much care must be taken in the placement of campers who are coming into a camp situation for the first time. Although each individual case may present unique problems, two generalizations are presented here for consideration. When two or more campers come from the same foreign or uniquely different home environment, it may be wise to place them in the same cabin, at least initially, to provide each one with support during the early adjustment period. If a group of campers are from a different cultural background, it is not recommended that they all be placed together in the same cabin. To do so may simply result in a minighetto in which they become isolated from the mainstream of the camp. For example, in Quebec, children whose first language is English may attend a French-speaking camp or vice versa. Their parents usually select a given camp because of a desire to have their children learn the second language through total immersion in the camp setting. If a group of English-speaking children are all placed in the same living unit, it is almost certain that most of the communication within the group will be in their first language. This is a problem that may face any director of a camp that attracts an international clientele.

DIRECTOR AND STAFF
Administrative team

Some camps have borrowed an idea from the field of education that is very common in schools today: the establishment of an administrative team. The word *team* gives a clue to its purpose. It comprises a group of people who have administrative responsibilities within the camp and who endeavor to work cooperatively in the interests of good camp administration. The administrative team concept is predicated on the premise that administrative decision making is improved when it is the result of group effort.

Not all camp directors favor the establishment of an administrative team because of their personal style of leadership, but the advantages that may accrue from such cooperative effort make the idea worthy of serious consideration. These advantages, or outcomes, may be summarized as follows: (1) improved coordination of services, (2) improved communication between the various organization units, (3) shared decision making leading to better decisions, and (4) clarification of who is accountable to whom.

The camp director, as the senior administrative officer of the camp, should assume responsibility for the composition of the team. A wide range of patterns are possible, especially in a large camp in which many persons have administrative or supervisory responsibilities. Fig. 3-11 and 3-12 indicate but two examples of the possible composition of the team. In the first, the director brings together the heads of the five functional units within the camp to more clearly define the relationship between these units. The camp director must continuously strive to help the group operate as a team when cooperation is the keynote. When directors do not succeed in imbuing the group with the need for mutual respect and common purpose, they may find themselves confronted with five individuals whose primary motivation is to promote their own personal units to the detriment of the camp as a whole.

If the administrative team concept is to succeed, the director must refrain from dominating and controlling the group. Such an approach is not conducive to open expression and exchange of ideas. The role

Fig. 3-11. Administrative team comprised of director and heads of functional units.

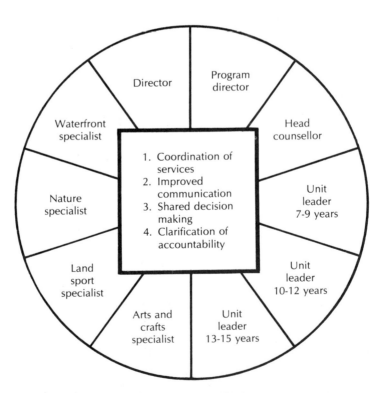

Fig. 3-12. Administrative team including unit leaders and program specialists.

of the leader is that of facilitator. The attempt should be to continually draw out members of the team and help each to make an optimal contribution to the organization.

Fig. 3-12 depicts an administrative team made up primarily of living unit leaders and those responsible for the program. The composition of this team assumes that much coordination is required among the large majority of staff members who have responsibility for conduct of the program as well as supervision of the living groups. Because counsellors are responsible to a unit leader for some part of the day and to a program specialist during other times, there is additional need to ensure that good communication, coordination of counsellor assignments, as well as clear lines of authority regarding decision making and accountability, exist between these two groups of administrative and supervisory personnel. This group should also play a primary role in staff evaluation as will be discussed in Chapter 11.

Staff meetings

The staff meeting has potential for being one of the best vehicles for communication and democratic problem solving. Unfortunately, it is often the most abused of all administrative activities. When badly conducted, the camp staff meeting leads to much criticism and dissatisfaction from all levels of the staff. Four basic weaknesses are most often identified by those who are critical of meetings.

1. Meetings are usually scheduled at night after the campers have retired when staff members are tired and lack patience.
2. Too often, meetings are little more than an excuse for disseminating information.
3. The meeting is often dominated by the camp director.

4. The meeting seldom provides for much staff contribution.

Perhaps the greatest problem hindering camp directors as they attempt to conduct a good meeting is the size of the staff. In small camps, with limited personnel, full staff participation is relatively easy to achieve. In large camps, with dozens of staff members, the all-camp meeting should be utilized mainly for two purposes: problem identification and decision making. The tedious work of investigating a problem, gathering data, and examining possible solutions should be handled by small committees who then bring their recommendations back to the full staff for final decisions.

The following are suggested as sound principles for the camp director to follow in the planning and conduct of staff meetings. They are also applicable for a chairman of a committee or subcommittee, as discussed in the next section.

1. Staff meetings should be conducted during the camp day whenever possible. The quiet hour immediately after the noon meal is frequently selected as a good time (A skeleton staff is required to supervise campers during the meeting.)
2. A meeting should only be called when there is sufficient agenda to warrant it.
3. The meeting should begin and end at a prescribed time.
4. Staff members should be encouraged to submit items for the agenda.
5. The agenda, and all relevant materials, should be distributed to the staff well in advance of the meeting.
6. Staff participation in the meeting should be welcomed by the camp director.
7. Minutes of all meetings should be taken, recording important arguments put forward, decisions reached, and questions yet to be resolved. Minutes

provide continuity from one meeting to another and prevent the need to review material covered earlier.

8. Minutes should be distributed to all relevant parties soon after the meeting to ensure complete understanding of decisions reached.

9. Directors must follow through on all decisions reached at the meeting. In some cases, they should initiate action themselves; at other times, they must supervise colleagues to be assured that the appropriate follow-up action is taken.

As to the actual conduct of the meeting, the skilled administrator uses several strategies that keep the meeting moving at a good pace while encouraging staff participation:

1. Creates friendly, nonthreatening atmosphere
2. Follows the agenda
3. Provides full opportunity for persons to actively participate
4. Clarifies questions and statements to avoid ambiguity
5. Diplomatically discourages disruptions and discussions that are not relevant
6. Summarizes progress periodically so the group knows where it is in relation to the task
7. Mediates differences of opinion

Often meetings are called, not for the purpose of identifying and resolving problems, but rather simply to impart information to the staff. Much of this data should be circulated by information memoranda or written notices posted strategically rather than by attendance at a meeting.

Valuable as the staff meeting may be, not all staff members need to meet on all camp matters. Only those involved with the items on the agenda should be brought together. It is annoying and frequently counterproductive for the staff to be asked to attend a meeting that does not concern them. Sometimes a more efficient approach is to convene smaller groups who then deal with more specific problems of direct concern to that group. These may take the form of unit meetings, committee meetings, or brainstorming sessions.

Unit meetings. There should be regular opportunity for members of a given functional unit to meet. Such meetings enable them to focus on the problems that are unique to their department. The greatest weakness of such meetings is that, too often, the agenda deals only with "housekeeping" items regarding the ongoing, day-to-day operation of the unit that can be better handled in a less formal manner. The camp director can play a significant role in this situation by encouraging the group to explore larger issues and new approaches. The director should work closely with each unit leader so that more important long-range problems become the central focus of its deliberations.

Committees. As has already been pointed out, formation of committees is an excellent administrative procedure for solving problems that, if tackled by the entire staff, would take far too much time. Through committees it is possible to achieve several important objectives:

1. Facilitate exchange of ideas
2. Encourage fuller participation of the staff
3. Promote better coordination
4. Ensure support and cooperation in the execution of a plan
5. Promote staff development and possible acquisition of new skills

Committee work also has its shortcomings. Newman[5] points out the three main limitations of committees when he states that (1) they are a slow and expensive form

5. Newman, W. H.: Administrative action: the techniques of organization and management. (Englewood Cliffs, N.J.: Prentice-Hall, Inc. 1963) pp. 240-245.

of decision making, (2) they may promote divided responsibility, and (3) there is always the danger of compromise decisions.

It is vital that, as committees are established, their role be clearly defined. For example, some committees may be empowered with decision-making authority; others are strictly advisory with some other body having the power for final decision making. This information must be made known to the members of the committee at the outset. Perhaps the greatest frustration that members of a committee can experience is to give conscientious and diligent attention to a problem only to have the camp director or some other higher authority display ambivalence and indecision regarding the implementation of the committee's recommendations. When a committee is asked to research a particular problem on behalf of the larger group, it should be assumed that, under normal circumstances, the recommendations of the committee will be adopted and acted on.

Committee size varies, but it is generally conceded that a group of three to eight persons is an effective number. The smaller the group, the easier it is to arrive at consensus. The larger the number, the greater the varying points of view, expertise, and insight that are brought to bear on the problem.

The key to a successful committee is the selection of the chairperson. Group leaders must be skilled in human relations so that they are able to get the most from each member of the committee while maintaining group cohesion. On the other hand, they must be attuned to the task the committee has been assigned and must possess the conceptual skills to clearly define the problem, gather the necessary data, and lead the group to the best solution available.

Brainstorming. Brainstorming is a method of attacking a particular problem by means of "free-wheeling," completely open-ended discussion. It is most successful with a small group of five to eight persons in which all members are encouraged to express any and every idea that comes into their head regarding the task. No idea should be considered "too far out" initially: another member of the group may pick up on that idea and refine it into something quite workable.

The brainstorming technique has been used with particular success in developing new and creative program ideas. For example, a small group of program staff members are challenged to come up with an original "all camp" program to celebrate the tenth anniversary of the camp. It is helpful to have a blackboard available on which each idea, no matter how preposterous, is listed. The success of brainstorming lies in other members of the group "taking off" on someone else's suggestion and developing it further until a workable solution takes shape. Many innovative programs have been developed through the use of this technique.

EXTERNAL ORGANIZATION

Up to this point, discussion of organizational patterns has focused on those within the camp that involve camp personnel. Attention will now be directed to structures that exist external to the camp itself but, nevertheless, play an important role in the total administrative structure of some camps.

The many sponsoring organizations that operate camps have traditionally established an advisory board or camp committee to assist in planning and formulating policy. There is great variation in how such advisory groups are structured, and it is beyond the scope of this book to deal with the many models that are found today. Suffice it to say that some camp committees operate 12 months of the year and undertake all the preseason planning. Members of the committee are responsible for many of the duties and responsibilities normally assumed by the camp director. In such cases, directors are hired annually and assume their duties only weeks before the camp opens and conclude their responsibilities days after the camp season formally ends.

At the other extreme are large organizations that operate one or more camps as part of a large community service program. Such an organization may have a large representative board of directors whose function it is to establish policy and approve decisions. Next in line of authority are several standing committees who are responsible for recommending policy to the board of directors. These committees serve essentially in an advisory capacity. Fig. 3-9 (p. 49) provides an example of a large organization with its standing committees and a subcommittee responsible for camping.

Between the two examples sited above are many different types of external organizational structure in which the division of responsibility is distributed according to the special needs of that organization.

While the discussion of external organization has dealt thus far with organizational camps, there is equal merit in establishing an advisory board or committee for independent camps. The reasons for an advisory group are as valid in the case of the private camp as they are for those supported by some sponsoring agency. The main reason why private camps have failed to use this administrative structure is that while it is relatively easy to find conscientious, public-spirited citizens who are anxious to render service, especially when children are involved, it is more difficult to engage volunteers to serve in an advisory capacity for a private organization.

The camp committee or advisory board

Composition and size. Members of the camp committee or board may be appointed or elected. A review of qualifications show a number of traditional weaknesses in the composition of camp committees. Members are usually beyond middle age, conservative in nature, and predominantly male. The recommended qualifications should be: (1) interest in camping and outdoor activity, (2) genuine concern for the welfare of youth, and (3) specialist skill and knowledge that will be of value to the committee. The size of the committee has traditionally tended to be large, but in recent years smaller groups have proved to be more efficient with numbers ranging from five to twelve members.

Functions. The terms of reference of the committee should be clearly spelled out in writing by the authority to whom it reports. Although it may have policy-making authority when serving a private camp, the usual practice in organizational camps is to limit its function to an advisory and recommending capacity. The following are the functions performed by most camp committees:

1. Formulation of a statement of the purpose and objectives of the camp.
2. Establishment of general camp policies that are consistent with camp objectives, camp standards, and government regulations.
3. Purchase, development, and ongoing maintenance of the camp site and all its facilities.
4. Planning the broad scope of the camp program and providing the necessary equipment and supplies.
5. Providing guidelines for the selection and training of the director and the staff.
6. Provision of a sound fiscal basis for the operation of the camp.
7. Assistance in developing a strong public relations program for the camp.
8. Guarantee of continuity in the ongoing operation of the camp. Because the director may change from year to

year, the committee provides stability for the operation.

9. Development of a safe and healthful environment for both campers and staff.

10. Arbitration of disagreements or disputes that resist solution at the administrative level.

The camp director and the committee

The role of the camp committee is largely advisory; the function of the camp director is executive. Both exist to provide the best possible experience for the campers. It is, therefore, essential that a very close and cooperative relationship exist between them. Directors should welcome the assistance that their committee is able to provide by making available a variety of talents as well as offering much needed continuity and stability to the long-range operation of the camp. At the same time, the committee should see its role as a facilitator in assisting the directors in executive function. The experienced director enjoys a relationship with the camp committee that is very different from the one enjoyed by a new camp director. The former guides and assists members of the committee in better understanding the total camp function, while the new director relies heavily on the committee for direction in the early stages of being in office. The critical point is that both directors understand clearly their respective roles. The committee should be wary of "meddling" in the director's administrative duties, just as the director must respect the policy-making role of the committee. A final point: nothing is more disconcerting to a director than to be required to give account to a committee whose members rarely, if ever, visit the camp when it is in operation.

ADMINISTRATIVE GUIDELINES

1. No camp organizational plan can function effectively without regard for the needs and expectations of the staff who are expected to implement the plan.

2. The various tasks that are required of most camps should be broken down into departments or functional units. Examples of camp functional units are business management, food services, health and safety, program, public relations, site and facility maintenance, and staff development.

3. Each camp organizational structure should be based on a number of widely accepted administrative principles that have been developed over many years.

4. Any organizational structure should result from a clear statement of purpose for a particular camp. The organizational makeup of the camp is designed to serve camp goals and should never dictate camp policy.

5. All lines of administrative responsibility must be open and direct to facilitate effective two-way communication.

6. The complexity of the organizational plan of a given camp should be consistent with the scope of the program offered. A small camp of less than 75 campers requires a much simpler administrative structure than the camp that involves several hundred campers of different ages.

7. Large camps should consider subdividing campers into homogeneous living units to preserve a sense of community and to avoid the impersonality that often characterizes the big camp.

8. Careful consideration must be given to the composition of tent or cabin groups since this sleeping unit replaces the campers' families during their stay at camp.

9. Camp directors should give serious consideration to the formulation of an administrative team to advise the director on many administrative matters.

10. Brainstorming sessions, camp committees, unit meetings, and all-camp staff meetings must be carefully planned if they are to serve as effective means of communication and problem solving.

11. The camp advisory committee or board has an important role to play in most agency camps, and its composition and function should be given very careful consideration.

Care must also be taken to ensure that an effective working relationship exists between the camp director and the camp committee.

SELECTED BIBLIOGRAPHY

Dalton, M.: Changing line—staff relations, Personnel Administration, pp. 3-5, March/April, 1966.

Gross, M.: Organizations and their managing. (New York: The Macmillan Co., 1968).

Hanson, R. J. and Carlson, R. E.: Organizations for children and youth. (Englewood Cliffs, N. J.: Prentice-Hall, Inc., 1972). Chapters 7 and 8.

Heller, J. H., et al.: Camping with a purpose— 4-H handbook. (Washington, D. C.: U. S. Government Printing Office, 1972).

Hjelte, G. and Shivers, J. S.: Public administration of recreational services. (Philadelphia: Lea & Febiger, 1972). Chapters 3 and 4.

Kraus, R. G. and Curtis, J. E.: Creative administration in recreation and parks. (Saint Louis: The C. V. Mosby Co., 1977). Chapter 3.

Luehrs, A. F.: Guidelines for effective cooperation between director and volunteers, Camping Magazine, 44(3):10-11, 14, March, 1972.

Rodney, L. S., and Ford, P. M.: Camp administration. (New York: John Wiley & Sons, 1971) Chapter 2.

Shalinsky, W.: Criteria used in cabin composition, Camping Magazine, 40(5):15, May, 1968.

Shivers, J. S.: Camping: administration, counseling, programming. (Englewood Cliffs, N. J.: Prentice-Hall Inc., 1971). Chapter 2.

CHAPTER FOUR

Personnel management

> It's not the critic who counts, nor the man who points out how the strong man stumbled or where the doer of deeds could have done better. The credit belongs to the man who is actually in the arena; whose face is marred by dust and sweat and blood; who strives valiantly; who errs and comes short again and again; who, at the best, knows in the end the triumph of high achievement; and who, at the worst, if he fails, at least fails while doing greatly, so that his place shall never be with those cold and timid souls who know neither victory nor defeat.
>
> **Theodore Roosevelt**

Once a camp has clearly defined its goals, the organizational structure that can best realize these objectives can be planned. As was seen in the previous chapter, the purpose of the organizational plan is to separate the many camp assignments into workable and manageable segments or units. These in turn provide specific positions requiring varying degrees of responsibility and authority.

The next step is to delineate, in some detail, each of these positions so that they may be classified and personnel may be hired and trained to perform the functions necessary to carry out the many tasks within the camp organization. This chapter deals with the recruitment and selection of the camp staff and the various facets of personnel management that assist individuals in making their optimal contribution to the organization.

There is almost total unanimity among writers within the field of administration that personnel management is the single most important role the administrator must

fulfill. This sentiment is echoed in equally strong terms by those associated with the camping movement.

Weather, location, facilities and equipment, food, program—all are important to the success of an organized camp. Even more crucial, however, in determining how well the camp is able to fulfill its multiple objectives is the quality of its leadership."[1]

An editorial in *Canadian Camping*[2] on staff hiring practices concludes with the following statement: "The future of your camp, and of camping in Canada, depends on the quality of leaders elected for our camp staffs."

FUNCTIONS OF PERSONNEL MANAGEMENT

The scope of personnel management is broad, but the ultimate aim is to provide

---

1. Percy, M. L.: Camp counsellor selection, Camping Magazine 36(3):22, Feb., 1964.
2. Editorial: Hiring staff? Here are a few ideas, Canadian Camping, 29(6):7, Dec., 1977.

members of the camp staff with the direction and guidance necessary to encourage their maximum contribution to the realization of camp objectives. Although the details of personnel administration vary from one camp to another, camp administrators should normally expect to assume the following functions:

1. *Position analysis, description, and classification.* This involves the assessment of the work to be performed in each position and a description and classification of each assignment in preparation for the recruitment of candidates.

2. *The staffing process, including recruitment, selection, and orientation of the new staff.* Individuals who apply for each position are screened, selected, and placed in positions commensurate with their interests, skills, and knowledge.

3. *In-service training and development of the staff.* Many camp staff members are young and inexperienced. In-service training is the process through which they are prepared, during the camp season, to do a more competent job.

4. *Development of job satisfaction and staff morale.* Team cohesiveness is critical to the camp operation. It is the function of personnel administration to promote high morale among the staff.

5. *Staff appraisal and promotion.* Good personnel management requires that methods be developed to recognize and reward those individuals who demonstrate superior performance by placing them in positions that will be personally fulfilling and of greatest advantage to the camp.

6. *Establishment of personnel policies regarding conditions of employment.* Conditions of employment include such matters as remuneration, work load, time off and separation.

7. *Professional conduct of the staff.* It is only natural that, from time to time, problems of discipline and grievance will arise within a large staff. The techniques used to overcome these difficulties is part of personnel management.

8. *Supervision and evaluation of personnel.* This involves the process whereby the performance of a staff member is compared with the expectations that were established when the job description was prepared.

The success or failure of a camp depends very substantially on the effectiveness of personnel management. If human talents are the most critical factor in the success of a camp, it naturally follows that much time and effort must be spent in selecting the best staff possible. Once the staff is hired, it is incumbent on the administration to ensure that each staff member is happy and feels a sense of purpose as a member of the camp team.

QUALIFICATIONS OF THE STAFF

With few exceptions, members of a camp staff are expected to lead. Just as the camp director and senior unit heads must accept administrative responsibility for a large segment of the staff, so too must intermediate staff members demonstrate their leadership capacity with counsellors and other support staff. In a similar manner, counsellors assume the leadership role as they work with campers in the living units and in the conduct of the camp program. This raises the interesting question as to what are the qualities of leadership that the camp director should seek when hiring the staff.

Kast and Rosenzweig[3] identified a total of 32 items that are required for effective leadership. Such an extensive list suggests that leadership is akin to sainthood. Other researchers conclude that it is fruitless to seek to identify human traits since leadership is

3. Kast, F. E., and Rosenzweig, J. E.: Organization and management: a systems approach. (New York: McGraw-Hill Book Co., 1970).

peculiar to a given situation. This theory of leadership suggests that an individual's capacity to lead varies greatly from one situation to another. As the objectives sought are altered and the makeup of the group changes, so does the individual's capacity to play the leadership role. Under this concept, leadership is a product of what the leader brings to a given situation, as well as the relationship that is established with the group in attempting to resolve a particular task or set of tasks.

Regardless of the particular theory one holds with respect to leadership, the camp director must hire enough people to effectively operate the camp. What general characteristics or qualities should be sought in the persons hired? The American Camping Association[4] recommends that directors look for five characteristics when hiring camp personnel: (1) liking and understanding of children, (2) enjoyment of outdoor living, (3) knowledge and skills for the position, (4) high level of physical fitness, and (5) maturity.

The *Canadian Camping Magazine*[5] points out that "previous camp experience and a high degree of skill in camp activities are not always necessary requisites" for a staff member. The article places greater emphasis on the personal qualities of the individual and lists self-confidence, friendliness, adaptability, leadership, and cheerfulness as desirable attributes to be sought.

POSITION ANALYSIS, DESCRIPTION, AND CLASSIFICATION

Once the goals of a camp have been formulated and an organizational plan developed, the director should group or classify

similar positions and then undertake a detailed analysis of each position. As was noted in Chapter 3, a large camp provides for many positions at many different levels of specialization. An important aspect of personnel management requires that each position be carefully analyzed as to general responsibility, specific duties, and relationships with others in the camp organization.

After a thorough analysis is complete, a written job description should be prepared that spells out position specifications including qualifications required.

Once job analysis and description has been developed, it should not be changed each time the position is filled by a new person. Staff members may change from summer to summer, but the position should remain reasonably stable. This does not preclude the need for periodic re-evaluation of the job description, however. Whenever such assessment is undertaken, those who have filled the position should be invited to participate in the review of it.

The next step is to classify various positions. Classification refers to grouping under one title those positions with similar responsibilities and duties. The classification of a group of positions implies that they require similar qualifications and that the experience, knowledge, and skill necessary to fill the position are sufficiently alike to warrant similar orientation and in-service training as well as comparable remuneration.

Advantages of job description and classification

The value of pursuing the three steps of analysis, description, and classification should be apparent. These procedures help provide a degree of objectivity and administrative efficiency when dealing with personnel problems and grievances. A thoughtfully prepared classification of positions:

1. Provides a sound basis for recruitment,

4. American Camping Association: Camp administration course outline. (Bradford Woods, Martinsville, Ind.: American Camping Association, 1961) p. 7.
5. Editorial: Hiring staff? here are a few ideas," Canadian Camping, **29**(6):5-6, Dec., 1977.

selection, and orientation of personnel

2. Clarifies use of terminology for all concerned when referring to positions
3. Ensures formulation of equitable salary schedules
4. Facilitates the identification of specific duties and responsibilities for both the staff members and the supervisors
5. Reduces inconsistencies in the application of personnel practices
6. Provides the basis of appraisal and evaluation of personnel

Format of a job description

A job description comprises a summary of the requirements and responsibilities assigned to a particular staff member in the performance of a given job. The description of the position should be based on a comprehensive examination of the actual tasks to be performed and the qualifications deemed necessary to fill the position. Job descriptions may be written in many ways but each should include (1) title of the position, (2) brief description of the position, (3) person

---

Program director. The program director is the senior executive person responsible for all facets of the camp program. These include developing, implementing, and coordinating the overall program of the camp. He is responsible for the supervision of each program specialist and activity head.

Accountability. The program director is responsible to the camp director and is required to submit a written program report at the end of the camp season.

Requirements. The program director should:
1. Normally be a minimum of 25 years of age and have at least 5 years of camping experience, two of which involve some administrative responsibility
2. Have a thorough understanding of the camp philosophy, its aims, and objectives
3. Possess a broad working knowledge of many, if not all, of the activities offered in the camp program
4. Whenever possible, possess a degree in recreation or physical education
5. Possess the ability to get along with people and have strong communication skills

Duties. The program director:
1. Assists the director in the recruitment, selection, and orientation of all program staff
2. Accepts primary responsibility for the planning and conduct of all staff precamp and in-service training that relates to program
3. Is responsible for supervising the planning and scheduling of all program activities within the camp as well as assigning staff for the conduct of these activities
4. Coordinates the various facets of the program as well as the facilities and equipment necessary
5. Develops and supervises all camper reports
6. Serves as liaison between the program department and other units of the camp
7. Is responsible for coordinating the supervision and evaluation of all program staff

Fig. 4-1. Sample position description for a program director.

to whom the staff member is accountable, (4) requirements for the position, and (5) duties or responsibilities of the position. Fig. 4-1 provides a sample job description for the position of program director. The American Camping Association[6] has prepared a helpful booklet in which job descriptions for many camp positions are outlined.

THE STAFFING PROCESS

Three distinct steps are involved in the staffing process: *recruitment* of applicants, *selection* of the best candidates, and *induction* of the new staff. Each will be discussed at some length in the following section.

Before the staffing process can be initiated, the camp director or the camp committee must examine carefully the interrelationship between three important types of data (Fig. 4-2):

1. *Purpose and objectives of the camp* de-

termine the types of staff members required.

2. *Salary budget available* influences the number and quality of staff members to be employed.

3. *Number and kinds of staff members necessary* to offer a program that will realize the camp goals.

Once the number and caliber of staff members required has been determined, the recruitment process can begin. Much time is required to scrupulously screen and interview many applicants, but it is time well invested when, as has already been stated, the caliber of staff is so important to a successful camp operation.

The democratization of administrative practice, in recent years, has lead many camps to form a staff recruitment and selection team. The team is usually composed of the camp director and several members of the staff who represent various levels of the camp hierarchy. The team often includes a member of the camp committee and in some cases a camper representative and/or

---

6. American Camping Association: Camp Staff Job Descriptions. (Bradford Woods, Martinsville, Ind.: American Camping Association).

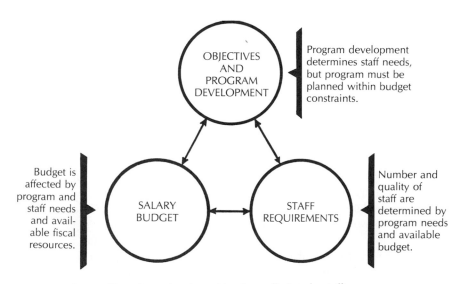

Fig. 4-2. Three interrelated considerations affecting the staffing process.

a parent. Two sound administrative principles are involved in formulating a staff recruitment and selection team: (1) it relieves a single person of the total responsibility for staff selection (two heads are better than one), and (2) camp personnel should have a voice in the selection of colleagues with whom they are expected to work closely.

Staff recruitment

Recruitment is the active pursuit of potential candidates for the purpose of persuading them to apply for positions available in a given camp. The object is to attract as many applicants as possible from the best candidates available.

Some camps experience difficulty each season in hiring competent, qualified staff members, while others are able to select personnel from a large number of applicants. This should tell camp directors something about their camp. There are several possible explanations for a camp's failure to attract high quality staff. The reason most often cited by camp directors who have hiring problems is the salary budget. They contend that their inability to pay salaries that are in line with other part-time summer positions is at the root of the problem. In some cases, this is a valid argument, particularly in agency camps in which the director may have little or no control over the salary budget but is expected to hire a strong staff with limited funds. In some cases, however, it may be a case of misplaced priorities. Money is sometimes available for capital improvements and equipment that might better be spent on improving the quality of leadership. A strong argument can be given for a higher salary budget: quality personnel provide a better program, which in turn attracts more campers.

The problem of recruitment of the camp staff is particularly acute when attempting to fill some specialist positions such as camp nurse, waterfront director, and qualified trip counsellors. The following suggestions should be examined as possible means of overcoming this recruitment problem:

1. Pay salaries that are competitive
2. Employ university students for longer periods by having them assist with pre-camp preparation
3. Explore cooperative program possibilities with colleges and universities in which students in education, physical education, and recreation may gain field experience credits toward their degree
4. Re-examine job descriptions to make positions more challenging and personally rewarding
5. Reassess CIT and junior counsellor training programs to provide a broader base from which to select junior staff members.

Another reason why camp directors may experience difficulty in recruiting competent staff is their failure to explore thoroughly all sources of possible applicants. Successful recruitment requires aggressive action on the part of those responsible for hiring practices. Where one camp director sends a form letter with accompanying job descriptions to the local college of education, a more enterprising colleague pays a personal visit to the same institution and attempts to set up a meeting with all undergraduates who are interested in learning about summer employment opportunities.

The following sources of possible recruitment are but a few of the many avenues available to the camp director; (1) returning staff, (2) former staff and campers, (3) referrals from current and former staff, (4) in an organizational camp, persons from other departments within the agency, (5) recruitment through the local camping association office, (6) state employment services, (7) announcements placed on bulletin boards in high schools, colleges, universities, churches, agencies, public libraries, and other appropriate locations, (8) personal contact with colleges of education, physical education, and recreation, (9) placement bureaus in high schools, colleges, and universities, and (10) paid advertisements through the media such as daily newspapers, weeklies, and radio stations.

Perhaps the single most important factor in successful staff recruitment is the general reputation of the camp. If a camp is widely known for its excellent camp program as well as its good working conditions, these two considerations will do more to enhance staff recruitment than any other single factor. While this observation may be obvious, it must be emphasized that unless a camp enjoys an excellent reputation as a quality camp all else in the way of staff recruitment may prove futile.

Staff selection

Staff selection involves five sequential steps (Fig. 4-3):

1. *Preparing position specifications.* The first step in the staff selection process is to determine the qualifications of the person the camp seeks to employ and then to define clearly the position to be filled. The specifications should also include the salary to be offered and opportunities for advancement at the camp. It is at this point that the camp director may wish to organize a *staff selection team,* so that a number of people may be involved in preparing the staff selection criteria.

2. *Publicizing the position.* The position must then be made known to the widest possible number of potential applicants. This should be done through a variety of contacts. Information regarding the application procedure to be followed should also be

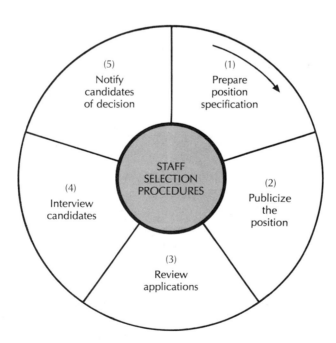

Fig. 4-3. Five steps in the staff selection process.

circulated along with the description of the position.

3. *Reviewing application papers.* The purpose of requiring various papers as part of the application is to gain information that will enable the staff selection team to determine which applicants should be invited for personal interviews. The papers most frequently requested are: (1) application form, (2) academic transcript, (3) written statement of camping philosophy, (4) standardized tests, and (5) letters of reference.

The *application* itself may provide a great deal of useful information, depending on how carefully it has been designed. Some of the information requested is factual and may be accepted at face value. Other information is quite subjective, and the selection team must be cautioned against drawing firm conclusions based solely on this data. Applicants are obviously anxious to convey the best image possible and will be very reluctant to include anything that might jeopardize their chances of securing a position. Arend[7] reports on a study in which he concluded that, for the most part, candidate's placement papers do not differentiate between effective and ineffective teachers. Arend's findings among teachers is supported by the work of Perry[8] who reports: ". . . very few items usually used in typical counsellor application blanks have been shown statistically to have any relationship with counsellor success." Gorton[9] sums up the real value of application papers when he states: "Perhaps the best use of placement credentials is to develop hypotheses and questions about

candidates, which can later be explored during the personal interview."

The practice of requesting *academic transcripts* from applicants is not widespread in the camping field. When they are required, it is assumed that they are the best and most convenient measure of the intellectual capacity of the applicant.

Some assessment of the applicant's *philosophy of camping* may provide limited insight into the applicant's capacity to fill a position at a given camp. This information may also be gained through the personal interview. Frequently, however, the selection team will request a written statement. In either case, to gain this information, it will probably be necessary to ask questions such as, "What do you expect to gain from a season at camp?" "What do you hope to be able to give to campers?" or "What do you believe are the important values of a camping experience for children?"

Many researchers have attempted to develop a single index or battery of *standardized tests* that will aid in predicting who will be successful camp counsellors. The tests may be written, oral, practical, or a combination of these. They include tests of general aptitude, intelligence, achievement, personality inventories, and vocational interest profiles.

In the field of camping, several studies have been conducted in an attempt to successfully select camp counsellors. Dimock[10] developed a leadership inventory that can be completed in less than 60 minutes and contends that "this inventory can predict who will be a successful camp counsellor better than 9 times out of 10."

Perry[11] reports on studies done in the

7. Arend, P.: Teacher selection: the relationship between selected factors and the rated effectiveness of second year teachers. An ERIC Report: Ed. -087-102, 1973.
8. Perry, M. L.: Camp counsellor selection, Part II, Camping Magazine **36**(4):17, March, 1964.
9. Gorton, R. A.: School administration: challenge and opportunity for leadership. (Dubuque, Iowa: William C. Brown Co., Publishers, 1976) p. 156.

10. Dimock, H. G.: How to choose only successful camp counsellors, Camping Magazine, **42**:(4):8, April, 1970.
11. Perry, M. L.: Camp counsellor selection, Camping Magazine, **36**(3) 25-26, Feb., 1964; 36(4):17-18, March, 1964.

summer of 1960 with 396 men and women camp counsellors who were employed at private as well as youth agency camps in southern California. The following quotation from Perry's report summarizes the most important conclusion drawn from these studies.

While this study revealed a number of personal and professional qualities which appeared to have a high relationship with the degree of effectiveness as a camp counsellor, it seemed equally apparent that persons with very different personality, interest and attitude patterns and with diversified environmental backgrounds can successfully perform the functions and responsibilities entailed in camp counselling.[11]

Although some interesting work has been done in attempting to predict counsellor success through the use of standardized tests, no definitive instrument has been developed for selection of camp staff.

After all the documents and papers of each applicant have been carefully reviewed, the selection committee should place each application in one of three groups: (1) strong candidate, (2) possible candidate, and (3) noncandidate. At this time, the persons in the third category should be sent a personal letter thanking them for their application but advising them that they are no longer being considered for the position.

The committee should then check out the *letters of reference* for each of the strong candidates. Some selection committees check on the references for all the possible candidates and even interview each of these individuals. However, if a large camp has many applications for each position, it becomes almost mandatory for the committee to do some initial screening so that only those who are considered reasonably strong candidates will go through the interview process. Under these circumstances, the *possible candidates* are temporarily set aside as a reserve group in case the position is not filled from the list of strong candidates.

Letters of reference may, or may not, provide valuable information regarding the applicant. It must be remembered that the reference persons are selected by the applicant and should therefore be expected to stress the positive qualities of the candidate. Unfortunately, many of these people do not state their true feelings regarding the potential staff member but comment on only the affirmative qualities and omit the weaknesses. Staff selection committees will find it a good investment in time if they prepare a standardized assessment form that may be mailed to each reference person. The form should make provisions for comments on the weaknesses of the applicant as well as the strengths. It is also strongly recommended that, whenever possible, members of the staff selection committee should make personal contact with the persons who provide references. Direct conversation has been found to yield a much more accurate appraisal of the candidate than use of a standardized form alone.

Camp directors and their senior staff members, should remember that when they are asked to provide a reference for someone, they have a professional obligation to give an honest and frank appraisal of the person. To fail to do so can only hurt the camping profession generally, and such action may come back to haunt the directors themselves when, at some later date, they expect a forthright appraisal from a camping colleague.

After all the references have been checked out for each strong candidate and personal contact has been made with at least one of the reference persons, the staff selection committee should be in a position to reduce the number of applicants to a short list of those whom they wish to interview.

4. *Interviewing candidates.* The personal interview is generally regarded as the most

important of all the procedures in the selection of new staff members. However, it is a time-consuming process, and some camp directors attempt to economize by conducting interviews by phone. A few even hire staff members without making any direct contact with the applicant. Neither of these practices is recommended. The interview should be a two-way process in which the organization learns a great deal about the candidate and the candidate has full opportunity to gain important information regarding the camp, its philosophy, as well as the position advertised.

The interview should be carefully planned if the time involved is to be used expeditiously. In some instances, directors may conduct the interview on their own. In other cases, two or three members of the staff seleciton committee meet with the candidate. In yet other camps, the full committee is involved in the interview. Clower,[12] in a study of the selection of teachers, underscores the importance of advanced planning for the interview. She reports that: (1) most interviews were not effective in revealing a candidate's ability to teach, his philosophy, or his basic preparation for teaching, and (2) applicants left the interview with only a hazy idea regarding the position.

Careful consideration of the types of information the interview should provide, for both the selection team and the candidate, greatly enhances the value of this procedure. The following questions are suggested as a guide to a well-planned interview:

1. What steps should be taken to ensure good rapport between the candidate and the selection committee? How are communication and candor facilitated?
2. What specific information does the committee seek from the candidate?

What questions should be asked to gain this information? How should the questions be sequenced? Who should ask each question?

3. What questions is the candidate likely to ask? What kinds of information does the committee want to convey to the candidate during the interview?

During the interview itself, it is important that the candidate be put at ease. This implies a warm, friendly atmosphere. At the same time, the members of the committee must realize that their primary function is to assess the candidate's suitability for the position. Members must be prepared to probe the weaknesses as well as the strengths of the candidate. It must be remembered that those interviewed will rarely volunteer information regarding their limitations.

Development of a simple evaluation form to be used during the interview will do much to make the interview procedure more objective. At the same time, it assists the interviewer to focus on the types of questions that should be asked. A sample assessment form, shown in Fig. 4-4 lists six areas in which valuable insight regarding the candidate may be gained.

Magee[13] lists six common weaknesses that should be avoided when conducting an interview:

1. Posing questions that can be answered by "yes" or "no," thereby eliciting little information from the candidate.
2. Asking unimaginative questions for which the astute applicant already has prepared answers.
3. Asking leading questions that suggest the "correct answers."
4. Asking questions that reveal the interviewer's attitude on the questions.

---

12. Clower, H. L.: The use of the personal interview in the selection of teachers. (Ed. D. dissertation, University of Southern California, 1963).

13. Magee, R. H.: The employment interview—techniques of questioning, Personnel Journal, pp. 241-245, May, 1962.

```
┌─────────────────────────────────────────────────────┐
│              STAFF INTERVIEW ASSESSMENT               │
├───────────────────────────────┬───────────────────────┤
│  Name of candidate            │  Date                 │
├───────────────────────────────┼───────────────────────┤
│            Item               │     Rating*           │
├───────────────────────────────┼───────────────────────┤
│  Self-confidence              │                       │
├───────────────────────────────┼───────────────────────┤
│  Communication skills         │                       │
├───────────────────────────────┼───────────────────────┤
│  Philosophy and values        │                       │
├───────────────────────────────┼───────────────────────┤
│  Experience with children     │                       │
├───────────────────────────────┼───────────────────────┤
│  Maturity and dependability   │                       │
├───────────────────────────────┼───────────────────────┤
│  Leadership potential         │                       │
├───────────────────────────────┼───────────────────────┤
│                     Total:    │                       │
├───────────────────────────────┴───────────────────────┤
│  Comments:                                            │
│                                                       │
│                                                       │
│                              Signature                │
└───────────────────────────────────────────────────────┘
```

*1 = Weak; 2 = Average; 3 = Above average;
4 = Strong

Fig. 4-4. Personal interview assessment form.

5. Asking questions that are unrelated to the task.
6. Asking questions that were already answered on the candidate's application form or résumé.

5. *Notifying the candidate of the decision.* Following each interview, there should be a discussion of the candidate's strengths and weaknesses by members of the staff selection team. Sometimes it is possible to make a decision at this point to offer the candidate a position or to reject the applicant. If, for example, a camp is interviewing ten individuals for eight counsellor positions, it may be quite in order to make a firm offer to a strong candidate at the time of the interview. Usually, however, all applicants should be interviewed before final decisions are made.

It must be emphasized that the staff selection team should keep a *written record* of all conference assessments. This record is of great value when final decisions are delayed for several days and many candidates have been seen in the interim. It is also helpful to have some written report in the event that a question is raised regarding the selection procedure.

Throughout the selection process, it is extremely important that those persons who are responsible for making the final selections retain a high degree of objectivity. Some research indicates that personal bias is a powerful factor in candidate selection. Merritt[14] indicates that school principals involved in the selection process are attracted to teacher candidates who show attitudes toward education that are similar to their own attitudes regardless of the candidates' quali-

14. Merritt, D. L.: Attitude congruency and selection of teacher candidates, Administrator's Notebook 19, Feb., 1971.

fications for the position. Highly qualified teachers were selected by principals only if their attitudes about education were congruent with those of the principal. The implications of this study are clear. If we assume that camp directors behave no differently from school principals when hiring staff members, we may also conclude that these directors will reject highly qualified individuals in favor of less qualified persons who have attitudes toward camping and the outdoors that are compatible with those of the director. While it is accepted that attitude congruency is desirable between administrators and their staff, this congruency should never be achieved at the cost of rejecting highly qualified personnel. As has been stated earlier, there are real advantages in hiring staff members who demonstrate some degree of diversity of thinking. The director of a large camp should perhaps deliberately seek to employ individuals with diverse backgrounds that reflect a broad range of attitudes and philosophies.

The final step in the staff selection process is to notify the candidates of the decisions reached. Too often, only the fortunate candidates are advised of the decisions. A personal letter should be sent to all unsuccessful applicants thanking them for their interest in the camp and advising them that their application will be kept on file. A file of all rejected application forms should be retained in case (1) another position is created before the season is concluded, (2) the camp wishes to consider the applicant next season, or (3) a colleague is seeking a staff member with the qualifications that one of these unsuccessful applicants possesses.

Staff contracts

It is strongly recommended that all camps, large and small, follow the practice of having every staff member sign a contract or letter of agreement covering the conditions of employment. Contract forms should include the name of the position, the dates of employment, and all details regarding remuneration and arrangements regarding board and lodging. Some camps include the rules and regulations covering staff conduct in the contract. Others include these in the staff manual or a personnel policies statement.

Many camps have found that when no formal contract exists some people assume that it is not unethical to accept a position, either verbally or in writing, and then renege if a more attractive job is offered. A contract helps these persons realize that they are assuming an important duty and that they have a moral obligation to live up to the terms of the contract.

Staff manual

Increasing numbers of camps have developed a staff manual as an aid to all staff, but particularly for new members. Its fundamental purpose is to inform personnel about many facets of the camp and to assist them in better understanding their particular role in the organization.

The manual serves as a ready reference that should be read numerous times by the staff. It should therefore have a complete table of contents for quick reference. It is recommended that the manual be mailed to new staff members well in advance of the camp season so that they may familiarize themselves with it contents before their arrival at camp. Much of the material in the manual will serve as the basis for the pre-camp training program.

Devitt[15] points out that "the most practical manual evolves over the years out of the shared experience of a specific camp group." He states that the manual is never complete

---

15. Devitt, E. H.: A counsellor's manual, Canadian Camping, **25**(2):13, Winter, 1973.

but should be under constant revision. This suggests a loose-leaf format in preference to a bound copy that is "much too final and discourages revision." A staff manual is valuable because it:

1. Orients new staff members to the camp and its unique features
2. Interprets the camp's philosophy, objectives, and traditions
3. Describes personnel policies and procedures that directly affect each staff member
4. Assists in preparing the staff to fulfill their new position
5. Helps avoid misunderstanding and frustration among the staff regarding the discharge of their responsibilities.

CONDITIONS OF EMPLOYMENT
Work load

One of the important factors that affects staff morale is fair and equitable distribution of work. Each camp administrator should make a sincere and conscientious effort to (1) place staff members in positions for which they are best suited, and (2) balance work, not only within a particular job classification, but between various classifications.

Occasionally an individual or a group of staff members may be asked to undertake some additional duties beyond the normal scope of their job description. When this occurs, compensatory time off may be given.

Over the years, camps have been criticized for overworking their staffs. This is particularly true in small camps in which many duties must be assumed by a limited number of personnel. An excellent, but overworked, staff will probably produce only mediocre results. If the camp experience is to be a rich and rewarding one, the director cannot afford to conserve on personnel.

New staff members should receive a reduced work load for the first week or two of camp so that they effectively orient themselves to their new position. In addition, all staff members should be consulted at the end of each session regarding any change of interest in their work assignment. For example, it is not uncommon for an inexperienced counsellor to be assigned to a living unit for 13 and 14 year olds only to find after a summer that he or she prefers to work with younger campers.

Salary

For a camp to attract a competent staff, salaries must be competitive, not only with other camps, but also with other types of summer employment such as playgrounds, pools, and recreation centers. Many young men and women rely on summer positions to defray the cost of college tuition. It is only natural that they seek positions that pay the most attractive salary. When camp directors are unable to match salaries paid by other employers, they may need to give serious consideration to cutting back selected camp services to hire first-class staff members.

Salaries are determined by evaluating factors such as the degree of difficulty and responsibility of a given position, the qualifications necessary for the position, and the availability of qualified individuals. The entire salary schedule should be predicated on a thorough analysis of each position and careful classification of these positions. Salary should rarely be determined on the basis of the personal merits of the individual. The latter becomes a significant factor only when promotion is being considered.

Once the job description and classification has been completed, the salary schedule may then be determined. Three factors must be considered in establishing the schedule: (1) comparison of salaries in other camps and organizations for comparable position classifications, (2) assessment of the camp's ability to provide a comparable level of compensation, and (3) establishment of minimum and maximum limits for each classification.

The basic purpose for establishing a salary range for each position is to provide a monetary incentive and reward system for good performance. Annual increments within a position classification should be automatic if the individual has performed satisfactorily. In addition, merit increases are sometimes provided in recognition of outstanding performance.

Promotion

Promotion refers to the advancement of staff members to a position of greater responsibility on the hierarchical pyramid. It may also involve a change of title and an increase in salary. The fundamental purpose of promotion is to fill more responsible positions with the most qualified personnel within the organization. Promotion *from within* the camp staff enhances staff morale and reduces the risks inherent in bringing in an unknown and untried person to the position. In rare instances, it may be necessary to offer a position to someone outside the organization. Such action suggests that a careful examination of the camp's in-service staff development program is in order. When promotion from within is *not* part of normal camp policy, staff loyalty and morale are jeopardized and overall staff performance is likewise threatened.

Separation

Separation is the termination of a staff member's contract with the camp. It may be initiated by the employer or by the camp. When individuals make the decision to leave the camp, they give due notice of resignation. If the camp initiates the severance, it is called *dismissal* or *termination*. In some instances, resignation by the employee may

be proposed in lieu of dismissal to avoid a negative report on the individual's personnel report.

The problem that an administrator may have to face is the question of whether it is worth the disruption to the campers and staff to release a staff member or whether the camp should tolerate inferior performance for the balance of the session. If the decision is made to dismiss someone, it may be wise to prepare a clear and unbiased statement as to the reasons for termination and distribute this to the staff. Not surprisingly, many staff members tend to side with a colleague, particularly if all the facts of the case are not known.

If the camp director dismisses individuals "on the spot" because of a flagrant violation, every effort should be made to have them leave the camp as quickly as possible. Every hour that they remain in camp increases the possibility that they may attempt to undermine staff morale before their departure.

STAFF DEVELOPMENT

A unique aspect of camp administration is that the majority of staff members are hired for a position for which they have little or no professional training. Most are young men and women who are still in high school or college, and many will come to camp for only a single season. This poses a special challenge to the camp director and senior administrators of providing on-the-job training for the staff to form them into a knowledgeable, cohesive unit.

The first step in the successful preparation of the staff is to employ a group of individuals who are anxious to learn and improve their personal performance level. Directors must instill in all their staff members a contagious need for personal advancement and development that spreads to all members of the team. Unless there is a sincere desire on the part of the staff to learn and improve, the training program is doomed to failure.

A comprehensive staff development program involves three phases that occur sequentially. The first phase consists of the steps that are taken before the staff arrives at camp. The second, and most important phase, is the precamp training program. The third phase is the in-service training program that is promoted during the camp season itself.

Staff development before the camp season

Staff development begins immediately following the signing of the employment letter of agreement or contract. A number of preliminary steps should be taken to assist staff members in gaining a better insight into their camp position. The first step, in the case of new staff members, is to mail out a copy of the staff manual. This should be read before coming to camp in preparation for the precamp training session.

Many camps have adopted the practice of mailing out regular bulletins or camp newsletters during the off-season. In some cases, a separate staff newsletter, containing many helpful hints and suggestions, is sent only to the staff.

Increasing numbers of camp directors encourage the staff to take special courses in the off-season to increase their expertise for the camp season. These may be theory courses, offered by a college or university, in such areas as child and adolescent psychology, group dynamics, and leadership training. There are also more practically oriented clinics or workshops in almost all phases of the camp program such as canoeing, archery, orienteering, crafts, drama, and dance. Many such clinics and workshops are conducted by regional camping associations. Yet another means of improving competency in the off-season is to encourage staff members to undertake some form of

volunteer work with youth groups. The experience gained working with a group of youngsters at a local agency, church school, or recreational center usually proves very rewarding.

Some directors bring their entire camp staff together several times during the off-season for training sessions on a particular topic. Others schedule meetings of each functional unit for preseason advanced planning. I am familiar with one camp director who gathers members of the senior administrative level together at least once monthly during the off-season for planning and evaluation sessions.

Most regional, state, and provincial camping associations hold annual conferences in the early spring, and several camp directors encourage, and even require, selected staff members to attend these meetings each year as yet another form of staff development.

Precamp training program

There is general agreement that potentially the most effective form of staff development is a staff precamp training program. The program consists of bringing all staff members to camp for a period immediately prior to the camp opening for the purpose of developing personal skills and competency for the job. At the same time, it is designed to form the entire staff into a functional team.

Several factors determine the length of the program: (1) amount of staff training offered during the off-season, (2) percentage of new staff members, and (3) amount of time available for training purposes. The minimum recommended length of a staff training program is 3 days, and camps that strive for excellence will wish to devote 5 to 7 days to this important endeavor.

Weaknesses of precamp training programs. In spite of the importance placed on staff precamp training by most camps, much criticism has been leveled at many programs by those for whom they are designed. Although there are many condemnations that staff members voice, the major criticisms seem to be the following.

1. *Staff are passive observers.* For effective learning to take place, the learner must be actively engaged in the process. Unfortunately, too many precamp sessions involve meetings in which large groups are "talked at," making staff participation virtually impossible. An excellent article appeared in *Camping Magazine* that stressed the importance of active participation of all staff members during development sessions. The following quotation sums up the writers' concern.

Many orientation programs* include philosophies, procedures, recipes, do's and don'ts, staff handbooks and housekeeping details which are told to, or discussed with, the staff member. This approach makes him a consumer, listener, observer, but rarely an actual participant. The value and retention of this type of presentation may diminish with each day of the camping season.[16]

2. *Too much covered too quickly.* Whenever a camp devotes only 2 or 3 days to the precamp training program or utilizes the staff energy and manpower to physically prepare the site for the camp opening, there is great danger of attempting to cover too many topics in the time available. It takes time to prepare a young, inexperienced staff. To argue that it is too costly to conduct a 5- to 7-day training program may be a serious case of misdirected economy. If it is not feasible to lengthen the period for the

development program, the best compromise may be to delete those topics that are somewhat superfluous to the actual role the counsellors must play and to handle fewer areas in greater detail. Some discussions may have to be postponed until the camp season is under way.

3. *Program is overstructured or, in some cases, nonstructured.* Too often, because of pressure of time, it is believed that formal lectures are the most efficient means of presentation, and little or no time is provided for "rap sessions" or general discussion on topics of real concern to the staff. The other extreme is sometimes found when the camp director and the administrative assistants do no advanced planning for the training program in the naive belief that the entire development program should "emerge from counsellor needs." The staff can only provide effective input when they have some very clear understanding of the roles they are expected to play.

4. *Overreaction to new training techniques.* Camp directors should be open-minded regarding new ideas and techniques that may be of value in the camp setting. By the same token, they should be cautious about adopting training techniques such as "T" groups, sensitivity training, and group dynamics unless they are knowledgeable and adequately schooled in the use of these techniques. Too often, when a particular technique is considered a valuable means of staff training because it is the "in" thing, it is allocated more time than is warranted in the total training program.

Establishing objectives. To develop and conduct an effective staff training program, it is necessary to formulate clearly stated objectives. While the objectives or anticipated outcomes for such a program may be planned by the director alone or in concert with a few senior staff officials, the program will almost certainly be more successful if all

---

* Rotman and Clayman use the phrase "orientation programs" to refer to "precamp training."

16. Rotman, C. B., and Clayman, C. S.: Human relations training for camp staff members, Camping Magazine, **43**(4):10, April, 1971.

levels of the staff share in the design of projected outcomes.

Wasserman, in writing about the precamp training program at her camp, reduces the objectives to three fundamental concerns. She states these simply and directly:

1. We want to get to know new counsellors and have them get to know us.
2. We want to have staff informed concerning our campers, our camp and our way of doing things.
3. We want to unify the staff as much as possible in the short time we have.[17]

A much more detailed list of objectives is provided by Smith of the National Council of Y.M.C.A.s in which strong emphasis is placed on staff participation in planning.

1. To gain knowledge and understanding of the characteristics of children 8-15, their physical, spiritual and emotional needs, and to gain skills to work with them as individuals and in groups.
2. To learn more about theories of working with groups.
3. To add to the self-understanding of each staff person.
4. To improve skills in camp program activities: crafts, ecology, evening programs, rainy day programs, special day programs and so on.
5. To become more familiar with program and administrative procedures and policies, through compiling and printing for each staff member: personnel, business, program and health policies.
6. To gain orientation to all sites and facilities of the camp-village area, camping sites, hike routes, etc.
7. To build *esprit de corps* and pride in the total staff and camp community through mixing staff, working together to build a strong team.

8. To develop refinement of unit programming, building in progression, unit themes and identity, and understanding of the philosophical base for programing.
9. To enhance staff understanding and skills in relating religious emphases to the totality of camp life, through chapel services, vespers, evening devotionals, staff reflection periods and so on.
10. To impart training in health, safety and first aid, through basic courses for new staff and seminars for old staff.[18]

Each camp must develop its own set of guidelines that best meet the needs of their particular situation. Such objectives should be cooperatively planned.

The program. It is not realistic to attempt to outline a specific program that is suitable as a model for all precamp training sessions; each camp must develop its own program. It is possible, however, to suggest several guiding principles that should be applicable to most situations.

1. *Plan for variety in the training sessions.* Variety can be achieved by utilizing a multiplicity of session leaders. The owner, director, section heads, unit leaders, program specialists, camp nurse, doctor, dietition, business manager, experienced counsellors, and outside guest leaders are all possible sources of leadership for the various sessions.

A second means of maintaining interest through diversity is by varying the format of the session itself. This may include lecture, panel discussions, small buzz groups, role playing, case studies, demonstrations, active participation sessions, as well as the use of films and other audiovisual aids. One word of caution is in order: do not use a particular method of presentation just because it is different. You must be able to justify a given

17. Wasserman, R. B.: How one camp operates its successful counselor training program, Camping Magazine, **41**(4):26, April, 1969.

18. Smith, D. I.: Use staff in planning training to gain greater acceptance, Camping Magazine, **44**(3):28, May, 1972.

methodology as the best means of presentation that can be devised for that topic.

2. *Follow regular camp routines during some part of the training session.* One of the best means of orienting staff to some camp patterns is to follow the actual procedure during precamp training. For example, the best way to learn about all the peculiarities of the dining hall routine may be to observe the actual format as the staff eats each meal during the precamp sessions. Similarly, an effective method of learning how to conduct a cookout or a sleepout may be to actually participate in one as it would be handled with campers. It is doubtful if trip counsellors could spend their time more profitably during precamp than by taking a short trip under skilled leadership and following all the routines and procedures recommended for use with campers.

3. *Involve experienced counsellors as instructors and leaders whenever possible.* Nothing can lead to grumbling and poor staff morale faster than to ask large numbers of returning staff members to sit passively through training sessions in which they have already participated several times. Experienced counsellors should be invited to share in the conduct of the training program. To assume responsibility commensurate with their knowledge and ability achieves several desirable objectives: (a) it ensures their interest in and support of the training program, (b) it adds variety to the presentations, and (c) it provides opportunity for leadership experience and encourages new staff members to aspire to similar responsibility.

4. *Whenever possible, plan sessions that involve small groups.* No matter how carefully planned and how well presented, a large group session negates the possibility of general participation by significant numbers of staff members. The more often gatherings can be broken into small work groups, the greater the chance for individual participation. Active participation invariably means greater sustained interest.*

5. *Utilizing staff members for work parties during the precamp program should be approached with caution.* Two arguments have been presented in defense of using staff members as a work force to prepare the camp for the arrival of the campers. The first is a legitimate one that states that much preparation is necessary before camp opening and the cost of hiring additional labor may be prohibitive. The other defense of this practice is that to place old and new staff members together on a work party is an excellent way for them to get acquainted and thus form strong personal relationships. It seems to me that *any* project that brings two groups together toward a common purpose can achieve this end—it does not have to be a work party. The question of work parties takes us back to objectives and purposes. If the primary purpose of the training program is just that—to train the staff to execute the responsibilities of their position— the program itself should reflect that emphasis.

Some types of work can be justified as meeting the overall objectives of the training program. One example will suffice. It may be difficult to justify the practice of requiring the staff to set up tents as part of precamp training. It would, however, be quite reasonable to expect tent counsellors to participate in a practice session in which they learn correct tent maintenance. In such a session, they would learn when and how to roll tent walls, how to tighten guy ropes so that there is adequate air space between

---

*For further information on active staff participation in the staff development program see: Rothman, C. B., and Clayman, C. S.: Human relations training for camp staff members, Camping Magazine, 43(4):10, 28, April, 1971.

the tent roof and the fly, and how to batten down the tent for a pending storm.

Each camp director must determine how much precamp training time will be usurped so that program staff may assist in preparing the physical site for the camp opening. If the director and the staff believe that too little time is already provided for adequate staff development, it is difficult to justify encroaching on that valuable time for work parties. Surely the answer is to hire some of the program staff 2 to 8 weeks before the camp is scheduled to open to complete most of the physical preparation prior to the precamp session.

6. *Special consideration should be given to the integration of old and new staff members.* Reference was made to this particular problem in the section on induction of new staff members. Because the turnover of counsellor staff may be substantial from year to year, it is not uncommon to find that cliques of old and new counsellors tend to form unless steps are taken to prevent it. As long as camp directors are aware of this phenomenon it is a fairly simple matter to structure the precamp training period in such a manner that the two groups integrate quite naturally.*

Staff development during the camp season

Once the precamp training program has been completed and camp is under way, there is a natural tendency for some new staff members to feel that they have "arrived." This is coupled with the fact that, with the rush of camp opening, those who should now play the supervisory role are busy with many other duties that make demands on their time. The result is that, too often, the staff development program comes

*For further details as to how one camp overcame this problem, consult: Welch, R. et al.: Integrating new staff with old, Camping Magazine, **44** (4): 10,12, April, 1972.

to a grinding halt. An effective staff training program must be an ongoing process that continues throughout the entire camp season.

At this stage, the *supervisory* role of senior and intermediate staff members becomes vital. It is here that human skills are of paramount importance for unless new staff members have confidence in and respect for their superiors, there is little hope of the supervisor providing much assistance to the counsellor. The supervisor must know and understand as much as possible about the needs and expectations of each staff member. Because supervision invariably involves aspects of evaluation, the relationship between superior and subordinate can become a very sensitive one requiring the supervisor to utilize considerable expertise in human relations. Several important procedures should be followed if new and inexperienced staff members are to get off on the right foot.

Directed observation. One effective course of action is to have new staff members observe experienced staff members during the first few days of camp. This training technique can be structured so that several new counsellors are assigned to observe a skilled colleague conduct a program or teach an activity to campers. This, in educational parlance, is the equivalent of the demonstration lesson taught by the master teacher. The phrase *directed observation* implies more than casual observation. It is very important that, when this technique is employed, the observer be given specific instructions as to what to observe. For example, the beginning counsellor might be asked to pay particular attention to how the instructor gets the attention of the group, how the instructor encourages and handles questions, how much group versus individual instruction is provided, and how maximum participation by campers is encouraged.

The next step is to give new staff members assignments in which they assume an assisting role under an experienced person. For example, new counsellors would not be asked to take charge of swimming instruction for a group of campers in the first week or two of camp, but they might serve as assistants to returning staff members. In this way, they are able to observe such things as the manner in which the instructor organizes the class, establishes rapport with the campers, and initiates good teaching progression. Over a period of several days or weeks, new counsellors assume more and more responsibility for the planning and conduct of a program until they are ready to accept full responsibility for at least some phase of the activity. As their confidence and experience grows, they are given more scope and responsibility until they are eventually capable of leading a group. At this point, they are ready to move to the next step in their training: the handling of a group under the observation of the supervisor.

Supervisory teaching. Throughout the directed observation period, new counsellors should have been receiving direction and guidance from someone in a supervisory role. They are now ready to assume primary responsibility for a group of campers while the supervisor observes and informally evaluates their performance. This first supervisory teaching may involve little more than taking a group of campers on a nature hike or organizing a small horseshoe competition. The important point is that new staff members must be given responsibility as they are ready for it. Great individual differences will occur, and the supervisor must judge when the individual is ready to accept additional responsibility.

Supervisory conference. Following one or more supervisory teaching periods, the novice instructor and supervisor should get together for an informal but carefully planned meeting. It is here that human relations skills are so important if effective dialogue is to result. Supervisors must be supportive and constructive in their comments and at the same time help new counsellors to recognize their limitations as well as their strengths. A good technique that has proved effective in such conferences is to have the supervisor ask numerous questions, so that in answering the questions, staff members are led to identify their own assets and deficiencies. Questions that might be directed to the individual include: How do you feel the assignment went? What do you think were the best features? What were the weakest aspects? How would you handle a similar situation another time? With questions of this type, the tone of the meeting is one of introspection and self-evaluation rather than criticism from the supervisor. This procedure of maintaining a close supervisory relationship between staff member and supervisor should be continued as long as the individual requires this type of support, always keeping in mind that the supervisor's role is primarily that of consultant and facilitator rather than "snoopervisor."

Other aspects of in-service training

The precamp training program and a carefully modulated supervisory program during the early part of the camp season should comprise the main thrust for staff development. However, a number of other steps may be taken to assist in the preparation of the staff. A useful technique is to arrange for selected mmembers of the staff to visit neighboring camps and observe some aspect of their operation. This is particularly useful for intermediate and senior staff members who have responsibility for the conduct of some element of camp life. For example, if a camp is considering introducing pottery for the first time, it might be helpful to visit one or more camps at which pottery has been offered for some time to observe and discuss with the pottery staff all facets of their program.

Each camp should have a library of professional reference material at the camp-site that is available to the staff at all times. Such an investment will provide rich returns if staff members are encouraged to review current literature related to their particular area of interest.

An increasing number of camps have duplicating equipment on the camp site so that it is possible to prepare mimeographed material for circulation to the staff on a particular topic both before and during the camp season. This material serves as a supplement to the staff manual and usually deals with topics of a specific nature.

A number of camp directors encourage their staff members to take memberships in the local or regional camping association by subsidizing part or all of the membership fee. This again is considered a wise investment of camp funds since many new ideas come from attendance at conferences and workshops or subscription to periodicals such as *Camping Magazine* and *Canadian Camping*.

Counsellor-in-training (CIT) program

Ever since the inception of the camping movement in North America, camp directors have recognized that experienced senior campers comprise one of the best potential sources of new staff members. For many years, however, it was believed that campers could automatically be transformed into effective counsellors because they had participated in the camping experience. As Hennessey[19] so aptly points out, if we follow that line of reasoning then anyone who has

attended school for 12 or 13 years should automatically qualify as a certified school teacher. The advantages of having been a camper for several years are great. Camp routines are familiar, something of the camp philosophy should have "rubbed off," and many important skills will have been learned. But to suggest that such experiences automatically qualify an individual to assume a leadership role in a camp is assuming too much.

Definition of terms. Confusion exists regarding terminology. A counsellor-in-training (CIT) program refers to a planned course of leadership training for future counsellors. In many cases, those permitted to pursue the program are senior campers, usually 15 or 16 years of age, who retain a semicamper/semicounsellor role. That is, they follow many of the rules and regulations laid down for campers and may engage in some camper programs. At other times they enjoy certain privileges beyond those accorded regular campers and participate in a special leadership program for much of their time in camp. A few camps charge no fee while a youth is enrolled as a CIT, some charge only a percentage of the regular camper fee, while still others assess the full tuition rate.

Although *counsellor-in-training* is the most common terminology used for those engaged in this type of program, they are sometimes referred to as *counsellor apprentices*. CITs should not be confused with *junior counsellors* or *counsellor's aids*. The latter terms are used synonymously and normally refer to 17 or 18 year olds who are not enrolled as campers but are hired as junior staff members who undergo on-the-job training and are paid a reduced salary.

Qualifications for candidates. The minimum age for a regular counsellor is 18 years as required by the A.C.A. and provincial camping associations of Canada. Because many

---

19. Hennessey, P., Be specific when you plan your C-I-T program, Camping Magazine, 44(1):26, Jan., 1972.

camps are finding it increasingly difficult to attract senior campers of 15 and 16 years of age back to camp, we find that a prevalent practice is to offer a CIT program for 16 year olds (or 15 and 16 year olds) and then to hire the best of the CIT candidates as junior counsellors the following summer.*

The other qualifications that a CIT should possess include the same qualities that are sought in any staff member: (1) sincere liking for children, (2) love of the outdoors, (3) balanced personality, (4) leadership potential, (5) usable skills, and (6) robust physical and emotional health.

Leadership of CIT program. The person chosen to lead a CIT program cannot be just anyone. A project of such importance should be assigned to a highly respected member of the staff who has considerable seniority; to do less would be to down-grade the program. Leaders should have demonstrated a capacity to work effectively with young adults or teenagers and must possess superior skills in human relations. They should also be able to organize efficiently and be capable of demonstrating a wide range of camp skills. Finally, they must be willing and able to draw their young charges into all phases of planning and evaluating the program.

Questionable practices. Unfortunately a number of camps have established devious schemes under the guise of CIT programs that have been looked on with disfavor by members of the camping profession and the general public. One of these questionable practices is that of exploiting adolescents as a form of cheap labor in some camps. The scheme involves enrolling a group of senior campers in a so-called CIT program, fre-

quently at some cost to the parents, and then requiring them to paint boats, rake shoreline, wash dishes, and set tables for much of the summer. Another unfortunate pattern that is sometimes observed is that which Guerard[20] refers to as the "tag-a-long" CIT program. In this psuedo-training program, each CIT is assigned to a regular counsellor to become, at best, an assistant, at worst, a flunky. This scheme provides little or no guidance or supervision of the new counsellor.

Recommended program. A comprehensive CIT program should be conducted for a minimum of 4 weeks of the camp season; 8 weeks in one summer or 4 weeks in each of two summers would be better. Much of what was described in the conduct of the *precamp training program* for all staff members is applicable to this program as well. The following principles are proposed as guidelines when planning the CIT program.

1. Those enrolled in the program should participate actively in the planning of its content. Only as the group works toghether on common projects will they gain an understanding of the group process that will be invaluable to them as counsellors.
2. Opportunity should be provided for the CITs to work directly with campers of different ages.
3. Leadership experiences should be planned to provide progressively increased responsibility.
4. Those in the program should be exposed to a wide cross section of camp staff.
5. The training sessions should offer a broad range of instructional techniques.

---

*In those camps in which no CIT program exists but junior counsellors are hired at 16 or 17 years of age, the following discussion of the CIT program can serve as the basis of a training program for junior counsellors.

20. Guerard, E. R.: Revamped CIT program trains for all camp staff positions, Camping Magazine, **44**(4):13, April, 1972.

6. Small group organization is recommended as it encourages full participation by the individual trainee.
7. Only meaningful duties should be assigned to CITs. There is no place in a CIT program for routine tasks.
8. Careful attention must be given to facilitating the transition from camper to counsellor. Some youth experience real difficulty in this adjustment.
9. Those participating in the program should play a significant role in the evaluation procedure. This includes not only assessment of the program but also evaluation of peers as well as self.

ADMINISTRATOR-STAFF RELATIONS

The camp staff must be more than the aggregate of the individuals who are employed by the organization; it should be a stable, cohesive, and effective team. Dimock[21] stated it well 30 years ago when he wrote "The camp staff possesses—or should possess—a collective, personality, conceived, not as the 'sum' of the personalities of its members, but as an entity that is a blending of these individuals." One of the most important characteristics of this "collective" personality is staff morale.

Staff morale

The camp administrator must demonstrate the ability to maintain a high level of staff satisfaction and morale. Morale significantly affects the performance of each staff member. Strong morale contributes directly to high productivity, whereas low morale means that staff members contribute just enough to get by. Even in a camp with the best of working conditions, including generous time off and excellent salary, there may be other factors causing low morale so

Table 4-1. Satisfaction and dissatisfaction factors among teachers

Satisfaction	Dissatisfaction
Achievement	Poor relations with colleagues and students
Recognition	Incompetent administrative policies and practices
Responsibility	Outside personal problems

that the entire camp operation is affected adversely.

How does the camp administrator develop and maintain a high level of staff morale? This is a difficult question, and answers are vague at best. Most of the reasearch on employee satisfaction and morale has been done in the field of business. More recently, several interesting studies have been conducted in education, examining teacher morale. The following discussion is based on the latter work on the assumption that findings among camp staffs should not be unlike those reported in the teaching profession.

The first step is to identify those qualities or behavior patterns that characterize high staff morale. A review of the literature on teachers suggests that the following qualities may be valid among camp staff members:

1. Demonstrates a sense of pride in the camp
2. Displays an enthusiasm for the work
3. Displays a sense of loyalty to the camp
4. Works cooperatively with colleagues
5. Respects and supports the camp administration
6. Accepts the camp philosophy

The work of Sergiovanni[22] on over 3,000 teachers provides some interesting findings regarding teacher satisfaction. His results are summarized in Table 4-1. Sergiovanni's

21. Dimock, H. G., editor: Administration of a modern camp. (New York: Association Press, 1948) p. 93.

22. Sergiovanni, T.: Factors which affect satisfaction and dissatisfaction of teachers, Journal of Educational Administration, **5**:66-82, May, 1967.

study suggests that the conditions that create staff satisfaction are associated with the job itself, whereas the factors that result in dissatisfaction seem to be related to the work environment, particularly the interpersonal relations elements of the environment.

A review of a number of other studies in the field of education suggests that the following factors may be important for camp administrators to consider as they seek to promote high staff morale.

1. A quality camp in which the staff may take pride
2. The administrator's recognition of each staff member as an individual
3. Staff confidence in the professional competence of the administration
4. Staff participation in formulation of policies affecting them
5. Individuals assigned to positions commensurate with their abilities
6. Good rapport with happy, contented campers
7. Fair and equitable distribution of work
8. A comprehensive in-service training program
9. Support by supervisory personnel
10. Adequate time off policy
11. Adequate facilities and program equipment
12. Salaries comparable with other types of part-time summer employment

Two major implications may be drawn from the research on staff satisfaction and morale. First, the camp director who seeks to build good staff morale should look to the overall quality of the camp program. If staff members believe that they are associated with a first-class camp, many factors that might otherwise lower staff morale will be overlooked. Secondly, all the studies underscore the importance of the camp directors' administrative leadership and their interper-

sonal relations with staff. Gorton[23] proposes six guidelines to assist administrators in their interpersonal relations:

1. Be sensitive to the needs of the others.
2. Attempt to explain the reason for your actions.
3. Try to involve others in decisions about the school.
4. Be open to criticism; try not to be defensive.
5. Be willing to admit mistakes and to make changes.
6. Be honest and fair in your interactions with others.

Administrator-staff problems

In any large organization, problems relating to administrator-staff relations occasionally arise. Such problems may be divided into two categories—those in which the employer demonstrates concern regarding staff performance or conduct and those in which the employee has a grievance against the organization. Dealing with staff problems of this nature is perhaps the least enjoyable of the camp administrator's responsibilities, but such differences must not be ignored in the hope that they will go away. Each problem must be confronted and brought into the open so that differences may be quickly and fairly resolved.

Staff performance and conduct. There are many offenses that, when committed by a staff member, are cause for concern. These offenses range from minor misdemeanors to serious acts that may endanger human safety. Infractions such as tardiness, laziness, carelessness, breaking of camp rules, and damage or loss of property are minor acts in themselves, but when they occur regularly, they assume greater importance. Other infractions include incompetence, insubordination, failure to enforce an im-

---

23. Gorton, R.: School administration: challenge and opportunity for leadership. (Dubuque, Iowa: William C. Brown Co., Publishers, 1976) p. 172.

portant camp policy or rule, gross misconduct, and gross negligence. Each of these breaches of conduct requires some action on the part of the administration. The actual steps taken will depend on the seriousness of the offense. The camp administrator has several possibilities.

1. *Verbal admonishment* should be given in the case of minor infractions that are not serious enough to warrant further action. In such cases, it is assumed that verbal counselling is all that is required. For a somewhat more serious offense, a reprimand or rebuke may be advised.

2. *Written reprimands* should be considered for more severe infractions. In these cases, following a meeting with the staff member, a written statement is placed in the individual's personal file and the person is given a copy of the reprimand. Most administrators remove the written statement from the file at the end of the camp season if no other infraction occurs.

3. *Transfer* may be deemed necessary in certain cases, particularly if personal friction is evident between the individual and co-workers. This may also be the wisest course of action if a person demonstrates incompetency in a given position but is believed to have qualities that could be utilized in a different assignment within some other area of the camp.

4. *Demotion* is a transfer that involves reduction in responsibility, status, and, in some cases, salary. Demotion occurs when a staff member is incapable of filling a particular position. This usually may be attributed to unsatisfactory initial placement.

5. *Discharge* is termination of employment. This should be resorted to infrequently, and only when all other recourse fails. In extremely serious cases, immediate dismissal is warranted as soon as the allegations are verified. A more common practice is to release the individual at the end of the first camp session following a probationary period.

Some of the more common personnel problems confronting almost every camp director include the following.

Lack of staff initiative. In any large camp staff, it would be surprising not to find one or more persons who demonstrate little or no initiative and appear to be downright lazy. Administrators who are confronted with this problem must make it clear that they expect intense staff involvement as a matter of policy. Specifically they must: assign appropriate tasks, set challenging goals, expect high standards of performance, and recognize achievement. By providing ongoing encouragement and positive reinforcement, the camp director can usually rejuvenate the sluggish staff member.

The staff agitator. Nothing can cause staff morale to deteriorate more quickly than the chronic complainer who drags colleagues down with a negative attitude. The first step in such cases is to seek out the cause of the grievance and bring it into the open. Open channels of communication are imperative to determine whether the complaints are real or imaginary. If there is just cause for concern, appropriate solutions should be explored at once.

Opposition to authority. This phenomenon may be either overt or covert. If the agitation is concealed, it is the administrator's first responsibility to locate the source and encourage the individual to voice his concerns openly. No camp can operate effectively with hidden dissension. Once the problem is in the open, the administrator must objectively assess whether the opposition is justified. If it is, one effective remedy may be to ask the dissident for his solution. If the lines of authority have been clarified and yet the problem persists, it may be necessary to make a leadership change or remove the dissatisfied staff member. If the action of a dissident is clearly construed as disloyalty by denigrating the camp or its administration, termination of contract is warranted. No organization should be expected to tolerate subversion, and certainly disloyal individuals contribute nothing positive to their position.

Staff grievance. For a variety of reasons, the camp staff may have real or imagined grievances against the administration. Again, every attempt must be made to have staff members express their grievances. In many cases, examination of the problem reveals that it is based on misunderstanding as a result of lack of effective communication. Each grievance should be handled quickly and at the lowest supervisory level possible. The object in each case is to resolve the grievance before it becomes a major issue.

It is important for the camp staff to know that a mechanism exists for the handling of a grievance and that any grievance will be treated with tolerance and compassion. Because nobody exists to represent the employee in a summer camp, supervisors and administrators must be completely professional in their conduct so that absolute objectivity is maintained in the interest of a just solution. The grievance procedure must ensure equity for each side without deterioration of staff performance of duties or lowering of staff morale.

There are no easy answers or simple formulas to be applied in the solution of problems of staff grievance and conduct. Each must be evaluated on its own merits, and decisions must be made in light of the particular circumstances of that case.

ADMINISTRATIVE GUIDELINES

1. The single most important role that the camp administrator must fulfill is that of recruiting, hiring, orienting, and training the camp staff.
2. A job description and analysis should be prepared for each position within the camp so that there is complete understanding between the applicant and the administrator regarding the duties and responsibilities to be assumed.
3. It is recommended that camp administrators establish a recruitment and selection committee comprised of a representative group of the camp staff.
4. Camp directors must be prepared to spend many hours recruiting and selecting personnel; it is time well invested. All available sources of new staff should be explored.
5. Staff selection involves five sequential steps: preparation of job specifications, publicizing the position, reviewing the applications, interviewing the candidates, and notifying applicants of the decision.
6. The development of a staff manual for camp personnel is a valuable means of orienting all staff, but particularly new staff members.
7. Camp administrators must be careful to develop fair and equitable workloads for the staff. In the past, too many camps have overworked their staff members to the point that efficiency deteriorated and the program suffered.
8. Camp directors must be prepared to pay salaries that are competitive with other forms of summer employment if they are to attract the best men and women available.
9. Opportunity for promotion and advancement should be available to outstanding staff who return to camp year after year. Whenever possible, promotion should come from within the camp organization if high staff morale is to be maintained.
10. Opportunities should be provided for all staff members to participate in a general development program designed to assist them in the performance of their job.
11. The most widely adopted form of staff development is the precamp training program. This should be conducted for a period of from 3 to 7 days and include all camp personnel.
12. Ongoing supervision and regular conferences are an integral part of a comprehensive staff development program.
13. Senior campers comprise an excellent potential source of future counsellors. Camps should

conduct CIT and junior counsellor training programs that assist promising campers to prepare for a staff position.

14. Those responsible for camp management must take all steps necessary to maintain high staff morale. Without strong morale and high job satisfaction among the staff, a camp cannot hope to operate at a high level of efficiency and productivity. Conversely, low staff morale invariably leads to poor staff performance and conduct as well as an increase in staff grievances.

SELECTED BIBLIOGRAPHY

American Camping Association: A guide to a counsellor-in training (CIT) program. (Bradford Woods, Martinsville, Ind.: American Camping Association, 1975).

American Camping Association: Camp counselor course outline for colleges and universities. (Bradford Woods, Martinsville, Ind.: American Camping Association, 1962).

American Camping Association: Camp leadership kit A & B. (Bradford Woods, Martinsville, Ind.: American Camping Association).

Ball, A., et al.: Staff recruitment, Camping Magazine, **51**(2):38-41,Jan., 1979.

Clarke, B. C., and Davis, J.: Staff management and morale, Camping Magazine, 39(5)10-11., May, 1967.

Gorton, R. A.: School administration. (Dubuque, Iowa: Wm. C. Brown Co. Publishers, 1976). Chapters 8 and 9.

Hjelte, G., and Shivers, J. S.: Public Administration of recreational services. (Philadelphia: Lea & Febiger, 1972. Chapters 8 and 9.

Jubenville, A.: Outdoor recreation planning. (Philadelphia: W.B. Saunders Co., 1976). Chapter 11.

La Roque, L., Wasserman, R. B.: Pre-camp counsellor training can be as different as day and night, Camping Magazine, 41(4):8-9, 2b, Apr., 1969.

Ledlie, J. H.: Camp counsellor's manual. (New York: Association Press, 1969).

Michel, E.: How to plan your C.I.T. program, Camping Magazine, **47**(4):10-12, Feb., 1975.

Mitchell, A. V.: Camp counseling. (Philadelphia: W. B. Saunders Co. 1970). Part II.

Rodney, L. S., and Ford, P. M.: Camp administration. (New York: John Wiley & Sons, Inc., 1971). Chapters 7 and 8.

Rotman, C. B.: The camp director's role in staff orientation, Camping Magazine, 42(4):11, 24, Apr. 1970.

Shivers, J. S.: Camping—administration, counseling, programming. (Englewood Cliffs, N. J.: Prentice-Hall Inc., 1971). Part II.

Silverman, M.: Professionalizing your staff development, Camping Magazine, **43**(3):13-14, Mar. 1971.

Welch, R., et al.: Integrating new staff with old, Camping Magazine, **44**(4)10, 12, Apr. 1972.

CHAPTER FIVE

Selection, development, and maintenance

The outdoors lies deep in the American tradition. It has had immeasurable impact on the Nation's character and those who made its history. . . . When an American looks for the meaning of his past, he seeks it not in ancient ruins, but more likely in mountains and forests, by a river, or at the edge of the sea. . . . Today's challenge is to assure all Americans permanent access to their outdoor heritage.[1]

One of the great problems facing the camping movement in America today is that suitable land for campsites is becoming scarce. Since World War II there has been a tremendous increase in the demand for wilderness space to meet the needs for highways, resorts, private cottages, preserves, and camps. Large cities and towns continue to push their boundaries outward as housing projects, shopping centers, and industrial parks devour land that only a few years ago was part of the countryside.

The 1962 Outdoor Recreation Resources Review Commission Study Report 22 points up the problem in dramatic terms as it projects that land use in the United States will equal 5.4 acres per person in the year 2000 A.D. as compared with 12.8 acres in 1950. The Report makes it abundantly clear that space for future camp development will continue to shrink rapidly. As urbanization persists at a relentless pace with all the de-

mands that commerce and industry impose on the need for vast tracts of land, North Americans are in danger of losing that which has characterized their way of life: "freedom to roam."

It is not surprising that those contemplating the purchase of land for a campsite no longer have the choice of unlimited tracts of ideal property. Good land is still available, but the cost increases each year, and the need to move further away from population centers is evident in some parts of the country.

SITE SELECTION
Camp development committee

In the case of agency or organization camps, it is routine practice to appoint or elect a committee to plan for the selection, acquisition, and development of the campsite. Private or independent camps would do well to follow this practice since the decisions are too important and complicated to be left to a single individual.

The camp development committee is a

1. Outdoor Recreation Resources Review Commission Study Report 22, Washington, D.C., 1962, quotation taken from back cover of the report.

88

working group with a task that may take several years. The committee itself should be fairly small—perhaps five to eight persons—with power to seek advice from consultants and experts as needed. The committee should include individuals who are familiar with large construction projects and who appreciate the importance of drawing on outside expertise. Above all, members must be enthusiastic and dedicated to the project to sustain their interest over the long period the committee must work.

The range of responsibilities of the camp development committee is broad, and it may be necessary to form several subcommittees to deal with specific aspects of the total assignment. The committee should:

1. Review the rationale that led to the decision to establish a new or expanded camp
2. Become familiar with the fiscal constraints of the project
3. Develop a long-range plan for the establishment of the camp (10 years minimum)
4. Conduct careful studies of sites available, which must be consistent with the requirements of the master plan
5. Select the site and authorize the finance committee to complete the purchase
6. Supervise legal matters related to the land acquisition
7. Establish an accounting procedure with the finance committee
8. Choose an architect and provide guidance for preparation of the preliminary plans
9. Prepare initial cost estimates, solicit bids, and award the contract or contracts
10. Supervise the entire construction of the project
11. Provide regular progress reports to the executive board for approval
12. When the project is completed, turn over to the camp maintenance committee all drawings, layout plans, and other documentation regarding the site.

The camp development committee must work in close association with several other committees such as those responsible for camp program, public relations, and finances. The latter committee should be responsible for providing funds for the project. However, the development committee must prepare rough estimates and a timetable of when monies will be required. If a campaign is required to raise capital funds, careful cooperation is necessary to ensure that the finance committee receives all the sketches, plans, and other details needed for the campaign literature.

Long-range planning. The importance of a master plan for the long-term use of a camp must be underscored. It is astonishing how many camps operate from year to year on an ad hoc basis with no preconceived thought regarding future development of the program or facilities. The long-range plan serves several important purposes:

1. It provides a catalog of future needs and identifies a logical, sequential development of them.
2. It capitalizes on the natural features of the site and provides the best utilization of the available space.
3. It provides for a pattern of development that preserves the natural landscape and aesthetic beauty of the site. Mistakes will be avoided that could lead to erosion problems, contamination of the camp's recreational or drinking water supply, and other forms of pollution.
4. It provides a long-term guide for future construction and development. Because a campsite is usually in the process of development over several

years, the committees and board responsible for the plan may vary in their constituency during this time. The master plan provides the continuity that is often lacking within these groups.

5. It is the best guarantee that funds are wisely spent. Sound financial planning is impossible without a long-range plan. It also serves as the basis for any campaign to raise capital funds.

An interesting question that confronts many camp development committees is whether the site becomes a reflection of a predetermined set of program needs or whether the master plan grows from the site. Although it is vitally important that the committee be thoroughly familiar with the prospective camper clientele and the basic camp philosophy, it should be determined to what extent members of the camp committee bring with them predetermined ideas and plans regarding the types of buildings, their relative locations, and the program content. There are very compelling arguments that suggest that the master plan should be largely determined by the landscape rather than by any preconceived plan. Wright and co-workers state:

The soils, topography, vegetation and water conditions of the site are the basis upon which the plan is formulated. By considering the natural conditions of the site, the planner allows possibilities for retention of desirable features and at the same time eliminates possibilities of later problems.[2]

The planning committee should begin their deliberations with a topographical map of the area. The next step is to examine the water and soil conditions on the site itself. Complete information in this regard may re-

quire percolation tests to establish the porosity of the soil in addition to determining the presence of streams, ponds, or swamp as well as the danger of flood in case of a flash storm. Vegetation also is an important consideration, particularly as it relates to the possibility of erosion. Only as the committee examines in detail the natural physical properties of the proposed site is it possible to evolve an effective master long-range plan.

Preliminary considerations. The need to develop a plan that is in harmony with the physical site does not preclude the importance of examining several factors prior to the actual site selection. For example, it would seem unrealistic to prepare a long-range plan without at least having a general idea of the financial resources available. Even when a fund-raising campaign is contemplated, it would be shortsighted not to make initial estimates of the potential from such a campaign. If the most optimistic prediction of funds from all sources over a 3-year period is $250,000, it is important for the camp development committee to know this and plan accordingly.

On the other hand, consideration of economic factors should not become such an overriding consideration that they are a limiting factor creating "tunnel vision" as the committee prepares the plan. Long-term financial planning is an essential element of site selection and must exist concurrently with other aspects of long-range development.

It is equally important for the committee to have as complete information as possible regarding the clientele to be served. Is it to be a day or resident camp? How large an enrollment is anticipated in the first year of operation? What is the potential for growth in enrollment? Is the camp to be an 8-week seasonal operation, or will it function for 12 months? Will the clientele be boys, girls, or

---

2. Wright, S., and Wright, R.: Building a new camp? The plan should grow from the site, Camping Magazine, **40**(7):11, Sept./Oct., 1968.

coeducational? What is the age range of the campers? The answers to these and other questions will greatly facilitate the work of the development committee.

Those persons responsible for developing the long-range plan must also have some indication of the camp philosophy and objectives, at least in general terms. If it is intended that out-tripping by canoe be a major program focus, the committee must seek a site with a suitable labyrinth of lakes and short portages. If on the other hand, the camp plans to promote aquatics and build its program around water activities, the committee has a clearer understanding of its responsibility and must give priority to a site with excellent waterfront facilities.

Factors in site selection

Several criteria should be considered when selecting a campsite. No piece of property provides all the characteristics described below, but to the extent that the committee is aware of these criteria, it is in a better position to evaluate various sites and make a judicious selection. The factors are not listed in order of importance since each camp must place its own value on the criteria discussed.

Size of property. It is recommended by the American Camping Association that a ratio of one acre per camper be provided for resident camps. In the case of day camps, the suggested ratio is one half acre per camper. These may appear to be very generous allocations, but several factors affect this recommendation. Camping by its very nature implies space and "room to roam." The idea of "lebensraum," or space for living, has always been a paramount consideration in the layout of camp facilities. It must be remembered that in most wilderness tracts of land some areas are too rocky, too swampy, too steep, or somehow unsuitable for living and program use. In addition, most committees

seek to provide a "buffer area" around the perimeter of the camp property to ensure privacy from neighbors. If a camp plans to decentralize its various living areas, additional space is required.

Long-range planning allows for future expansion. It is unrealistic to assume that by purchasing a small parcel of land initially it may be possible to acquire additional, adjacent property some time in the future. The quantity of available land is decreasing, and what is for sale becomes more costly each year. Everything dictates that enough acreage should be purchased at the outset. It should be remembered that the cost of extra acreage is usually very small when compared with the total investment.

Large acreage provides a feeling of privacy and seclusion and protects the camp from future encroachment by the public. Camp development committees should be encouraged to seek a generous piece of land even though at the time of purchase it may appear to far exceed the long-range needs of the camp. Such property should be self-contained to optimize the degree of protection against future development on the camp's borders.

Physical characteristics. Variation in topography is vitally important to a good campsite. The committee should seek a site with an interesting contour to the land including open fields or meadows and gentle hills as well as more rugged terrain that ensures an attractive and adventurous setting. Every camp must have enough level land (maximum of 10% grade) to accommodate the various living areas as well as program areas with even less grade. Ponds, brooks, streams, wetland, and rock outcroppings offer additional, interesting program possibilities.

The site should also have a contrast between mature tree cover and open areas. A good site offers sunny areas for cold days and cool, shaded spots for hot weather. Open, level areas are needed for many program activities, whereas tall trees offer an excellent break in areas in which prevailing winds are strong. Low bush cover helps prevent erosion of some soils and also furnishes an excellent natural buffer between living areas.

Soil and drainage conditions are important for several reasons. First, soil and slope of the land combine to determine drainage after rain. A heavy, nonporous, clay soil causes much standing water during and after inclement weather resulting in wet footware and clothing. Ideal soil conditions for a camp consist of firm, porous, sandy, or gravel subsoils that guarantee good natural drainage. Care must also be taken to ensure that facilities are not located in gulleys or swales that are susceptible to flooding.

A second important consideration that relates to soil condition is the problem of waste disposal. Heavy soils greatly increase the problems of sewage removal and often result in costly installations. All locations for waste disposal latrines, septic tanks, grease traps, and leaching fields should be located on higher ground than the immediate surrounding area. Care must also be taken to ensure that they do not contaminate either the drinking or swimming water.

Soil conditions must also be capable of withstanding the impact of extensive foot traffic, especially in the living and program areas. The soil must sustain a good turf cover so that footpaths do not have to be relocated on a continuing basis. While low marsh and swamp lands may prove to be valuable program assets, under no circumstances should these be located within or adjacent to the main living or program areas.

Environmental elements. Inquiries should be made regarding neighbors adjacent to the proposed site. An industrial plant, air-field, garbage dump, or junk dealer could each depreciate the land value of the camp. As suggested earlier, sufficient property around the perimeter of the camp site is good insurance against this possibility. Even better is a natural boundary such as a river, ravine, or high ridge separating the two properties.

Another environmental condition that should be explored is the presence of natural hazards on the site, including cliffs, white water, or the danger of flash flood or fire. The latter two may be of sufficient concern to rule out a site entirely. Poisonous plants, reptiles, and insects may also be deterrents but these can usually be controlled with careful planning

Climatic conditions should also be a consideration. Some regions of the country may be ruled out as potential sites because of excessive heat in the summer and little shade cover, inaccessibility in the winter because of the volume of snow, or too much low-lying acreage, making the proposed site continually damp and humid. Higher elevations are generally preferred during the summer months when gentle, prevailing winds make the heat more tolerable and do much to reduce the problem of mosquitoes and other flying insects. Data regarding a particular locale is readily available from the U.S. Weather Bureau, and the local office should be consulted.

Water supply. No site should receive serious consideration unless there is an adequate and safe supply of drinking water. Tests should be conducted early to determine (1) the potability of the water and (2) if there is sufficient quantity.

The potential source of water for domestic purposes may come from a ground or surface supply. The latter includes lakes, streams, and springs and are generally considered less reliable than ground sources such as artesian wells or city water systems.

Regardless of the available source, some technical advice should be sought concerning the potential water supply. This guidance is available from state or university geologists, water engineers, or the water resources commission. It may also be necessary to have a legal firm explore the water rights in the area.

The volume of water required in a given camp varies greatly with the type of camp. The need will be greatest in camps in which flush toilets, showers, and a swimming pool are provided. Day camps require less than residence camps. It is estimated that most residence camp requirements range from 30 to 50 gallons per person each day. A new camp that uses the higher figure should have little difficulty in providing an adequate water supply. Day camp estimates run at 20 gallons per person per day.

Accessibility and services. The distance that a camp is located from the source of population to be served is an important consideration. In the case of day camps, when campers must travel daily to the site, it is generally agreed that the camp should be located no more than an hour's drive from any pick-up point. In the case of resident camps, the distance may be greater depending on the type of camp. Generally speaking, agency camps have sessions of 5 days to 2 weeks and tend to use the site a great deal throughout the year. This type of camp should require a maximum driving time of approximately two hours for the campers. Private camps on the other hand, may draw their campers from a large geographic area with travel by plane, train, bus, or car. In the latter case, the camp may choose to locate a considerable distance from large population centers to preserve a true wilderness setting for the camp.

An excellent task for any camp committee to undertake is that of preparing a time/distance map overlay on a constitutent location map. By drawing concentric circles around the anticipated centers of camper population, the committee should be in an excellent position to initiate its site search.

Regardless of the geographic location of the camp, it should be approachable by a good highway and directly accessible by means of well surfaced and well-maintained secondary or tertiary public roads. Road building and maintenance is very costly and the committee should avoid selecting sites to which access roads must be constructed over any significant distance. Public roads or rail lines that bisect the camp property also pose awkward security and safety problems.

Consideration must be given to utilities such as electricity and telephone. When either facility is not present on the site, enquiries should be made regarding their availability.

One disadvantage of a remote site is the problem of having supplies and services readily available. Building materials, maintenance supplies, as well as food items that can be procured in the local community are a great convenience. Of even greater importance may be the necessity of using the local town or village for fire and police services as well as medical support from a local doctor, hospital, or medical clinic. In summary, overall costs of the total camp operation tend to increase proportionally with the degree of isolation from population centers.

Program resources. While the natural characteristics of a site may suggest many interesting program possibilities, it is important, nevertheless, that the site chosen be in congruency with the basic philosophy and objectives of the camp. A camp that plans to specialize in mountaineering must have available surrounding country that is suitable for this purpose. If sailing is to be featured, a lake of sufficient size is required as well as weather conditions that are conducive to such a program. To the extent that members of the camp development committee have some clear indication of proposed program emphases, they will be in a much stronger position to locate a site that meets at least some of these needs.

Aquatic areas. Consideration of suitable facilities for swimming and boating activities clearly belong in the program resources category described above. However, aquatics is so prominent in most summer camps that it deserves to be treated separately. Many camp owners and camp committees place such a premium on aquatic activities in the total camp program that it frequently becomes one of the most important criterion in site selection.

Throughout North America, many types of aquatic resources are utilized by organized camps. These include the ocean, gulf or bay, stream, river, pond, or lake, and of course the commercial swimming pool. The ideal situation is for a camp to purchase acreage with its own self-contained lake and assurance that the watershed is not subject to pollution in future years. Waterfronts on rivers or streams are usually not as safe as lakes for several reasons. First, the danger of upstream contamination may be beyond the camp's control. In addition, the problems of developing a suitable shoreline and swimming bottom are greatly magnified. It may also be difficult, if not impossible, to conduct any type of boating program.

One advantage of a lake site is the opportunity to find a natural beach area or one that can be developed. The ideal site provides an expanse of sandy beach with a firm bottom slope of between 5% and 10% to a maximum swimming depth of 12 feet.

Whenever possible, man-made lakes and dammed streams or rivers should be avoided. Neither of these projects should be undertaken without the guidance of experts. Even when consulting services are available, suitable construction is invariably costly.

Existing structures. It is not uncommon to find some existing buildings on a site that is under consideration. Care should be exercised in evaluating the potential value of these structures. There is always a danger that they are given greater value than they actually warrant. It would be a rare stroke of good luck if existing buildings were placed in precisely the location the camp desires. Even if they are well positioned, it is almost certain that they were designed for some purpose other than that anticipated by the new owners. Such buildings are therefore usually a poor substitute for new structures that are designed and located to fulfill a specific need.

Regulatory agencies. Before the camp development committee progresses very far along in its deliberations, a thorough check should be made to determine whether there are any licensing or zoning restrictions that might jeopardize a site selection. These restrictions include local building codes, rights of way, riparian rights, and easements.

Inquiry should also be made with the appropriate authorities concerning proposed super highways or roads in the area. In addition, public utility companies should be questioned regarding long-range plans for water and sewage lines as well as electrical power lines. Some of the following agencies may have to be consulted depending on the site location: watershed board, pollution control agency, environmental quality council, state board of health, state natural resources board, property owners association, and others.

In summary, many factors must be considered when selecting a campsite. The persons responsible for this selection must be prepared to spend considerable time and deliberation assessing the merits of various sites before making the decision to purchase a given tract of land.

SITE ACQUISITION

After the camp development committee has explored all possible sites and has made its decision, a property survey should be conducted before initiating purchase of the property. The camp owner or the executive board must know exactly what is being purchased, and the survey map provides much valuable information. The survey should include the installation of permanent property corner markers. These establish clearly defined property lines and help avoid future boundary disputes with neighbors. The survey map should be kept on permanent file as it will be used to assist in planning the actual layout of the site.

After the survey is complete, the development committee must submit a comprehensive report to the camp executive board with a recommendation to purchase. After the board has studied the committee's report and decided to act on it, the board then advises the development committee and the finance committee to jointly proceed with the purchase. At this point, an attorney must work with those responsible for carrying out the transaction. The attorney determines whether clear title can be delivered and is responsible for the preparation of all agreements concerning water, timber, and mineral rights.

SITE DEVELOPMENT

Once the land has been purchased, the camp development committee must again swing into full operation. Whether a new site has been acquired or an established site is already functioning, all future development should be based on the long-range master plan. This plan is the blueprint for present as well as future use of the site.

Technical services

It cannot be emphasized too strongly that camp owners and executive boards should not attempt to develop the site without the services of several technical experts. Too often in the past, camp committees have relied solely on their own initiative and the building talents of local contractors when starting a new camp. Available technical services must be utilized if the plan is to have purpose and direction.

Architect. The services of a reputable architectural firm can usually save the camp more than the cost of its fees. The architect, more than any other technical expert, is a necessity because of the wide range of services provided. The architect:

1. Interprets building codes and health requirements
2. Determines building design and prepares preliminary drawings
3. Prepares initial cost estimates
4. Prepares working drawings and specifications
5. Assists in obtaining bids and letting the contract or contracts
6. Supervises construction on behalf of the owners
7. Assists in obtaining other technical services
8. Approves any changes
9. Endorses completion of each phase of the project and authorizes payment

Engineers. Engineers may need to be consulted on several matters, including road construction, water and drainage problems, waste disposal, and design of swimming facilities.

Health officials. Many regulations, both state and local, must be adhered to when developing a camp site. The appropriate representatives should be consulted early in the planning stages.

Conservationists, landscape architects, and environmental control representatives. Several experts may need to be consulted during the early stages of site planning regarding such problems as soil erosion, woodlot management, and protection of wildlife. One of the most helpful is the U.S. Soil Conservation Service.

Steps in site development

Plans for the actual site development should proceed according to a logical and orderly plan. The following steps ensure such a systematic approach to site development and their adoption can avoid many needless pitfalls.[3]

Step 1. Gather all data related to the site. The first step in site development involves obtaining several maps and documents related to the site. No matter how small the acreage, it is impossible to effectively plan the layout by simply walking over the ground. It would be equally unrealistic to expect to locate the buildings and other facilities without making an on-site inspection of the property.

The first document required is the boundary or survey map, which should have been obtained before the land purchase. This clearly indicates the boundaries of the property, names of neighbors, and the scale of the map. The survey map should also indicate highways, power lines, and rights-of-way affecting the property.

Perhaps the most important single document required is a topographical map. Frequently, when such a chart is not available, small camps are hesitant to go to the expense of having one made. However, whenever a camp owns property exceeding 100 acres, the use of the topographical map should prove invaluable.

Some large camps find it helpful to obtain aerial photographs of the entire camp site. These provide another dimension of the natural features of the property and are valuable in planning maximum utilization of the acreage available.

Conservationists, foresters, naturalists, and others can provide much helpful material regarding the effective conservation of land, vegetation, and wildlife. Some land is not capable of supporting heavy camper traffic year after year, and those persons responsible for planning must be aware of this fact. Other areas require reforestation to prevent erosion, while still others need constant thinning of existing woodlots. Improving the habitat and streams of the wildlife can have a significant effect on the number of birds, animals, and fish on the camp property, and the opportunity for campers to observe and study the wildlife of the area is a richly rewarding experience that should not be denied them.

In addition, several state and local officials should be approached to provide information related to the water system, waste disposal, health and sanitation problems, installation of utilities, and other practical considerations.

Step 2. Prepare a priority list of needed facilities and improvements. Keeping in mind that 3 to 5 years may be required to develop a complete camp site, an orderly approach to construction is mandatory. Several factors play a predominant role in determining what facilities are required. These include consideration of the constituents the camp will serve, main program emphases, type of camp operation (short-term or long-term, day or resident), nature of the site, and existing facilities and resources.

Several factors may impinge on the actual schedule for the construction program, including availability of funds to enable work to continue on time, size of the initial camp and anticipated growth rate, and weather conditions that influence construction schedules in some parts of the country. Regardless of these considerations, certain

---

3. The following material is adapted from *Campsites and Facilities*, No. 3679, Publications Division of the Boy Scouts of America, pp. 27-52.

basic elements must be part of any first-stage construction, including access road into the camp property, available water supply, electricity for heat, light, and power, and waste disposal facilities.

It is not uncommon to give early priority to construction of the camp custodian's residence and the maintenance facilities. This makes it possible to have the custodian on the site during all phases of construction as well as providing suitable storage for building materials and supplies. Throughout construction, it is wise to avoid the building of temporary structures: it is too easy for them to become permanent.

Step 3. Develop plans for the physical layout. At this point the committee is ready to "flesh out" what up to now has been the bare skeleton of the site. Consideration should be given to location of, and space for, camper living quarters and program areas, in that order. These are followed by development of administrative and other central service areas.

The layout for a given camp is determined to some degree by the physical characteristics of the site. However, there are proven principles that have been established over the years in the development of many sites. The following standards serve not as hard and fast rules, but as guidelines for locating camp facilities.

1. The natural beauty of the site should be maintained.
2. Buildings should be pleasantly spaced. Natural terrain and tree cover provide excellent baffles for separating buildings.
3. The need for utility lines and their location must be considered as new facilities are situated.
4. Conscious concern for conservation and antipollution measures must be maintained as the site plan is developed.

5. Camper living units should be given first priority when locating facilities. All other facilities should be located in relation to the tents or cabins.
6. Generous space between living and sleeping units should be preserved.
7. Location of some program facilities is determined by the nature of the activity. Careful inspection of the site will determine the best location.
8. Administrative services should be central to all areas of the camp and should be accessible by good service roads.
9. The camp entrance should be located where it can be easily seen and should permit safe entrance to, and exit from, the camp.
10. Roads and trails should blend with the terrain so they are inconspicuous.
11. Living units for married staff members should provide a degree of privacy from the rest of the camp.

Fig. 5-1 illustrates a layout plan for a decentralized camp in which the principles outlined above have been incorporated. The camp has four living units and accommodates about 150 campers. The legend at the right locates, by number, the major facilities on the site.

Step 4. Select architectural treatment and construction materials. Camping is epitomized by vigorous experiences located in the outdoors. Camp buildings therefore should be essentially supportive and serve primarily as a means of shelter. They should be simple but functional in design and should harmonize with the landscape to blend in with the natural environment. It should therefore be apparent that there is no one best design or style of building. The wide range of landscape in America dictates different types of architecture that are consistent with a given setting. Many of the oldest organized camps attempted to preserve

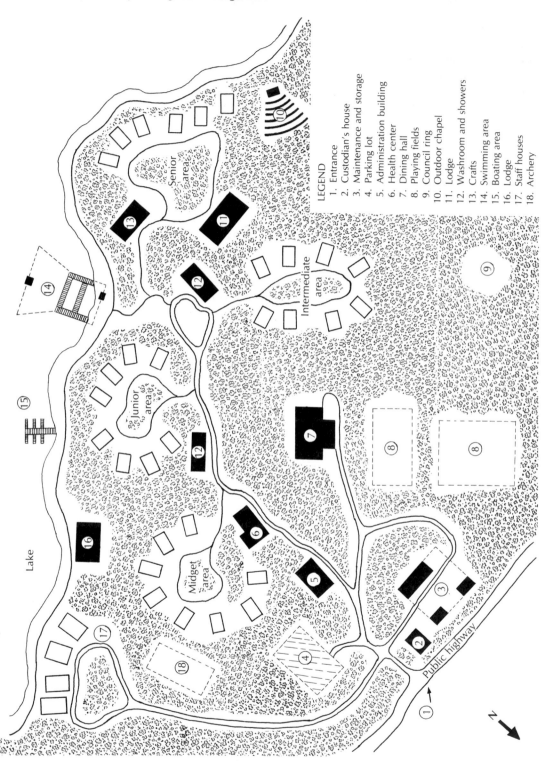

LEGEND
1. Entrance
2. Custodian's house
3. Maintenance and storage
4. Parking lot
5. Administration building
6. Health center
7. Dining hall
8. Playing fields
9. Council ring
10. Outdoor chapel
11. Lodge
12. Washroom and showers
13. Crafts
14. Swimming area
15. Boating area
16. Lodge
17. Staff houses
18. Archery

Fig. 5-1. Model layout of decentralized camp.

the traditional appearance of pioneer cabins and other early American structures. These buildings, while attractive in appearance, were soon found to be nonfunctional and difficult to maintain. Today, camp buildings combine simple, conservative and, hopefully, traditional design with modern, long-lasting materials.

The following basic considerations should assist the development committee and architect in determining the type of design that is most suitable for camp structures.

1. Establish a coordinated design pattern for all camp buildings that gives the total site a planned appearance.
2. Locate facilities to blend in naturally with the landscape. Do not crowd buildings. Select an architectural treatment that is appropriate to the physical characteristics of the site.
3. Exterior color of buildings is an important consideration. It should be chosen to harmonize with the surroundings.
4. It may be desirable to plan a given building to serve several functions. When this is done, design it to fill specific needs. Do not erect a multipurpose building, the exact use to be determined as need arises.
5. Avoid combinations of services in one building that result in heavy traffic concentrations at the same time.
6. Construct buildings to last. A camp is a long-term investment, and durable, high quality materials greatly facilitate maintenance and reduce costs over the years.
7. Avoid two-story construction. It looks out of place in a camp and also poses additional fire hazard problems. Camp buildings should generally be low in contour and mass.
8. Careful design and construction greatly reduces safety hazards, including lack of emergency exit from buildings, failure to install proper handrails, slippery floors, insufficient ventilation, improper electrical wiring.
9. Provide enough openings (screen and glass) to ensure that interiors have good natural light and ventilation. This is a major shortcoming in many older camps.
10. Plan for expansion of building structures for future enlargement of the camp.

One of the tasks that is frequently overlooked when planning new buildings is the allocation of funds for landscaping. Not only is landscaping necessary to restore the aesthetic beauty of the site, it is equally important to prevent erosion problems. All construction scars should be graded so that they will hold grass and other surface cover. Native shrubs and trees should be planted informally around buildings and over utility lines, leeching fields, and other unsightly areas.

Step 5. Present the layout plan for approval. In many independent camps, final authority for the entire project resides with the development committee. In this case, Step 5 is not required, and the committee can ask the architect to start preparing construction drawings and specifications.

However, most public and parapublic camps require the development committee to seek formal approval at all stages of site selection, purchase, and development. The committee asks the architect to prepare preliminary drawings of the site layout and structures. These are then presented to an approving authority such as the executive board. All members of the development committee, as well as the architect, should be present to fully discuss the (1) layout plan describing why the various structures are located as they are, (2) function of each building, (3) architectural treatment of each facility, and (4) cost estimates and proposed construction schedule. After all questions have been answered satisfactorily, the committee seeks board approval of the entire project as presented or with any modifications that have been agreed on at the joint meeting.

Step 6. Prepare construction drawings and specifications. The architect now proceeds with detailed construction drawings for all proposed structures, while the engineer works out specifications for roads, water system, and other projects. During the preparation of the drawings and specifications, regular consultation should take place between the architect and members of the development committee. Final approval of each drawing should be required by the camp development committee.

Step 7. Invite bids and let the contracts. The committee's legal consultant should assist in all contract preparations. Once these are prepared, the committee should call for competitive bids from selected reputable contractors. The lowest bid is not always accepted, but the contract should go to the firm that is best able to do the work at a competitive price. The entire project can be let to one contractor, who may then subcontract some parts of the work to other firms. In other cases, the project is prepared in a number of smaller contracts and let to several companies.

Occasionally, building material vendors will furnish items at cost or donate them to agency camps. These donations should be suitably recognized. At the same time, care must be taken to see that the donated materials meet the architect's specifications and can be delivered according to schedule.

The practice of using volunteer labor, although laudible, should not be adopted when undertaking major projects. There are unlimited smaller jobs of repair and maintenance that are better suited to dedicated volunteers. The main building assignments should be left to professional workers.

Step 8. Supervise the construction and keep accurate records. While the architect is usually on the site continuously to supervise construction, the development committee should also appoint someone from within their group to supervise the building program. The purpose of this supervision is to:

1. Assure compliance with the construction drawings
2. Assure that material specifications are met
3. Prevent unnecessary damage to the site
4. Resolve questions regarding changes or revisions in the plans
5. Verify completion of work for approval of payments to the contractors.
6. Provide progress reports to the rest of the committee and executive board
7. Maintain accurate records of the entire project.

One of the most important responsibilities of the supervisor of construction is the establishment of a businesslike method of filing all records. Many of these records will eventually be turned over to the camp maintenance committee once the camp begins operating. Records include a complete financial statement of receipts and expenditures, a daily log of on-the-job transactions and happenings, a correspondence file related to the project, a complete set of construction drawings, and a file containing all installation and operating manuals, warranties, and parts lists for all pieces of camp equipment purchased. This file also includes the name of suppliers as well as the company that services the equipment.

Step 9. Turn over records to the camp maintenance committee. Once the project is completed, the final responsibility of the development committee is to turn over all pertinent data to the property management and maintenance committee. This file should include all the documents listed in Step 8. In some camps, the development committee is also expected to arrange for a ground breaking and dedication ceremony. More often, however, the public relations or finance committee is responsible for this ceremony.

DEVELOPMENT OF FACILITIES
Sleeping units

Most camps today house the campers in tents or small cabins. The question of which is more desirable seems to be largely a philosophical one. Those who favor tents argue that this is the essence of real camping. To sleep with only a layer of canvas between oneself and the elements epitomizes what camping is all about, namely getting closer to nature. The supporters of cabins, on the other hand, contend that tents do not provide sufficient protection from the elements and force the camper to endure certain hardships that should be eliminated if the camping experience is to be truly enjoyed.

Regardless of whether tents or cabins are provided, there is general agreement in support of decentralizing sleeping units. This means that not only is sufficient space provided between living units, but a degree of privacy is also offered to individual tents or cabins.

Tents. A great variety of tents are available on the market today, but the majority are not suitable as sleeping quarters in a resident camp. When tents are used as permanent sleeping units throughout the camp season, they should possess the following characteristics:

1. Large enough to house three to six persons
2. Located on a permanent wooden platform that is at least 18 inches off the ground, which reduces dampness, permits good circulation of air, and reduces rodent infestation
3. Have high enough side walls to permit standing with comfort

4. Have a fly or large piece of water-repellent material suspended above the tent roof to divert the main force of the rain (If the fly is to serve its purpose, there must be an air space between it and the tent roof.)
5. Fire and mildew resistant and commercially waterproofed.

Tents that are placed directly on the ground, either with or without a canvas floor, are unacceptable as permanent sleeping quarters. The recommended wooden platform should be set on concrete footings or masonry blocks so that the floor has a slight pitch to assist in water drainage.

Solid canvas tents should have side walls that can be rolled up and tied in fair weather so that the camper truly experiences the feeling of sleeping under the stars. In the event of a sudden rainstorm, the overhang provided by the fly prevents all but the most violent driving rain from penetrating the tent platform.

Tents are available that combine some elements of the cabin with those of the tent. One type of construction has walls of wooden frame construction up to a height of about 3 feet and upper walls and roof of canvas. Another variation that has proved very functional is a wooden platform and a regular asphalt-covered roof supported by four corner posts. The four walls are made of canvas that are attached by grommets at the top and bottom to taut horizontal wires. In good weather, the side walls can be pulled to the corner posts, thus providing maximum ventilation and fresh air.

Whenever canvas tents are used, great care must be taken to ensure that the tents are completely dry before taking them down for storage, otherwise mildew can destroy a costly investment.

Cabins. When cabins are used, construction and style should be kept simple. The most common construction is wood frame with unfinished interior for summer use.

When cabins are used all year, insulation and interior panelling may be required. The winterized cabin also requires an insulated floor and ceiling or roof. Windows and door screens should be large enough to provide good, natural lighting and cross ventilation. Some cabins are screened on all four sides on the upper walls. A generous roof overhang protects the cabin from driving rains.

Cabins are usually built to accommodate four to eight campers. The interior dimensions should be large enough to provide 40 square feet of space per camper. Beds should be arranged so that there are at least 3 feet between them when placed side by side and a minimum of 1 foot when placed end to end. The beds should be further positioned so that there is at least a 7-foot horizontal separation between the heads of sleepers. This necessitates a head-to-foot or foot-to-foot arrangement. If double bunks are used, the upper bunk should be at least 36 inches from the ceiling.

Sleeping accommodations are usually provided by metal folding cots or built-in bunks. The use of double-decker bunks conserves space but provides an additional safety hazard with young campers. A safety rail should be mandatory on all upper bunks used by children under 10 years of age.

Shelves, lockers, or closets should be provided for each camper's clothing and personal belongings. When tents are used, the popular practice is to invite campers to bring their personal belongings in a small steamer trunk or large suitcase that is kept at the end of or under the bed. The latter arrangement is far from ideal since it requires pulling out and pushing back a large, heavy container several times each day.

Some camps require the counsellor to sleep in the tent or cabin with the campers, while others locate the staff in separate sleeping units within the living area. When the former practice is followed, it is recom-

mended that there be at least a semipartition separating the counsellor's quarters from the campers, thus providing the staff member with a modicum of privacy.

The location of toilets and hand-washing facilities is also a matter of debate. It is certainly more convenient when a toilet and wash basin is located in each sleeping unit. However, it is much more economical to place toilet and washing facilities in a central location within the living area, to be shared by all campers and staff in that immediate vicinity.

Program facilities

A wide variety of structures, designed primarily as program areas, are required in any camp. The extent of these facilities is determined by the program philosophy, camp size, and available fiscal resources. Although certain facilities are used for a variety of activities, each should be designed with specific program functions in mind. The following sections describe program facilities that are found in the majority of camps.

Unit lodges. Many camps provide a structure within, or immediately adjacent to, each living area. It is designed as a multipurpose program facility for use in inclement weather and for evening activities. Camps have a variety of terminology for this structure, the most common perhaps being the *lodge*.

The size and construction of this shelter differs greatly within camps. Sometimes it is nothing more than a roof supported by corner posts with all four sides open and a natural, hard-packed earth floor. Others are enclosed on all sides up to a height of 3 or 4 feet so that the semiwalls serve to bound the floor area for certain games. Some large camps provide a lodge for each living unit, while others locate one or two centrally for use by all campers.

More sophisticated lodges include such

supplementary facilities as toilets, wash basins, and even a small kitchenette. Storage space for program equipment is usually provided, and some camps partition off a small, secluded section that serves as a quiet area for games and reading. Many lodges include a fireplace or a freestanding heating unit such as a Franklin stove. The fireplace is an important consideration since the lodge is used mainly in poor weather or after dark when a little heat is much appreciated.

Recreation hall. In addition to unit lodges, there is a need for one large facility that can be used for all-camp programs. It can be a very simple building with few distinguishing features. It is generally rectangular in shape so that a variety of indoor court games can be played. At other times, it serves as a theatre, chapel, dance hall, meeting hall, craft center, or room for games that require little organization. Many camps find it useful to build in a raised stage area with a proscenium arch at one end. In the absence of a recreation hall, the dining hall, or even the indoor chapel, may have to be used for these activities. Multiple exits should be carefully planned for the recreation hall since it must accommodate the entire camp on many occasions.

Special activity centers. Depending on the size and affluence of a camp, one or more separate structures may be constructed for selected program specialties, including arts and crafts, dance, drama, gymnastics, Indian lore, music, nature study, photography, and wood and metal work. Each special activity may have certain unique construction requirements as well as specialized equipment installations. Program specialists should be consulted regarding these particular needs.

Aquatic facilities

The waterfront is considered one of the primary program assets of nearly all camps. Earlier in this chapter, consideration was given to the various waterfront possibilities. These include natural lakes, ponds, rivers, streams, ocean or tidewater, man-made lakes, and swimming pools. Table 5-1 outlines some characteristics of each type of waterfront site. Every waterfront presents a unique set of characteristics that must be accounted for when designing the layout. Regardless of the physical conditions that exist, the following general guidelines should apply to any waterfront installation.

1. Safety must be the paramount consideration when designing an aquatic facility layout.
2. Swimming and boating areas should be kept separate by at least 200 to 300 feet. No small craft used for recreational purposes should be allowed in the swimming area.
3. Sailboats should be docked or moored on the leeward side of the swimming area with respect to the prevailing winds.
4. Canoes and kayaks should be beached further downwind from the sailing docks.
5. Powerboat use and water skiing should be conducted well away from both the swimming and boating areas.
6. All facilities should be maintained in an attractive and functional manner.

A model layout for a camp waterfront that incorporates the principles outlined above is provided in Fig. 5-2.

Piers and docks. The basic structures of any waterfront are the piers or docks that are used to enclose the swimming and the boating areas and provide access to each area from the shore. The shape and size as well as the type of construction and installation varies tremendously according to particular needs. In general, however, piers and docks should have the following characteristics:

1. The assembled pier must be stable and of sufficient strength to withstand se-

Table 5-1. Characteristics of camp waterfront areas

Lake	Stream or river	Tide water	Man-made lake	Swimming pool
Lakes generally provide the best camp waterfront.	It is usually difficult to develop a satisfactory waterfront on a river or stream.	Saltwater bodies rarely provide good camp waterfronts.	Construction of a man-made lake should never be undertaken without consulting experts such as a water engineer and the U.S. Soil Conservation Service.	Swimming pools provide optimal control and safety for campers.
A lake totally within camp property ensures privacy and some degree of pollution control.	Program opportunities such as canoeing and fishing may be excellent.	Ocean surf may offer some excellent program choices for campers with superior aquatic skills.		Limited numbers of campers can be accommodated at a given time.
Control of the watershed guarantees protection against pollution.	Flood danger is a potential hazard.	Tidal action severely restricts scheduling of aquatic activities.	Provision should be made to drain any artificial lake.	Boating is not possible.
Small bodies of water are more easily polluted.	Fluctuating water levels present irritating problems.	Tides and currents create dangers for both swimmers and boaters.	All trees and low bush cover should be removed from the planned lake bed, but sod and topsoil need not be removed.	Bacterial contamination can be controlled.
Very large lakes frequently provide adverse weather conditions.	Water currents can make swimming hazardous.	Storms and heavy seas can suspend water programming for long periods.		Swimming pools provide freedom from most environmental hazards.
Natural sandy beach areas are desirable.	Water movement may bring debris and waste into the camp area, but natural flow may also be helpful in maintaining "clean" water.	Beach area is difficult to maintain and keep free of debris.	Beach area should be graded before the lake is filled.	Design and construction is complex and requires experts.
A relatively constant water level is an asset.		Saltwater and marine growth increase equipment maintenance and human safety problems.	Artificial lakes tend to be turbid. An upstream silting basin may be necessary in some areas.	Swimming pools should not be located on low ground where surface run-off can contaminate pool water.
Lakes with turbid water, many weeds, or a sharp drop-off in the swim area should be avoided.	Problems of installation and maintenance of facilities are magnified.	Waterfront facilities are costly to construct and maintain.		Swimming pools should be located away from ground cover that may cause leaves and bark to interfere with the filter system.
				Guard tower should face north or east whenever possible for improved visibility.
				Construction is costly.

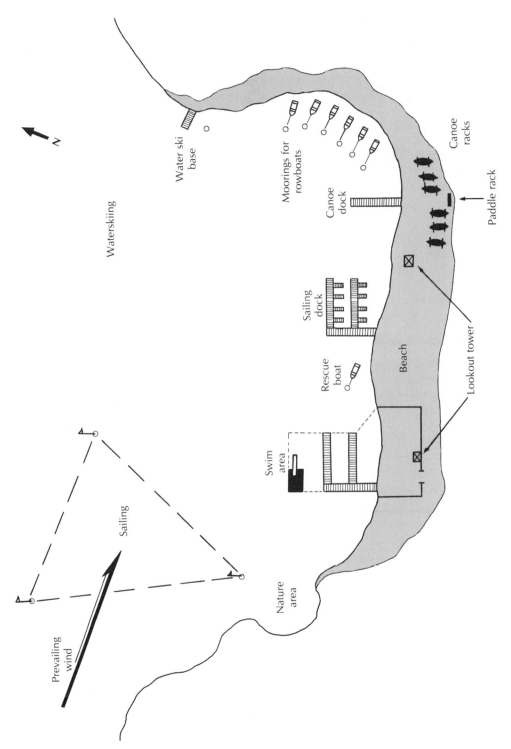

Fig. 5-2. Model layout of a camp waterfront.

vere weather as well as the knocks of various types of smallcraft.

2. Piers should be easily erected and taken apart.
3. Sections of the pier should be of modular construction with interchangeable parts.
4. Sections should be capable of simple and efficient assembly.
5. Sections should be lightweight so that four persons can handle any module.

Piers can be constructed of wood, aluminum, steel, or any combination of these. The characteristics of each are shown in Table 5-2.

Piers are of three general types: permanent piers, stanchion piers, and floating piers. The decision as to which installation is best for a given camp depends on condition of the underwater terrain, tidal or water level fluctuations, and climatic conditions.

Permanent piers. Large wooden piles are driven down into the lake, river, or ocean bottom, and a platform is then constructed just above the surface of the water on top of the piles. In shallow water, a crib or long wooden frame may be built up from the bottom and the pier constructed on top of the box. The crib is usually filled with stone or sand to prevent it from shifting. Fixed piers of this type are most suitable in moderate climates because there is no annual installation, removal, and storage required. However, in areas in which there are severe ice conditions in winter, maintenance and repair costs make this type of construction prohibitive.

Stanchion piers. Stanchion, or removable piers, are used in areas in which fixed piers are impractical because of icing. Removable piers have permanent stanchions or legs on which the piers are placed, or the supports may be removed during the off-season along with the platforms. When the foundation structure is fixed, the supports are driven down into the bottom of the lake or river to the point of refusal. Frequently, cylindrical legs are fitted into permanent sleeves that are set in concrete (Fig. 5-3). When temporary stanchions are used, the base of each support is fitted with a large rectangular pad that sits on the lake bottom. A level, hard surface is necessary if pads are to be used. In most setups that use stanchions, the installation provides for adjusting the sections of dock to the water level. A typical arrangement is shown in the insert in Fig. 5-3.

Floating piers. Free floating piers are required when the level of the water varies during the camp season, the terrain is unsuitable for stanchion piers, water depth is excessive, or the pier installation is to be ex-

Table 5-2. Characteristics of waterfront pier construction materials

Characteristic	Wood	Aluminum	Steel
Cost	Least expensive of the three	More expensive than wood and about the same as steel	Approximately the same as aluminum
Weight	Lighter than steel but heavier than aluminum	Much the lightest of the three	Heaviest of the three
Strength	More durable than thin-guage aluminum but less durable than steel	Generally, the least durable	Most durable of the three
Maintenance	Little maintenance required if well constructed	Little or no maintenance required; not satisfactory in saltwater because of oxidation	Highest maintenance costs of the three

tensive. Floating piers are more easily assembled than most stanchion docks but do not have the same degree of stability. They must be anchored to the shore or the bottom of the lake or stream.

Floating piers are built in sections and are hinged together with heavy cotter pins for easy assembly. When a floating raft is attached to a fixed pier, large, eliptical ring assemblies should be used to permit the floating section to rise or fall with changing water level (Fig. 5-4).

Docks, rafts, and piers should be inspected regularly for loose boards, protrud-

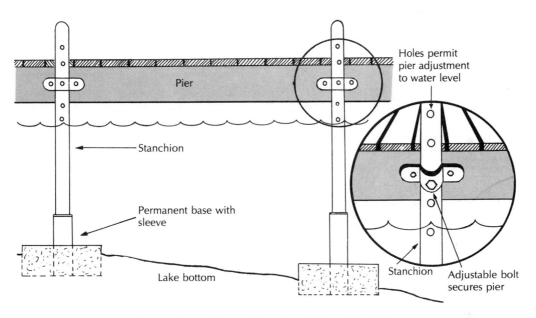

Fig. 5-3. Removable stanchion pier with fixed foundation.

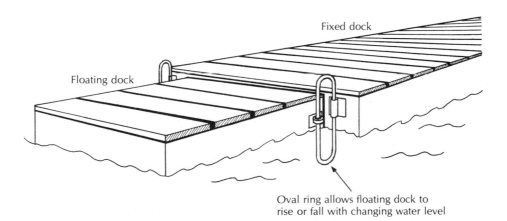

Fig. 5-4. Floating and fixed docks.

ing nails, wood slivers, and slippery spots. Wet surfaces on docks and rafts can present a serious hazard if finished lumber has been used on the upper exposed surface. One effective solution is to paint the surface with special nonskid paint that contains fine aggregate in the paint itself. The maintenance staff can do the job themselves by using regular paint and sifting fine sand over the freshly painted surface. Another solution is to lay down outdoor carpeting or cocoa or rubber matting. The use of adhesive-grip strips is also effective.

The swimming area. At most camps, swimming includes both an instructional and a recreational program. This must be kept in mind when planning the physical layout of the area. Piers should be placed on the windward side of the nonswimming area to reduce the possibility of waves. Many camps also rope off a 25-meter area in which older campers and counsellors can train on a measured course.

The overall size of the swim area naturally varies with the size of the camp. A rough guideline provides 50 square feet of water surface for each swimmer. Three separate areas should be clearly defined as follows:

Nonswimmers: Maximum depth of 3 feet, 6 inches or, in the case of very young campers, no deeper than chest level for the smallest campers.

Beginners: Maximum depth of 6 feet.

Swimmers: Maximum depth of 12 feet when diving boards are no higher than 1 meter from the water.

The bottom of the lake or river should have a gentle slope of no more than 10% grade and should be completely free of all obstacles such as rocks, logs, and anchors. Fig. 5-5 shows the recommended depth and lake bottom for the swimming area.

If diving boards are included in the swimming area, they should not be mounted on floating rafts or platforms because of the risk created by the motion of waves and the action of persons moving on the raft. When diving boards of more than 1 meter from the water are installed, care must be taken to ensure sufficient water depth below the end of the boards.

At least one lookout tower should be provided for a senior lifeguard to supervise the entire swim area. It must be high enough to permit excellent visibility of the area and should face north or east so that sun glare on the surface of the water is minimized. The base of the tower can be enclosed to

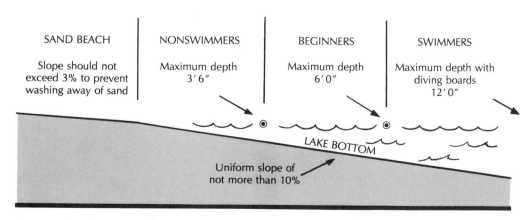

SAND BEACH

Slope should not exceed 3% to prevent washing away of sand

NONSWIMMERS

Maximum depth 3′ 6″

BEGINNERS

Maximum depth 6′ 0″

SWIMMERS

Maximum depth with diving boards 12′ 0″

LAKE BOTTOM

Uniform slope of not more than 10%

Fig. 5-5. Profile of recommended swimming depths.

provide a storage area for emergency waterfront equipment.

The beach area. The beach should be cleared of trees, shrubs, and any other impediments that reduce the lifeguard's visibility and create problems if emergency rescue is required. The waterfront area must be accessible by road in the event that an emergency vehicle is needed. The beach immediately in front of the swimming area should be enclosed with a restraining rope or fence with a single entrance wide enough to accept pairs of swimmers. A "buddy" or "check-off" board should be located at the entrance. Fig. 5-6 illustrates two popular swimming area layouts.

The boating area. Boating facilities, including piers, moorings, canoes, oar and paddle racks, and boat houses for storage, are an integral part of waterfront planning. A separate location, well away from the swimming and waterskiing areas, should be set aside for boating and canoeing.

Canoes and kayaks should be carried up on shore and placed on conveniently located racks. Racks should be located in shady areas and constructed low to the ground for young campers. Fig. 5-7 shows a recommended rack for four canoes.

The actual boating area on the water should be clearly defined by buoys or some other suitable markers. Many camps have a safety procedure whereby a red flag is raised on shore whenever the waterfront director wishes to have all smallcraft brought in to shore. This warning system is effective in the event of impending bad weather.

Watercraft may be stored in the off-season in special boathouses located at the waterfront or in an appropriate building such as the recreation hall, lodge, or even dining hall if one of these is located in close proximity to the boat dock area.

Playing fields. Every camp requires open, level play areas of varying sizes and shapes.

The extent to which these open areas are developed is determined by two factors: the program philosophy of the camp and the availability of suitable areas within the site.

The size and variety of areas that might be developed is only limited by the imagination of the program staff. Small level openings throughout the main parts of the camp may be used to promote badminton, tetherball, horseshoes, boccie, croquet, and other similar activities. Some areas should also be developed for the exclusive purpose of participation in one specialized activity. Examples of these are archery, riflery, horseback riding, and tennis. A few camps place such a premium on organized court games that they construct special hard surface areas of asphalt or concrete for volleyball, basketball, and similar sports. The majority of camps, however, are content to have several large open fields that can serve as multipurpose areas. These game fields should be relatively level and free of roots, stones, logs, and rocks.

Archery range. Archery is only one of many activities that require special facilities at camp. It is included here because so many camp administrators fail to appreciate the inherent danger in this activity and permit archery to be conducted by staff members with little knowledge of the sport. Archery is potentially as dangerous as riflery, and the range should be organized with a high degree of care.

The first requirement is a large, open space, with relatively level ground, preferably some distance from the main parts of camp. An area of 150 by 250 feet will accommodate six targets at a range of up to 50 yards. This provides for considerable open space around the shooting range itself for good visibility and safety. The area should be free of all rocks and logs to keep arrow breakage to a minimum. The grass in front of and behind the targets should be kept

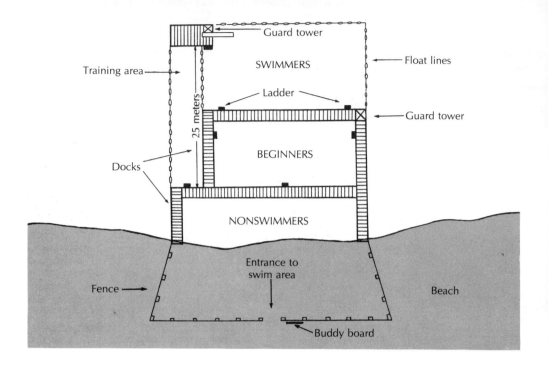

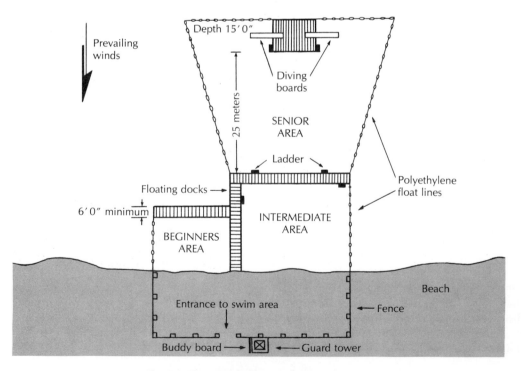

Fig. 5-6. Two sample layouts of swimming area.

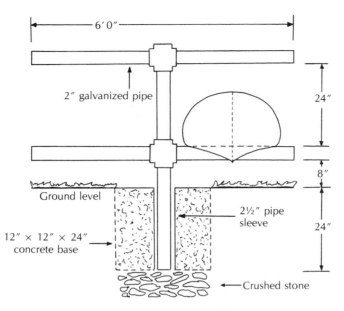

Fig. 5-7. Canoe rack.

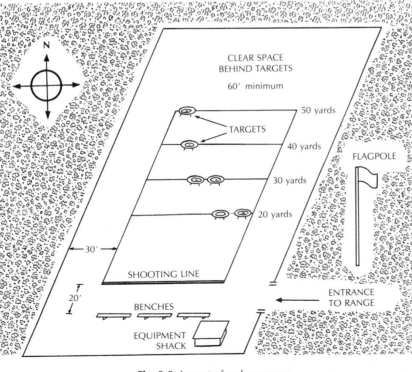

Fig. 5-8. Layout of archery range.

short so that arrows do not "snake" into it and become lost.

The single most important consideration in the layout of an archery range is to stagger the targets when campers are shooting at different distances. Many camps make the fundamental mistake of staggering the shooting line. This is a hazardous procedure. The shooting line is fixed regardless of the distance of the shooters (Fig. 5-8).

A restraining rope or fence should be erected to enclose the range and placed a minimum of 30 feet from the range proper. Warning signs should also be posted around the perimeter of the range alerting everyone that this is a danger zone. Some camps follow the practice of locating a flag pole just outside the entrance to the range. A red flag is flown to advise others in the camp that the range is in use.

Council ring. A traditional weekly program in many camps is Indian council ring. It involves bringing the entire camp together for an evening program in which a formalized Indian ritual ceremony is followed. The location of the council ring is important. It should be somewhat removed from the main areas of camp so that it must be approached by a quiet wooded trail. Seclusion is an important aspect of the council ring. The ring itself should be in an attractive wooded area with an opening large enough to accommodate the entire camp. The ring should be on level ground or form a natural amphitheater. In the latter case, care must be taken to avoid flooding after a heavy rain. The floor of the ring should be level and hard since it is used for stunts, combatives, dancing, and other rites.

Seating should be arranged in concentric circles or semicircles to provide intimacy to the area. The seats themselves take the form of elevated split logs or rustic planks. A sacred council fire is located in the center of the ring or at the head of the semicircle. A special chair for the chief is customary, and some council rings are surrounded with totem poles that have been carved by chiefs and braves over the years. No artifical lighting should intrude on this area. All light should come from the council fire, elevated fire platforms at the head of the amphitheatre, or fire pots located around the edge of the ring.

Chapel. Most camps are concerned with the spiritual welfare of their campers and therefore provide for some form of spiritual or religious service. In developing the facilities for religious observance, it should be possible to plan a sanctuary that meets the requirements of many faiths and can also be used in a single, interdenominational service or by each group at different times. Some chapels are located completely in the outdoors with no shelter or covering. In the event of inclement weather, the service must then be moved to the lodge, recreation hall, or dining room. Other camps, in keeping with the requirements of some faiths, provide an altar that is covered by a shelter, while still others also cover the seating area but leave the structure entirely open on one or more sides.

As in the case of the council ring, the chapel should be located away from the busy areas of the camp in a quiet and sequestered site with an attractive view, preferably of the lake. This should be a place of quiet meditation for an individual camper at any time. The ideal location provides a gentle grade of about 10% and good drainage. The structure should include an altar, lectern, or pulpit as required by particular faiths. The architectural treatment should be rustic and simple in keeping with the total camp decor.

Central services

Although sleeping and program facilities are of primary concern to campers, there are many other supporting services that are essential to a well-organized camp. The camp development committee must keep in proper perspective the role that these supporting services play, always bearing in mind that such facilities have only an indirect impact on the camp program and the campers themselves.

Administration area. This area includes a complex of services that are sometimes located in a single building or dispersed throughout several smaller structures. Regardless of the layout, these administrative services should house the director's office, business office, including central office staff and reception area, program staff office or meeting room, program equipment storage, camp store, and camp post office.

The administrative area should be in close proximity to the parking lot so that visitors to the camp have no difficulty locating an office where they can get necessary information. The area should also be fairly central to the entire camp for purposes of general supervision and emergencies.

The area for the business office and staff naturally depends on the size of the camp. In a very small operation, the camp director's office, reception area, and central office area may comprise a single room, whereas a larger camp might have six or more full-time office staff requiring more space. Regardless of the size of this structure, it should include all camp business files and whatever business equipment the camp rents or owns.

Many administrative structures include an office or meeting room in which senior program personnel meet to plan and assess the total camp program. All program charts, schedules, files, and other records should be located here.

Health center. Every camp should have a permanent structure that serves as an infirmary or hospital. This facility is referred to as the health center throughout this book and is discussed in some detail in Chapter 7. It should be centrally located and easily accessible to campers as well as camp vehicles.

Dining hall and kitchen. The dining hall–kitchen complex is usually the largest single building on the camp property. A few camps, with large enrollments, may have two or more dining halls. In other cases, meals are served from one facility, but in shifts.

The dining hall and kitchen are described in detail in Chapter 8. It is sufficient to point out here that this facility should be within walking distance of all living units. It should also have convenient access by service vehicles so they do not have to pass through living units and general program areas to make deliveries. Both the kitchen and dining hall should have good natural lighting and ventilation and must be thoroughly screened against insects. They must also be rodent proof.

The recommended floor area for a camp dining room is between 10 and 15 square feet per person. The latter allocation provides generous space for aisles between tables. The standard for the kitchen recommends between 2.5 and 4 square feet per person served. This figure does not include the space required for storage and refrigeration.

Because of the specialized function of these areas, food service planners and consultants should be invited to advise on the construction and equiping of these facilities.

Shower facilities. Camp standards require that facilities be available for all campers and staff to have a warm shower or bath on a regular basis. The recommended ratio of shower heads or tubs per person is 1:20. Shower units should be located to meet the following criteria: convenient to camper and staff living areas, in sunny, open areas, and where sewage disposal can be handled effectively.

If the camp has a swimming pool, showers should be located adjacent to the shallow end of the pool since warm, soapy showers should be required of all persons before entering the pool.

Good natural light and ventilation is very important in shower buildings. Too often these facilities are dark and damp, thus fostering accelerated bacterial growth. A 6-12-inch open space between the floor and walls is one solution. Another answer is to construct open gables. Some excellent shower facilities have no roof, permitting the sun to dry the area naturally.

The size and type of hot water heater will be determined by local conditions and total daily demand. Regardless of what size and type of tank is used, a temperature control valve should be installed limiting the water temperature to approximately 110°F.

Staff lodge. The staff house or counsellor cabin is a structure that frequently has low priority when a new site is planned. Staff members need a facility where they can get away from campers and relax or socialize among themselves when they are off duty. It should be well away from camper living units and "out of bounds" to campers. The lodge should be part of the central complex, however, so that staff members can be easily located when needed.

Staff living quarters. Camp staff members deserve proper housing accommodations if good morale is to be maintained throughout the camp season. Important considerations when planning staff living quarters are adequate space and privacy. In this latter regard, kitchen staff and custodial personnel should be housed well away from camp and counsellor staff quarters since they often begin their workday at a very early hour and retire early in the evening. No sleeping quarters for food services staff should be located in the building that houses the kitchen. Fire laws prohibit sleeping quarters above the kitchen in most states and provinces.

The facilities for families of married staff members should be segregated from the main camp areas and form a somewhat self-contained community. Most camps invite spouses and children of employees to take their meals in the dining hall with the rest of the camp. Others arrange for the families to pick up prepared camp food before every meal but to eat it in their cottages. A few camps permit the families to pick up food supplies from the kitchen, but all preparation must be done in the cottages.

Maintenance area. Maintenance is a critcal feature of any camp operation, and the camp custodian or superintendent is a key member of the staff. In many camps today, he or she is repsonsible for the year-round supervision of the site as well as its total maintenance. The superintendent is usually responsible for his or her house, the maintenance yard and shop, equipment, camp vehicles, and storage of flammable materials.

Because the camp custodian fulfills such a pivotal position at camp, a comfortable home should be provided to attract and keep a good person. It should be located away, from the central areas of the camp and afford some degree of privacy. The house should be strategically located close to the camp entrance, providing a control point for the main access road. It should also be close to the public highway for year-round accessibility.

An enclosed maintenance yard should be located close to the custodian's house but screened from the camp road. The yard should be large enough to store all maintenance equipment as well as building materials and supplies. The entire area must be well fenced with one or two entrances that can be secured. The yard and its access road should have an all-weather surface for year-round use.

Within the yard, there should be several structures for repair and storage. A workshop area that is fully winterized and heated is a necessity for the custodian and the staff. It contains a work bench with both hand and power tools. In addition, storage areas should be provided for equipment such as beds, mattresses, tents, and many types of maintenance materials and supplies.

A special word is in order here regarding mattress storage. Open, slatted shelving, with 36-inch clearance between shelves and the bottom shelf at least 6 inches off the floor is recommended. Approximately eight rolled-edge mattresses can be placed on each shelf. More than this number stacked horizontally causes those on the bottom to become spread and misshapen. The weight of many mattresses can also cause a heat buildup so that they become a fire hazard.

Every camp has the need to store some flammable materials such as gasoline, kerosene, paints, and varsol. These should be kept in metal containers and stored in a separate facility at least 50 feet from all other buildings. The structure should be built of fire-resistant materials, kept locked at all times, and have limited access.

Utilities

Water supply. An adequate and clean water supply should be assured before the purchase of camp property. Drinking water must not only be free of pathogenic organisms, but palatable and aesthetically appealing. Camper acceptance of the water supply is seriously jeopardized by such characteristics as color, turbidity, odor, and taste.

Tests to determine the bacterial content of the water must be made when the supply is first located and at regular intervals thereafter. These tests should be conducted by state or local authorities or a reputable commercial laboratory. It cannot be emphasized too strongly that one or two satisfactory test results does not ensure a permanent safe supply of water. Coliform bacteria may enter the water supply system in a variety of ways, and the only insurance against contaminated water is regularly scheduled water tests. It is important to remember to take water samples for testing from various points where the water is drawn and not just at the source. The safest procedure is to draw samples at the extreme end of the water system farthest from the source. This will catch any contamination that has entered the water distribution system.

The source of a potable water supply may be a drilled or shallow well, spring, lake stream, or town system. The camp development committee must investigate all possible sources with care since one source will almost certainly prove preferable to the others. Generally speaking, drilled wells are the safest sources. Shallow wells, lakes, streams, and springs are more prone to some form of surface contamination. Shallow wells and springs frequently can serve as an auxiliary or short-term water source. The problem with both is that they rarely provide a sufficient quantity of water in times of drought.

The selection of a water system for a camp is a complex project and usually requires the help of a water system engineer as well as state and local health authorities, since many local ordinances influence the actual installation. Such questions as what is the best source of water when several are available, is filtration of water necessary to remove suspended material, what type of chlorination is recommended, what types of pumps can best meet the camp needs, and what is the most desirable layout of the distribution system can only be answered by a qualified expert in light of the conditions within a given camp.

Every camp should make provisions for some form of water storage within their system. The loss of the water supply for a day or two as a result of a defective pump or power failure can create an emergency situation. It is recommended that a storage tank capable of holding a 48-hour supply of water be installed in all camps that must rely on pumps to draw their water.

The actual layout of the water distribution system should involve close collaboration between representatives of the development committee and the engineer. Whether or not the system or part of it is to be winterized is a primary consideration. This will have a bearing on the type of pipe to be laid, the depth at which it should be buried, the location of drainage outlets, and the types of fittings to be used.

Waste disposal. Many misconceptions and misunderstandings regarding sewage and waste disposal have led to major problems in camps. As in the case of the water supply system, waste disposal is a technical problem necessitating the expertise of a sanitary engineer.

Proper sewage treatment and disposal has implications not only for the camp community but also its neighbors. An inadequate system could result in one of the following: contamination of the camp drinking water or that of its neighbors, pollution of the recreational swimming water, rodents and insects infecting food or water supplies, parts of the system may be unsightly in appearance, cause unpleasant odors, or result in soft, spongy ground conditions.

All waste disposal systems are subject to many local health regulations necessitating close collaboration between camp representatives, camp engineer, and state or local health authorities. Each installation must conform to all existing ordinances and standards. The system that is eventually installed depends on such factors as (1) nature of the terrain, (2) type of soil, (3) size and layout of the camp, and (4) volume and types of waste.

In addition to the normal problems that must be confronted when planning for waste disposal, the camp situation is further aggravated by the great distances between facilities. To effectively handle sewage disposal over an area of several hundred acres is no easy task. This raises the question as to whether a central disposal system should be installed or whether individual decentralized units should be used throughout the camp. The sanitary engineer is the best person to answer this and similar questions.

A wide variety of toilet installations are used in camps today. These include flush toilets, pail-a-day toilets, chemical toilets, as well as pit and vault latrines. Whatever type is used, toilet facilities must be vermin proof, well ventilated, and well maintained in a clean, sanitary condition at all times. In residence camps, the number of toilets should be one seat for every 10 persons. One seat for every 20 persons is recommended in day camps. Hand-washing facilities must also be provided adjacent to all toilets. Special attention should be given to hand-washing facilities for kitchen personnel.

Another problem that confronts many camps is the difficulty in disposing of the large quantities of waste water produced by central shower installations as well as the kitchen dishwasher. A variety of schemes is possible. The waste water may be piped to a septic tank and the effluent eventually dispersed in an absorption field. Another possibility is to first remove the water to a grease trap and then combine it with the effluent from toilet waste as it enters the absorption field. Regardless of what system is recommended, all septic tanks and drainage fields must be located a minimum of 150 feet from drinking and recreational water sources. It must not be assumed that effluent, when leaving the septic tank, is bacteria free and therefore safe.

The removal of rubbish and kitchen garbage can be achieved in several ways. Where state and local regulations permit, combustible rubbish can be easily burned in a simple outdoor incinerator. Noncombustible items must be taken to a local dump or buried. The preferred method is to have the custodial staff haul garbage to a public dump or contract with a local firm to carry it. Burying camp garbage is the least desirable method because of the large quantities that must be handled.

Electricity. Defective electrical wiring is one of the greatest causes of fire in the camping industry. One of the reasons has been the failure to hire qualified electricians to do repair and extension work with the result that the camp becomes a hodgepodge of overloaded switch boxes and fuses. All wiring should conform to the National Electrical Code. Established camps would be well advised to have a qualified electrician do a complete inspection of the entire system every 2 or 3 years just before camp opening.

The use of electric light in camp should be limited to selected areas. Indiscriminate use of artificial light can negate the camp atmosphere. There is little need to install electrical lights in sleeping units. Outdoor light should be limited to the maintenance yard and possibly the parking lot, administration building, and health center. The use of floodlights for outdoor program areas should be undertaken only after careful deliberation.

Communications. Every camp must have telephone communications with the outside community. This service should be connected to the custodian's house and the administration center. Whether the health center is included is a personal decision. Staff and camper phone calls should be made in the administration center, and rules should be established so that only essential calls are permitted.

In addition to the outside phone, an internal phone system should connect key centers in the camp. These include the administration building, kitchen, health center, custodian's house or maintenance building, and the waterfront.

Roads and trails. Roads and trails within the camp should be kept to a minimum for two reasons: road construction is costly, and a labyrinth of roads and trails detracts from the natural wilderness setting of the camp.

The main camp road should be of all-weather construction and built to carry heavy buses and delivery trucks. It should be approximately 18 feet wide and provide good drainage. This main road terminates at the camp parking lot. Secondary and tertiary service roads are also required. The former provide for camp deliveries, service vehicles, and exit in case of an emergency. This road network should pass all major facilities. Tertiary service roads are reserved only for camp vehicles, such as a pickup truck or jeep. They are only 8 to 10 feet in width, require no special surfacing, and need minimal grading, tree removal, cutting, and filling. The only maintenance should involve minor clearing of brush each spring.

Foot trails offer access to all facilities on camp property. Each trail should be part of an all-camp plan: trails should not just happen. It is important that trails or paths do not pass through living areas or playing facilities. They should lead to or around these areas.

Some camp signs are necessary to identify major buildings and to provide directions to various facilities. Again, each camp sign should be part of a larger plan. They should be uniform in pattern, large enough, and professional in their appearance.

When planning each of the camp utilities described above, it is very important that detailed layout drawings be made during the planning stage. Once the utility has been completed, these drawings should be placed on file with the camp custodian so that as maintenance problems arise, reference can be made to the exact distribution pattern for that utility.

MAINTENANCE AND PROPERTY MANAGEMENT

The property, buildings, other structures and equipment represent a substantial investment in any camp, regardless of its size. It therefore follows that this physical plant should be managed in a systematic, businesslike manner. Only if carefully developed methods and procedures are followed can a modern camp expect to maintain its property, facilities, and equipment at peak operational efficiency. A scheduled preventive maintenance program can extend the life of camp structures and equipment many years and thus save the organization considerable money.

Many camp directors and committees make the false assumption that new buildings need no maintenance, and they therefore allocate a paltry amount for this purpose. It is true that new facilities require less initial maintenance than older facilities, but in any large camp operation there is a need for continuous preventive maintenance, and this should begin at the time new facilities are put into operation. Failure to take certain preventive maintenance steps when closing the camp for the winter may cause faster deterioration of some equipment than occurs when it is in full use.

Apart from the fact that prudent fiscal practice demands a well-planned property management and maintenance program, such a program should be followed for other reasons as well:

1. Well-maintained facilities and equipment ensure better program service and satisfaction.
2. Health and safety of campers and staff is optimized when hazards related to the property, facilities, and equipment are eliminated.
3. Public relations are enhanced when parents, campers, neighbors, and visitors are impressed with an attractive, well-maintained site.
4. Morale and respect for camp property is strengthened when staff and campers are proud of the campsite and its facilities.

A good maintenance program begins with the selection of the site and a carefully planned layout and development of facilities in accordance with the principles stated earlier in this chapter. If shortcuts are taken during the various planning and development stages or if the budget is cut in the interest of initial economy, the result, in the long run, may make a maintenance schedule financially disastrous.

Maintenance supervisor

The camp director has primary responsibility for securing qualified staff to implement the maintenance program. Such a program must be headed by one person who possesses the management as well as the technical skills to carry it out. The person assigned to fulfill this management role is given various titles in camp. In a very small organization the appointment may be part-time and, in such cases, the terms *caretaker* or *handyman* are common. In larger camps, maintenance may be a year-round responsibility with a number of part-time staff members hired to assist during the camp season. In these cases, the job designation may be *custodian* or *maintenance supervisor*. In very large camps, a corps of specialists including carpenters, painters, grounds-keepers, plumbers, stone masons, automotive mechanics, and others may comprise the maintenance team. In the latter case, the staff may be headed by the *maintenance engineer* or *superintendent*. For purposes of clarity and consistency, the person in charge is referred to as the *maintenance supervisor* in this chapter.

In many small camps, the maintenance supervisor is directly responsible to the camp director. In larger camps, the director frequently delegates maintenance supervision to the business manager. Whatever the line of responsibility, regular weekly, biweekly, or, in some cases, daily meetings must be held between the maintenance supervisor and the administrative superior to ensure coordination of the total maintenance program.

The maintenance supervisor in a small camp must be a "jack-of-all-trades." It is highly desirable to find a person who has practical experience in carpentry, plumbing, electrical work, and mechanics since routine maintenance and repair is required in all these areas. In seeking to fill this position, the director or business manager should look for a person with the following qualifications:

1. Graduate of a vocational technical program or equivalent formal skill training
2. A minimum of 3 years practical experience preferably in the combined areas of carpentry, electrical work, plumbing, and general maintenance
3. Possession of a valid chauffeur's license
4. Ability to maintain accurate records and inventories
5. Ability to get along well with people

Responsibilities of maintenance supervisor. The range of responsibilities that supervisors must undertake varies with the size of the camp operation and whether or not it is a year-round position. Full-time maintenance supervisors who live at the campsite will have many very diverse responsibilities, including the following:

Protection of camp property. Campsites vary in size from less than 100 acres to over 10,000 acres. To oversee such large tracts of land is a difficult assignment. Specifically, the supervisor must be responsible for screening visitors, both in and out of the camp season. In the off-season, camps frequently attract curiosity seekers and sometimes vandals. There are no easy solutions to the problems of trespassers and vandalism. However, the following suggestions should be of some assistance in forestalling this problem:

1. Locate the supervisor's home at the main camp entrance with clear visibility of the camp service road.
2. All camp boundary lines should be clearly marked and the brush cut away from these lines.
3. Post "Private Property" or "No Trespassing" signs at frequent intervals around the property lines.
4. Plant a "living fence," such as multiflora rose, on camp boundaries.
5. Erect a sturdy fence at points of ready access to camp property.
6. Patrol the campsite regularly by vehicle or on foot.
7. Report all trespassers to local law enforcement agencies at once with accurate descriptions, license numbers, and other useful information.

Protection of camp property also includes prevention of natural hazards such as fire, storm, flood, and the effects of snow and ice. In the event that a disaster befalls the camp, the maintenance supervisor plays a central role in coping with the emergency. In some cases, this is the best person to lead the planned emergency procedure.

A third responsibility of the supervisor regarding protection of property is care of the natural resources of the camp. Preservation of the natural conditions of the campsite should be the primary objective of any good maintenance program. This includes concern for soil erosion, water pollution, and woodlot conservation. The aesthetic appearance of the property is also inextricably related to the preservation of the natural setting.

Ongoing operation of the facilities and property. This responsibility includes the many "housekeeping" responsibilities that must be undertaken by the maintenance staff. These responsibilities should never be neglected for the sake of maintenance tasks or new construction. Operational duties include the routine inspections and checks that are part of every camp operation and are distinguished from maintenance tasks in that they do not require any repair.

Maintenance of facilities and property. Repair of existing facilities and equipment is the primary function within this category of responsibilities. These tasks, unlike operational duties, require some corrective action and many cannot be anticipated. Preventive maintenance, on the other hand, is designed to prevent breakdown or deterioration of equipment and facilities through planned action. Examples of maintenance and operational tasks are contrasted in Table 5-3.

New construction and major renovation. Each of the three groups of responsibilities listed thus far are of greater importance in scheduling the supervisor's time than new construction or improvements. Too often, existing structures are permitted to deteriorate while maintenance personnel give their time to new projects. Only after careful appraisal of the work schedules of the maintenance staff can a decision be made as to whether the maintenance supervisor should undertake new construction or supervise the work of others who have been given the contract.

Table 5-3. Typical regular operational and maintenance responsibilities

Regular operational responsibilities	Maintenance responsibilities
Cleaning buildings on a predetermined schedule	Cleaning out clogged drains and the like
Cleaning up debris after a storm	Painting and staining buildings and equipment
Cutting out dead trees and branches	Planting ground cover for erosion control
Distributing firewood where required	Repairing defective railings, steps, and docks
Disposing of garbage and trash	Repairing results of storm damage
Maintaining roads, ditches, and trails	Repairing defective mechanical equipment including automotive breakdowns
Making routine preventive maintenance inspections	Replacing worn-out equipment or burned-out motors
Mowing grass and cutting brush	Replacing broken windows and screens
Providing routine service to all mechanical and program equipment	Reroofing camp structures
Patrolling the site regularly in the off-season	Repairing broken waterlines
Removing snow from roofs	

Community relations. A resident maintenance supervisor is the one continuing contact that the camp has with its neighbors throughout the entire year. To the extent that the resident employee of the camp takes an active interest in, and cooperates fully with, the local community, the public relations of the camp are greatly enhanced. Interest in local affairs can do more to cement good relationships than perhaps any other single public relations step.

Selection and training of maintenance personnel. The camp director or business manager consults with the supervisor regarding the need for additional maintenance personnel. The supervisor's recommendations should carry considerable weight since he or she is the person most familiar with the range of duties and the time schedules required to complete the jobs. The supervisor must also establish the orientation and training program for the new staff. Duties must be effectively allocated so that the work is of high quality and completed with dispatch. The evaluation of maintenance employees is a further responsibility.

Records and reports. Any well-planned camp maintenance program requires the keeping of accurate and complete inventories and other records. Supervisors are responsible for the ordering of construction materials and large quantities of maintenance supplies. In addition, they issue equipment and tools during the camp season. Supervisors are responsible for all these materials and equipment and must observe established bookkeeping procedures for all these transactions. In addition, they must plan and organize the work schedules of the maintenance staff in a businesslike manner. They must also manage the workshop and general maintenance area efficiently.

Supervision of personnel. In addition to the maintenance supervisor, large camps may have one or more assistants who are hired during the camp season to do relatively unskilled work. Frequently, these part-time workers are from the local community. It is the supervisor's responsibility to plan and oversee the work of these seasonal personnel.

It is not uncommon, especially among camps run under the auspices of service organizations, to have teams, of volunteers assist during the precamp period and on weekends in minor construction projects as well as regular maintenance assignments. It is usually the responsibility of the maintenance supervisor to help plan and oversee these workers.

Many times, specialized skills are needed to complete a maintenance task involving repair or renovation. This work may be contracted to an outside firm that specializes in this type of work, but the camp supervisor is expected to oversee the project and certify its satisfactory completion.

The work schedule

The planning of an effective and efficient maintenance schedule involves three factors: (1) the work to be done, (2) the personnel available, and (3) the funds allocated. Through careful, deliberate planning, a step-by-step schedule can be put into effect. Maintenance schedules can be classified into three general categories: routine operation schedule, maintenance schedule, and long-term projects.

Routine operation schedule. These tasks include the routine housekeeping chores that can be scheduled well in advance since most can be anticipated. A few occur as a result of some emergency, such as a storm, and cannot be predicted. The first step is to list all known routine tasks and then determine the frequency with which they must be performed. This data can be compiled on 5 × 8 inch index cards (Fig. 5-9), and the cards can be filed alphabetically by job description or job number. A daily or weekly schedule of all operational tasks can then be drawn up and posted. In a large camp, the name of the person assigned to each job should be included.

Maintenance schedule. A systematic maintenance schedule also makes use of individual maintenance job cards for each assignment. This system has the advantage of consolidating all relevant data in one place, and the cards can be easily filed according to job description, job number, location, or priority. The card should provide for a little more information than is needed on the operational card (Fig. 5-10).

As a result of inspection tours before, dur-

```
┌─────────────────────────────────────────────────────────────────┐
│                      OPERATIONAL JOB CARD                         │
├──────────────────────────────────────────┬────────────────────────┤
│ Job_____ │ Job number_____ │
│                                          │                        │
│ Location_____│                        │
├──────────────────────────────────────────┼────────────────────────┤
│ Originator_____ Date_____  │       Frequency        │
├──────────────────────────────────────────┼────────────────────────┤
│ Description:                             │ Daily      _____   │
│                                          │ Weekly     _____   │
│                                          │ Monthly    _____   │
│                                          │ Annually   _____   │
│                                          │   (spring)             │
│                                          │ Annually   _____   │
│ Materials, supplies, and tools           │   (fall)               │
│ needed:                                  ├────────────────────────┤
│                                          │   Estimated time       │
│                                          │      for job           │
│                                          │    _____ Hours      │
└──────────────────────────────────────────┴────────────────────────┘
```

Fig. 5-9. Sample routine operational job card. (The back of each card provides space for the date the job was done, the time required, and the initials of the worker.)

```
┌─────────────────────────────────────────────────────────────────┐
│                      MAINTENANCE JOB CARD                         │
├──────────────────────────────────────────┬────────────────────────┤
│ Job_____ │ Job number_____ │
│                                          │                        │
│ Location_____│                        │
├──────────────────────────────────────────┼────────────────────────┤
│ Originator_____ Date_____   │       Priority         │
├──────────────────────────────────────────┼────────────────────────┤
│ Description:                             │ Immediate    _____  │
│                                          │ Short term   _____  │
│                                          │ End of camp  _____  │
│ Tools and equipment needed:              │ Beginning of _____  │
│                                          │   camp                 │
│                                          │ Long term    _____  │
│                                          ├────────────────────────┤
│ Materials to be ordered:                 │ Estimated time for job │
│                                          │    _____ Hours      │
│                                          ├────────────────────────┤
│ Labor to be done by:                     │ Cost estimate for job  │
│                                          │    _____ Hours      │
└──────────────────────────────────────────┴────────────────────────┘
```

Fig. 5-10. Sample maintenance job card.

ing, and after the camp season, a number of job cards should have been prepared. These are then scrutinized carefully and placed in priority order. The steps to be followed in the completion of any camp maintenance task may be summarized as follows:

1. Determine what jobs need to be done
2. Gather all pertinent information, such as estimates of materials required and costs
3. Check on availability of funds and submit a budget estimate when required
4. Prepare a work schedule for camp maintenance staff, ouside contractor, volunteers, or camp staff
5. Complete the job and any follow-up action that my be required

Long-term schedule A number of maintenance jobs occur infrequently but should nevertheless be scheduled. These include such projects as painting or reroofing buildings, replacement of electrical wiring, repointing masonry, and tent replacement. The importance of scheduling these projects along with all the short-term tasks cannot be emphasized too strongly. Failure to do so could result in major costs being incurred in any given annual budget. For example, the roofs of several buildings might require replacement all at one time. Good planning enables the camp to distribute such costs over several years by reroofing two buildings per year for a 5-year period. The schedule in Table 5-4 shows how long-range projects may be staggered to keep budget costs relatively constant.

Records and reports

Permanent records are an important aspect of responsible camp maintenance. It is

Table 5-4. Sample long-range maintenance schedule

	Specific year scheduled										Year when next scheduled
Project	1981	1982	1983	1984	1985	1986	1987	1988	1989	1990	
Painting (ext. bldg.)											
Administration	X										1986
Arts and crafts		X									1987
Custodian's house			X								1988
Dining hall/kitchen				X							1989
Health center					X						1990
Lodge						X					1991
Shower houses							X				1992
Staff cottages								X			1993
Reroofing											
Administration						X					2006
Arts and crafts						X					2006
Custodian's house							X				2007
Dining hall/kitchen							X				2007
Health center								X			2008
Lodge								X			2008
Shower houses									X		2009
Staff cottages									X		2009
Equipment replacements											

not enough to depend on the camp supervisor's memory as to the exact route of the waterline from the lodge to the staff houses or which of the camp buildings have not been reroofed for over 20 years. Even if memories were infallible, individuals leave the camp and continuity of information is lost.

The number and type of records required is innumerable. Many have already been alluded to in this chapter. The following list includes a summary of the important ones.

PROPERTY RECORDS
1. Surveyor's map of property
2. Topographical map
3. Aerial photographs
4. Camp layout plan of facilities
5. Map of each utility and its distribution
6. Conservation and land-use plan
7. Deeds and other legal papers
8. Property and building insurance

STRUCTURAL RECORDS
1. Building construction drawings
2. Individual building cards
3. List of other structures

EQUIPMENT RECORDS
1. Manufacturer's catalogs
2. Operational manuals
3. Inventory of all mechanical equipment
4. Individual equipment cards

MAINTENANCE RECORDS
1. Maintenance inspection checklist
2. Weekly work schedule
3. Routine operations job card
4. Maintenance job card
5. Inventory of materials, supplies, equipment, and tools

OTHERS
1. Reports of all camp emergencies (fire, storm, flood)
2. Safety and sanitation records
3. Business records including payroll, purchase orders, deliveries, and receipts.

ADMINISTRATIVE GUIDELINES

1. The selection, acquisition, and development of a campsite is too important to be left to a single person. A representative camp development committee should be formed to undertake these tasks.

2. Whether a new camp is being established for the first time or an existing site is in full operation, each should have a master plan for development. Immediate, short-term goals should always be developed in light of the long-range plan.

3. Several criteria should be considered when selecting a campsite, including (1) the size of the property to be acquired keeping in mind both immediate and future use, (2) the physical characteristics of the proposed site, (3) environmental elements such as neighbors, natural hazards, and climate, (4) available water supply, (5) accessibility and availability of local services, (6) suitable waterfront and other program areas, (7) presence of existing structures, and (8) licensing and zoning restrictions.

4. A property survey should be conducted before any land purchase is undertaken.

5. Actual site acquistion should be subject to the approval of some advisory group such as the camp board, council, or committee.

6. Site development is a complex task; it should not be undertaken without the help of a number of technical consultants such as architects, engineers, health officials, and conservationists.

7. Site development involves nine recommended steps and each should be followed in sequence:
   a. Gather all information pertaining to the site
   b. Develop a priority list of facilities and improvements to be undertaken
   c. Prepare a detailed plan for the physical layout of facilities
   d. Select architectural design and construction materials to be used
   e. Take plans to board or council for approval
   f. Have drawings and specifications prepared
   g. Invite bids and let the contracts
   h. Supervise the construction project
   i. Turn over all records to the camp maintenance committee at the completion of the project

8. The decentralization of sleeping units is recommended for the majority of residence camps.

9. Each development committee should carefully consider the advantages and disadvantages of cabins versus tents as sleeping units.

10. Program facilities comprise a fundamental component in campsite development. Careful deliberation must be given to their selection, location, and construction.

11. Of all program facilities, none is more important, in most camps, than the aquatic layout. Many factors determine the optimal location and development of swimming and boating facilities.

12. Each camp must provide a number of central support services such as the administration area, health center, dining hall and kitchen, shower facilities, and maintenance area. In addition, provision must be made for staff living accommodations. Each should be planned as an integral part of the master plan for the entire site.

13. Camp utilities include the following important services: adequate and clean water supply, effective disposal of all camp wastes, electricity, internal and external communications, and maintenance of camp roads and trails. Historically, many camp problems have centered around these utilites. Careful, long-range planning can preclude most of these potential irritants.

14. Camp maintenance should be handled in a systematic, businesslike manner. The key to a sound maintenance program is a maintenance supervisor who possesses not only the necessary technical skills but also management experience.

15. The range of tasks to be undertaken by the maintenance staff is so varied that it is helpful to classify them in three categories: routine operational duties, maintenance responsibilities, and long-term projects. Once all the tasks have been identified, realistic work schedules should be developed so that assignments are undertaken in some logical sequence.

16. Accurate record keeping is an important part of any good camp maintenance program.

SELECTED BIBLIOGRAPHY

American Camping Association: Conservation and the campsite. (Bradford Woods, Martinsville, Ind.: American Camping Association, 1960).

Armstrong, R. J.: Camp maintenance is a year-round job, Camping Magazine, 47(7):14 May, 1975.

Athletic Institute and American Association for Health, Physical Education and Recreation: College and university facilities guide. (Chicago, Ill.: Athletic Institute, 1968).

Athletic Institute and American Association for Health, Physical Education and Recreation: Planning areas and facilities for health, physical education, and recreation. (Chicago, Ill.: Athletic Institute, 1966).

Beryle, M. K.: Planning waterfront facilities, Camping Magazine, 37(7):11-12, Sept./Oct., 1965;37(8):19-20, Nov./Dec., 1965.

Boy Scouts of America: Camp property management (No. 3688). (North Brunswick, N.J.: Camping and Engineering Service, Boy Scouts of America, 1978).

Boy Scouts of America: Campsites and facilities (No. 3679). (North Brunswick, N.J.: Camping and Engineering Service, Boy Scouts of America, 1964).

Bruning, W. F.: Your landscaped areas need efficient maintenance today, Camping Magazine, 44(2):18, 26, Feb. 1972.

Christofero, L.; Camp conservation, Camping Magazine, 51(3):10-11, Feb., 1979.

Devlin, W.: Designing a camp health center, Camping Magazine, 47(1): 12-13, Sept./Oct., 1974.

Ezersky, E. M., and Theibert, R.: Facilities in sports and physical education. (St. Louis: The C. V. Mosby Co., 1976).

Flynn, E.: What's with your storage? When and how to store for winter, Camping Magazine, 46(1):14-15, Sept., 1973.

Jackson, W.: Planning your years—a good maintenance program, Canadian Camping, 30(2):8-9, 12, Apr., 1978.

Keller, R. J.: Modern management of facilities for physical education. (Champaign, Ill.: Stipes Publishing Co., 1973).

Loheed, P. S.: Redesigning multiple camp facilities for year-round programs, Camping Magazine, 51(5):17-19, Apr., 1979.

Mittelstaedt, A. H.: Realistic master plan aids long-range camps growth, Camping Magazine, 47(1):18-19, Sept./Oct., 1974.

Nathans, A. A.: The handbook of camp maintenance. (New York: Association Press, 1959).

Nielsen, R.: Your camp caretaker, Camping Magazine, 44(7):13, 29, Sept., 1972.

Rasmussen, B. L.: Multiple use management of land, Camping Magazine, 39(1):24-25, Jan., 1967.

Sears, B. G.: Camp building trends, Camping Magazine, 40(2):21, Feb., 1968.

Stevenson, J.: Maintenance man wears many different hats, Camping Magazine, 48(5):31-33, Mar., 1976.

Swift, W. C.: A camp manager's view of the maintenance program, Camping Magazine, 45(3):18-19, Aug., 1973.

Temple, E. S.: Facts and fallacies in camp sanitation, Camping Magazine, 41(1):28-29, Jan., 1961.

CHAPTER SIX

Program administration

> . . . Program includes *all* activities, conditions, and relationships that affect the camper: the planned activites as well as the unplanned; the subtle conditions that surround him as well as the more obvious conditions; the relationships that he has with other campers and with counselors; the counselor's attitudes toward him as well as the methods that the counselor uses.[1]

This statement made by Dimock over 30 years ago defines program in the broadest sense. It includes all activities, experiences, and associations that make up the camper's daily routine. It is not limited to organized or structured activities that are designed to reflect camp philosophy and contribute to camp objectives, but includes all those spontaneous, informal, and unplanned moments that constitute a large part of the campers' day. In essence, program includes the sum total of everything that happens at camp.

The camp administrator must accept that all experiences have some impact on campers and help shape their impressions and attitudes toward the camp. At the same time, the administrator must realize that it is the planned experiences that most profoundly influence the campers' feelings regarding their stay at camp. In the eyes of the campers, the success of the summer experience is measured largely by their reactions to the formal camp program. Program development, therefore, becomes a preeminent consideration for the camp administrator since

the success or failure of the entire camp venture may rest on how the program is perceived by the campers.

This raises a fundamental question of those responsible for planning the program: to what extent should the camp program be determined by program specialists hired for this purpose and to what extent should it cater to the interests of the camp clientele?

Some directors take the position that activities should be almost totally predicated on the wishes, and even demands, of those for whom the program has been planned. Others believe that staff members have been carefully selected for their expertise in program planning and are, therefore, best able to develop a balanced and attractive schedule of activities. Most camp directors subscribe to a camp philosophy somewhat different from that advocated in our schools. Educational curricula tend to be developed largely by pedagogical experts who are regarded as the group best qualified to achieve educational goals. On the other hand, a few recreational agencies see their role as one of providing facilities and only enough program leadership to ensure safe conduct of the activities.

---

1. Dimock H. S.: *Administration of the modern camp.* (New York: Association Press, 1948) p. 123.

Most leaders in camp programming take a middle course between those described above. They accept the need for certain types of facilities and equipment being available for informal self-organized activity or "free play." They also recognize the necessity of providing planned programs with active leadership for specific groups of campers. Through a careful blending of informal and more structured activities, it is believed that the objectives of the camp can most effectively be realized.

The camp administrator, who is vitally concerned with program development, carefully assesses the need for program change. There is little virtue in making program innovations until the need for change has been carefully evaluated. The basis for determining the efficacy of program modification is the extent to which it reflects camp philosophy and helps realize camp objectives.

This chapter is concerned with the administrative considerations related to the organization and conduct of the camp program. Little space is devoted to the actual content of the program itself since this is not within the purview of a book on administration. Rather, the focus is directed toward those factors that should assist the administrator to facilitate sound program development and implementation.

FACTORS INFLUENCING PROGRAM SELECTION

Frequently, those persons responsible for camp program development rush into the assignment with great enthusiasm and dedication. This is laudable and predictable; however it may result in the implementation of a program that is doomed from the outset. Many factors must be considered when developing a program. To overlook any of these factors may mean something less than a successful experience for many of the campers. The following section deals with a number of these influences. Each may vary in the effect it has on the total program, and every camp operation must be analyzed to determine the relative importance of each at a particular time.

Camp philosophy and objectives

Program planning and implementation can proceed only after the basic philosophy of the camp has been clearly enunciated. Once a definitive statement of purpose has been developed and specific objectives outlined, it then follows that all program planning should articulate very closely with these philosophical concepts. The program must be planned to harmonize closely with the philosophy of the organization if it is to contribute toward the realization of each of the stated objectives. Several examples should serve to point up the importance of this relationship between objectives and program.

In a camp that places paramount importance on bringing the world of nature and the world of humans into closer consonance, one would expect to find programs in which nature conservation is a prime consideration. One should also anticipate a strong emphasis on activities that lead campers into direct contact with their natural environment. Such a program might be expected to include cookouts, hikes, overnight trips, and trip camping.

On the other hand, if a camp stresses concern for individual differences among campers, one could look for a broad, well-balanced program of activities that takes into account the tremendous range of differences among campers. The total program should include competitive and noncompetitive situations, informal and structured experiences, and activities that contribute to the social, cognitive, and physical development of the campers. The creative interests of the individual would hopefully also receive favorable consideration in such a camp.

Program staff

It is generally conceded by camping authorities that the single most important factor in the development of a camp program is the quality of the leadership. The experience and imagination of a resourceful staff can overcome many obstacles in the development of a strong program.

There is a natural tendency for a camp program to reflect the interests and competencies of those responsible for planning that program. If the program director is a high school physical education specialist during the school year, one should not be surprised if the camp promotes a highly structured, competitive games program. Similarly, a waterfront director with a strong background in sailing may be expected to encourage the administration to initiate an intensive sailing program.

It would be a shortsighted program director who did not take advantage of such special talents among the camp staff. However, the program should not be formulated exclusively on the basis of staff competencies. Intelligent program development results from careful consideration of a variety of factors. It is difficult to justify the promotion of competitive team sports if such competition is not consistent with the camp's philosophy. In a like manner, attractive as an extensive sailing program might appear, financial constraints may make it impossible to acquire the craft necessary to promote such a program. Enlightened program leadership implies that staff interests are utilized whenever they are consistent with the camp philosophy and other important program considerations.

Camps vary in the degree to which they seek to hire program specialists. The obvious advantage of specialists is the expertise they bring to a particular activity as well as promotional enthusiasm. This latter quality may sometimes work to the detriment of the overall program, however. If a camp hires a number of specialists, the program director must be alert to the possibility of these specialists promoting their own activity so aggressively that it is harmful to the evolution of a balanced, total camp program. The overzealous trip director may wish to schedule so many out-trips that the in-camp program is threatened. The ardent sailing specialist may appear to make unreasonable demands on limited equipment funds. The riding specialist may be unwilling to cancel instruction on the day of a carnival that is planned for the entire camp. Program specialists can add much to the promotion of certain desired activities. However, the person responsible for supervision of the camp program must continuously be aware of the need to preserve balance and harmony within the total offerings of the camp.

Under no circumstances should an activity be promoted without competent leadership. To do so may not only jeopardize the safety of the camper in high adventure activities, but it will invariably result in a deterioration of that program. It may take only one unfortunate program experience of this type to dull a camper's enthusiasm for returning the following summer.

Geographic location and climate

Terrain, natural resources, climate, and auxiliary community resources may all exert a significant influence on the selection and organization of the program. The campsite itself may be so small and heavily wooded that little opportunity exists for activities requiring large open areas or level terrain. Conversely, a campsite that lacks significant wooded area immediately eliminates many trail game possibilities. Some camps are located on lakes that are so small that the opportunities for water skiing or sailing are greatly restricted.

The camp that is fortunate enough to have a diversity of natural resources on its site enjoys many possibilities for enriching the camp program. These might include a densely wooded stand of large trees necessary for the construction of a hebertisme or aerial obstacle course, swampy wetland for nature study, an abundant supply of softwood trees for an axemanship program, or rock outcroppings suitable for mountaineering.

Climate provides another variable that affects program selection and organization. In a hot climate, some form of aquatics becomes almost mandatory and may, in fact, be the central focus of all program planning. In more temperate regions, the swimming program will have much less appeal, particularly if the camp is located on a large, deep lake where the water temperature discourages daily swimming.

In locales where cool mornings and evenings are the norm, it may be necessary to schedule more vigorous physical activities at those times of day. Camps that experience very hot summer weather should plan for relatively passive activities during the heat of the midday, including a long siesta or rest period immediately after the noon meal. Excessive hot, dry weather may cause closing of the woods in some areas so that all trip camping is suspended during certain periods of the summer. Likewise, if the camp is located in an area of high precipitation, it may be necessary to plan many rainy day programs. This may require more indoor facilities for these activities.

Finally, the enterprising program director should not overlook the availability of auxiliary facilities in the community adjacent to the campsite. Some camps have found it expedient to offer activities such as horseback riding and waterskiing at a neighboring sta-

ble or lake. Others have scouted the terrain bordering the campsite and located excellent mountain climbing or nature study facilities that a neighbor is willing to make available for camp use.

Financial resources

It must be apparent that without some capital outlay for equipment, certain activities cannot be offered. It is difficult to suggest to the camp administrator what percentage of each camp dollar should be spent on program resources. Problems such as the choice between the purchase of a new powerboat for waterfront supervision or asphalting the entrance road to camp or between replacing several canoes or acquiring a new dishwasher for the kitchen are the types of endless choices that confront most camp administrators operating within fairly tight budgets.

The enterprising administrator explores every means at his or her disposal to maintain a quality program in spite of facility and equipment costs. Some camps utilize the resources of their woodcraft program to supplement program equipment. I was associated with a camp in which the older campers made their own bass wood paddles, lemonwood bows, and cedar arrows. These were quality items of which each boy could be justly proud. This same camp employed its custodian year round, and during the off-season, he constructed cedar rib canoes at a considerable saving to the camp.

Several camps have adopted the practice of encouraging camper-staff improvement projects during the summer. Such projects might include the construction of a tree house, an outdoor chapel, an Indian council ring, or an adirondack lean-to made from local trees felled on the site. I am familiar with a camp in which local sand, gravel, and clay was used to construct four tennis courts. Campers frequently report that the hours spent on camp improvement projects of these types provided some of the most cherished memories of a camp season.

Camp clientele

The camp program must be in harmony with the campers for whom it is planned. Those persons responsible for program planning must take into account the age, sex, physical and mental maturity of campers, as well as the size of the group. Care must be taken to ensure that activities are not so elementary that they provide no challenge and participants become bored. By the same token, the program should not be so advanced or difficult that campers become discouraged and "turned off." Eight-year-old campers may have so much difficulty nocking an arrow and keeping it on the arrow rest as they draw the bowstring that after a few unsuccessful efforts, they give up in frustration. The greater danger is that, having failed to experience initial success, they will not return to archery at 10 or 12 years of age when they would have been physically able to master the necessary motor coordination.

It is quite unrealistic to expect that all program counsellors will have extensive preparation in child and adolescent psychology. However, it is not unreasonable to expect that part of their precamp training should include some information on the growth and development characteristics of the age group to whom they are assigned. For example, counsellors who do not recognize that young children generally tend to have short interest spans may be in for some difficult times unless they plan accordingly.

Many of today's camps cater to exceptional or atypical persons. Each group of atypical campers has its own particular set of needs and, in many cases, limitations. A group of educable mentally retarded camp-

ers requires not only special care in the presentation of an activity, but it may also be necessary to give careful consideration to the suitability of the activity itself. Likewise, counsellors working in a camp for diabetic children must learn that these children require fairly vigorous activity immediately after eating, whereas most camps plan a relatively sedentary period following meals.

One of the most important factors that influences program selection is the socioeconomic background of the campers. Children from a relatively affluent suburban community bring very different kinds of interests and experiences to camp than do children from a disadvantaged, inner-city community. A child from a rural setting would profit little from a camp animal farm, whereas the child from the inner city could learn much from seeing cows being milked, sheep being sheared, or chickens sitting on eggs.

Camp committee or board

In some organizational camps in which an advisory committee or board is responsible for the general supervision of the entire camp operation, one of the committee's duties may be to determine the broad scope of the camp program. Difficulties sometimes arise as to whether the advisory committee or the program staff has ultimate responsibility for determining program content. The program staff may believe that they are stifled in attempting to introduce new program ideas because of a more traditional, conservative position by the board. When the two groups are in disagreement, a review of the statement of purpose and objectives of the camp and the terms of reference of the advisory committee usually helps resolve any differences.

Length of camp session

The period that each camper spends at camp has a bearing on program planning.

Those camps that provide short-term sessions of 5 to 14 days should be very selective in determining what is to be included in the available time. Any camper projects that are initiated must, of necessity, be relatively simple so that they may be completed within the camp session. In camps in which the session is from 4 to 8 weeks, a more detailed progression of instruction can be provided and a somewhat less hurried approach taken toward the accomplishment of program objectives.

Regardless of the length of the camp session, the staff must acknowledge that several factors determine camp program, beginning with camp philosophy and including staff stengths and limitations, camp location, natural and fiscal resources, nature of the camp clientele, length of the camp season and, when applicable, the influence of the camp advisory committee or board.

STEPS IN PROGRAM DEVELOPMENT

In many camps, program planning is superficial and unsystematic. Too often, program experiences are selected on the basis of tradition or current fads, rather than careful, step-by-step examination of camp objectives and camper needs. The following section provides a systematic approach to program planning. Whether a new camp is developing its program for the first time or an established organization has decided that its overall program should be reexamined, the steps outlined below should serve as helpful guides.

1. *Establish a program planning group.* The first step in program development is to determine the composition of the group that will plan the camp program. There is little disagreement with the assumption that those members of the staff who administer the program comprise the most important segment of the planning group. Since staff members, in many cases, were hired be-

cause of special program expertise, they should logically be intimately involved in the planning process.

The staff should also be represented by someone fairly high in the camp administrative structure, frequently the camp director. "The administrator's role should be that of consultant and facilitator."[2] Other members of the staff may possess greater expertise in some areas of program development, but the director can provide the support and leadership to help the committee work cooperatively toward its goals. The director can also be instrumental in providing necessary resources and generally removing obstacles that may stand in the way of the group.

While camper opinion can be sampled in a number of ways, there is still great value in having camper representation on the committee itself. Only in this way can the camp administration demonstrate its desire to truly democratize its operation.

Others to be considered for inclusion in the group are parent and community representatives. Some organization camps also invite the camp advisory committee or board to appoint a member to assist the group in its deliberations.

The number of members on the program planning committee varies depending on the size of the camp and the scope of the intended program. Obviously it is out of the question to include all counsellors involved in the program. However, as subcommittees begin to struggle with the detailed planning of specific aspects of the total program, many program counsellors may be invited to participate at this level of planning.

2. *Examine camp objectives.* The initial task for the planning group is to carefully re-

---

2. Walen, H. L.: A principal's role in curriculum development, *Bulletin of the National Association of Secondary School Principals,* **51:**37, Nov., 1967.

view the philosophy and the general objectives of the camp. This examination should provide a clear statement of purpose and thus a sound rationale on which to base the program. Since every camp program should be inextricably related to sound camp objectives, the entire process of program formulation begins with an examination of the desired ends or outcomes.

3. *Assess camper needs and interests.* Unless the activities provided are compatible with the physical, psychological, and sociological characteristics of the campers for whom they are planned, there can be little hope of realizing the desired ends. Camper program interests may be surveyed in many ways. The first step is to make the decision that such information should be sought. Unfortunately, too often program directors believe that their staff members are the experts on program selection, and it is therefore their responsibility to determine the entire program. Much valuable information regarding interest in program can be acquired from the campers. Just as the world of business is vitally concerned with consumer feedback, so camp personnel must be alert to the interests and needs of the campers.

4. *Appraise available program resources.* Three types of resources are necessary to develop a comprehensive camp program. The first of these is a high calibre staff capable of conducting a wide range of activities in an efficient and competent manner and, at the same time, able to inspire camper participation. This implies that once program needs have been determined, those persons responsible for hiring personnel must seek to engage a team of program counsellors who, collectively, possess a wide range of special competencies that the camp needs for the conduct of the program.

To be successful, a camp program also requires the proper mix of physical resources such as open playing areas, wooded areas, suitable waterfront, and appropriate surrounding country for trip camping. Although considerable improvement may be made to an existing site, the availability of ideal physical resources is largely determined at the time the original campsite is selected.

Thirdly, the camp must have available the fiscal resources to be able to hire a strong team of program personnel and make the necessary improvements in the physical site. In addition, funds will be required to construct or purchase program facilities and equipment such as tennis courts, sailboats, or a pottery kiln.

5. *Formulate general and specific program objectives.* Once the planning group has reviewed the broad, general camp objectives, appraised the needs and interests of campers, and determined the resources available for implementing the program, it is now in a position to develop broad, operationally defined program objectives. These objectives are distinct from the general camp objectives because they relate specifically to program outcomes. They must be stated in the clearest possible terms so that the program itself may be accurately evaluated against statements that are easily understood and interpreted. Operationally defined program objectives might include such statements as:

- Program should provide for individual, small group, and total camp experiences.
- Program should include structured and informal learning experiences.
- Program should reflect balance between active and quiet pursuits.
- Program should include time for individual, unscheduled activities.

6. *Select program experiences.* The next step for the program planning group involves the careful examination of many different program experiences and the selec-

tion of those that can assist in the realization of the operationally defined objectives. This selective process should, whenever possible, be based on objective evidence that supports the inclusion of certain activities and learning experiences.

The program should allow for some new activities each summer that the individual returns to camp. Although repetition of activities is unavoidable and, in fact, desirable, it should be so arranged that campers sense a continuous progression not only during the camp season but from year to year. It is only in this way that they will feel fully challenged to return and strive for higher achievement levels.

Once the various program areas have been selected, specific, operationally defined objectives should be developed for each activity. In addition, careful consideration should be given to determining how the activities selected can best be presented. This includes considerations such as motivation of campers, optimal size and age of the group, length of program sessions, and actual methods used to present the activity. Here, the expertise of veteran camp program staff, especially those with teaching experience in schools or recreation agencies, is invaluable in assisting new staff members to develop sound principles of program management.

When an activity is to be offered for the first time, it may be wise to run a pilot program for one session of campers. This approach has the advantage of testing the real interest of the campers and suggesting appropriate motivational devices. It also should enable the staff to work out some of the unforeseen problems before the activity is offered to large numbers of campers with the sizable outlay for capital equipment that may be required. For example, a camp that contemplates offering pottery for the first time might invite one knowledgeable and highly motivated person to initiate a limited program with a select group of campers to test the program before hiring additional staff and purchasing expensive equipment.

7. *Evaluate the program.* The final step in program development is the establishment of procedures for continuous assessment and revision when necessary. The extent to which any phase of the camp program may be impartially evaluated depends on how clearly program objectives have been operationally defined. When objectives are nonexistent or are stated in vague terms, there is little basis for measuring the success of the program.

PROGRAM STRUCTURE AND ORGANIZATION

There are many variations in the manner in which camp programs are structured and administered. Some camp directors place almost complete responsibility for program development in the hands of the staff, who are considered the program experts. Others encourage "grass roots planning," with all program ideas emanating from the campers. A few camps plan every moment of the camper's day; others free them "to do their own thing." Some camp directors may place a high premium on the instructional content of program; others encourage the recreational, or free play, philosophy of camp programming.

There are arguments to support or refute each of these positions. It is probably safe to say that most farsighted camp directors attempt to develop a program structure that incorporates the best of each of these ideas. Individuals are so diverse in personality, temperament, and interests that discerning camp administrators must plan varied, flexible, and innovative programs to meet these widely disparate needs.

Structure by group

One of the ways in which the camp program can help cater to the great range of personal differences among campers is to encourage scheduling of activities for many different-sized groups. These vary from providing opportunities for campers to engage in some pursuits on an individual basis to planning programs in which the entire camp participates together. The following represent the most common groupings found in camps today.

Individual camper. There was a period in the evolution of organized camping when camping philosophy seemed to be patterned very closely on that of the schools. It was believed that every waking moment of the campers' day should be planned to keep them fully occupied and therefore contented. Educators and camp administrators now realize that, just like adults, children need to have periods when they are free to follow their own individual pursuits. These may include the need to be alone, the need to contemplate, or the need to do virtually nothing.

Opportunities should be scheduled, therefore, so campers may get away by themselves to engage in self-directed activities such as fishing, boating, reading, or taking a nature hike. Such pursuits should be possible with little or no apparent staff supervision. The program staff should make available the facilities and equipment, establish the necessary rules for the safe conduct of the activity, and then provide encouragement for campers to engage in these individual pastimes. Some opportunity for such activities should be provided irrespective of what the rest of the camper's tent or cabinmates are doing or wish to do.

Those persons responsible for camp programming should also recognize that there needs to be time during the day when the camper has complete freedom to engage in apparently "nonproductive" endeavor such as contemplation, introspection, or reminiscence. However, the staff must also be on the alert for campers who exhibit an unnatural propensity to keep to themselves. Since the camp seeks to contribute to the social development of the individual through adjustment to effective group living, efforts must be directed toward involving each camper in a variety of group settings.

Tent or cabin group. The campers who share a tent or cabin comprise a second program group. Many camp administrators consider this small aggregation, of usually four to six persons, to be the most important of all program groups. They maintain that this is particularly true when the living unit has been carefully selected for compatibility. These administrators also argue that this congenial group engages in so many things together, such as sleeping, eating, and maintaining the bunk or cabin, that it is only natural that they should play together. It is also suggested that for those individuals who are coming to camp for the first time or who have previously had a very limited circle of friends, the adjustment to large program groups may overwhelm them. A further argument contends that tent or cabin units develop strong loyalties that are desirable for promoting competition between tents or cabins. I believe that such rivalries may, in fact, be antithetical to sound program philosophy if carried to excess.

The countervailing argument in support of other program units is that since campers within the living unit already do so many things together in the course of each day, a conscious attempt should be made to broaden their sphere of social contacts when planning the program.

Special interest groups. Flexible program planning provides for a group of any two or more campers to pursue a common interest project. An interest group may be drawn from different living units and, more uniquely, may bring together persons from different age groups. The sole criterion for existence is that the group share a mutual interest in undertaking a given project or activity. Sometimes the plan is short-lived, and its demise is as abrupt as its spontaneous birth. Other special interest groups may come together on a recurring basis for several days or even the entire camp session.

Most projects of this type require little or no supervision, and in some cases, staff assistance may be viewed as unwanted interference. In other cases, the nature of the project is such that staff support is necessary for safety and is welcomed by the campers themselves. For example, it is difficult to visualize a group of young campers being encouraged to embark on the construction of a tree fort without some outside help. Not only is there the question of its safe construction, but the camp must almost certainly provide tools and materials if the project is to be brought to a successful conclusion.

Instructional groups. Many activities offered in the typical camp program lend themselves to organized group instruction. These include archery, diving, first aid, riflery, sailing, and swimming. Instructional groups are frequently more organized than special interest groups since they must be scheduled at a given time and place, and regular attendance is usually expected. Again, care must be taken not to formalize instruction so that it becomes repetitious, mundane, and boring. Campers should be invited to attend activities of their choice.

Instruction is usually more beneficial when campers are placed in homogeneous groups according to ability. If the group is composed of novice, intermediate, and advanced participants, additional burdens are placed on the instructor in attempting to meet individual needs within the group.

One of the great advantages of scheduled instruction is that the potential for enhancing the developmental value to the camper is increased when a careful progression of learning experiences is provided at regular intervals.

Sectional groups. Some camp programs should be planned for large groups in which all campers within a sectional unit make up the program module. Examples of programs that are enriched by participation of large numbers include cookouts, hikes, boating regattas, swimming, and athletic meets, as well as many group-chasing and combative games. An obvious advantage of large groups is that they have the capacity to widen the range of social contact of each camper.

It is also possible to further increase the size of the participating program group by combining two or more sectional units. In small camps, each sectional unit is composed of campers of different ages and maturity. It is important to remember that some types of interunit competition should not be encouraged when the two groups are not comparable in ability or maturity.

Total camp group. Most camps provide at least a few events that include the entire camp community. Some all-camp activities may be held on a regular or recurring basis and include picnic day, chapel, movie night, and entertainment or theatre night. Many smaller camps often schedule regular evening camp fire programs for the entire camp.

Program leaders have learned from experience that some provision should be made for all-camp special events. These program "spectaculars" give spice and change of pace to the program. A carnival, circus, or woodsman's competition may be planned for the entire camp and could be scheduled for a full day. A few camps schedule at least one super extravaganza such as olympic or interplanetary games.

I am familiar with one camp that annually conducts Indian Tribal Games extending over part of 3 days. Every camper is assigned to one of six teams, or tribes, and each tribe is further subdivided into papooses, braves, scouts, and warriors according to age. This subclassification provides for more equal competition between groups. Tribes are encouraged to make up tribal yells, songs, and banners. Each tribe is identified with characteristic facial markings in "war paint," and each group has its own color headband. The tribal games are further highlighted by such traditions as no talking during meals throughout the games. All communication at meals is by sign language. The game's program itself consists of war canoe races, lacrosse, archery competitions, and other activities indigenous to the North American Indians.

Some camps sponsor events that require many days of preparation such as a special demonstration of skills learned, exhibits of objects made or collected, theatrical performance by groups in front of the rest of the camp, or a parade to commemorate a special day or event.

It is important to stress that a well-planned camp program provides a careful balance between regularly scheduled activities and special projects or events. When the program consists only of scheduled, recurring activities, it tends to become too regimented and may be seen by campers as dull and boring. Inevitably interest wanes and camper participation drops. On the other hand, if those persons responsible for programming attempt to schedule many special events that require much preparation, joy and spontaneity may be lost as a result of the pressure involved in putting on the event. The answer is to work for a happy balance between recurring activities interspersed with enough special events to maintain a high level of camper enthusiasm.

Scheduled versus unscheduled program

It was noted earlier that there was a period in the history of organized camping when it was believed that a good camp program should be patterned after the school curriculum in which the child's day was programmed from school opening until closing. When this philosophy was carried over into the camp setting, it meant that campers moved routinely from wakeup to bedtime through the camp "curriculum." Such rigid scheduling of the daily routine often became boring and, indeed, frustrating to many campers. Some revision was in order.

The change, in many cases, took the form of a complete swing to the other extreme where campers had virtually no scheduled activities and were free to do as they pleased for much of the day. The argument for this degree of freedom went as follows. Individuals need to be offered opportunities to develop self-discipline and responsibility, and to learn these traits requires freedom to make personal decisions. It was therefore concluded that campers should be given complete liberty to do as they wished for much of the day. This meant that, in some isolated cases, the child did almost nothing at all for days at a time.

In referring to programs offered by public recreation agencies, Hjelte and Shivers[3] polarize these two extreme viewpoints when they question the role of the agency:

Is their responsibility limited to the provision of facilities and to the exercise of essential control, to the protection of public property, and to the regulation of the patron's behavior? Or is it their responsibility to assume full control of the recreational program and to permit on the public recreational facilities only activities that they have organized and promoted in accordance with certain pre-conceived objectives?

Clearly the response to each of these alternatives must be 'no.' The real answer lies somewhere between the two extremes. Today most camp administrators recognize the need to schedule some aspects of the daily

---

3. Hjelte, G. and Shivers, J. S.: *Public administration of recreation services*. (Philadelphia: Lea & Febiger, 1972) p. 437.

and weekly routine. Scheduled activities include morning wakeup, meals, and the bedtime routine. Others may include tent or cabin cleanup and rest period as part of a fixed schedule.

The vast majority of camps recognize the need for providing facilities for unscheduled activity, or free play, in which the game, project, or event is unscheduled and requires some organization on the part of the participants. This may be thought of as self-directed activity in which staff planning is nonexistent and supervision is not apparent to the camper. Staff members provide only that degree of supervision that ensures the safety of those taking part and protection of camp property. At the same time, nearly all camps offer scheduled programs while attempting to provide for a high degree of flexibility and spontaneity within the program.

Program organization

It should be clear from foregoing discussions that an important basic principle of organizing a program is the need to democratize the selection and planning process. Today, nearly all camps assign someone to the role of program director. In small camps it may be the director who assumes, this responsibility, but large camps often provide one or more program assistants whose major assignment is program planning and implementation. In addition, there is a trend toward hiring increasing numbers of program specialists to work with a large group of program counsellors.

Staff-camper planning. The staff team should not assume total responsibility for program selection and organization but should work coopoeratively with those for whom the program is planned—the campers. When program organization is a joint project, the staff role becomes primarily one of consultant and animator. In this type of cooperative approach to program development, the staff contributes much experience and expertise that, when taking into account the desires and needs of the clientele, should guarantee vigorous and enthusiastic support by the campers.

The respective role that each group plays varies in different circumstances. During the first few days of camp, new campers may be reticent to take an aggressive approach to program planning. They have little or no experience to provide the basis for program selection and planning. In such circumstances, the staff must be expected to assume a more dominant role, at least initially. On the other hand, the older, experienced campers have been "through the mill" and are usually quick to make known their wishes when given the opportunity. Not only are they anxious to select many of their programs, they are also capable of planning and even directing the activity or project. Self-directed programs should be encouraged whenever possible since these experiences are invaluable in fostering such desirable qualities as independent thinking and self-reliance.

A word of caution is in order at this time. When campers are given too much freedom in program selection, they sometimes have a tendency to limit their choices to those activities with which they are most familiar and most successful. If a group of children have played a great deal of organized basketball in the city and enjoyed considerable success in this activity, they have a natural desire to play basketball at camp since high achievement level brings recognition and personal satisfaction. In this situation, the staff must play a very diplomatic role and tactfully open up new program possibilities to the group.

There may be other occasions when just the opposite is true. Young campers frequently leap into something new just because it is different and unknown. When this happens, they are often inclined to drop the project as fast as they took it on. The staff must be prepared to provide some guidance by pointing out that a project should not be undertaken unless the individual or group is prepared to see it through to completion.

All program counsellors should be continuously on the alert for any hints as to camper program interests. The attentive staff member can pick up many valuable cues regarding program interest from the casual conversation of campers at meal time, in the cabin, or while sunning at the waterfront. These tips should be passed on to those who have responsibility for planning the program for that particular group of campers.

Centralized versus decentralized planning. The selection and formulation of program content may take place at a variety of levels. There are a small number of camps, even today, where all program is organized by the camp director and the activities for the day come from that office. In other camps, a small team of program staff members draw up a schedule of activities, on a daily or weekly basis, for all sections of the camp. This is known as centralized program planning and usually provides for minimal camper participation in the selection of activities. At best, campers may expect to have a token representation on this central planning committee.

The central program group not only selects the activities for each segment of the camp, but they also assign program supervisory staff and allocate facilities and equipment. This method has some administrative advantage since the assignment of all human and material resources is in the hands of one small coordinating group.

A more popular model is one in which the responsibility for program planning rests with each section of the camp. This level of program administration usually provides for better balance between camper and staff participation. However, care must be exercised to ensure that counsellors do not outnumber camper representatives so that the latter feel intimidated and contribute little.

As the program planning role is decentralized, the problem of distributing staff becomes more complex. The usual practice is to expect each section to operate as an autonomous unit so that all program staff members come from within the section itself. This does not solve the problem of equitably utilizing program specialists who are expected to serve all parts of the camp. In this case, it may be necessary to set up an all-camp schedule for specialists to ensure that each section has access to their services. Another solution is to require each section to request a specialist at least several days in advance.

The same dilemma exists regarding use of facilities and equipment. If several sections decide independently that they wish to use the tennis courts on a given afternoon, there is obviously a problem. The most common solution is to submit requests for program facilities at least a day in advance to one person who is responsible for allocating facilities on a proportionate basis.

Program planning may be further decentralized, and hopefully democratized, by locating this responsibility for planning in the individual tent or cabin. When this is done, several things usually happen. A great deal more spontaneity is introduced into the programming. A group of four or five campers can decide, on a whim, to engage in a particular project as long as there is no conflict over facilities or equipment. This type of "grass roots programming" invariably results in a much more individualized program in which the interest of small groups are met more effectively. Furthermore, the opportunities for campers to make democratic choices are greatly increased as long as the camp philosophy is one that encourages the counsellor to play a low-key guidance role rather than autocratically assuming all responsibility for program selection.

Democratic decision making at the cabin level is not without its problems. It is not always easy to lead a group of individuals to a common decision regarding program. What if three of the group want to go sailing, two wish to challenge the cabin next door to a game of soccer-softball, and one child wishes to go fishing.? This is the predicament that faces cabin counsellors almost daily. They must possess the sensitivity and diplomacy necessary to bring the group to consensus or provide for these divergent interests in some other way.

It should be evident that centralized program planning, like most forms of autocracy, provides for an element of administrative efficiency. This may be more than offset, however, by its failure to adequately meet the needs and interests of the campers it is designed to serve. It must always be remembered that people are more likely to engage in those activities that they have helped to select and organize.

National programs. Some organization camps such as the Boy Scouts, Girl Scouts, Camp Fire Girls, and 4-H have progressive educational programs that have been developed by program experts at the national level. The requirements of these programs are usually spelled out in such detail that leaders, with minimum training, can follow the syllabus with little trouble. Most national programs have a strong awards system that operates in conjunction with the program, and the awards are used as an extrinsic motivating device to promote maximum participation in the various programs.

There are two apparent weaknesses of national program plans. There is little oppor-

tunity for the members of the organization to asssist in the planning and development of the program since it is the product of the national office. Such a "tailor-made" program may prove excellent for use by voluntary, inexperienced staff, but a hardworking group of veteran leaders may resent having the program "parachuted" in from the head office.

The second shortcoming is that it is difficult for nationwide programs to adequately provide for individual and local needs as they vary from one part of the country to another. Such variations may also exist even within a given community. One authority[4] claims that the national programs of the scouting groups have proved more successful with middle-class children than those from other socioeconomic levels.

These limitations have been recognized by camps that conduct national programs, and they now attempt to augment them with a local program adapted from the larger plan. In this way, the local organization can better meet the specific needs of their participants by inviting them to assume an active part in the selection and formulation of their own program content.

Program records. Administrators who are primarily responsible for camp programming should make a practice of developing charts and keeping accurate records of what transpires from season to season. The specific form in which program records are kept will differ from camp to camp. The following are recommended as minimal suggestions.

Individual program file. Some form of permanent record should be maintained of all camp activities, projects, and events. A useful practice is to describe each activity on a separate 5 × 8 inch index card and arrange these alphabetically in a card file,

4. Hanson, R. F., and Carlson, R. E.: Organizations for children and youth. (Englewood Cliffs, N.J.: Prentice-Hall Inc., 1972) p. 62.

```
┌─────────────────────────────────────────────────────────────┐
│                                                             │
│   ───────────────────────────                               │
│    Name of activity                    Age group            │
│                                      ──────────────────     │
│   ───────────────────────────                               │
│   Category (water, field games, etc.)  No. of participants  │
│                                      ──────────────────     │
│   Equipment:                                                │
│                                         Location            │
│   ──────────────────────────────────────────               │
│   Description of activity:                                  │
│                                                             │
│                                                             │
│                                                             │
│   Recommendations:                                          │
│                                                             │
│                                                             │
│                                                             │
└─────────────────────────────────────────────────────────────┘
```

Fig. 6-1. Sample program card.

(Fig. 6-1). Each card indicates the age group for which the activity is recommended as well as the suggested number of participants. This makes it possible to further classify all activities according to age. Space is provided at the bottom of each card for the program counsellor to describe any recommended modification of the activity. Once the program file is prepared, it should be modified and updated from one season to another.

Program charts. Program directors should be encouraged to prepare daily, weekly, and sessional program charts. (Fig. 6-2). Whereas it may be impossible to record programs for the various sections in advance, all special events and recurring campwide programs can be included as they are planned to preclude the possibility of facility duplication. The master schedule also provides clear indication of the degree to which each section is participating in a balanced program.

In the chart in Fig. 6-2, campwide special events are shown as shaded blocks. These can be scheduled days ahead and, in some cases, even before the camp session begins.

Each morning, except Sunday, is reserved for instruction in eighteen different activities. Campers sign up for the two instructions of their choice on Sunday. This provides the program director with the necessary time to assign the appropriate number of staff members for each activity. In some activities, it may be essential to limit numbers of participants. For example, in sailing it would be unrealistic to allocate more campers than there are craft to accommodate them. Six 45-minute periods of instruction are offered in each activity, Monday through Saturday. The camp has a sailing and a craftshop specialist, and one period per week is scheduled for the four sections in each activity. If weather conditions do not permit sailing, it would be rescheduled at a later date. Both specialist are available during other program periods for nonscheduled groups of campers. The remaining blocks provide for planning of programs by section or by living units within each section. It is quite possible that several programs might be scheduled concurrently for campers within a given section to provide more choice for the campers.

Fig. 6-2. Sample weekly program chart for camp with four seasons.

	SUNDAY	MONDAY	TUESDAY	WEDNESDAY	THURSDAY	FRIDAY	SATURDAY
MORNING PROGRAM—9:30-11:00 A.M.	Chapel · · · Free period: all facilities available	Each camper selects two areas of instruction from 18 activities and attends each for 45 minutes Monday to Saturday					
AFTERNOON PROGRAM—3:00-4:30 P.M.		Section I / Section II / Section III Sailing / Section IV	Picnic and supper out of camp	Section I / Section II Sailing / Section III / Section IV	Section I Sailing / Section II / Section III / Section IV	Woodman's competition for entire camp by section	Section I / Section II / Section III / Section IV
EVENING PROGRAM—7:00 P.M.-BEDTIME	Section I Craftshop / Section II / Section III / Section IV	Section I / Section II Craftshop / Section III / Section IV	For entire camp	Indian council ring for entire camp	Section I / Section II / Section III Craftshop / Section IV	Section I / Section II / Section III / Section IV Craftshop	Theatre night for entire camp

Program participation. A well-organized program director should keep accurate statistical data regarding the number of participants in each program. The director may also request that each counsellor who is responsible for a given activity comment briefly on camper interest in the program.

Special events file. It is strongly recommended that a detailed file be maintained on each major special event or project offered during the summer. This file should include: (1) content of the event, (2) organizational plan, (3) staff resources required, (4) facility and equipment needs, and (5) recommendations for change One final word of caution: Overuse of the master schedules leads to regimentation. It preempts freedom of choice and innovation in the camp program. Program schedules are only a plan and to cling tenaciously to preconceived plans may devitalize the program. A flexible program is capable of meeting unforeseen needs and being adapted to each new situation as it arises.

Scope of program

The range of program activities offered at camp is almost unlimited. Those persons responsible for the administration of the program should offer a broad, balanced program that caters to the wide range of interests typically found among any group of campers. Such a program must account for not only the physical needs of the individual, but must include activities that meet artistic, intellectual, social, and, in some cases, spiritual and religious interests. A balanced program also implies that some activities should be primarily instructional, while others may be competitive in nature. The majority of activities fall somewhere in between and may be considered essentially recreational. The important point to remember is that the program should accommodate various degrees of competence within a given activity.

In attempting to describe the scope of camp programming, it is difficult to classify all activities in neat, self-contained categories. Many activities could be placed in several program areas. The following groupings do not represent a carefully developed taxonomy. They do, however, give some indication of the potential range of events and skills that might be offered at camp.

Sports and games. This category probably comprises the most popular and, therefore, the most widely promoted area of camp programming. Land sports and water activities are included in this category. Land sports and games encompass a vast range of organized individual and dual activities as well as many of the traditional team sports. The former include archery, badminton, horseback riding, riflery, and tennis. The organized team games, which are an important component of the school athletic program, are also included in many camp programs. These include basketball, lacrosse, soccer, softball, touch football, and volleyball. In addition to these established sports and games, there are many low-organization games and activities that have developed over many years. These activities range from such well-known activities as horseshoes, table tennis, and tetherball to a large number of games generally considered to be indigenous to the camp setting because they utilize wooded areas. Included in this group are the chase, hunt, and trail games.

Wherever hot summer weather predominates, water sports comprise an important component of the total camp program. As well as the traditional swimming and diving program, the list includes synchronized swimming or water ballet, skin and scuba diving, and water polo. A variety of small-craft activities such as canoeing, kayaking, rowing, sailing, fishing, and waterskiing may also be included. In addition, a large number of low-organization games utilizing waterfront facilities have also been developed in local camps.

Nature and outdoor activities. This category includes those activities that are largely indigenous to the camping movement and are popularly referred to as *camping skills*. The list includes axemanship, firelighting, preparing meals over the campfire, tent pitching, construction of lean-tos and bow-bed—making. These skills, once learned, may then be put to good use as the program is expanded to include orienteering, trail-blazing, hiking, mountaineering, and all forms of out-tripping. In addition, this classification includes many forms of nature study such as animal lore, astronomy, butterfly collecting, study of marine life, ornithology, rock climbing, and nature conservation.

The arts. A number of specialized camps use one or more of the art forms as their main program focus. For example, an organization may call itself a dance or music camp and build most of its programs around one or both of these categories. Any other activities that are offered are secondary and serve to supplement and provide variety to the main program thrust. Other camps include dance, drama, music, literature, and creative writing as an integral part of the total camp program.

Arts and crafts. Included in this category are those activities that lead to the production of utilitarian objects. Ceramics, leatherwork, lapidary, metalcraft, weaving, and woodcraft are typical examples of arts and crafts programs found in camps.

Hobbies. A hobby may be distinguished from arts and crafts as an interest that is pursued for pleasure or recreation and not as a main occupation. Clearly, this definition suggests that all the pursuits described as arts and crafts above should more accurately be classified as hobbies when viewed in the camp setting. Nevertheless, many

camps refer to the above activities as part of their arts and crafts program. Hobbies, on the other hand, might include photography, stamp collecting, gardening, or bird-watching. Some program specialists prefer to include the latter two hobbies under nature and outdoor activities.

Social recreation. This aspect of camp programming emphasizes sociability and human interaction as the skills to be promoted and developed. Rarely are special facilities required since the main focus is on how campers relate to one another. Many of these activities are conducted in the tent or cabin and include quiet games between small groups of two or more individuals. Typical examples include table games, card games, charades, and other humorous presentations. Much of the programming planned around the campfire is in this category. Cookouts and banquets usually involve a high degree of socialization and so could be included in this classification.

Spiritual and religious activities. These may be found in varying degrees within organized camps. In church-sponsored camps, they usually comprise the cornerstone around which all other programming is built.

Special events. Reference was made earlier in this chapter to special projects that usually involve a large segment of the camp and in many cases the entire camp. The possibilities are limitless, and many can be classified in one of the program groups described above. For example, a mass boating regatta is a water activity, a woodsman's competition is a nature activity, and an olympic competition can be included in the land and water sports. However, some forms of festivals, pageants, parades, and special holiday programs cannot be easily placed in any of the categories already outlined and perhaps deserve a separate category.

The program areas described above are

typical of those found in most camps today. The groupings and the activities themselves are by no means exhaustive and other forms of program could easily be included. This underscores the fact that program possibilities are boundless for counsellors who are creative and open in their search for new program ideas.

Program methodology

Throughout this chapter the need for great care in the selection of program content has been stressed. Unless the camp program is seen by campers as attractive and exciting, there is ever probability that many will not voluntarily return the following summer. But to select inherently appealing and appropriate activities is not sufficient. The program chosen must be planned and conducted in a manner that ensures enthusiastic acceptance by the participant. If program counsellors are to conduct activities in an exciting and challenging manner, careful attention must be paid to details of planning.

Selection of physical setting. Each program should be conducted in the atmosphere most favorable to the success of that event. An evening cookout is doomed to failure if the site chosen is in the middle of dense woods where the air is humid and oppressive and biting insects are out in great numbers. Similarly, a game of water flag raid, usually played in waist-deep water, will be a disaster if the area selected is strewn with live clams almost guaranteeing numerous cut feet among the players. These two examples point up the necessity of carefully scouting a potential site to determine that all the conditions are optimal to ensure the success of the program.

Timing and sequence of events. For some programs, judicious timing may greatly enhance the pleasure derived by the campers. Experienced program staff know that it is very important to culminate a sequence of instruction with a special feature. For example, participation in a tennis tournament after a week of instruction or the opportunity to show macramé or leatherwork products at a display before returning home can do much to increase the campers desire to return to camp next year and continue that particular interest.

Program counsellors must also be sensitive to what is topical. If interest among campers is high at a given time, the staff must be prepared to capitalize on it. Some years ago, the movie "Moby Dick" was shown to campers one rainy evening. The next afternoon a "new" water program entitled "The Great White Whale Hunt" was announced, and virtually every child in the section turned out to participate in the hunt.

Maximum participation. Nothing can thwart enthusiasm for a program faster than to have campers stand around watching or waiting their turn rather than actively participating. Children want and need to be actively involved in the program. There is an old axiom "we learn by doing." Here again, wise planning is the key:—activities that do not provide for maximum participation should be avoided. In this regard, the use of elimination games should be discouraged.

A child who selects archery as a program goes to this activity expecting to shoot arrows. The first meeting should not involve a talk for the entire period about the parts of the bow and arrow and safety rules for the range. An objective of the first lesson in archery should be the release of at least a dozen arrows by each camper.

If young campers have been scheduled for a tour of the lake in the camp motorboat but the boat only seats six persons, those planning the program should assign at least one additional counsellor to the 12 youngsters on shore so that they may participate in some land game while waiting their turn for the tour.

When more campers show up than can be effectively accommodated in the game or activity, it may be wise to divide the group into two or more smaller groups and play several games concurrently. This assumes that there are sufficient facilities, equipment, and staff to supervise each group. Similarly, if 24 campers are scheduled to go for a walk on a nature trail, four groups of six children, each with a leader, would be far superior to one large group, as long as each counsellor is knowledgeable about the trail.

Homogeneous grouping. It must be recognized that individuals possess not only different interests but also great variation in rates at which they learn. This implies that instruction must be highly individualized to meet the different levels of interest and competency within a group. This again suggests the need for small group instruction within a given activity. In swimming instruction, it would be unwise to attempt to combine nonswimmers with those who have already attained their junior swimming badge. Similarly, a group of children of the same age may need to be divided into beginner, intermediate, and advanced groups for chopping instruction. Where the opportunity for more individualized instruction is provided, it must always be possible for campers to move easily from one group to another consistent with their capabilities. Homogeneous grouping should not preclude the possibility of the more skilled and knowledgeable campers assisting the less skilled to improve their performance level. This is particularly helpful in arts and crafts, hobbies, and the arts in which involvement of the advanced campers provides great incentive to the novice.

Team teaching. If campers in a large class are to be divided into subgroups according to ability, it follows that a corps of counsellors must be available to move each subgroup along at its own optimum pace. This is referred to in educational parlance as *team teaching*—two or more leaders combine to better utilize staff talents and more effectively meet individual differences. Going back to the example of the swimming lesson—a recommended procedure might be to ask several staff members to work regularly with nonswimmers because they possess a thorough knowledge of the techniques involved as well as the patience and empathy required at this level. Similarly, someone who has had competitive experience in swimming might bring a high level of motivation to the coaching of campers at a more advanced level.

Camp administrators must realize that very few counsellors have had any formal preparation in teaching. As a result, if they are left to their own devices, the methods they use to conduct camp activities will be largely hit or miss. Program directors must recognize this danger and utilize those staff members who are full-time teachers or recreation leaders throughout the rest of the year to instruct the staff in sound principles of methodology during the precamp training period.

Special problems

Rainy day programs. Perhaps one of the most vexing problems that face camps is the question of how to productively occupy campers when it rains. Since most camp activities are designed to be conducted outdoors, very few camps enjoy the luxury of spacious indoor facilities in which to offer programs. Several days of inclement weather can challenge the adaptability and resourcefulness of even the most imaginative staff. The problem arises when large numbers of campers must be accommodated in limited indoor facilities. Several suggestions are in order that may help to minimize the problem.

First, a thorough inventory should be made to determine just what facilities may be utilized during inclement weather. In addition to the obvious sites such as lodges, recreation hall, gymnasium theatre, and cabins or tents, other possible locations should be explored. Perhaps the camp has several water-proof adirondack lean-tos, tree house, or covered area at the rifle range. Each could house a small group. Some camps place the dining hall and chapel "out of bounds" except for the specific purpose for which they were designed. It is hard to defend the practice of limiting use of the dining hall to three or four hours in the day when it is a superb program facility during bad weather.

The program staff should not be too quick to re-schedule activities indoors. Many camp activities can be conducted outdoors in the rain as long as campers have good rainwear. Swimming in the rain on a warm day adds an exciting ingredient the first time it is experienced. A nature walk on a rainy day uncovers some wonders of nature that can only be experienced under these conditions.

There are days, however, when discretion demands that even the most adventurous program staff reschedule activities under cover from the elements. The secret is to plan well in advance for such occasions and not have to improvise on the spot. A well-organized program staff has at its fingertips a large repertoire of rainy day activities that can be implemented on very short notice.

Needs of teenagers. A second concern of an increasing number of camps is that of attracting and keeping older youth at camp. Many directors report that the single greatest problem they face today is to attract campers of 13 to 16 years of age back to camp.

When attempting to analyze the reasons for this decline in interest among teenagers, the recurring answer seems to be the inability of camps to adjust to the changing needs and interests of young people. Too often the camp program for older campers is simply an extension or continuation of those activities offered for campers of 10 to 12 years of age. As Hanson and Carlson[5] so aptly point out: "Youth organizations do have to be careful not to provide the older members with the 'same old thing warmed over' if they hope to hold the interest of a boy or girl from ages eight to 18." Part of the problem has also been the tendency for camps to introduce many activities too early so that by the time campers reach their teens there is nothing new for them to try.

Many camps have turned increasingly to older campers to ask them what it is they seek from the camping experience. Results of these studies reveal four main responses.

1. *Youth want to have increasing responsibility for self-direction.* They accept the need for adult guidance, but they want more freedom to have responsibility for their own decisions and to permit leadership to emerge from within the group.

2. *Programs must have a high adventure component and must challenge youth.* Activities such as mountaineering, white water paddling, scuba diving, and surfing are high on their list because they see them as involving some element of hazard or risk. No longer are older campers content to participate in out-trips that differ from earlier trips only in the length of the excursion. They now want to engage in survival or wilderness camping, which implies greater challenge and therefore greater rewards.

3. *Teenagers want to participate in more*

5. Hanson, R. F., and Carlson, R. E.: Organizations for children and youth. (Englewood Cliffs, N.J.: Prentice-Hall, Inc., 1972) pp. 64-65.

coeducational programming to satisfy the natural interest in the opposite sex. Many camps have shied away from planning wholesome, co-recreational activities for fear that to do so would create more problems than it would solve.

4. *Today's youth is greatly concerned with the larger social problems of our times.* Questions relating to conservation education, poverty, race, religion, and sex are of particular interest to these young adults. Program administrators should capitalize on these concerns and develop program elements around them.

Indigenous programming. If camps are going to promote programs that identify them as uniquely different from other camps, program administrators must examine the physical resources and historical traditions that set them apart from other organizations. This unique programming may be developed in unlimited ways. Careful examination of the campsite may open up a variety of possibilities. For example, a shallow, sandy shoreline suggests the possibility of playing many water games that would have to be confined to land in another camp. A wooded area comprised mainly of deciduous trees and minimal undergrowth lends itself to a vast range of tracking and trail games. If the camp is located in a region with a rich history of Indian folklore, the program director would be shortsighted not to build some camp program around these traditions. Nature study should be related to the flowers, plants, trees, birds, and animals that are common to the area. If a good quality clay is found on the campsite, this may provide the impetus for a ceramics program. Similarly, a camp that has rich driftwood resources along its shoreline or that of neighboring lakes may have little difficulty initiating a unique driftwood carving program for interested campers. In short, each camp should seek to identify distinctive program ele-

ments. It becomes a matter of determining which characteristics can best be exploited and then providing the initiative to capitalize on them.

Bus programming. The problem of how to entertain a busload of energetic and excited day camp children is a challenge to even the most innovative program staff. Nevertheless, there are good reasons why such a program must be given careful thought. First, children go to camp to have fun. This objective may be largely stultified if the first and last hour each day is spent in a dull and monotonous bus trip. Second, a good bus program may serve as an excellent form of public relations. Parents view this as an extension of the camp program. Third, a strong bus program is the best guarantee for maintaining order and control on the bus and thus contributing to safety.

The real challenge is to determine what program is to be offered. The following suggestions may prove helpful.

1. Campers utilize the bus trip to renew acquaintances and talk. The first part of the trip should not require a planned program.
2. Staff ingenuity may not extend to new program ideas every day; space bus programs judiciously.
3. If program materials are to be used on the bus, they should be selected with discretion. In a moving vehicle, sharp objects increase the potential for injury.
4. Remember that the number of campers increases as the trip progresses to camp and vice versa; select activities accordingly.
5. Whenever possible, avoid allowing each bus stop to interrupt the program. In some cases, it may be possible to make the stop the focal point of the activity.
6. Plan for quiet, individual, and small

group activities as well as activities for the entire bus.

Awards. The practice of giving awards has long been the subject of much controversy among camp administrators. Those condemning the practice argue that children should engage in a camp program for the intrinsic joy and satisfaction of the activity itself rather than for some outside reward. However, if the award has little extrinsic value it is difficult to defend a rationale that states that the award becomes more important than the inherent pleasure of the activity itself. As long as the award is seen as a *symbol of achievement* and serves as an incentive to greater participation and improved performance, it would seem there can be little criticism of this practice. Just as the ancient Greeks recognized athletic prowess with the awarding of the laurel wreath, so an award of little monetary value may do much to enhance the camp program by instilling in campers a pride of achievement.

ADMINISTRATIVE GUIDELINES

1. The camp program is more than the formal experiences offered by those responsible for planning activities. It is the sum total of everything that occurs during the child's waking hours at camp.
2. The camp program should grow out of the camp philosophy and objectives. Once a clear statement of the aims and objectives has been developed, the program should provide the means of realizing these objectives.
3. Many factors should be considered when developing the camp program, including staff competencies, location and climate, financial resources, clientele to be served, interests of the camp committee or board, and length of the camp session.
4. The camp program should be sensitive to the wishes of the campers it is designed to serve.
5. Several logical and sequential steps should be followed in developing the camp program, including setting up a representative group to plan the program, reviewing camp objec-

tives, assessing camper needs and interests, appraising available program resources, formulating specific program objectives, selecting program experiences, and evaluating the new program on an ongoing basis.
6. Program planning should provide for participation by groups of differing sizes. The possibilities range from individualized activity to programs for the entire camp.
7. A balance should be sought between informal, unscheduled activity and prescheduled structured programs. To plan every waking hour of the camper's day is as undesirable as complete freedom for campers.
8. Camp program planning should be a cooperative endeavor between counsellors and campers. The staff provides expertise and often much experience, while the campers make known their needs and interests.
9. Joint camper-staff planning is usually most effective when program development is decentralized so that it takes place in the living units and, hopefully, at the cabin level.
10. The camp program should reflect a broad scope of activities that meet the divergent needs of campers. Program content is drawn from eight broad areas: sports and games, nature and outdoor activities, the arts, arts and crafts, hobbies, social recreational activities, spiritual and religious programs, and special events.
11. Program administrators must remember that the most popular activity may be unsuccessful if careful consideration is not given to the manner in which it is presented. Factors such as selection of the physical setting, timing of the activity, planning for maximum activity, careful grouping of the participants, and effective utilization of available staff are all important considerations in determining the success of a given program.
12. Rainy day programming presents unique problems at many camps and requires much advanced planning. Another concern of many program directors is that of providing challenging activities for older campers. Day camps face the special program challenge of keeping campers productively occupied while travelling to and from camp each day.

SELECTED BIBLIOGRAPHY

Bacon, E. M.: Make your woodlands work for you, Camping Magazine, 43(1):13-14, Jan., 1971.

Barnett, J.: Creative activities, Convention Report of the Ontario Camping Association, pp. 123-126, 1976.

Barnett, J.: Dramatics, Convention Report of the Ontario Camping Association, pp. 127-132, 1976.

Berger, H. J.: Program activities for camps. (Minneapolis: Burgess Publishing Co., 1969).

Carlson R. E.: Ecology programs—how ecology affects all camp attitudes, Camping Magazine, 46(1):11-12, Sept./Oct., 1973; 46(2):12-13, Nov./Dec., 1973.

Clarke, G. A., and Eells, E. P.: Early findings on values of camping now available, Camping Magazine, 47(2):8-11, Nov./Dec., 1974.

Corbett, M.: Survey reveals camper interests, Camping Magazine, 47(2):6-7, Nov./Dec., 1974.

Council for National Cooperation in Aquatics: Lifeguard training—principles and administration. (Bradford Woods, Martinsville Ind.: American Camping Association, 1973).

Cousineau, C.: Outdoor living, Convention Report of the Ontario Camping Association, pp. 132-135, 1976.

Hanson, R. J., and Carlson, R. E.: Organizations for children and youth. (Englewood Cliffs, N.J.: Prentice-Hall Inc., 1972). Chapters 6 and 8.

Glascock, M. McE. and Scholer, E. A.: Camping for older adults, Camping Magazine, 41(3):15-16, Mar., 1969.

Heller, J. H., et al.: Camping with a purpose a 4-H handbook. (Washington, D.C.: U.S. Government Printing Office, 1972).

Kraus, R. G., and Curtis, J. E.: Creative administration in recreation and parks. (Saint Louis: The C. V. Mosby Co., 1977).

Lawden, J.: Landsports, Convention Report of the Ontario Camping Association, pp. 117-122, 1976.

Lea, T.: Programme logistics in day camps, Convention Report of the Ontario Camping Association, pp. 181-194, 1976.

Mitchell, A. V., et al.: Camp counselling. (Philadelphia: W.B. Saunders Co., 1970). Part III.

Palm, J.: Waterfront, Convention Report of the Ontario Camping Association, pp. 115-156, 1976.

Rodney, L. S., and Ford, P. M.: Camp administration. (New York: John Wiley & Sons, 1971). Chapter 9.

Schainman, S. B.: Making a bus ride part of the camp program, Camping Magazine, 51(4)14-16, 32, Mar., 1979.

Shivers, J. S.: Camping—administration, counselling, programming. (Englewood Cliffs, N.J.: Prentice-Hall Inc., 1971). Part III.

van der Smissen, B., and Goering, O. H.: A leader's guide to nature oriented activities. (Ames Iowa: Iowa State University Press, 1965).

CHAPTER SEVEN

Health and safety

The law prohibits careless action: whatever is done must be done well and with reasonable caution. Failure to employ care not to harm others is a misfeasance.[1]

For most parents, the single most important consideration in the selection of a camp is the health and safety of their child. As substitute parents, camp directors and their staff have an obligation to provide a safe environment in which the well-being of each camper is guarded zealously. Most camps strive to create a relaxed camp atmosphere that is free from rigorous constraints and application of rules. However, whenever health and safety of campers is at stake, there can be no compromising of the regulations. Strict adherence to all such rules is essential if prevention of accidents and personal health is to be preserved.

The maintenance of a safe healthy environment is a cooperative responsibility of all members of the camp community. While the medical staff of the camp has this as its primary function, the camp physician and nurse can achieve little without the full co-operation of the administration, counselling staff, and the campers themselves.

This chapter discusses health and safety under three topics—camp health services, preservation of a safe and healthy camp environment, and legal implications related to accidents.

HEALTH SERVICES
The health center

Every camp, regardless of size, must have a facility that serves as the camp hospital. A variety of different names have been used to identify this center. They range from hospital and infirmary to sick bay and first aid cabin. I prefer the term *health center* in the belief that it has a slightly more positive connotation than the others.

The health center should be strategically placed. It should enjoy a central, convenient location and yet be quiet. Some camps have met these apparently conflicting criteria by placing it between the general living area for campers and the dining hall, but moving it 20 to 50 yards off the main camper traffic routes. Convenient location is highly desirable so that campers are not dissuaded from stopping at the health center for what, to them, may appear to be a very minor condition. Young campers often believe they have more important things to do than visit the nurse or physician for medical attention. In some locales, it is also advisable to select a wooded area so that the center is in the shade during the heat of the day.

---

1. National Education Research Division for the National Commission on Safety Education: Who is liable for pupil injuries? (Washington D.C.: National Education Association, 1950) p. 6.

The use of a tent or some other temporary structure is not recommended for the health center. Rather, it should be a permanent building that is carefully planned to be functional and orderly. The interior should be painted in a bright, attractive color and be the essence of cleanliness. It should provide for excellent ventilation during the hot weather and, depending on the geographic location of the camp, have some form of auxiliary heat for cold nights and mornings.

It is highly desirable to have a telephone in the health center with emergency numbers posted clearly on the wall beside the phone. These should include local physician, hospital, fire and police departments, ambulance service, and poison center. When a local intercommunication system is used to connect various segments of the camp, the health center should be included in this system.

A typical health center includes the following areas: (1) a ward with enough beds to take care of peak needs, (2) an isolation room for at least one patient, (3) a waiting room or covered porch area, (4) an examination room, (5) toilet and bathroom facilities, and (6) adequate storage space for all equipment and supplies. The center should be equipped with hot and cold running water. A shower stall or bathtub is strongly recommended. The entire health center should have adequate lighting with particular attention given to the examination room. Quality beds and mattresses should be placed throughout the center, and it is recommended that beds be spaced a minimum of 4 feet apart.

Staffing the health center

The composition of the staff responsible for the operation of the health center varies with the size and nature of the camp. Some large camps for crippled, diabetic, or otherwise handicapped children have a team of physicians and nurses and a fully equipped hospital on the campsite. Small resident camps and many day camps have only a graduate nurse or a nurse-in-training, and in a few cases, someone with only advanced first aid certification. More typically however, a physician is at the campsite at all times. The camp physician may be assisted by one or more registered nurses or nurse's aids. Other camps have a registered nurse at the site and a hospital or 24-hour medical clinic within a few miles of the camp. Some camps have a written agreement with a physician in the immediate vicinity of the camp who agrees to be on "24-hour call" if the camp nurse requires special services.

When a camp is large enough to warrant a team of physicians or nurses, it is recommended that the senior person be hired first, and he or she should then work closely with the camp director in the recruitment and selection of the other medical staff.

Camp nurse. One of the most vexing problems confronting camp directors in recent years has been the difficulty of recruiting a camp nurse. This problem is not unique to camps; the shortage of nurses is prevalent in almost all parts of the United States and Canada. The following suggestions have been made with regard to recruiting the camp nurse:

1. Place advertisements in nursing journals
2. Contact local schools of nursing for new graduates as well as instructors in the school
3. Explore the university graduate schools of nursing
4. Investigate private duty nurse registries.[2]

Camp directors have also had success by posting job descriptions on nurse's hospital notice boards. If all these sources prove fruitless, it may be necessary to consider a

2. Zielarth, L., and Wurzell, C.: Recruiting the camp nurse, Camping Magazine, 38(8):18, Nov./Dec., 1966.

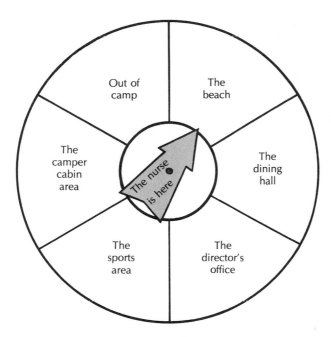

Fig. 7-1. Location of camp nurse.

student nurse who has at least completed maternal-child health preparation. It must be remembered, however, that a student nurse may not legally accept the responsibilities of a qualified registered nurse, and the camp director must be careful to ensure that such a person has the necessary support resources available in the immediate community.

Whenever possible, the nurse should live in quarters that adjoin the health center or are immediately adjacent to it. In this way, it is possible to supervise patients who may be required to stay in the center overnight. When the nurse is off-duty, a sign should be posted prominently outside the health center indicating where the nurse can be located (Fig. 7-1).

The following is a list of recommended qualifications that the camp administrator should seek when hiring a camp nurse.

1. A valid license to practice in the state or province in which the camp is located.
2. Several years' of experience in nursing, preferably in pediatrics, public rehabilitation, or community nursing.
3. Minimum age limit because of the vast range of responsibility required.
4. Qualities of responsibility, leadership, versatility, and flexibility.
5. Above all, a genuine concern for children.

Duties of the medical staff

Whether the health center is staffed by a registered nurse, a camp physician, or a team of physicians, several duties must be performed. These responsibilities begin before the camp season and are not completed until after the campers have returned to their homes. In most camps, the medical staff fulfills these assignments in close cooperation with the camp director. A few directors leave these responsibilities entirely in the hands of the camp physician or nurse on the assumption that this is a very technical area about which they know very little. As the senior administrator of the camp, however, it is the director's obligation to consult regularly with the medical staff regarding the efficient operation of the unit.

Precamp responsibilities. Several things must be done well in advance of camp opening and continue right up to the day the campers arrive.

1. *Establishment of job descriptions for each member of the health care staff.* There must be clear understanding of the responsibilities and limitations of each member's function.

2. *Selection of staff.* This must be completed well before the camp season, and the senior medical person should play a primary role in recruiting staff for the health center.

3. *Determination of the health service budget.* This must be done in consultation with the camp director and possibly the business manager.

4. *Review of possible facility and equipment changes.* The medical staff report of the previous summer should be consulted to determine if there are any recommendations regarding the improved operation of the health center for the coming season.

5. *Revision of camper and staff policies relating to health and safety.* All policies regarding health and safety should be under continuous review. For example, it may have been noted that last summer a large number of cuts were sustained by young campers while they were whittling. A review of this problem may result in the whittling policy being changed or more careful instruction being given regarding safe whittling technique.

6. *Ordering of equipment and supplies.* Each year new supplies are required to stock the health center. The order should be based on a careful review of the inventory of equipment and supplies on hand at the close of the previous camp season. When the budget is limited, the possibility of donations from local businesses, hospitals, or pharmaceutical companies should not be overlooked. The list of supplies includes some medications. It is essential that all medications be properly labeled and stored in a locked place. To ensure adequate security, only members of the health center staff should have access to this storage area.

7. *Precamp health inspection.* Each year, prior to the opening of camp, the director and the camp physician or nurse should make a thorough check of the sanitary condition of such areas as the kitchen, food storage areas, garbage storage area, dining room, toilets and washrooms, bathhouses, and cabins. All should meet rigorous standards of cleanliness.

8. *Training and supervision of subordinate health care staff.* This begins in the precamp period and continues throughout the entire camp season. It includes orientation of the staff to the health care center, review of all procedures, rules, regulations, and duties, and delegation of the specific tasks and responsibilities.

9. *Training of general counsellor staff.* During the precamp staff training program, the medical staff should play a significant role in covering such topics as: camper clinic hours, night calls, visiting campers, appropriate camper footwear and clothing, symptoms of overfatigue and heat exhaustion, immediate first aid, use of first aid kits, first aid instruction for out-trips, and instruction in mouth-to-mouth resuscitation.

10. *Collection of resource material in the health center.* The camp health center should be equipped with a selection of available reference materials. These should include books on fundamentals of nursing care, pediatrics, community health nursing,

infectious communicable diseases, pharmacology, and American National Red Cross first aid manuals.

11. *Establishment of relationship with local physicians, hospital, or medical clinic.* Many camps enter into a contractual agreement with a doctor who is located close to the camp and is willing to be "on call" during the camp season. The health center personnel should also determine what additional medical resources are available within reasonable proximity to the camp for more serious cases. Clear directions describing the location of each emergency service should be prepared. In fact, it would be desirable to have the health center staff personally visit emergency centers during the precamp period.

12. *Gathering and filing staff health certificates.* Many camps are careless about requiring *all* staff to present a medical certificate before the beginning of the precamp staff development program. All staff, including senior personnel, should present a certificate signed by a qualified physician before they engage in any precamp activity.

Responsibilities during camp season. Once the campers arrive, the staff of the health center must concern themselves with the immediate needs of the campers and the total camp staff.

1. *Maintain accurate record of all health files.* The health center staff must keep several types of records for both campers and staff. The first of these is the health examination record. This form is usually sent in by the parent or guardian prior to the camp season. Some camps collect the forms from the parents on the opening day of the camp session. Other camps require the camper to present the health record to the health center staff on arrival at camp. An effective system must be developed for the collection of these forms that does not involve campers

handling the form; they are too easily misplaced or lost.

It is important that the health center staff keep a written record of every patient seen. This should be done by inscribing the camper's name, date, time of visit, and a brief notation of the complaint and treatment in a hard-cover *daily logbook*. A typical entry might read:

Name	Time	Diagnosis and treatment
Tom Brown	1:30 p.m.	Complains of sore throat. Temperature normal, throat appears normal. Given salt water, gargle and told to report after evening meal.

In the case of a potentially serious injury, an accident report form should be completed. In addition, records should be kept of insurance forms, equipment and supplies inventories, as well as special diets for those campers with food allergies or diabetes.

2. *Gather camper medications.* Again, these should be given directly to the nurse or other senior staff member by the parent or guardian. Under no conditions should young campers be given custody of their own medications. All prescribed medications should be stored in the health center and dispensed by those persons responsible for the health care of the campers. When going on an out-trip, the camper's medications should be the responsibility of the senior trip counsellor.

3. *Establish clinic routine for the health center.* Most camps provide fixed times during each day when campers and staff are encouraged to come to the health center for routine treatment. The most common pattern is immediately after each meal. At this time, the entire medical staff is usually on

duty to dispense medications, handle ongoing treatment, and diagnose any new conditions that have arisen since the last clinic.

4. *Post standard treatments for health center staff.* Some camp physicians follow the procedure of posting "standing orders" for the handling of many routine injuries and illnesses.

5. *Routinize care of campers confined to the health center.* During the course of the camp season, some campers are admitted to the health center for observation and treatment. Such confinement normally requires that the medical staff take the camper to a physician or have the physician come to the camp when necessary, write a letter to the parents advising them of their child's condition, keep a progress report on the child's personal health record, provide some form of recreational therapy such as books, games, or puzzles during the convalescent period, and require the camper to report to the clinic daily up to 48 hours after discharge.

6. *Inspect camper living units.* A few camps adopt the practice of asking the medical staff to assume responsibility for periodic, or even daily, health checks of each tent or cabin group. This is usually done during cabin cleanup or rest hour and is another screening device to uncover any undiagnosed health problems among campers. The majority of camps, however, rely on each tent or cabin counsellor to be on the alert for any unusual symptoms.

7. *Inspect entire camp regularly.* The physician or nurse should accompany the camp director on regular camp tours to inspect the sanitary condition of certain key areas. Included among the duties that the medical staff may be asked to assume are taking samples of the drinking water and swimming water for laboratory analysis, checking the drinking water chlorinator regularly, and supervising the use of chemical additives when a swimming pool is in oper-

ation. In many camps, this is the responsibility of the waterfront director.

8. *Provide detailed instructions to out-trip counsellors.* Members of the medical staff should be required to give comprehensive in-service training to all staff who participate in out-trips. Such instruction should include water purification, treatment of poison ivy, poison oak, snake bites, sunstroke, and hemorrhage, dressing of lacerations and abrasions, and so on. All counsellors should be thoroughly knowledgeable in mouth-to-mouth resuscitation and familiar with each item in the first aid kit and its use.

Postcamp responsibilities. After the campers leave, the medical staff still has several duties to perform.

1. *Make detailed inventory of all equipment and supplies.* Only when this is done, can the staff plan and order efficiently for the following season.

2. *Close health center for the off-season.* This includes such details as packing away all bed linen and collecting and storing all other equipment appropriately. It must be remembered that items must be inaccessible to rodents. In addition, some liquids must be stored where they will not freeze, while the shelf life of others may indicate that they be discarded.

3. *Prepare a final report with recommendations for the following year.* The best time to evaluate the summer's operation is immediately after the end of camp. Such a report should include the strengths and weaknesses of the season just concluded and suggestions for improvement.

4. *Store the daily logbook and all accident forms in a safe place.* For legal purposes, these files should be retained until campers reach the age of maturity in some states.

CAMPER HEALTH AND SAFETY

The medical staff of a camp assumes considerable responsibility for accident prevention. Still, the physician and/or nurse cannot possibly guarantee an effective preventive program without the full support of all staff members and campers. This section discusses the many ways in which all members of the camp community work to provide a safe and healthy camp environment.

Counsellors's role in health and safety

Camper health and safety is the responsibility of all camp personnel. It is one of the most important concerns of cabin counsellors who are directly responsible for a small group of campers. The following points underscore this important role.

1. *Inspection of physical setting and supervision of safety regulations.* It must be impressed on counsellors that they are in a very favorable position to observe any undesirable or dangerous conditions regarding the physical environment of the camp and report them immediately to the appropriate authority. They must also remind campers of camp safety regulations when violations are noted.

2. *Continuous daily inspection of campers.* The counsellor is in the best position to make continuous observation of campers to discover any irregularities that may require medical attention. Symptoms that should be easily observed include skin rashes, sunburn, cuts or lacerations, infected bites, coughing, sneezing, bloodshot eyes, listlessness, and overfatigue. The counsellor should also inquire about regular bowel movements. In the case of young campers, counsellors should accompany them to the health center. With older youngsters, it is the counsellor's responsibility to check on whether the camper attended the clinic. If a camper is admitted to the health center overnight, it should be camp policy that the counsellor visits the youngster at least once each day. The counsellor should also ensure that the child has proper clothing and toilet articles.

3. *Camper personal hygiene.* Campers often view camp as an opportunity to abandon all rules of personal cleanliness. A counsellor once uncovered a conspiracy within a tent of 10-year-old boys in which each boy had pledged not to change his socks or undergarments for the month he was to be in camp. The tent or cabin counsellor is the only sure check against whether campers bathe regularly, wash their hands before each meal, change their clothing, and clean their teeth at least twice daily. Counsellors should discourage the practice of campers sharing personal items such as towels, combs, and toothbrushes.

With young campers, the counsellor should also make regular, inconspicuous checks for bedwetters and take the appropriate action when one is discovered. Checks should also be made to see that no child sleeps in a damp sleeping bag.

4. *Camper clothing appropriate to the weather.* Campers must be carefully supervised regarding appropriate clothing and footwear in excessively hot, cold, or rainy weather. It should be a daily responsibility of the counsellor to check on such things as a warm sweater or jacket on cold mornings, raincoat and rubber boots for precipitation, and suitable clothing to cover the head and exposed areas when in the hot sun for prolonged periods.

5. *Adequate rest and sleep.* Most camps follow the practice of scheduling a rest period during the day, usually immediately following the noon meal. Counsellors should be expected to ensure that campers observe this quiet period. They should also provide sedentary breaks during very strenuous activity programs such as soccer, lacrosse, and touch football. Each counsellor should be alert to conditions of overfatigue, especially among young campers.

Rules regarding bedtime hour are usually established by the camp administration. It is the counsellor's responsibility, however, to settle campers as efficiently as possible and to remain at the cabin or tent after "lights out" until all campers are completely quiet. Similarly, in the morning the counsellor must discourage early risers from disturbing other campers as well as the staff. It should be suggested to campers who wake early that they remain in their cabin and engage in some quiet activity such as reading a book or writing a letter. It is also the counsellor's duty to see that there is adequate fresh air in the cabin at all times.

6. *Dining hall behavior*. The dining hall should provide a relaxed atmosphere in which campers eat at a leisurely pace. Children should be encouraged to try all kinds of food that is served, but little is gained by forcing children to eat food they dislike. Counsellors should be expected to set an example with regard to food consumption as well as general dining hall deportment.

Another aspect of food consumption has to do with "food packages from home." Many camps adopt a policy of insisting that all food and sweets be shared equally by all members of the cabin or tent. This practice has two virtues: it minimizes the candy and rich food that is received and it encourages campers to accept, as normal practice, the principle of sharing with others.

Types of camp hazards

Many potential danger areas within the camp setting may jeopardize a camper's health or safety. Some of these are natural hazards, indigenous to the camp locale and its rugged wooded terrain. In other cases, the hazards are man-made, but are no less threatening.

Natural hazards. One of the primary considerations in the selection of a campsite is the choice of property that has a minimum number of natural hazards. No matter how thorough and careful new owners are in the selection of their property, they must be

reconciled to the fact that some forms of hazards will exist. Having identified these dangers, the staff must take effective precautions to minimize each hazard. The following are some natural hazards that are most commonly found in camps.

Questionable drinking and swimming water. It is difficult to imagine acquiring a new camp site in which either water supply is polluted. However, once the camp is in operation, there is always the possibility that what was once a source of clean water is no longer safe. Regular laboratory tests must be conducted to ensure the safety of both swimming and drinking water.

Camp terrain. Several natural hazards that may be inherent in the physical site include rock promontories and cliffs, exposed roots or rock outcropping in heavily trafficked areas, and steep trails that become slick in rainy weather. Each may be a real source of concern, especially with young campers. To remove or reduce these hazards, some areas may have to be placed out of bounds and roped or fenced off. In other cases, it may be wise to white-wash rock outcroppings or hazardous roots on trails.

Obstruction in the swimming area. There are times when it is impossible to locate a swim area that is completely free of natural impediments such as sunken logs and rock outcroppings. These may constitute a hazard to swimmers, depending on the depth of the water. The first attempt should be to remove all such obstructions. Sometimes it may be necessary to have a professional come in and dynamite them. If this is not possible, their locations should be clearly marked by placing floating buoys directly above them. All campers and staff must then be advised to keep well clear of these obstacles.

Swamps and other dangerous wetland. Although such areas may be a wonderful resource for nature study programs, they are sometimes a threat to camper safety. Such areas may need to be placed out of bounds.

Dead trees. Camp directors frequently overlook the potential hazard of large dead trees on the camp property. When these are located in heavily trafficked areas, there is always the danger of branches or the entire tree being blown down in a strong wind. A tour of inspection should be made each spring, and all dead trees should be felled, cut up, and cleared away.

Noxious plants. Poison ivy, oak, sumac, and different forms of nettle are found in many parts of North America and are a real threat to campers. Since there is not always quick, effective treatment, prevention should be emphasized. The camp director must first determine whether any of these pernicious plants are on the campsite, its environs, or the areas in which the camp conducts out-trips. The staff must then learn to identify each plant. If the plants are found in small quantity, they can be eradicated by carefully digging them up by the roots. They may also be killed with the use of chemical preparations. Frequently, however, they cover such a large area that the only solution is to learn to recognize them and avoid direct contact with the plant. When hiking in new areas, it is wise to require all camp personnel to wear long trousers and long-sleeved shirts.

Poisonous reptiles. Very few poisonous snakes are found in the United States and Canada, and those that are harmful are found in limited regions of both countries. If a camp is located in an area in which poisonous snakes are known to exist, several precautions are recommended. Snakes do not have ears but are sensitive to ground vibrations, so it is wise to carry a hiking stick to tap on the ground as one travels. The tapping alerts the snake to the presence of a human being, and it will then move out of the path as it is a very shy creature unless cornered. A sturdy pair of high walking boots is also recommended since over two thirds of all snake bites occur on the foot or leg. A snake bite kit should also be carried and all staff members taught how to use it.

Other poisonous pests. Bees, hornets, wasps, leaches, spiders, woodticks, scorpions, centipedes, mosquitoes, and other pests may be at least as great a threat as snakes. There are now excellent commercial repellents that when used as directed are effective deterrents. If a group is travelling where such insects are common, special attention must be given to clothing so that very little skin is exposed. A good repellent should be applied to exposed skin areas and to the clothing on the edge of areas such as the neck, waist, cuffs, and tops of socks.

Extreme hot or cold weather. Although severe weather conditions rarely result in bodily injury, they may cause considerable discomfort and impair health. Heat exhaustion and heat stroke must be guarded against in very hot, humid weather. There is particular danger when exposed directly to the sun's rays for long periods on the water. Several precautions should be taken to protect campers from overexposure, including:

1. Wear loose-fitting, light colored clothing.
2. Protect the head and neck from the direct rays of the sun.
3. Schedule vigorous activities early or late in the day.
4. Provide more frequent and longer rest periods in hot weather.
5. Remember that high temperature and humidity cause heat stroke and exhaustion. Both can also occur in the shade.

Similarly, extreme cold weather in certain geographic locations may leave the camper open to exposure unless appropriate clothing and bedding is provided.

Natural disasters. Fire, flood, landslides, tornadoes, hurricanes, electrical storms, and earthquakes are camp hazards. Every camp should have a carefully conceived disaster plan. Of these natural phenomena, the hazard of fire is the greatest, and drills should be conducted regularly with campers and staff. It is especially important that a fire drill be scheduled when the entire camp is in the dining hall or camp theatre to be certain that an orderly and efficient exit can be made.

Lightning is another hazard that confronts many camps each summer. Some campers, and even counsellors, have a great fear of lightning because they do not understand it. Summer camp offers a unique opportunity to teach a healthy respect for electrical storms. The following guidelines should help allay camper fear and provide the basis for rules of camp procedure, especially on out-trips.

1. Staff members should help campers develop a respect for lightning. Every attempt should be made to downplay their fear.
2. Campers and staff should move indoors as soon as an electrical storm breaks.
3. Stay away from open doors and windows. Close them.
4. Avoid contact with electrical devices such as telephone, lamps, radios, televisions, hair dryers, and razors.
5. Stop all dishwashing, showers, and baths during a storm and avoid touching water taps.
6. Do not stand in any water during the storm.
7. If outdoors lie flat on the ground, preferably in a ditch or culvert. Never seek the shelter of a tree.
8. When on water, be overly alert to all approaching storms. Head for shore so that you can beach quickly.
9. When in a car, bus, or truck, pull over to the side and wait out the storm. Stay in the vehicle; it is about the safest

place to be in a storm. Do not park on the crest of a hill or under a large tree.

In case of electrocution, the following steps are recommended: (1) send for the doctor and remain calm, (2) remove the victim from the source of electrocution with great caution, (3) apply mouth-to-mouth resuscitation at once, (4) keep the victim covered and warm, and (5) give first aid for electrical shock without stopping resuscitation.*

Persons lost, missing or runaway. Although it may be argued that none of these is a natural hazard but man's doing, the heavily wooded terrain around camps greatly magnifies the problem. Campers and staff must be given explicit direction on how to avoid getting lost and exactly what step they should take in the event that they lose their bearings.

Each camp must develop a search and rescue procedure for persons lost, missing, or runaway. The following is an example of the type of procedure that might be developed for such an emergency.

1. When a camper is believed missing, it should be reported to the camp director immediately.
2. The person reporting the incident should return to regular duty to avoid undue concern.
3. The director (or designate) should determine the last known whereabouts of the missing individual.
4. The director should then initiate one of the following actions:
   a. determine whether the camper may have left camp property with per-

---

*Camp directors may wish to order a booklet entitled: "In Time of Emergencies" published by the Defense Civil Preparedness Agency, Department of Defense, 2800 Eastern Blvd. (Middle River), Baltimore, MD 21220. This booklet has excellent directions on how to cope with natural disaster.

mission of a staff member (for example, by camp vehicle).

b. initiate a search of the immediate area of last known whereabouts.

c. activate the camp search and rescue team in anticipation of a large-scale search.

5. If the camper is not located within 30 minutes, the search and rescue team should reassemble and assess the situation.

6. Police and other agencies in the local community should be notified.

7. The director should ensure that the camp routine is maintained so that the possibility of panic is held to a minimum.

8. As soon as the missing person is located, it should be reported to the director who notifies all personnel involved.

Man-made hazards. Humans are guilty of creating many situations that are potentially harmful to themselves and those around them. Several of these self-inflicted hazards may be found in many camps, and some of the most common are discussed here.

Public highway bisecting camp property. A few camps have acquired property that has a road or even a railway line running through it. This forms a dangerous situation if campers must cross such a road or line in moving from one part of the camp to another. Several steps may be taken to reduce the danger. The camp should request highway officials to post appropriate signs to reduce speed or, better still, bring traffic to a full stop. The camp should also post its own signs on either side of the crosswalk and cut away all brush on both sides of the highway to improve pedestrian and driver visibility. Finally, the camp should establish very firm rules regarding crossing the road, which should be posted at the site.

Facilities requiring repair. Camp buildings require continuous inspection and maintenance to reduce the hazard of accidents. Such conditions as a rotting floor board on a tent platform, a broken window pane, a loose stair riser, or a defective handrail are but a few examples of the many conditions that require continuous repair. In addition to regular inspections by the camp director, all staff members should be asked to report immediately any condition that they consider potentially hazardous. All repairs should be carried out at once. When this is not feasible, the area should be placed out of bounds until the problem has been rectified.

Movable hazards on the site. Many materials, when found on the campsite, constitute a hazard to personal safety, including such items as broken glass, rusty tin cans, or nails in scrap lumber. Piles of cut, dry brush, or slash, represent a fire hazard as do oily rags. The solution in each case is to remove the danger. If flammable materials such as gasoline, coal oil, paint thinner, and paint are kept on the site, they should be secured in a separate storage room that is out of bounds to all campers and staff. Only selected personnel should have access to this storage area.

Lack of effective rules regarding camper safety. Camps must establish several rules to minimize the danger of accidents. Some camps deplore the need to set rules, but to fail to do so is to invite very serious consequences. A few examples should suffice to convince the reader of the inherent dangers. There should be a rule forbidding the throwing of stones except in selected areas of the camp and then only with supervision. Most camps now prohibit soft drink bottles in camp. Campers should not be permitted to carry matches except in the campcraft area and under supervision. Footwear should be worn at all times except at the waterfront.

Selection of high adventure programs. All

program activities lie along a continuum from very safe to high risk. Activities such as mountain climbing, trampolining, white water paddling, archery, and riflery are considered more hazardous than softball, badminton, or a nature walk. Each program director must make some decisions regarding the relative merits of the high-risk activities to determine whether the values of the activities outweigh the potential hazards.

Use of electrical, motorized, and mechanical equipment. As a camp uses more power equipment in the kitchen, maintenance shop, or as a means of camp transportation, the risk to staff and campers increases.

Use of power boats on lake or river. In some areas, the volume of power boats on the lake or river where the camp is located poses an increasing hazard from year to year. Some camps have had to place additional float lines beyond their swimming and diving areas to provide a "buffer zone" as a means of safeguarding their campers and staff.

Procedure for handling hazards

Recognizing that there are many potential natural and man-made hazards in most camps, the director must have a clear plan of action to remove or reduce the risk involved. Fig. 7-2 depicts a sequential plan of action that should be followed to effectively cope with existing hazards.

1. *Identify the hazard.* The first step is the recognition that certain hazards do exist. This usually involves regular inspection by various senior staff members. For example, the waterfront director should continuously be on the alert for any potentially dangerous

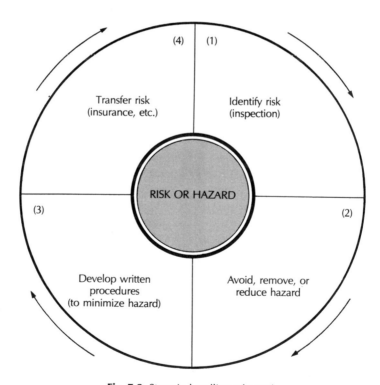

Fig. 7-2. Steps in handling a hazard.

conditions that are associated with activities conducted in this area. Similarly, the food services manager must make regular inspections of the entire food service operation to detect hazards related to kitchen staff working conditions or the possibility of food-borne illness threatening members of the camp community. It has already been pointed out that the identification of specific risks should not be left to selected staff members alone. The camp custodian may be primarily responsible for the maintenance and repair of many conditions relating to the physical site, camp buildings and equipment. However, every staff member should assume responsibility for reporting any situation that is viewed as potentially hazardous. A ruptured water pipe, a rotten floorboard, a defective fire extinguisher, or a frayed climbing rope becomes the responsibility of each member of the staff.

With regard to identifying existing perils, it is often very helpful to have an outsider tour the camp and assist in the recognition of risk situations. Often those in charge of a given program sometimes fail to foresee the danger simply because they are too close to the problem and assume all is well. In this regard, local and state government inspectors, camping accreditation visitors, insurance representative, and other qualified experts can be of great assistance in not only identifying areas of concern but in suggesting solutions to problems.

2. *Avoid, remove, or reduce the hazard.* Once a problem has been identified, there are several ways of dealing with it. One possible solution is to avoid the hazard altogether. For example, the program director may be urged by several staff members to introduce mountain climbing into the camp program. However, after careful examination of the climbing area and the competency of the available staff, it may be decided that the risks are too great at this time and so the hazard is avoided.

Another means of dealing with a risk may be simply to remove it. If the planks from the discarded sailing dock constitute a hazard because of rusty nails and jagged ends, the best answer is to eliminate the problem by having the boards burned or moved to the dump.

A third means of disposing of a hazard is to find means of reducing the risk. This is the method usually adopted when dealing with program. If a high adventure activity is considered worth retaining, means must be found to reduce the risks involved while retaining the excitement of the activity itself. The dangers are usually circumscribed in one of several ways: (1) the use of only qualified personnel to conduct the activity; the better qualified the staff, the more likely they are to foresee the dangers and find solutions, (2) modification of the activity and its rules, or (3) ensuring that the facilities and equipment are appropriate to the activity and the campers engaged in that program.

3. *Develop written procedures to minimize the hazard.* Whenever a high-risk situation is identified, it is wise to have a written, carefully developed set of procedures or rules to be followed. Written procedures help ensure a carefully developed plan of action rather than ad hoc arrangements. Written procedures should be kept on file and therefore be available another year in case different staff members return. If a group of staff members have carefully worked through certain safety procedures, it would be foolish not to have available the fruits of their effort for their successors. In case of legal action against the camp and its staff, such written procedures may be invaluable evidence in a court of law. These procedures should also be posted at the site of the activity. If the camp stores large quantitites of gasoline for use of a power mower and power boats, it would be expedient to establish firm rules about where the gasoline is

stored, who has access to it, and under what conditions. Similarly, if the camp decides to include field archery as an activity, careful consideration should be given to who may engage in field archery, at what times, under what supervision, and according to what set of rules.

4. *Transfer the financial risk to another agent.* In spite of all that may have been done, there still may be some risk involved and yet the camp wishes to continue that activity. Therefore, it would be appropriate to take out some form of insurance.

Program safety

Conduct of a safe camp program implies careful attention to a number of considerations that constitute a potential hazard to camper health. These areas of concern include provision of safe facilities and equipment, equal competition, responsible instruction, and judicious selection and supervision of high adventure activities.

Facilities and equipment. Too often, the camp director has attempted to justify inferior program facilities and equipment by using the rationale that camping is rustic and primitive, and therefore a small, rock-strewn, open area should suffice for a game of touch football. Such reasoning will carry little weight in a court of law if the cause of injury can be attributed to the unsatisfactory condition of the playing surface. The following questions should be raised by every camp administrator with respect to outdoor play areas.

1. Are all playing areas reasonably level and do they have a surface suitable for the safe conduct of the activity?
2. Are all playing surfaces free of natural hazards such as trees, roots, and rock outcroppings?
3. Are the playing areas properly maintained—removal of stones, branches, glass, tin cans, and the like?

4. Are play areas well marked, using safe marking materials?

Similar questions should be asked regarding indoor facilities.

1. Is each area free from obstructions such as posts, drinking fountains, fireplaces, and the like?
2. Have adequate precautions been taken to ensure that the playing surface is not warped, splintered, or unduly slippery?
3. Do all doors open outward off each play area but not onto a set of stairs?
4. Is there adequate lighting?
5. Are court boundaries sufficiently far from walls and other obstructions?
6. Is there sufficient floor space for the number of participants using the area?

In addition to providing safe facilities, the administrator must give careful attention to the type and condition of camp equipment that is provided for the use of campers and staff. The director must be able to give an affirmative answer to each of the following questions.

1. Does the camp purchase high quality protective equipment to ensure the safety of its clientele? Flotation devices? Headgear for horseback riding?
2. Does the camp provide sufficient quantity of equipment so that there is no danger of a camper receiving ill-fitting protective equipment?
3. Is there regular inspection of all safety equipment to ensure that it is well maintained and in good repair at all times? Are outmoded items discarded?

Equal competition. One of the dangers observed in some camp programs is the practice of thrusting campers of different ages into activities in which bodily contact is an integral part of the contest. This occurs most frequently in smaller camps in which there are insufficient numbers of children of a given age and maturity to enable only those campers of similar height and weight to play together. As a result, it is not uncommon to find campers of 11 or 12 years of age pitted against older campers who outweigh them by as much as 50 pounds. In combative-type activities where physical contact is prominent, the danger of injury is greatly increased. Those responsible for program planning must be alert to this danger and either modify the rules of the game so that the risk of injury is reduced or discard the activity altogether.

Another practice that should be examined is that of allowing, or even encouraging, counsellors to play contact games with the campers. When this procedure is followed, it is argued that staff participation heightens the interest and excitement of the game. This may be true, but this advantage must be carefully weighed against the potential danger of having a young camper injured as a result of the overzealous play of an 18-year-old counsellor.

Safe instruction. Experienced teachers of physical education recognize that good instruction leads to skillful performance that, in turn, reduces the incidence of injuries. It is vital that campers receive good instruction to alert them to the dangers inherent in some activities and provide them with the skill and knowledge to avoid potential hazards. This is only possible when the staff members themselves are aware of the latent hazards in a given activity and are able to preempt many possible dangers. A few examples should suffice to make the reader fully aware of the problem. Campers should be discouraged from running to touch a wall in a relay. The danger of tripping and pitching into the wall headfirst cannot be overlooked. Campers should not be permitted to carry bows and arrows from the equipment shack to the range without supervision. The temptation to nock an arrow and shoot it is just too great. Children should not be permitted to use an axe until they have had some basic chopping instruction, including practice, under supervision.

High-adventure activities. On the question of adventure versus risk, Pestolesi and Sinclair state:

In a sound instructional setting, curriculum should be dictated by desired outcomes rather than by fear of legal implications. Since there are very few absolutes in life, it is inevitable that some participants will sustain injuries despite the instructor's vigilance. The goal therefore should be to minimize this number as much as humanly possible.[3]

Once it has been accepted that some high-adventure activities are to be included in the camp program, it then becomes necessary for the camp director and program staff to minimize all risk factors without totally divesting the activity of its inherent excitement.

Program activities lie along a risk and high-adventure continuum. Quoits is not as dangerous a game as horseshoes, while horseback riding implies considerably more risk than bicycle riding. A canoe is a more hazardous water craft than a row boat, just as a distance swim across the lake involves more adventure than swimming laps within the confines of the swim area. If camp directors and their program staff are to include those activities that have some element of risk and high-adventure component, it follows that precautions must be taken to ensure the health and safety of the participant.

Camp administrators must carefully assess each activity they contemplate offering to determine where the potential risks lie. Once the dangers have been identified, it should not be difficult to establish rules and procedures to minimize these hazards.

One high-adventure area of camp pro-

3. Pestolesi, R. A., and Sinclair, W. A.: Creative administration in physical education and athletics. (Englewood Cliffs, N.J.: Prentice-Hall Inc., 1978) p. 234.

gramming has been selected to suggest how policies may be developed to reduce potential hazards. The activity selected is trip camping.

Trip camping. There is probably no activity that causes camp directors more concern than out-tripping. Trip camping poses particular problems insofar as the health and safety of campers is concerned:

1. It is usually conducted in an area where, in case of emergency, help may not be readily available.
2. It involves a high level of physical activity. As a result, fatigue is more likely to occur.
3. The trip camping staff are on their own and may have to make judgments that would be the responsibility of more experienced senior staff members in camp.

Because of the above considerations, it is imperative that trip counsellors undergo an extensive training program including several out-trips during which they serve as apprentice to a seasoned counsellor.

The following is a checklist for trip counsellors designed to ensure the health and safety of campers.

1. Does the camp make known to the campers all safety procedures relating to the trip before the group leaves camp?
2. Are all members of the trip required to have a physical examination by camp medical staff on the day of departure and the day of return from the trip?
3. Is the leader of the trip at least 21 years of age with special competence to lead such a group?
4. Are there a minimum of two staff members on all trips?
5. Is the equipment for trip camping appropriate to the campers using it, and is it maintained in good repair?

6. Is protective shelter provided for all members of the group against the natural elements?
7. Does each member of the group have protective clothing against the natural elements?
8. Is each member of the party equipped with suitable sleeping equipment against the natural elements?
9. Have the trip counsellors been provided with the necessary procedures to deal with such matters as purification of drinking water, food preparation and storage, travelling on white water, use of the compass and steps to be taken if lost, and emergency first aid treatment?
10. Whenever campers engage in aquatic activity, are they supervised by a staff member with adequate water safety training? Does the staff member refrain from participating in the activity while supervising?
11. Is an adequate first aid kits provided for all groups when leaving the main camp?
12. Is a detailed itinerary filed at the camp, including the anticipated site for each night away from camp?
13. In the case of an emergency, are the exact locations of help identified on the trip map?

Although trip camping represents one of the greatest threats to the camp director's peace of mind, there are other high-adventure activities that have much to commend them and are therefore included in many camps. These include such selected programs as archery, axemanship, horseback riding, mountaineering, and the entire waterfront program. Each has its own particular risks, and each requires thoughtful consideration as to how these risks may be minimized while still preserving the excitement and adventure inherent in the activity.

LEGAL RESPONSIBILITY

The preceeding section indicated several ways in which the health and safety of campers and staff must be safeguarded. However, regardless of the degree of care the camp director and staff exercise, since much of the camp program usually involves physical activity, it follows that some injuries will occur. When accidents do occur, it is the duty of the camp administrator to understand under what conditions the camp and/or the staff may be found legally responsible. Directors must do everything within their power to minimize the possibility of legal action against the staff and/or the camp. Failure to take every reasonable precaution against accidents is to invite not only possible serious injury to campers but also financial ruin for staff members and the camp. It should be pointed out that the purpose of this section is not to threaten camp administrators but rather to make them fully aware of their legal obligations so that they may develop effective policies and procedures to minimize the frequency of accidents.

The general public is becoming increasingly aware of its rights regarding legal liability, which is causing many parents to pursue legal action whenever injury or damage occurs. Increasing numbers of malpractice suits are being brought against the medical profession. In addition, the legal and teaching professions are being subjected to a tremendous volume of legal suits. It is only human that parents should also blame camps and camp owners for personal injury or property damage and seek redress through the courts. It becomes essential therefore for camp administrators to make themselves thoroughly knowledgeable about all aspects of legal responsibility. Ignorance does not offer any protection in a court of law, and camp administrators who avoid becoming well-informed in this area do so at their own risk and that of their employees.

One of the problems confronting the camp administrator is that interpretations and judgments regarding legal liability vary from state to state. It is therefore necessary for directors to become knowledgeable about the law as it applies in a particular part of the country. In spite of the fact that laws concerning liability are vested primarily with the state or provincial legislature, there is enough universality regarding litigation to make it possible to discuss liability generally as it pertains to all parts of the country. Camp directors have a responsibility to educate themselves and their staffs so that all facets of the camp operation are conducted in such a way as to minimize the danger of court action.

Legal concepts

To have a clear understanding of their responsibilities regarding liability, camp directors must be familiar with the most widely used legal terminology.

Civil and criminal law. All legal matters within a state are classified as civil and criminal law. The latter involves offenses against the general public or the state, whereas civil law involves a wrong against an individual or group of individuals. In criminal law, guilt must be determined "beyond a reasonable doubt," whereas in civil cases only a "preponderance of evidence" is necessary for conviction. In the latter case, the defendant's guilt may be partial or shared. Legal action against camps nearly always comes under civil jurisdiction.

Liability. This term refers to a condition of legal responsibility either by a person or a group of persons for their actions as they relate to the safety and well-being of others. When a camper or staff member is injured as a result of proved negligence by a staff member or the camp, either or both may be sued to obtain compensation for the injury.

It is interesting to note that the courts

have consistently ruled that members of governing boards or committees are not liable as long as *reasonable diligence* can be demonstrated. This can be interpreted to mean that individual members of camp boards or committees are rarely found liable since they act in a corporate capacity and not for themselves. The law states that they should not be held responsible for the actions of their agents (camp staff).

Tort. This is the legal term for a civil wrong that infringes on the rights of another. Thus a tortious act is a legal wrong that results in either physical or mental injury to another individual or group or damage to property. A tort may result from an act of malfeasance, misfeasance, or nonfeasance.

Malfeasance. This term refers to an act of *commission with intent* to hurt, cause harm, or otherwise injure another party or his property through misconduct or misuse of authority.

Misfeasance. This refers to when a person is actively involved, and liability results from either an act of *commission* or *omission* without malicious intent. An act of *commission* occurs when the injury to the second party results from incompetence in the execution of a lawful act, while an act of *omission* occurs when an individual owes a duty to the participant but does not fulfill that duty.

Nonfeasance. This refers to the *omission* of a lawful act or failure to execute a legal duty when passively involved in a situation that results in damage or injury to persons or property.

In loco parentis. This Latin phrase means "acting in place of the parent." In camps, the director and those staff members who have responsibility for the camper act as a guardian does in the case of a minor. It is assumed by the courts that those persons responsible for the child will act as a "reasonable prudent parent" would behave toward the child. This assumption places considerable responsibility on camp directors in their role as guardian to ensure that all campers receive this high degree of care owed them.

Foreseeability. A great deal of legal importance is attributed to the principle of *foreseeability,* a term that refers to an event or action that could have been anticipated and prevented by a reasonably prudent person. Camp staff members who have direct responsibility for the supervision of campers must attempt to anticipate every situation that has some inherent risk and take the necessary steps to alleviate the danger. This means that counsellors must be capable of anticipating camper behavior that could lead to injury. They must know their campers well enough to preclude any rough play and irresponsible behavior that might result in litigation.

Attractive nuisance. An attractive nuisance is any contrivance that may be alluring to children and potentially dangerous to them. In most states the doctrine of attractive nuisance does not apply to children beyond 7 years of age. Older children are expected to have enough maturity to anticipate the inherent danger.

Defendant. This term refers to the individual or corporate body against whom legal action is taken. In a court case involving a camp, the defendant may be the camp owner or any member of the camp staff.

Plaintiff. This is the legal term for the party (individual or group) that initiates legal action against the defendant.

Precedence. This is a legal practice wherein lawyers, or the judge, may refer to an earlier court decision if two cases appear similar in many respects. Legal precedent carries much weight since nearly all cases of liability draw on earlier judgments.

Negligence. This occurs when an individual owes a duty to another to protect against unreasonable risk and there is failure to exercise reasonable and prudent care toward that person in relation to the situation. Negligence is the primary consideration in any case of liability before damages can be assessed. The courts therefore put great stress on such words as "prudence" and "reasonableness" and the appropriateness of the standard of care performed when attempting to establish whether there has been negligence. Just because an accident occurs and someone is injured does not mean that a staff member was negligent and therefore liable. It must be clearly established that the injury was related to some *negligent act*.

Factors necessary for proof of negligence

Commission of a tort. Obviously unless some wrong has been committed, there can be no negligence. The tort may include physical, mental, or emotional injury, property damage (clothing, personal possessions, and so forth), or character defamation. In the camp setting, the tort usually involves a case of physical injury to a camper.

Duty toward plaintiff. For negligence to be proved, it must be clearly shown that the defendant has a duty toward the plaintiff. Camp administrators and all program staff clearly have such a duty toward their campers.

Breach of duty. The person who has a duty must have breached that duty either by an act of omission or an act of commission. The counsellors who have a duty to campers cannot absolve themselves of responsibility by doing nothing when some action on their part is clearly dictated. The person who acts unwisely may be as guilty as the one who fails to act. A simple example should make this distinction clear. A camper trips and falls while playing a chasing game in the woods. A deep laceration is sustained on the inside of the thigh and there is profuse bleeding. The counsellor in charge who fails to employ any emergency first aid treatment to stop the bleeding is guilty of an act of omission. If, on the other hand, a tourniquet is applied on the thigh incorrectly, which leads to further complications, the counsellor again may be guilty of negligence; in this case an act of commission.

Proximate cause of injury. The act of commission or omission described above must be directly related to the injury by an unbroken chain of events. Only a direct relationship between the imprudent action, or failure to act on the part of the counsellor, and the injury itself can provide grounds for negligence. Simply stated, was the act, or failure to act, the proximate (legal) cause of the injury?

Defenses against negligence

It should be evident that camp staff members may fail to act or may act unreasonably, but if no tort or harm results, there is no legal grounds for litigation. In cases in which a staff member behaves unwisely, the follow-up action should be administrative, not legal. That is, the imprudent counsellor should be cautioned regarding the potential consequences of the indiscrete behavior.

It is strongly recommended that campers be advised verbally and that written regulations be posted at the site regarding potentially dangerous areas or activities within the camp. Such verbal or printed instructions are an effective means of reducing the number of accidents among campers. In the event of litigation printed rules may also serve to demonstrate the staff's concern for camper safety in their role as prudent substitute parents. Such regulations do not, however, absolve the staff member of liability in the case of a tortious act.

When an accident has occurred, several legal defenses are available to the defendant. Each is discussed in the following.

Act of God. Some injuries that occur are beyond human control. These are said to be acts of nature or acts of God. This legal principle has profound implications in the camp setting when natural elements such as wind, electrical storms, floods, landslides, or earthquakes might lead to a camp disaster and can be clearly shown to have contributed to unforeseeable injury.

For example, a counsellor takes a group of campers out on a lake and an unexpected windstorm results in a capsized canoe and a drowning. This, in all probability, would be construed as an act of God over which even the most reasonable person had no control. If, on the other hand, it was apparent that the storm clouds had been building on the horizon for some time and the counsellor virtually ignored the warning signs, there may be solid grounds for legal action against the counsellor.

Assumption of risk. This principle of civil law relates to individuals' voluntary participation in a situation in which they recognize the possibility of some hazard as a result of their involvement. If it is accepted that there are inherent risks in nearly all physical activities, it follows that camps offer certain activities because the benefits derived from participation are believed to outweigh the possible dangers. Regardless of how reasonable the quality of supervision is, injuries may occur as a result of widespread participation in some activities.

Most parents send their child to camp with the full knowledge that the youngster will engage in many vigorous, physical activities and that the possibility of injury is present. Similarly, if parents choose to send a child to a camp in which all children are invited to take trips by canoe, the parents accept the fact that even though there may be some additional danger in this experience, the values that accrue from it far outweigh the inherent risks, because they have

confidence in the camp and the quality of supervision provided.

Contributory negligence. This refers to action taken by the *injured party* that falls below that of prudent behavior and contributes to the resulting injury. Contributory negligence occurs most frequently when campers ignore rules regarding an activity, and their subsequent action is a contributing factor in causing the accident. In such cases, even when there has been an act of omission or commission on the part of the staff member, the person responsible is absolved of liability. The age of the injured party is of primary consideration in cases of this type since contributory negligence is predicated on the assumption that the actions of the injured party fall below those expected of prudent persons of similar age and maturity. In such cases, the courts have usually ruled that children above the third grade level are deemed to be responsible persons who are able to read, react to directions, and demonstrate an ability to reason. Children below the age of reason cannot be guilty of contributory negligence.

There are many examples of contributory negligence in the camp environment. If a camper, in spite of boating rules to the contrary, stands up in a canoe and an accident results, he or she will almost certainly be guilty of contributory negligence.

In some states, the principle of *comparative negligence* applies. This doctrine states that if both parties are at fault, the court may find each negligent and assign a percentage of the damages to both the plaintiff and the defendant.

Lack of proximate cause. As was pointed out earlier, for negligence to be present, it must be shown that the behavior of the defendant was directly related to the injury in an unbroken chain of events. When this direct relationship between the defendant and the injured party cannot be established, there is no grounds for litigation even though the defendant may have been guilty of negligent action.

A camper falls from a tree and is moved to the infirmary by the counsellor in charge before consulting with the medical staff. Subsequent examination shows no evidence of serious injury, but after returning to the city, the child's back is reinjured in another accident resulting in permanent disability. The counsellor and the camp cannot be held responsible for damages because there is no continuous chain of events that ties the counsellor's negligent action to the second accident.

Trespassing. Whenever persons are in a given location without an invitation or right to be there, they are trespassing. Once individuals trespass, they give up much legal protection against any damage sustained during their unauthorized presence. An owner owes a duty to trespassers to warn them of ultrahazardous dangers, and if trespassers, once discovered, are allowed to remain, they become licencees to whom a duty is owed to be warned of hazardous dangers. A child may be guilty of trespassing at any age.

Sudden emergency. This is a less common legal defense in which it is assumed that in an emergency, certain behavior may be condoned that normally might be considered negligent. If a staff member is confronted with an emergency situation that requires immediate and dramatic action and as a result an accident occurs, the counsellor may be free of responsibility for the second accident on the grounds that the primary emergency required exceptional conduct an the staff member's part.

A lifeguard on duty during general swim suddenly sees a camper in trouble in deep water. While rushing to get a reaching aid, the guard accidentally pushes another child off the dock who sustains a head injury in the fall. If the parents of the child who was injured by the fall take legal action against the camp, the defense may be based on the principle of a sudden emergency.

The examples just cited make it apparent that the age of the camper has a profound bearing on the position the courts take regarding negligence. Those persons responsible for young campers must realize that they have a great obligation for the safety of the child. What would be considered reasonable supervision for teenage campers may be considered negligence when dealing with young children.

Areas of potential negligence

There are many potential areas of litigation in the typical camp environment. It therefore behooves camp administrators to make themselves familiar with the most common causes of lawsuits so they may take the necessary steps to minimize the possibilities of injury and the ensuing threat of legal action. The following section outlines some of the most common areas of jurisprudence.

Inadequate supervision. Negligence is frequently associated with failure to provide standards of supervision normally expected of a person in a given activity with a particular group of persons. One of the most frequent causes of litigation occurs when counsellors are temporarily away from their supervisory role and an accident occurs in their absence. Obviously, the mere presence of the counsellor is not enough; the staff must take all reasonable steps to safeguard the campers in the pursuit of that activity. Since there are many times when direct supervision of each camper is impossible, the law has been interpreted to mean that "area" supervision is satisfactory. For example, if children are playing a chasing game in a wooded area, it would be almost impossible to supervise the movements of each child. The fact that one or more counsellors are in that area supervising the game and that clear instructions as to expected behavior by campers has been provided is considered adequate supervision by the courts.

Inappropriate selection of activities. Wise selection of activities is contingent on the physical and mental maturity of the participants as well as the skill level they bring to the activity. If the camp staff is insensitive to this fact, the result may be an injury for which the camp is legally responsible. This implies that some high-risk activities should not be offered to children until they have developed the cognitive process to the point where they can appreciate the dangers inherent in a given activity. For this reason, many directors do not permit campers to participate in archery or riflery before 10 years of age.

The camp program staff must also be aware of individual differences among children. Campers should never be placed in a position in which they are shamed into attempting something beyond their capabilities in front of others. Extending campers' capabilities and forcing them to go beyond their limitations are two very different things. To require a boy to attempt a hand-over-hand traverse on a suspended rope when he lacks the arm and shoulder strength to support his body weight would be irresponsible.

Inadequate control. Occasionally, the actions of a camper constitute a hazard to the welfare and safety of the group. Program leaders must accept responsibility for controlling the actions of persons whose behavior may create such a danger. For example, a child who persists in running on swim docks and pushing other campers into the water must be disciplined in a firm manner when these actions jeopardize the safety of others. Failure of a lifeguard to take appro-

priate action may be grounds for negligence.

Hazardous facilities and equipment. Whenever camp facilities or equipment are unsafe or defective, the organization and those staff members directly involved are vulnerable to legal action if the unsafe equipment results in an accident. This points up the importance of regular inspection of facilities and equipment. All defective equipment should immediately be removed or made inoperable. It is not enough to set the equipment aside where an unsuspecting camper may use it. Personal protective equipment such as headgear, pads, life belts, and mountaineering ropes should also be carefully inspected at regular intervals.

Transportation. The transportation of campers to and from camp, as well as trips during the camp season, pose a very serious area for litigation. In the case of day camps, when children are transported daily to the campsite, the chances of an accident are significantly increased. It is therefore imperative that camp administrators give careful consideration to the implications of various modes of transportation available before establishing camp policies.

Chartered commercial vehicles are generally recognized as the most desirable means of transporting campers. Care must then be taken to confirm that the commercial carrier selected is a reputable firm with an outstanding safety record. This is not a case in which the lowest bid should be accepted. Camp directors must be prepared to do some thorough research into the background of the firm, the condition of its vehicles, and the experience of its drivers. In addition, the camp representative should expect to see a copy of the firm's license to transport persons and its insurance coverage.

Medical examinations. No camp director should permit campers or staff to come to camp without having a thorough physical examination, and yet there are a surprising number of camps in which a current health certificate for every camper and staff member is not a precondition for attendance at camp. Only through such an examination is it possible to determine which campers are authorized to engage in all camp activities and who should be on a restricted program, either temporarily or for their entire stay at camp. Failure to have a physical examination does not in itself constitute negligence. It would have to be proved that failure to have an examination was proximate cause.

After an injury or illness requiring supervision by the medical staff of the camp, campers should be permitted to resume activites only with the permission of the camp doctor or nurse. To allow a child to resume normal activities and then find that resumption of play has resulted in further injury or illness may be grounds for legal action.

Corporal punishment. As stated earlier, camp personnel serve in loco parentis: in place of the parent. This raises the question as to whether staff members have the authority to use corporal punishment as a means of disciplining campers. For an answer, we must look to the precedent found in the schools. Some states and schoolboards sanction the use of corporal punishment, but generally this is seen as an undesirable and ineffective means of discipline. A second important reason for abandoning all forms of corporal punishment as a means of discipline is to eliminate one more source of legal action against the camp. When corporal punishment is condoned, the following conditions should prevail:

1. The camper's behavior should clearly warrant such drastic action.
2. The punishment should be administered without anger or malice and must not result in physical abuse (harm).

3. The staff member is assumed to be acting in good faith, and the punishment must not be excessive.
4. Whenever corporal punishment is resorted to, it should be administered by a senior staff member.
5. All corporal punishment should be witnessed by another responsible staff member.

Handling camp accidents

Emergency routine. When an accident occurs, every member of the staff should know how to deal with the situation effectively. The following steps will help ensure that a systematic and efficient procedure is followed in such emergencies:

1. The nearest staff member should proceed to the scene of the accident immediately.
2. A quick examination of the injured party should be conducted to determine the general nature and extent of the injury.
3. The counsellor in charge of the activity should administer immediate first aid if necessary.
4. The person in charge of the activity should be notified and the camp doctor or nurse summoned when necessary. (When in doubt, err on the side of caution.)
5. A staff member should stay with the injured person until the camp doctor or nurse arrives.
6. In the case of a potentially serious accident, an injury report form should be completed, including the names of two witnesses. All less serious accidents must be recorded in the daily logbook.

First aid treatment. Camp directors have long recognized the value of having several individuals on the staff who have certification in first aid. The larger the number of persons with this specialized preparation, the better since any staff member may be the first person on the scene of an accident that requires emergency first aid treatment. This is especially important for those camps that have an extensive out-tripping program.

All emergency numbers should be posted conspicuously near every phone on camp property, including those of the fire and police departments, doctor-on-call, hospital, or medical clinic.

Accident reports. Accident report forms should be used in every camp to record all accidents and injuries of a serious or potentially serious nature. Such reports are basic to the safety program of the camp not only because they focus on the causes or accidents, but because they may be the single most important piece of evidence that can be provided by the camp in its defense against a liability suit. The report should include the name and address of the injured party, date and time of accident, and location of the activity that was taking place, nature of the injury, circumstances leading to the accident, name and location of the staff member in charge, treatment given, and names and addresses of two witnesses. Statements by the witnesses regarding any *contributory negligence* on the part of the injured party would greatly strengthen the report. Some camps have developed a separate form providing a statement by the witness. It is essential, however, that no statement of cause of injury be included, since this may be construed as evidence of negligence.

It cannot be stressed too strongly that these reports may be invaluable whenever there is the threat of litigation. In addition, they provide strong statistical evidence regarding the need to modify building structures, play areas, and camp equipment. They may also be used to review some facets of the camp program in which injuries

are occurring with considerable frequency. Some programs may need to be modified; others discontinued. Injury report and statement of witness forms should be kept on file for the period of federal and state statutory limitations. Some state laws permit litigation proceedings to be initiated years after the accident.

Consent and waiver forms. A permission or consent form is an authorization, usually signed by the parent, permitting the child to engage in camp activities. A waiver or release form, when signed by the parent, is designed to free the camp of any legal responsibility in the event of an injury to the child while travelling to and from the camp or participating in any camp activity. The consent form should be made up of three parts: (1) acknowledgment of the nature of the activity, (2) agreement to follow the leader and the rules of the activity, and (3) affirmation of satisfactory physical condition. The waiver form, on the other hand, is of no legal value whatsoever if the parent proceeds with litigation. A parent has no legal authority to waive the rights of a child under majority age. By signing the waiver form, parents forfeit their right, as parents, to sue for damages, but no parent can legally waive the right of the child to sue as an individual. Most camps continue to use the waiver form on the assumption that many parents believe they have waived the right to initiate legal action. The waiver form, therefore, acts as a strong deterrent against lawsuits.

The health and safety of campers participating in all aspects of camp life must be a paramount consideration not only for the director but for all camp personnel. Parents have entrusted their most valued possession—their child—to the care of the camp. Directors and their staff must do everything possible to warrant this position of trust by providing an exciting, but safe, environment in which the camp program can flourish.

ADMINISTRATIVE GUIDELINES

1. As substitute parents, camp administrators are obliged to ensure a safe environment for all campers and staff. The provision of a healthy and safe camp experience is a prime consideration for many parents when selecting a camp for their children.

2. The provision of a safe, healthy environment is the responsibility of all camp personnel, not just the medical staff.

3. Camps should provide a permanent structure to serve exclusively as a health center. It should be attractive, efficient, and sanitary.

4. Camps are obligated to provide some form of health supervision and medical service on the site. This may be a licensed physician, registered nurse, or nurse-in-training. At all times, there should be someone on the site who is officially qualified to provide first aid service.

5. Health center personnel have a variety of duties to fulfill. These can be classified as precamp, during camp, and postcamp responsibilities.

6. Cabin counsellors have an important role to play in camper health and safety. These responsibilities include daily inspection of the physical site, implementation of camper safety regulations, continuous visual inspection of campers, and supervision of camper hygiene, wearing apparel, and dining hall behavior. Counsellors should also monitor the amount of rest and sleep campers receive.

7. Many natural and man-made hazards are found at a typical campsite. Administrative personnel must take the necessary steps to either remove these hazards or control the risk factors associated with each of them.

8. When hazards exist that cannot be removed, it is recommended that written procedures or rules be prepared for the handling of each of these hazards.

9. Certain conditions arise in camp programming that may leave individuals and/or the organization open to legal action. These include quality of facilities and equipment, unequal competition between groups, inadequate instruction, and selection and control of high-adventure activities.

10. Laws regarding liability vary considerably from state to state. It is imperative that camp administrators familiarize themselves with regulations that apply in their area.

11. Four factors must be present for proof of negligence: an injury must have occurred, someone must have a duty toward the injured party, there must have been a breach of this duty, and someone's act, or failure to act, must have been the proximate cause of injury.

12. Camp administrators should familiarize themselves with the various defenses against negligence, including act of God, assumption of risk, contributory negligence, lack of proximate cause, trespassing, and sudden emergency.

13. Surveys of litigation against camps over the years pinpoint nine major areas of potential negligence: camper supervision, selection of appropriate camp activities, inadequate camper control, hazardous facilities and equipment, transportation, medical examinations, and corporal punishment.

14. Camp administrators must be conversant with the values and limitations of accident reports as well as permission and waiver forms.

15. The camp staff should be encouraged to develop written safety codes for their camps. The code should comprise specific policies and procedures designed to promote optimal health and safety of all campers and staff.

SELECTED BIBLIOGRAPHY

Appenzeller, H.: Physical education and the law. (Charlottesville: The Michie Co., 1975).

Appenzeller, H., and Appenzeller, T.: Sports and the courts. (Charlottesville: The Michie Co., 1979).

Auld, M., and Ehike, G.: Guide to camp nursing. (Bradford Woods, Martinsville, Ind.: American Camping Association, 1974).

Bolmeier, E. C.: Legality of student disciplinary practices. (Charlottesville: The Michie Co., 1976).

Caden, C.: Risk management insurance, Camping Magazine, **50**(6):15-16, 19, 21, May, 1978.

Chafin, M. B.: Camp emergencies, Camping Magazine, **48**(7):8-9, 22, May, 1976.

Department of Defense: In time of emergency (H-14).

(Baltimore: Civil Defense Preparedness Agency 1977).

Dobec, P.: Health care in camp, Convention Report of the Ontario Camping Association, pp. 59-64, 1976.

Drowatzky, J. N.: Liability: you could be sued, Journal of Health, Physical Education and Recreation, 49(5):17-18, May, 1978.

Frakt, A. N.: Adventure programming and legal liability, Journal of Physical Education and Recreation, 49(4):49-51, Apr., 1978.

Hamessley, M. L.: Handbook for camp nurses and other camp health workers. (Bradford Woods, Martinsville, Ind.: American Camping Association, 1977).

Leibee, H. C.: Tort liability for injuries to pupils. (Ann Arbor, Mich.: Campus Publishers, 1965).

Means, E.: Helpful hints from a camp nurse, Camping Magazine, 42(4):20,22, Apr., 1970.

Melamed, M.: Day camp busing, Camping Magazine, 42:(5):17-18, May, 1970.

Palm, J.: Adventure versus risk, Canadian Camping: National Directory Issue, pp. 5-7, Jan., 1976.

Papp, L.: Build a safe camp, Camping Magazine, 46(1):25,29, Sept./Oct., 1974.

Putt, A. M.: The most important element in camping must be our concern for camper's health and safety, Camping Magazine 45(2):20, 22, Feb., 1973.

Rankin, J.: The legal system as proponent of adventure programming, Journal of Physical Education and Recreation, 49(4):28-29, Apr., 1978.

Resick, M. C., et al.: Modern administrative practices in physical education and athletics. (Reading, Mass: Addison-Wesley Publishing Co., 1979). Chapter 4.

Roos, N. R., and Gerber, J. S.: Government risk management manual. (Tucson, Ariz.: Risk Management Publishing Co.). Section IV.

Schmidt, E. F.: Camping Safety. (Bradford Woods, Martinsville Ind.: American Camping Association, 1971).

van der Smissen, B.: Legal liability of cities and schools for injuries in recreation and parks. (Cincinnati: W. H. Anderson Co., 1968).

van der Smissen, B.: Legal liability—adventure activities. (Albuquerque: ERIC/CRESS, University of New Mexico, 1980).

CHAPTER EIGHT

Food service management

The camp dining hall should be an intrinsic part of the program facilities. Time spent in the dining hall can be filled with fun, satisfaction and good food. Camps should attempt to create a pleasant atmosphere of leisurely good companionship at mealtime.[1]

No matter how rich and varied the experiences offered at camp, none is more paramount to a successful season than camp food. After all, what other camp program involves 2 to 3 hours daily for the entire camp session. Any camp administrator who doubts this, need only eavesdrop on conversations between campers and parents on visitor's day. One of the first questions asked by a parent is likely to be: "How is the food Billie?" or "Are you getting enough to eat, Mary?" When Billie inquires, "Mom, do you think you could make pizza the way the chef cooks it?" the director can be assured that the kitchen staff has at least one strong vote of confidence.

Even if the quality of the food served was not a vital consideration in the eyes of the camper, it deserves the camp director's careful attention since it comprises between 30% and 40% of the annual operating budget of most camps. This amount varies with the size of the camp and whether the camp is eligible for government surplus food. Some agency camps are forced to operate on a low-budget menu while other camps offer more elaborate meals as one of their main promotional thrusts. Regardless, any item that absorbs approximately one third of the camp budget deserves considerable attention from those involved with administrative planning.

The camp menu also plays a significant role in the health of each camper. Parents have a right to expect that their children will receive a nutritious, balanced diet while at camp. Furthermore, an outbreak of a foodborne illness at camp could do irreparable damage to the reputation of an otherwise excellent organization.

Finally, the 40 to 60 minutes spent in the dining hall three times each day should be a pleasant relaxed experience in which social interaction is featured. Unfortunately, camp meals are often characterized as too regimented, too rushed, and a time when a state of constant bedlam prevails. It is difficult to conceive how such conditions can contribute to camper digestion and general good health.

FOOD SERVICE PERSONNEL

The size of the food service staff varies greatly from one camp to another. A small camp serving less than 100 meals per sitting

1. Shivers, J. S.: Camping administration, counselling, programming. (Englewood Cliffs, N.J.: Prentice-Hall Inc., 1971) p. 51.

may have one cook who is assisted by several kitchen helpers. Someone must also act as relief cook to provide the regular cook with time off. On the other hand, a large camp may have a full-time dietitian, several chefs, baker, salad cook, meat cook, and multiple cook's helpers. This staff is invariably supplemented by dishwashers, waiters, and cleanup personnel.

Regardless of the size of the kitchen staff, it is important to designate one person to supervise the total food service operation. In a small camp, this may be the cook; while in a larger organization, the dietitian usually assumes this responsibility. Very large camps may have one or more dietitians. For purposes of clarification, throughout the balance of this chapter, the person responsible for the total food service management is referred to as the coordinator.

Food service coordinator

Food service management involves a variety of duties including planning the menu, ordering, preparing, and storing the food, serving the meal, supervising cleanup, and ensuring careful sanitation practices. It is vital that these various functions be coordinated smoothly under one administrative head.

Qualifications. Because food service managment is so vital to a successful camp, the person chosen should be selected with considerable care. It is recommended that camp directors look for applicants with the following credentials:

1. A minimum of 25 years of age (This ensures the recommended maturity as well as time for the necessary "on the job" experience.)
2. Several years' experience in planning and serving meals in quantity
3. Formal training in nutrition or dietetics as well as management skills
4. Ability to supervise the food service

staff effectively as well as relate to the rest of the camp staff and campers
5. Ability to work within a planned budget
6. Maintenance of a sanitary kitchen and dining room
7. Experience in planning cookouts and trip menus

Responsibilities. The role of the coordinator is diverse and depends to some extent on the size of the camp, the style of meal service, and the nature of the facilities and equipment available. Typically, responsibilities include the following:

1. Assist in the hiring of the food service staff.
2. Plan all meals within the established budget and supervise their preparation
3. Supervise the purchase and storage of all food supplies
4. Organize and supervise the food service staff
5. Plan and supervise the dining room management
6. Assist in the planning of all meals eaten outside the dining room
7. Consult with the medical staff regarding special diets
8. Maintain an accurate inventory of all equipment and food supplies
9. Maintain a sanitary kitchen and dining room including the supervision of the personal hygiene of the food service staff
10. Close up the food service operation at the end of the camp season

Staff participation in camp life

In too many camps, the kitchen staff is viewed as a group apart from the rest of the camp. This pattern is established during the precamp training program and perpetuated throughout the camp season. The food services staff should be included in all staff training sessions that relate to general camp policies, safety, and public relations. There is little point in advising all counsellors of the importance of staff deportment in the local village if the kitchen staff then cause a disturbance. Nor is there much sense in outlining a set of safety policies regarding the waterfront to all campers and counsellors, but excluding the food service staff. If swimming in pairs or wearing a life preserver in a sailboat is important policy for counsellors, it must be equally vital for personnel assigned to the kitchen.

The food service staff should be an important part of the camp team. The same rules must apply to them, but similar privileges should also be extended to them. They should have the same use of facilities as other staff and should be drawn into total program participation. When they are encouraged to participate in the camp program, it is wise to mix them with other members of the staff rather than have them play as a kitchen team. The object is to strengthen the overall staff morale and this can best be achieved by playing *with*, rather than *against*, each other.

Staff morale

One of the biggest headaches confronting camp administrators is the retention of a strong cooperative team in the food service operation. Turnover of staff during the season and from summer to summer is probably greater in the kitchen than any other unit of the camp. Camp owner/directors must give more careful attention to hiring practices and general conditions of employment if this problem is to be overcome. The following points should help resolve the problem of poor morale in the food service area:

1. Sufficient personnel to provide adequate time off and avoid overwork and fatigue

2. Careful job analysis to ensure clear division and chain of responsibilities
3. Recognition of work done so staff members take a real pride in their work
4. Integration of kitchen staff into the general stream of camp life
5. Good facilities and equipment with which to work
6. Comfortable living quarters, including bathing and toilet facilities
7. Proper working conditions in the kitchen such as an adequate heating and cooling system
8. Thorough medical care for minor injuries and illness
9. Prompt payment of competitive wages

Hiring food service personnel

The first person to be hired within the food service unit must be the person who will have administrative responsibility for the unit: the food service coordinator. The coordinator should then play a major role in the recruitment of all other personnel. Similarly, once a head chef or cook has been hired, he or she then collaborates with the coordinator in the selection of other food preparation personnel.

Perhaps in no phase of the recruitment and selection process is the need for references more important. As prospective cooks, assistants, and specialty cooks are invited to apply, letters of recommendation should be mandatory for each applicant. It is further recommended that the food service coordinator make personal contact with previous employees to get a confidential, first-hand report on prospective candidates before engaging them at the camp.

PLANNING THE MENU

Effective menu planning is not a simple exercise. It requires training and experience and is a detailed time-consuming assignment. If the camp does not have a dietitian on staff, the menu should be submitted to one for approval and suggestions. When developing a menu for the first time, it is wise to consult with colleagues from other camps or agencies to get sample menus as a guide.

Systematic menu planning. As the dietitian or food service coordinator prepares to develop the menu, a number of factors should be kept in mind.

1. *Food preference varies with the age and sex of the camper.* Whereas young campers may rave about canned pork and beans with hot dogs sliced in them, that same meal would probably have little appeal for young adults. The latter group might prefer a well-spiced dish of barbecued spare ribs, which would probably have limited appeal for 6 to 8 year olds. Similarly, teenage girls will have different needs regarding quantity and even type of food than those of their male counterparts.

2. *Climate may have profound influence on menu planning.* On cold mornings, hot cereal and cocoa is preferred to ready-to-eat cereal and milk. Warm days suggest the need for fewer hot entrees but larger quantities of cold beverage. Since it is impossible to predict changes in climate with any accuracy, it is necessary to provide a degree of flexibility within the menu plan that allows for these variations in weather.

3. *Food budget allocation may place restrictions on menu planning.* If a given camp allocates $20,000 to the food budget for the camp season, this allows considerably greater freedom and flexibility in food selection and preparation than if the budget is only $15,000.

4. *The range of foods available is a consideration.* If fresh fruits and vegetables are supplied by local farmers, significant savings may be realized.

5. *The types and sizes of storage facilities is a determining factor in menu planning.*

The camp that wishes to use frozen, prepared foods requires considerable freezer space for this purpose. Similarly, large refrigeration compartments permit more quantity buying and the resultant savings in purchase costs.

6. *The size and competence of the food service staff is a factor in menu planning.* One cook may have little difficulty in preparing 100 frozen entrees, whereas two cooks would have considerable difficulty preparing the same number of individual salad molds at one time.

Principles of menu planning

Keeping in mind the constraints that have been outlined above, several guidelines are important.

Planning early. It has already been pointed out that menu planning is a complex procedure. It cannot be done on a week-to-week basis, but should be planned well in advance of the camp season. Since all food supplies that are to be ordered must be determined from the menu, it must be ready early enough to allow ample time to place orders and receive delivery of foods purchased outside the local area. Menus that are planned at the last minute invariably result in haphazard buying of food, which frequently results in more costly purchases. Economical food purchase requires careful planning to avoid overbuying. It also enables the camp to take advantage of special prices.

Using standard recipes. It is strongly recommended that every camp standardize their recipes and keep these in a permanent file. One effective method of filing is to place each recipe on a 5 × 8 inch index card (Fig. 8-1) and keep them in duplicate, one set in a metal index box in the kitchen, and the other with the coordinator's permanent files. The set in the kitchen should be covered with a plastic envelope for longer life.

Standard recipes are usually prepared for

```
  _____        _____
     Name of recipe              Category

  Size of pan _____      Cooking time _____

  No. of servings per pan___  Temperature  _____

  No. of servings to be      Time of preparation____
               prepared  ___
  Ingredients:



  Preparation:


```

Fig. 8-1. Standard recipe card information.

Table 8-1. Conversion of household recipe to standard recipe

6 Servings	Conversion factor	25 Servings
4 eggs	4.18	16.72 = 17 eggs (1½ lb)
⅓ cup sugar (2.3 oz)	4.18	1⅓ cup sugar (10 oz)
¼ teaspoon salt	4.18	1 teaspoon salt
3 cups milk	4.18	12½ cups milk = 3 qt plus ½ cup
1 teaspoon vanilla	4.18	1 tablespoon + 1 teaspoon vanilla

multiples of 25, 50, and 100 servings. If a camp consistently requires a different yield such as 40, 80, 120 servings, these conversions should be made on each recipe. Too many errors result and too much time is wasted if the cook must do the conversion during preparation.

Household recipes may also be converted for quantity preparation. The first step in converting a recipe designed for six persons, is to express the measurements in 25 servings or some workable yield for a particular group size. To determine the conversion factor, divide the desired number of servings (25) by the number of servings in the household recipe (6) to give a factor of 4.18 as shown in Table 8-1. Each of the ingredients in the recipe is then multiplied by the conversion factor to give the new measurements for 25 servings.

In developing standard recipes for large numbers, it is often necessary to test and refine the recipe. For example, the amount of vanilla may be reduced to only one tablespoon. Once the recipe and ingredients are standardized the recipe card should reflect each of these changes.*

Nutritional need and food value. Before the camp menu can be planned, the person responsible for the menu must have a thorough knowledge of the food needs of growing, active children. An examination of camp

---

*For further information on standard recipes see *Standardizing Recipes for Institutional Use*, American Dietetic Association, 620 North Michigan Ave., Chicago, Ill., 60611 (50 cents).

Table 8-2. Nutrients required for health*

Nutrient	Important sources of nutrient	Build and maintain body cells	Some major physiological functions	
			Regulate body processes	Provide energy
Protein	Meat, poultry, fish Dried beans and peas Egg Cheese Milk	Constitutes part of the structure of every cell, such as muscle, blood, and bone; supports growth and maintains healthy body cells	Constitutes part of enzymes, some hormones and body fluids, and antibodies that increase resistance to infection	Supplies 4 calories per gram
Carbohydrate	Cereal Potatoes Dried beans Corn Bread Sugar	Supplies energy so protein can be used for growth and maintenance of body cells	Unrefined products supply fiber for regular elimination; assists in fat utilization	Supplies 4 calories per gram; major source of energy for central nervous system
Fat	Butter, margarine Salad dressing Shortening, oil Sausage	Constitutes part of the structure of every cell; supplies essential fatty acids	Provides and carries fat-soluble vitamins (A, D, E, and K)	Supplies 9 calories per gram
Vitamin A (retinol)	Liver Carrots Greens Sweet potatoes Butter, margarine	Assists formation and maintenance of skin and mucous membranes that line body cavities and tracts, increasing resistance to infection	Promotes healthy eye tissues and eye adaptation in dim light	
Vitamin C	Broccoli Oranges Grapefruit Papaya Mango Strawberries	Forms cementing substances that hold body cells together, thus strengthening blood vessels hastening healing of wounds and bones and increasing resistance to infection	Aids utilization of iron	

Nutrient	Food sources	Functions	
Thiamin (B₁)	Lean pork Nuts Fortified cereal products	Promotes the utilization of carbohydrate; promotes normal appetite; contributes to normal functioning of nervous system	Aids in utilization of energy
Riboflavin (B₂)	Liver Milk Yogurt Cottage cheese	Functions as part of a coenzyme in the production of energy within body cells; promotes healthy skin, eyes, and clear vision	Aids in utilization of energy
Niacin	Liver Peanuts Meat, poultry, fish Fortified cereal products	Functions as a part of a coenzyme in fat synthesis, tissue respiration, and utilization of carbohydrate; promotes healthy skin, nerves, and digestive tract; aids digestion and fosters normal appetite	Aids in utilization of energy
Calcium	Milk, yogurt, cheese Sardines Salmon with bones Collard, kale, mustard, and turnip greens	Combines with other minerals within a protein framework to give structure and strength to bones and teeth	
Iron	Enriched farina Prune juice Dried beans and peas Liver Red meat	Combines with protein to form hemoglobin, the red substance in blood that carries oxygen to and carbon dioxide from the cells; prevents nutritional anemia; increases resistance to infection	Functions as part of enzymes involved in tissue respiration Aids in utilization of energy

*Adapted from National Dairy Council: Nutrients for health, ed. 4. (Rosemount, Ill.: National Dairy Council, 1977).

menus reveals that the nutrients most often lacking are protein, calcium, iron, iodine, and vitamins A, B, B_2, and C. There is usually no problem with vitamin D during summer camp since campers receive ample supplies from sunshine. As young people pass through the accelerated "growth spurt" in early adolescence, they require increased quantitites of protein and calcium.

About 50 different nutrients are required by the human body for optimal growth. These chemical substances build and maintain body cells, regulate body processes, and supply energy to the body. Of these 50 nutrients, ten are considered more important than the others, and every menu must be planned to ensure that these "leader" nutrients are provided in sufficient amounts in the daily diet. Table 8-2 provides a list of the leading nutrients, important food sources, and some of the bodily functions they affect.

The carefully planned menu provides for the inclusion of each of these major nutrients on a daily basis. To achieve this, foods have been divided into four major groups and anyone responsible for planning the camp menu must develop a diet that includes a variety of foods selected from each of the following groups: milk and milk products, meat and meat alternatives, fruit and vegetables, and cereal, bread, and pastas. In addition, certain foods and condiments should be included to compliment, but not replace, foods from the other four groups. These supplementary foods and condiments supply carbohydrates and fat nutrients.

By judiciously selecting foods from each of the major food groups everyday, and preferably for each meal, the nutritional needs of campers can be guaranteed. Whether the menu calls for roast beef, ground beef, or a fresh banana, the food value is much the same. The important thing is to select something from each major group.

Preparing attractive meals. It has been stated that "children eat with their eyes." Food is not appetizing if it does not look attractive. Studies indicate that if food looks good, it is perceived as tasting good. Color, therefore, becomes an important consideration when preparing an attractive meal. It is helpful to plan combinations of colors that contrast well. Baked whitefish with mashed potatoes and cauliflower will not appeal to campers as much as baked whitefish, browned potatoes, carrots, and green beans.

Texture of food is another important consideration. Here again, contrasts between crispy and creamy or firm versus soft foods will invariably add to the attractiveness of a meal.

A third consideration in guaranteeing that a meal is appetizing is the flavor itself. This is particularly true for young campers who, generally speaking, have not developed likings for strongly flavored food. The desire for seasoning and spices is usually acquired only after some years. Young children normally show preference for reasonably bland types of food.

Many camp cooks do not take the trouble to dress up desserts to make them more appealing. These same cooks would be amazed at the increased consumption of caramel or chocolate pudding when a whipped topping is added. Jello is far more attractive with a similar adornment. A tablespoon of sauce converts plain ice cream into a sundae, just as icing on a chocolate cake makes it much more appetizing.

Overcooked foods tend to be unappetizing once they loose their bright, interesting color and texture. For this reason, it is better to undercook vegetables and fruits and to avoid preparing food for long periods before it is to be served.

Planning for variety. Perhaps nothing causes camp meals to be classified as institutional food as quickly as the knowledge that every Tuesday and Friday morning is orange juice, hard-boiled eggs, and toast, and that every Monday evening means macaroni and cheese and canned peaches. Those persons responsible for menu planning should be encouraged to develop an odd day menu cycle of 11, 13, or 15 days so that a particular meal is never served on the same day of the week. The length of the cycle should be such that a camper whose stay is 4 weeks will only have the same meal two or, at the most, three times during that period.

Another way to provide some much needed variety in the menu is to vary the style of service periodically. This might include changing to cafeteria-style service on certain occasions if family style is the prevailing pattern in the dining hall. Serving meals in places other than the dining hall is another means of breaking the monotony. Some camps serve Sunday morning "brunch" occasionally on a come-and-go basis during a 2-hour period. The menu for the brunch may differ quite dramatically from the normal breakfast or lunch meal.

One practice that appears to be gaining popularity is the provision of a salad bar in many camps. Some camps offer this variation once or twice a week, while others provide a salad bar daily for at least one meal. The salad bar requires some additional preparation but has several advantages:

1. It provides the needed variety to break up the mealtime routine.
2. It is possible to provide a variety of vegetables and dressings that would otherwise be difficult to serve.
3. It is an excellent means of offering a balanced, nutritious diet. It has been found that children will eat raw, fresh vegetables under these conditions, perhaps becuase they are free to select that which appeals to them.

A "partial" buffet once or twice a week is another means of introducing variety into camp meals. Here, the buffet is combined with a limited set menu so that the campers again have greater freedom of choice. Many camps find the buffet is an excellent means of using up yesterday's leftovers.

Additional menu-making tips that should be considered when first undertaking this task include:

1. Select dishes and food that campers like. The menu should not reflect the personal likes and dislikes of the person preparing it. There is little to be gained by serving liver just because it is nutritious if no one eats it.
2. At the beginning of each session, serve proven, popular meals such as chicken, pancakes, or French toast.
3. Consider the cooks' workload and available equipment. There must be a balance within each meal in food preparation and availability of cooking space.
4. Usually, something hot should be planned for each meal; the necessary steps should be taken to see that it is served hot.
5. Allow enough flexibility in menu planning to account for weather variance and special program needs.

Other considerations

Noon or evening main meal. Much discussion has centered around the question of when to serve the main meal. Some camp directors have theorized that because the main meal is usually served in the evening in most homes this practice should be continued at camp. Others claim that if the main meal is served at noon, the snack at bedtime is more costly. Some believe that if a substantial breakfast is served, the major meal should be delayed until the evening. It has been reported that a number of cooks prefer the main meal at noon so they can prepare the evening meal at the same time. In this way, the kitchen staff has some free time during the heat of the afternoon.

Surely the most rational approach to this question lies in examining the caloric needs of the camper. If, as one would expect to find in most camps, the daily schedule of activities places relatively equal demands on the camper throughout the day, the three meals should reflect this fact and be well-balanced. This can most easily be achieved by planning a heavy entree with a light dessert and vice versa.

Emergency menu. Electrical storms occur with considerable regularity in some locales. As a result, power may be lost for as much as 48 hours or more. In areas in which this phenomenon is common, contingency plans should be made so that the kitchen and dining room continue to operate efficiently. The best way to handle an emergency is to plan for it. Brief interruptions in power are annoying in that they may delay the normal eating routine, but loss of electrical power for more than several hours calls for other measures.

When the power goes off, the first step is to attempt to determine from the utility company how long the interruption will last. It is then possible to simply delay the meal or make other plans. If the kitchen relies heavily on electrical power, it may be a wise precautionary step to have a portable gas stove available for heating water for a hot beverage or soup.

Many camps plan an emergency menu and set aside specific food supplies that have been purchased for this purpose. These items should be labeled for emergency use and stored together. The types of foods that can be used for this purpose include canned ready-to-eat meats and seafoods, canned fruits and juices, sandwich fillings such as peanut butter, jam, and honey, dry cereals, and dehydrated foods.

Special diets. It seems that each year camps are faced with the problem of coping with an increasing number of requests for special diets. These requests generally fall into two categories: those from persons who have specific food allergies and those from persons who follow a vegetarian or natural food diet. A third, somewhat different group, is comprised of campers who have many personal food dislikes. Camps have sought a number of solutions to the special diet problem, and several of the most common are:

1. Placing complete responsibility with the camper or staff member to avoid the "forbidden" foods (This requires that the kitchen provide some choice of food.)
2. Using the buffet and salad bar
3. Assigning one member of the food service staff to be responsible for all special diets
4. Refraining from enrolling campers, or hiring staff, with special food requests with which the camp is unable, or unwilling, to cope

Snacks and cookouts. Whereas some camps provide a midmorning and afternoon snack as well as some refreshment before retiring, the majority of camps offer only an evening snack. The evening snack may be served in the dining hall or in some other part of the camp such as around the evening campfire. This light refreshment takes many forms including popcorn, cold punch, cookies, hot chocolate, crackers and cheese, cinnamon toast, bread and peanut butter or jam, a candy bar, or a piece of fresh fruit.

Cookouts are considered by many food service coordinators as the most difficult problem for the kitchen staff. They need to be planned well in advance, and careful thought must be given to the menu since many "novice" cooks will be involved in the meal preparation. The preparation should be kept simple and the cooking time reduced as much as possible. Many camps provide precamp training for the staff by conducting several cookouts before the campers arrive. It is also recommended that separate utensils be provided for cookouts. Following the meal, the cleanup is done by campers and staff, and the utensils are cleaned in the dishwasher. Some camps use disposable paper dishes for all meals that are eaten outside the dining hall to avoid the problem of haphazard dishwashing practices.

FOOD PURCHASING, RECEIVING, AND STORING

The food service coordinator should supervise the ordering, purchasing, receiving, and storing of all camp food supplies. Food purchase must remain within the financial limits of the food budget and yet meet the nutritional needs of active campers. The key, then, is to buy food of *good quality* at the *lowest price* and in the *correct quantity*.

To maintain the same quality of food service from year to year, the director or camp committee must be prepared to adjust the food budget in accordance with current food prices and staff salaries. Statistics are readily available that indicate the comparative costs of food from year to year. These statistics should be consulted before determining the camp food budget for a given season. It is also helpful to retain all past records of food purchases and refer to these as current food orders are being planned.

The person responsible for food purchases must also be aware of the range of suppliers available depending on the camp's location. These include retailers, wholesalers, institutional suppliers, sales representatives, product manufacturers, the local market, and the local farmer. To ignore any one of these possible suppliers may mean loss of food bargains.

Planning the food order

An accurate estimate of required food supplies is good economy. Overbuying results in having to dispose of unused items at the end of the camp season. It may not always be possible to return surplus items, especially if containers have been opened. Storing supplies during the off-season should be avoided whenever possible since the quality of nearly all food deteriorates with long storage. Underbuying, on the other hand, invariably requires several small purchases in the latter part of the season, and these orders result in higher prices than those for the same foods purchased in quantity. As the food service coordinator prepares to make up the food order, several things must be considered.

Food budget for the coming season. This is the basis of all fiscal planning and places the limit on expenditures for food supplies.

The menu. Since all foods to be purchased are determined from the actual detailed menu for the camp season, no systematic ordering can be done without it.

Inventory of food supplies on hand. In spite of every attempt to control purchasing, in a large camp it is impossible to use up all supplies at the end of the camp season. "Carryovers" from the previous season should be used first.

Number of meals to be served. It is important to work out in as much detail as possible the number of meals to be served at camp. This includes calculating any new groups and the number of persons out of camp at all times.

Yields from various packages and containers. Quantity cookbooks are available that provide charts on how much to buy for various numbers.

Camp standard recipes. Copies of all standard recipes must be available to the food buyer to determine how much food to order for each dish served.

Foods available in the marketplace. It is essential to know what frozen convenience foods are available or whether fresh fruits and vegetables can be purchased directly from the local farmers or market.

Planned use of each product. Top quality fresh vegetables may be required when served with a meat or fish entree, whereas a cheaper grade can be purchased for a stew without compromising the nutrient value. Similarly, a "standard" or "commercial" cut of beef will be just as flavorable and nutritious in the stew, but a "choice" or "good" grade of beef may be recommended for the entree.

Quality, grade, or other standard for food items. It is important that the food purchaser have a complete understanding of the quality of various foods. For example, turkey gives a better yield than chicken when cut up for creamed dishes. The syrup content and quality of canned fruits varies with the brand and grade. Grade differences in canned fruit and vegetables are based primarily on appearance. Lower grades of fruit are usually riper and somewhat broken, but are quite acceptable as pie filling.

Food cost comparisons

It must be apparent that food cost cannot be equated with nutritional value of foods. The best grade is not always needed, and it is therefore necessary to select the quality of food that is appropriate for its intended use. Food prices can be compared only when items have similar nutritional value, are the same quality, and have the same intended use. There are two methods by which food costs can be compared: unit pricing and cost per serving.

Unit pricing. This refers to the price per measure (pound, quart, kilogram, liter, and so forth).

$$\text{Unit price} = \frac{\text{Price of food package}}{\text{Number of market units}}$$

EXAMPLE: If fresh apples are priced at 5 lbs. for $1.65, the price per unit (lb) is $\frac{1.65}{5} = \$0.31$.

Unit prices can be used to compare food items that are available in two or more different size packages or containers and two or more brands of equal quality. Unit pricing *does not* take into account the amount of food needed for a serving, the amount needed to feed a given number of people, nor the total price of the item. Unit pricing is helpful in determining the minimum price per unit.

Cost per serving. This form of food cost comparison is generally more useful for camp purposes. To determine the cost per serving, the serving size, number of servings in a container, and price of the food item must be known.

$$\text{Cost per serving} = \frac{\text{Price of food item}}{\text{Number of servings per item}}$$

EXAMPLE: A standard serving of milk is 8 ounces and 1 gallon of milk provides 16 servings. If the cost of a gallon of milk is $2.40, the cost per serving is $\frac{\$2.40}{16} = \$0.15$.

Cost per serving is used to compare food items that are similar in nutritional value and quality, available in two or more size containers, and available in different forms: fresh, frozen, canned, or dried. Cost per serving comparisons focus on the quantity of an item to be eaten. This quantity can be the standard serving or the portion the camp plans to serve.

Preparing the food order

Once the information listed above has been assembled, the actual food order can be prepared. The quantity of each food item can be determined in many ways. The following is a simple two-step procedure that has proved effective. First, prepare a market order work sheet as shown in Table 8-3.

Working from the planned menu, list every food item needed in column 1. These should be organized alphabetically by food group. Record the number of meals at which a particular item is to be used in column 2. This figure should be multiplied by the number of times the menu is to be repeated (column 3) to find the total number of times the item will be used in the season (column 4).

Second, prepare a master food order form (Table 8-4). List items alphabetically by food group in column 1. Fill in columns 2 and 5 from the work sheet. Complete column 3 from the yield information. Determine column 4 by dividing 100 by the number in

column 3. Multiply columns 4 and 5 to give the final order in column 6. This process may appear time-consuming, but it is effort well invested. Once the food list has been developed, it will require only minor changes in subsequent years.

Specification sheets

The next step in food purchasing is the preparation and submission of bid specifications to several suppliers. As in other forms of purchase, it is only good business procedure to get prices from two or more suppliers before placing the food order. A specification is a clear, concise statement of the exact food items you wish to purchase (Fig. 8-2). Unless precise details regarding the items are provided, it will not be possible to accurately compare prices. Specification details vary with the type of food ordered. All specifications should include name of food item, grade or quality, size of container or package, number of purchase units, and other relevant information.

It must be emphasized that it is only possible to compare merchandise when one really knows the characteristics of each food item and the market. For example, the yield on meat and poultry varies with the amount of bone, fat, and breading. Whole fish provides one to two 3-ounce servings to the pound, whereas pan-dressed fish will yield

Table 8-3. Sample work sheet for food order

Food item	Number of meals	Number of times menu repeated	Total
Staples			
Canned juices			
Apple	4	3	12
Grape	1	3	3
Grapefruit	2	3	6
Tomato	3	3	9
Cereals			
Corn flakes	3	3	9
Corn meal	2	3	6
Oatmeal	3	3	9

Table 8-4. Sample food order form for camp meal averaging 100 servings per meal

Food item	Grade	Approximate serving per container	Number of containers per 100 servings	Number of times per seasons	Amount to order for season
Canned vegetables					
Green beans	A-Fancy				24 (No. 10)
	B-Extra	25 (No. 10)	4 (No. 10)	6	
	C-Standard				
Tomatoes	A-Fancy				12 (No. 10)
	B-Extra	25 (No. 10)	4 (No. 10)	3	
	Diced-A	25 (No. 10)	4 (No. 10)	3	12 (No. 10)
	Paste-A				

```
                        BID SPECIFICATION FORM
                                          _____
                                             Date

Name of supplier_____

Name of person completing bid_____


                              Container or    Quantity      Unit
    Food item        Grade      package     (No. of units)  price
_____

Corn, Golden, Cream  A-Fancy   4 x #10 Tins    4 cases
Corn, Golden, Whole  A-Fancy   4 x #10 Tins    2 cases
  Kernel
Flour, White, All-   Enriched  50 lbs.         2 bags
  Purpose
Margarine            Fortified 36 x 1 lb.      1 case
```

Fig. 8-2. Sample food order bid specification form.

two to three servings. Raw celery provides five to six servings per pound, but when cooked, it yields only four servings. In summary, comparing food prices is only part of the chore of effectively managing food resources. Equally important is the need to understand what kind of yield a particular item will provide.

When camps are somewhat remote from major suppliers, it may be practical to pay slightly higher prices to enjoy excellent delivery service. This is particularly true in the case of fresh produce, milk, meat, poultry, and fish that must be delivered on a regular basis.

The food purchaser must continually be aware of overbuying. There is often the danger that the purchaser will be persuaded to buy an extra large quantity of one or more items because they are offered at a good price. Sometimes a purchase is made impetuously just because it is on the truck. The best guide to follow at all times is to purchase on the basis of *planned need*. Food supplies that are not fully utilized do not constitute a good buy.

Finally, unless a camp is very small, it is wise to patronize several suppliers. Although there is some convenience in dealing with a single supplier, it is rarely as economical as spreading an order among several bidders. When suppliers know that they have only part of a camp's business, they tend to keep their prices much more competitive than if they are assured of a complete monopoly from year to year.

Food marketing tips

Space does not permit a comprehensive examination of all information that may be necessary regarding food selection and purchase. However, the following suggestions should prove helpful to those persons involved in camp food service management.

1. Big tom turkeys (20 lbs. and up) are the most economical form of poultry.
2. Chicken wings, necks, and backs are cheaper and meatier for making soup than beef soup bones.
3. Protein foods such as baked beans, fish, cheese, and milk can stretch meat dollars. Eggs are an excellent

substitute for meat as lunch and supper dishes.

4. When serving fruit and vegetables to 25 or more persons, buy No. 10 cans. This means fewer cans to store, count, and open.

5. Fruit juice has more nutritive value than fruit drinks.

6. Look for specials in fresh fruits and vegetables during the summer months.

7. Learn to substitute fruits and vegetables for others of comparable nutritional content (for example, cheaper cabbage for expensive tomatoes).

8. Look for bright color in vegetables and fruit. The deeper the green or yellow, the greater the vitamin A.

9. Frozen produce is generally more expensive than the same canned item.

10. Make sure frozen packages are solid block. Ice crystals in the package means that the food has thawed and been refrozen. Both flavor and food value are reduced.

11. Watch for store brand specials. They usually cost a little less and have the same food value as nationally advertised brands.

12. Avoid rusted, bulging, or dented cans. The food inside may be spoiled.

13. Buy canned fruit in light syrups. Heavy syrup has more calories and costs more per serving.

14. Cheeseburgers and pizza are high in nutritional value.

15. Uncooked cereals are less expensive than ready-to-eat cereals and provide a hot meal at breakfast.

16. When selecting cereals, choose at least half of the whole grain type, and the balance, enriched.

17. Bulk milk is cheaper, but state and local ordinances prohibit serving it in some areas.

18. Dried milk is much cheaper than fresh milk and is easy to use in cooking.

Receiving the food order

All too often, much time and care is spent in purchasing food only to have receiving procedures neglected. Frequently when a food order arrives at the kitchen, no one is assigned to receive the order. The first, and most important step, in establishing good receiving procedure is to assign one person to be in charge of receiving all supplies.

The receiver must check the order to make sure that the quality and quantity delivered is in agreement with the invoice. Each item should be checked for weight, count, and quality. Any item not meeting specifications should not be accepted. Torn packages or damaged cans should be rejected. The receiving clerk should also *record* all items for price count and weight. Any discrepancy should be recorded before the invoice is signed.

If the food service coordinator has delegated the responsibility for receiving to another member of the food service staff, this person should report any variance from the order to the coordinator immediately. It may be necessary to change the menu because of these discrepancies.

Food storage

To ensure that food is safe, wholesome, and appetizing, it must be stored properly. If, after having been received and checked, food is permitted to remain exposed to either extreme heat or cold for even a short period, deterioration of quality and infestation, or spoilage, may result.

General storage procedures. Adequate storage space is an important consideration. It is interesting to note that one food management survey of resort hotels indicated that nearly one in every three establishments

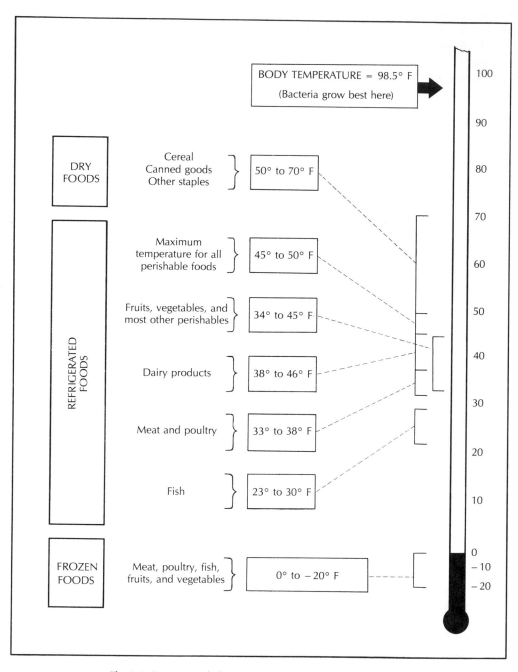

Fig. 8-3. Recommended temperature ranges for storage of foods.

lacked sufficient storage space for efficient food service operation. Without sufficient storage space, it is impossible to take advantage of bulk buying.

A second consideration is the location of storage areas. Adequate space should be located in close proximity to both the receiving and food preparation areas. A thoughtful floor plan should be developed so that food items are stored systematically by food classification. All supplies should be stored 6 to 12 inches off the floor at all times. It is very important that provision be made to rotate all stock. This means that old stock must be regularly moved to the front so that it is used before new supplies.

Care must also be exercised regarding ventilation, moisture, and temperature control. Circulating fans increase the efficiency of storage facilities and reduce the danger of spoilage by maintaining lower temperatures and discouraging the possibility of mold, mustiness, and rusting of metal containers. Temperture control is by far the most important consideration in food storage. To ensure that it is properly regulated at all times, every storage area should be supplied with an accurate thermometer, which should be located prominently.

Types of storage. There are three basic types of food storage, each requiring a different temperature range.

Dry food. This group includes cereals, beans, pasta products, canned goods, and other staples such as sugar and condiments. All dry goods keep well for the normal 8-week camp season when they are stored at temperatures of from 50°F to 70°F.

Refrigerated food. This second group requires temperatures between 32°F and 50°F. It includes all fruits and vegetables (except bananas), eggs, dairy products, fish, meat, and poultry as well as all other perishable products such as opened cans and most leftovers.

Frozen food. Frozen foods require a temperature of 0°F and lower. This group includes foods that must be kept frozen until used such as the convenience foods.

A chart of recommended temperatures at which foods should be stored is shown in Fig. 8-3.

Storing leftovers. Once a package or can has been opened, the danger of food spoilage increases sharply because of moisture, heat, and human contamination. Rodents may also be an added concern in the case of dry foods. The following suggestions will prove helpful in storing opened containers or foods that are kept for another meal.

1. Cover opened cans with tight-sealing plastic lids. Many vendors have these lids available in a variety of sizes.
2. Acid foods, such as citrus juice and tomatoes, should not be stored in the can since they tend to take on the metallic taste of the container.
3. Opened cans should be used within 48 hours before the quality of the food deteriorates.
4. Large plastic or metal refuse cans, when plastic lined, make an excellent container for 50 to 100 pounds of dry foods such as flour, rice, and sugar. As long as the container has a tight-fitting lid, it will keep out insects, rodents, and moisture.
5. Cheese should be tightly wrapped to prevent it from drying out.
6. Eggs should be refrigerated to allow good circulation of air around them.

Food odors. Some foods give off odors, while others absorb foreign aromas. These foods require separate storage or sealed containers. Among the foods emitting odors are cabbage, cantaloupe, melons, onions, fresh apples, peaches, and potatoes. Some common foods that absorb odors are butter, cheese, cornmeal, eggs, flour, nonfat dry milk, and rice. Cleaning items such as soap, waxes, and disinfectants may also be the source of unwanted odors.

Cleaning food storage areas. All storage areas should be swept daily with a nonpungent sweeping compound and mopped at least once a week. In addition, shelves, mobile food carts, and walls should be washed regularly. Any food that is dropped or spilled should be cleaned up immediately and the area scrubbed or mopped. Refrigeration and freezer units must be kept in good repair and inspected frequently.

THE KITCHEN

In the early days of the camping movement, most kitchens consisted of antiquated, used stoves and other inefficient and unsanitary food preparation equipment. Some of these outmoded kitchen operations are still in existence today, but the vast majority of camps have made great advances toward modern, efficient food service management.

With the high cost of labor, it is imperative that kitchen management be planned to provide quality meals with the least number of staff. This implies that the physical layout of the kitchen and the equipment must receive careful consideration. It may appear that some new, high-speed equipment is inordinately expensive for an economical operation, but it must be remembered that costs can be depreciated over a number of years whereas the payroll for food service personnel is always present.

For this reason, the guidance of professional food service consultants who specialize in camping and conference centers becomes a necessity. It is their job to study means of making food service operations more efficient. The camp food service coordinator should not hesitate to make use of their expertise. One such group is the National Sanitation Foundation (NSF). This is a nonprofit, noncommercial organization that conducts or sponsors ongoing research

to facilitate construction sanitation. Kitchen equipment may only be awarded the NSF seal of approval when it has met their stringent standards. It would be wise for camps to require the NSF seal on all new equipment purchases.

Physical layout

A camp food service operation should be patterned after large commercial food service establishments. Facilities should provide for a smooth, efficient flow from raw foods through the food preparation area to the dining room. The operation begins with the receiving area that should, whenever possible, provide a receiving platform at truck unloading level that is covered and protected from the elements.

Although many possible layouts may be used in planning a camp kitchen, generally speaking, the food preparation area should be located in the center of the room. In addition, all cooking equipment should be centralized so that plumbing, electrical, or gas installations may be made at minimal cost. Great savings in energy and time can also be made through the efficient use of space. When purchasing new equipment, it is advisable to consider modular-type preparation and serving tables. These tables provide for the addition of units at any time and offer great flexibility in the kitchen operation.

Most camps develop a kitchen design that enables the prepared food to be placed on mobile serving carts immediately adjacent to the preparation area. Again, the object is to provide efficient use of space with the minimum number of wasted steps. Strategic location of hot food holding equipment, milk or juice machines, and extra flatware can also save the food service staff additional work.

The floor surface for the kitchen area is an important consideration. It should be seamless and nonabsorbent for cleanliness and sanitation. At the same time, it must be a safe, nonslip surface.

The dishwashing system should be located adjacent to the dining hall to permit efficient return of dirty dishes. It should be removed from the food preparation area to avoid unnecessary congestion. The primary consideration is a layout that involves minimum movement and handling of dishes so that scraping, washing, and stacking may be done economically.

In addition to the main cooking, food preparation, and dishwashing areas, several other facilities are required. Toilet facilities should be provided for staff within the general kitchen area. This room should be kept spotlessly clean at all times. A small office should also be available for the food service coordinator and located so that the total food operation may be observed. The office should contain a desk, telephone, and appropriate filing system for the various food service records that must be kept. Many camps also provide a small lounge where kitchen personnel may relax and eat their own meal in relative quiet.

A well-ventilated refuse storage room must be constructed. It should be elevated on a solid concrete slab permitting easy removal of refuse. It must be fly and rodent free and washed down regularly with an antibacterial agent. A closet for cleaning equipment should also be provided away from the food storage and preparation areas.

Equipment and utensils

When purchasing kitchen equipment, a number of factors should be considered. The following material is based on recommendations made by the Consumer Education and Human Nutrition and Food Division of Cornell University.

Need. Before any new item is purchased, it must be determined whether the kitchen will operate more efficiently with it. A good guide when considering a new item is to expect that any piece of equipment must be used at least 7 hours per week to justify its purchase.

Performance. Efficiency of function is paramount for every new purchase. Does it meet the specific job requirements for which it is to be purchased? It must also be easy to operate, otherwise staff will avoid it.

Sanitation. All equipment must be easily cleaned and maintained in a sanitary condition. Equipment that is complicated to clean may lose much of its potential efficiency as a labor-saving device.

Flexibility. A piece of equipment that can be used for a variety of jobs is usually easier to justify as a new purchase.

Safety. All kitchen equipment should be designed to safeguard the user. Safety guards and valves and wheel locks on mobile pieces are all important considerations.

Cost. The cost of any item should include initial cost, installation charge if any, maintenance costs, operating costs, and depreciation costs. It is possible that the initial capital outlay on an item may be high, but energy saving and low service charges, defrayed over several years, make it a good investment.

Service. The availability of service and parts must also be considered. The best safeguard is to purchase from reputable dealers who stand by their products.

Kitchen equipment. Whenever possible, camps should install sinks, tables, dishtables and the like of stainless steel. They are easy to clean, require no painting or refinishing, and have negligible deterioration. In addition, stainless steel is not affected by food acids or alkalies, nor does it rust or scratch with normal scouring.

Consultants recommend different pieces of equipment for different camps, but several items seem to be almost universal in their acceptance.

Meat slicer. This is considered an essential item because of its versatility. When placed on a mobile carrier, it becomes even more adaptable.

Convection oven. This high-speed oven has a fan that blows the heat uniformly around the food, cutting cooking time by almost two thirds. The savings in both time and utility costs is further augmented by its large capacity.

Commercial foodmixer. This is another very adaptable item that comes in 30, 60, and 80 quart sizes. It has numerous attachments and can be used as a meat grinder, vegetable and fruit slicer, or blender.

Steam kettle and steam cooking unit. These units are capable of cooking large quantities of food with minimal power in a short period. The number of dishes that can be prepared using this low-pressure steam method is almost unlimited. An added virtue of the steam cooking units is that they require very little space.

Mobile carts. Every camp should consider the use of various sizes of movable carts.

They may be used to hold prepared hot food, in which case heated, thermostatically controlled carts are recommended. A supply of 18 × 26 inch tray carts can be wheeled to each table ensuring that food is maintained at predetermined temperatures until served. Tray carts may also be used as holding carts for desserts, salads, or prepared food to be refrigerated.

Refuse containers. These should be located strategically around the kitchen and stored under counters, shelves, or tables when not in use.

Kitchen utensils. Selection of pots, pans, and other utensils that are appropriate in size, material, and construction are important to the efficient operation of the kitchen. When selecting kitchen utensils, consideration should first be given to their intended use rather than purchasing solely on the basis of relative costs. Table 8-5 shows the comparative characteristics of the most popular utensils.

When selecting baking and roasting pans, sizes should be chosen that provide maxi-

Table 8-5. Comparison of kitchen utensil materials

Material	Advantages	Disadvantages
Aluminum	Good heat conductor; easy to clean; lightweight	Strong alkaline detergent and salt water pit the surface; lightweight aluminum dents easily; will scratch with severe scouring; discolored by some foods
Stainless steel	Does not rust or scratch with scouring; is not normally affected by food acids or alkalies	Excessive heat may cause oxidation stains; poor heat conductor; pans may develop hot spots where food sticks and burns
Cast iron	Good heat conductor; holds heat well; relatively inexpensive	Heavy; rusts; breaks upon severe impact
Glass and porcelain enamel	Relatively inexpensive	Unsatisfactory for camp because of breakage

mum use of oven space while still allowing for air circulation around the pans. Similarly, when purchasing stock pots, the diameter should be no larger than the distance between the centers of the individual burners. For example with a ten-burner, restaurant-size stove, it should be possible to use all ten burners with stock pots that do not exceed 11 inches in diameter.

Large dishpans, holding from 16 to 20 quarts, make excellent lightweight mixing bowls for salads and other ingredients.

Dishwashing. An efficient sanitary dishwashing procedure is mandatory. Most large camps have installed commercial dishwashers, but many smaller camps continue to wash dishes by hand.

Commerical dishwasher. This should be a heavy duty unit that includes a recirculating prewash cycle. It should also have an adequate thermostatically controlled heating unit to ensure a final rinse water of 180°F. In many cases, a separate booster may be necessary to guarantee sufficient hot water. An electrically operated detergent dispenser is also recommended as an economy measure. An exhaust fan should be installed over the dishwasher and good ventilation provided for the entire area.

All tableware and flatware should be handled as little as possible after washing to reduce the possibility of human contamination. Cups and glasses should remain upside down in the washing trays, which are placed on portable dollies. These can then be wheeled into the dining room for table setting. Flatware should be placed handles up in tote boxes with cylindrical containers for each type of silver.

*Washing by hand.** Thorough washing and rinsing significantly reduces the number

---

*This section is based on 1962 revised recommendations of the United States Public Health Service Sanitation Ordinance and Code.

of bacteria on dishes. For dishes to be considered safe, they should be *sanitized*, which can be achieved in one of two ways.

Dishes that are immersed for at least 30 seconds in water that is a minimum of 170°F will be sanitized. Pouring boiling water over dishes is *not* satisfactory. To sanitize flatware and tableware in this manner, it is necessary to provide long-handled, wire baskets to hold the dishes, a sink deep enough so that the 170°F water completely covers the dishes, a thermostatically controlled heater to hold the water temperature at a minimum of 170°F, and an accurate thermometer to test the water temperature. The disadvantage of this method of sanitation is that 170°F water will scald the washer's hands.

A second technique, and the one that is more acceptable, is to immerse dishes in a chemical sanitizing agent for a minimum of 60 seconds. In this method, the water temperature need only be 75°F or more. A variety of sanitizing agents are available, and food service coordinators should check to determine which are acceptable in a given state or province. It must also be remembered that food scraps and detergents interfere with the sanitizing action of all these chemicals. Dishes must therefore be scraped, washed, rinsed, and drained before they receive the sanitizing treatment. The rinse water containing the agent must also be changed regularly to ensure sufficient concentration of the antibacterial agent.

Dishes that are sanitized by immersion in 170°F water need not be towel dried since the dishes are hot enough to cause the water to evaporate very quickly. When dishes are immersed in a sanitizing agent, they should be air dried whenever possible. If, however, a camp does not possess sufficient counter space, it may not be feasible to air dry all the dishes. In this case, care must be taken to ensure that the towels are clean and sanitary. There is always a danger that clean dishes will become contaminated from bacteria on dirty towels.

To efficiently wash dishes by hand, the following are required: sufficient work space, a three-compartment sink (or three large dishpans) for washing, rinsing, and sanitizing dishes, plenty of hot water, and appropriate equipment including rubber scrapers, synthetic detergent, and plenty of sanitized towels if dishes cannot be air dried. Following are step-by-step instructions for washing dishes by hand:

1. *Scrape the dishes* to remove excess food particles.
2. *Rinse the dirty dishes*. If space permits, rinse or preflush the dishes: those with egg, cheese, or starchy foods in cold water; those with gravy, sugar, or syrup in hot water.
3. *Stack the dishes* by separating glassware, tableware, and flatware.
4. *Wash the dishes* in clean water and a synthetic detergent. The water should be as hot as the hands can stand (100°F to 120°F). Keep changing the water so it is clean and hot. Wash the glassware first and then the silver.
5. *Rinse the dishes* in clean, hot water.
6. *Sanitize the dishes* by one of the two methods described above.
7. *Air dry dishes* if possible. Otherwise dry them using plenty of clean, sanitized towels.
8. *Handle the sanitized dishes as little as possible*. Place them in mobile dollies that can be moved directly to the tables for setting.
9. *Wash dishcloths and towels and sanitize* using the same method as for the dishes. Hang towels where they will dry quickly and be free from insects. Store clean, dry towels where they are protected from contamination.
10. *Clean dishpans, sinks, and all work surfaces* using the sanitizing agent.

THE DINING ROOM
Physical layout

Several factors can contribute to a relatively serene dining hall. The first of these is the actual location of the hall. Insofar as possible, it is desirable to locate the building among a beautiful stand of trees with a fine view of the lake so that the building becomes a part of nature. At all costs, one should avoid the impression that this is a city cafeteria simply transposed to a country site. If an attractive location with a fine view is possible, it naturally follows that expansive window space should bring nature's beauty into the dining room.

Within the dining hall itself, control of camper and staff movement is an important consideration. If one quarter of the persons are continuously on their feet, this will not be conducive to a relaxed, leisurely meal. Much care must be given to smooth efficient traffic flow with sufficient space for persons to move freely without jostling or forcing others to adjust their chairs so they may pass. Equipment such as milk and cold drink machines, drinking fountains, or ice-making machines must be strategically located to minimize the number of steps required. In addition, an efficient style of serving must be developed to keep traffic to the very minimum.

The acoustics in the dining hall should also be a vital concern. Even when a careful plan of dining hall management has been adopted, with 100 or more vital, active, young people under one roof, there will be a considerable undercurrent of sound in the hall most of the time. Proper acoustical treatment of the facility can do much to minimize this factor. It may be necessary to consult with an expert in building design to solve this problem.

Furnishings

Perhaps no single factor is more important in establishing the decorum of the dining room than the proper selection of tables and chairs. The noise level in many dining halls could be reduced by as much as 50% with the discarding of long, rectangular tables and the adoption of square, octagonal, or circular tables. When rectangular tables 8 to 10 feet long are used, campers must raise their voices when requesting the salt and pepper if it is located at the far end of the table. As this process is multiplied ten or 20 times at other tables, the decibel count rises precipitously. Table 8-6 provides some of the strengths and weaknesses of various table shapes.

Whereas rectangular and square tables permit the use of benches or chairs, circular and eight-sided tables require the use of chairs. Chairs should be of the metal, stack-

ing variety so that they may be easily stored. Many camps advocate folding tables for the same reason.

Color adds much to the aesthetic appearance of the camp dining room. Children appreciate bright, lively colors, and an assortment of matching colors on table tops and chairs can greatly enhance the room.

When campers use wheelchairs at the dining room table, it is highly desirable to use adjustable tables so that the height of the eating surface can be raised or lowered to accommodate the chairs as well as meet the campers personal requirements.

Dining room equipment

Tableware. Attractive, durable tableware can be purchased in china, glass, and plastic.

Table 8-6. Comparison of dining room table shapes

Type	Number of settings	Size	Advantages	Disadvantages
Rectangular	8	72″ × 36″ (young campers) 72″ × 40″ (older campers)	Adaptable to banquet and other uses; low-cost construction	Poor communication; counsellor too isolated; difficulty reaching food at far end of table; square corners impede traffic flow
Square	8	48″ × 48″	Adaptable to banquet and other uses; fairly good communication; low-cost construction (This is a compromise between a rectangular table and the two types below.)	Only fair ease reaching food; square corners impede traffic flow
Octagonal	8	48″ corner to corner (young campers); 60″ corner to corner (older campers)	Excellent communication; excellent ease reaching food; equality—no "head" or "foot" at table	Costlier construction; unsatisfactory for banquet and other uses; difficult to set extra place
Round	8	48″ diameter (young campers); 60″ diameter (older campers)	Excellent communication; good ease reaching food; equality—no "head" or "foot" at table	Costlier construction; unsatisfactory for banquet and other uses

Each has its advantages and weaknesses so that food service coordinators must make their choice based on their particular needs and preferences.

When purchasing tableware, it is wise to select an "open-stock" pattern, which simplifies the task of procuring replacements. Narrow rim plates provide the same surface area for food, but require less storage space. A chart indicating the characteristics of each type of tableware is shown in Table 8-7.

Flatware. When selecting flatware, utensils should feel balanced and comfortable. Some patterns provide slightly smaller knives and forks for small children. A simple design should be chosen to facilitate cleaning. There are basically two choices available in flatware: silver plate and stainless steel. On nearly all counts, the latter is recommended for camp use. It is lighter more durable, and less costly than silver plate. Stainless steel resists tarnish, rust, and scratches and maintains its luster with normal washing.

Glassware. Lead glass is usually preferred over lime glass for camp use. It has a finer texture and higher luster and is less brittle. On the other hand, lime glass is usually heavier. Glasses should be chosen so that they cannot be stacked on top of each other. Glasses are also available in plastic, both transparent and colored. They are lightweight and resistant to breakage. They do, however, scratch easily and are therefore harder to clean.

Trays. These are available in a wide range of materials including anodized aluminum, fiberglass, hard rubber, laminated paper, melamine plastic, and stainless steel. The metal trays are noisy, and aluminum trays may dent. Fiberglass and plastic trays are the most widely used in camps. Dishes tend to slip on plastic trays, but they are less expensive than fiberglass. The recommended size for camp use in 14 × 18 inches.

Dining room management

Management of the dining hall involves setting tables, methods of serving the meal, return of dirty dishes, and dining hall cleanup. The first and last of these assignments are usually assigned to the same group of staff members.

Table setting and cleanup. There are several different practices regarding who sets tables and who cleans up after the meal, including: (1) paid waiters or waitresses, (2) dishwash-

Table 8-7. Comparison of tableware

Type of tableware	Advantages	Disadvantages
China (vitreous or porcelain)	Easy to clean—smooth, hard surface; stain resistant unless glaze is worn off; resists breakage fairly well (heavy duty best)	Heavy for campers to handle; expensive; cups must be stored in single layers
Glass	Stain resistant—no glaze to wear off; less expensive than china or plastic	Shatters dangerously; colors may fade with use
Plastic (melamine)	Lightweight; quiet to use; very little breakage; poor heat conductor so food does not cool off quickly; cups may be stacked	Scratches easier than china or glass; gloss is destroyed with heavy abrasives—more difficult to clean; picks up stains when gloss is removed; cost similar to hotel china

ers, (3) junior counselling staff (CIT), (4) selected group of campers who receive reduced tuition rates, and (5) all campers on a rotating basis.

Regardless of the method used, one person must supervise the operation. A popular practice is to lay out a sample place setting before each meal for all to follow. It is also vitally important that the person in charge train all table setters to practice scrupulous personal hygiene when handling tableware or food. It cannot be assumed that young men or women will pursue rigorous sanitation practices without encouragement and direction from the dining hall steward.

Methods of serving. There are several different methods of moving the food from the kitchen to the tables. Some camps employ waiters or waitresses, each of whom serves a number of tables; some appoint campers to carry the food; while others believe that all campers should be responsible for selecting their own food much as in commercial cafeterias.

Family-style service. This is by far the most common method of serving and usually involves the counsellor assigning one or more campers to bring the food from the kitchen to the table after all the campers have been seated. The campers carry the food in serving bowls, or on trays, or it may be delivered to the tables by mobile cart. The food is either served by the counsellor, or the bowls and platters are passed around the table for campers to help themselves.

Cafeteria-style service. In this method, all campers take a tray and line up for their own food, which is served by the kitchen staff from one or more serving counters. This is far less formal than family-style service and results in much traffic in the dining hall throughout the meal.

Camps also employ different types of seating plans. It is customary in family-style service to require all members of a sleeping unit to sit together at one table. However, when cafeteria style is used, it is fairly common to permit the campers to choose their own table, since the sleeping unit rarely goes through the food line as a group.

There has been considerable debate over many years as to which of the two methods of serving is preferable. Both sides contend that food saving is greater with their method. The law in many states prohibits the re-serving of any food placed on the tables if the package or container has been opened. This suggests that there should be less food returned to the kitchen in the cafeteria method. However, adherents of family-style service maintain that as long as the food is pre-portioned before it leaves the kitchen, there is little waste. They further contend that whereas young children may be hesitant to tell a relative stranger behind the counter how much of each item they desire, campers have no such inhibitions with their own counsellor.

The question of which method requires less paid staff is also open to debate. It is certainly true that family-style service requires many more serving bowls and platters, and these must be scraped and washed after each meal. This, however, may be offset by the fact that counsellors or campers do most of the individual serving in family-style service, whereas kitchen staff serve everyone in cafeteria-style service.

Return of dirty dishes. Regardless of the method chosen, it is recommended that main course dishes be returned to the dishwashing area before dessert is served. In this way, food is prevented from congealing on tableware and platters, greatly facilitating the dishwashing chore. Some camps follow the practice of having campers scrape all plates at each table before returning them to the kitchen, which saves the dishwashers much time. Unfortunately, it is seen by many as negating the very decorum that camps are striving to develop in their dining halls. A suitable compromise may be to have campers scrape the plates but in a secluded alcove just as they return them to the dishwashers.

SANITATION AND FOODBORNE ILLNESS

One of the major areas of concern for the camp food service coordinator is the possible threat of a foodborne illness or food poisoning. This is not a simple problem to overcome, because the microorganisms that cause foodborne illness are always present. Every food contains some active, or potentially active, microorganisms and virus. The real task is to *prevent their growth and transmission*.

It is estimated by the Federal Center for Disease Control that over 4000 customers in the United States contact foodborne illness every day. It is disturbing to examine these figures and learn that since the late 1940's there has been no reduction in these outbreaks. Clearly, food service establishments do not have bacterial growth in food under control.

Microbiological agents

Microorganisms require four basic environmental conditions in which to multiply. They must have *food*, which is usually a mixture of protein, sugar, and vitamins. They also require optimal *temperature*. Slow growth may begin as low as 44°F and increases up to 90°F to 115°F., where maximum multiplication takes place. As the temperature approaches 125°F., growth is again retarded. *Moisture* is also required in a neutral or mildly acid environment. Finally, optimal growth occurs over *time*. It should be noted that whereas all four conditions are necessary for optimal growth, bacteria may survive under extremely adverse conditions.

There is no such thing as zero contamination in a conventional camp food service

Table 8-8. Major microbiological agents of foodborne illness

Agent	Cases by percentage
Staphylococcus	32
Salmonella	31
Clostridium perfringens	16
Hepatitis (virus A)	4
Other (streptococcus, botulinum, and the like)	17

operation. This is no cause for concern, however, because at low levels there is no danger. Healthy persons continually ingest infectious microorganisms. It is the level of contamination that is important.

Cooked foods represent a far greater hazard than raw foods. The latter may have just as high a bacterial count and yet be safe because of the presence of nonpathogenic bacteria, which results in spoilage of the food. Spoilage bacteria cause raw food to smell and look bad when the count gets high enough, but as they multiply, they prevent the growth of contamination-causing agents.

A problem arises when a small number of pathogenic bacteria survive the normal cooking process, because that same process inactivates the nonpathogens. The important thing for the camp food service coordinator to control is the potential growth of pathogenic organisms and thus hold the danger of a foodborne outbreak to the minimum. The main causes of microbiological contamination are shown in Table 8-8.

Visual versus bacterial cleanliness

Work areas, equipment, and utensils in a camp kitchen may appear spotless but still harbor millions of pathogenic organisms. To be confident of bacterial cleanliness, the following steps must be observed by the staff:

1. *Use a clean, warm, detergent solution to wash*. This step helps remove the dirt or food particles on which bacteria feed. In the

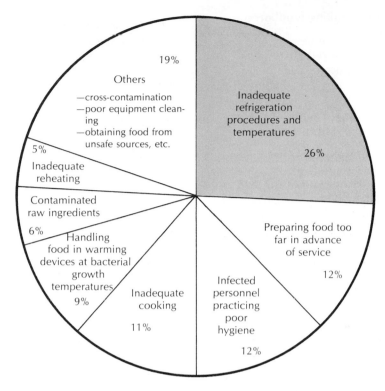

Fig. 8-4. Food preparation causes of foodborne illness.

cleaning process, dirt particles use up the detergent and so it must be replenished regularly.

2. *Use clean cloths or disposable paper towels.* Do not use sponges to apply the sanitizing solution because they cannot be cleaned and sanitized adequately. Cloths should be cleaned and sanitized regularly.

3. *Use separate containers for the clean and sanitized solution.* Protein destroys the sanitizing ability of chemicals and so the sanitizing solution must be changed regularly.

4. *Cleaning and sanitizing materials should be stored in a separate room or closet.* It is wise to permit access to these chemicals to only one person who is trained to mix the exact strength of the solutions.

5. *Sanitizing sprays are safe for food preparation areas.* The Food and Drug Administration has thoroughly tested the use of spray sanitizers and reports them safe for use on work surfaces as long as the concentrations recommended are not exceeded and the solution is allowed to dry thoroughly.

6. *Cross-contamination must be avoided.* The cleaning-rinsing-sanitizing sequence is particularly important after raw food is handled and before cooked food is prepared.

Causes of foodborne illness

The Federal Center for Disease Control has investigated the causes of food poisoning for several years and reports that lack of proper refrigeration and temperature control results in twice as many outbreaks as any other single cause. The top seven offenders are listed in Fig. 8-4.

Procedures for controlling foodborne illness hazards

As has already been stated, the food service coordinator cannot eliminate the existence of dangerous pathogens, but much can be done to contain the growth and transmission of these organisms. Reduced to its simplest equation this means that:

$$\frac{\text{Contaminated}}{\text{food}} + \frac{\text{Growth and}}{\text{transmission}} = \frac{\text{Foodborne}}{\text{illness hazard}}$$

The three main sources of hazards that can be controlled are: the time-temperature sequence, contamination of the food source, and human contamination.

Time-temperature control. The time-temperature relationship refers to the *time it takes pathogenic organisms to multiply at a given temperature*. Contamination can be arrested or retarded by either heating food rapidly to a temperature above 115°F or cooling it rapidly below 50°F.

When pieces of food are large, a mixture is thick and viscous, or the food is in large batches, special treatment is required to bring the entire mass from 115°F to 50°F within a 2-hour period. Solid foods such as meat and poultry should be cut into smaller pieces, placed in a shallow tray, and pre-cooled on ice or refrigerated at once. Liquids, such as soup and gravy, should be cooled in batches of no more than 2½ gallons. Cooling can be speeded up by placing the mixture in cold water and stirring continuously before refrigerating. Potato, egg, and meat or poultry salads, as well as puddings, should be cooled quickly in shallow pans.

During food preparation, some of the high hazard foods such as meat, poultry, fish, eggs, and milk may be held at dangerous levels (70°F to 100°F) for several hours. Within this range microorganisms multiply rapidly. Every possible precaution should be taken to have food in the 50°F to 115°F range for a maximum of 2 hours.

Food that is ready for serving should be held at temperatures above 115°F. If it is necessary to hold food for 1 to 1½ hours, the temperature should be at least 170°F when placed in warming equipment. Warming equipment is not normally capable of heating food. Freezing will destroy many, but not all, pathogens. Those that survive freezing are capable of growing after the food is thawed. It is not recommended that food be frozen on the camp premises unless the food can be prepared rapidly and frozen quickly. Cooked foods that are to be frozen should be heated to 170°F, cooled rapidly, and stored in small batches or shallow containers to accelerate freezing. Refrigerated food should be kept at 40°F, while all frozen foods must be held at 0°F or lower.

Frozen foods should be prepared in the frozen state whenever possible. When thawing is necessary, it should be done in the refrigerator or under cold running water. Commercially frozen food should be delivered in refrigerated trucks and transferred directly to the freezer. Items that show evidence of thawing should not be accepted.

Leftover food requires special treatment since the hazard of contamination is especially high. Cold leftovers should be refrigerated at once. When storing warm leftovers, they should be reheated to boiling temperatures, if possible, and then quickly cooled and refrigerated. Cooked food that has been refrigerated should be used within 24 hours.

Food source hazards. The best insurance against the hazards that food itself presents is to purchase from reputable suppliers. Because different food groups may be considered high or low hazard, it is necessary to examine each group separately.

Foods containing no protein and little or no moisture are low hazard, whereas foods with high protein that require refrigeration or freezing are high risk. Most dry goods such as flour, pasta, sugars, dried meat, and vegetables are safe. They are all contaminated with bacteria but lack sufficient moisture and nutrient to support growth. Oils are also safe because, although a liquid, they contain no water. Fresh vegetables are low hazard since they do not contain much protein for food. In addition, nonpathogenic bacteria offer too much competition. Vegetables should, however, be washed to prevent transmission of viruses. Although most of the above are low-hazard foods, they can contaminate dishes when mixed with high-hazard foods (for example, meat casserole or salad).

Canned foods are generally quite safe until opened. The exception may be dented or swollen cans. Home-canned food should be avoided.

Since freezing stops the growth of most bacteria, frozen foods can be considered safe while frozen. However, frozen food that has been defrosted and frozen again must be classified as high risk.

Of all groups, animal protein foods that require refrigeration are the most dangerous. These include meat, poultry, fish, and shellfish. Meats contain staphylococcus and perfringens, poultry harbors salmonella, and fish may support all three. The best safeguard is to purchase from reputable sources so that the initial bacterial count is low.

Dairy products are also considered high-risk foods, not because they are initially badly contaminated, but milk, eggs, and cheese can act as an ideal environment for the growth of pathogens.

Human contamination hazards. Whereas foods carry many microorganisms, humans harbor hundreds of thousands of bacteria. The main source of transmission is the *hands*. Sanitation regulations state that no person with a contagious disease may handle food. Whereas this principle is sound, it must not be implied that healthy persons do not carry food poisoning pathogens. The very slightest trace of human feces on the hands or under the nails is capable of transmitting hundreds of thousands of microorganisms. There is no more extreme source of potential contamination. Toilet hygiene, therefore, is a critical point in the control of potential foodborne illness. Camp food coordinators must be prepared to invoke the most stringent handwashing routine to minimize this hazard.

Refuse storage and disposal

A final step in ensuring good sanitation procedures is the storage and disposal of refuse. The objective must be to leave the total food service area clean and free of materials that might attract bacteria-carrying insects and animals. Perhaps the most important consideration in this regard is the control of flies, a common carrier of salmonella. By far the most effective means of eliminating flies, as well as vermin and rodents, is to follow good sanitation practices conscientiously. The guidelines below are recommended:

1. Clean and sanitize floors, walls, work surfaces, and food equipment regularly.
2. Store all refuse in 16- to 20-gallon metal or heavy plastic garbage containers. These should have a smooth surface and be cleaned regularly.
3. Place disposable, heavy plastic liners in each refuse container and fold the top back over the upper edge of the can so that no refuse comes in contact with the can itself.
4. Locate refuse containers in several strategic areas around the kitchen for convenient and efficient disposal.
5. When not in use, refuse containers should be covered with tight-fitting lids and placed under work counters or tables.
6. Seal refuse in the plastic liner and remove it from the kitchen after each meal.
7. Store refuse in a raised, completely fly-

Table 8-9. Guidelines for prevention of foodborne illness

Guide	Rationale
Food contamination	
Use only water from safe sources. Test frequently.	Contaminated drinking water may cause typhoid fever and other diseases.
Deal with reputable food suppliers.	All food carries bacteria. Reputable firms control the initial numbers of bacteria.
Purchase meats that bear the federal inspection stamp or have been inspected locally.	Inspection guarantees that animals were not diseased before slaughter.
Use only pasteurized dairy products.	Tuberculosis, typhoid fever, and undulant fever microorganisms may be carried by milk products.
Human contamination	
Food handlers should wash and scrub hands frequently with soap and water, especially after using the toilet	The gastro-intestinal tract harbors many bacteria. Human feces is particularly virulent.
Staff members with a sore throat or a recent case of diarrhea should not handle food.	Infected sores usually carry large numbers of staphylococcal bacteria.
Staff members should avoid coughing or sneezing on food or work surfaces. The mouth and nose should be covered with a handkerchief and the head turned away from food.	Bacteria-laden droplets may be spread as far as 9 feet when sneezing. Remember that hands become contaminated when they touch a dirty handkerchief.
Hands should be kept away from the mouth, nose, and hair. If contact is made, the hands should be washed thoroughly.	The mouth, nose, and hair are particular heavy sources of microorganisms.
The hands are the main carrier of human contamination. They should be kept out of food as much as possible and away from tableware that contacts the camper's mouth.	Clean hands are quickly contaminated as they touch any unclean object or surface.
When food must be handled with the hands, extra precaution should be taken to clean the hands.	Cross-contamination may easily result from the handling of raw food and then prepared food.
Hair restraints or a cover should be worn to prevent the temptation to touch the hair.	Hair is not washed as frequently as hands, but it may carry large numbers of bacteria.
Time and temperature	
Keep fresh foods and prepared foods in the refrigerator at a temperature of 40°F or lower, except when preparing them.	Temperatures of 40°F or below retard bacterial growth and hasten cooling of the food.
Cool leftovers quickly by placing in small shallow containers. Cut large pieces into small sections. Facilitate cooling by stirring or placing in cold water or ice.	Food in large batches cools slowly. Bacteria multiply quickly in foods between 50°F and 115°F. Food must be cooled to 50° F in 2 hours or less.
Use leftovers as soon as possible (within 24 hours).	Contamination is high and potential deterioration is therefore great.
Place cream desserts, milk puddings, potato salad, protein salads, and high-protein sandwich filling in refrigerator at 40°F or lower as soon as prepared.	Bacteria grow very quickly in high-protein foods at temperatures between 50°F and 115°F. Most staphylococcal poisoning results from improper time-temperature handling of this group.
Poultry should not be stuffed. The dressing should be prepared just before it is to be cooked and should be baked in shallow pans.	Dressing in stuffed birds remains between 42°F and 120°F for 5 or more hours.

Table 8-9. Guidelines for prevention of foodborne illness—cont'd

Guide	Rationale
Sanitation routines	
Wash, rinse, and sanitize all work surfaces after using them.	Cleaning and sanitizing reduces the danger of food contamination.
Keep the entire food service area free of rodents, flies, and other insects. Do not permit household pets in the kitchen or dining room.	Animals and insects are carriers of pathogenic organisms.
Do not use cracked or chipped tableware.	These dishes may harbor bacteria. In addition, they are unpleasant to look at and may be a safety hazard.
Follow a rinse-wash-rinse-sanitize cycle for all eating and cooking utensils.	Dishes that appear clean may carry large numbers of bacteria.
Dispose of refuse and other wastes after every meal. Keep all waste receptacles clean.	Food refuse attracts insects and rodents.

and rodent-free separate facility. The floor of the storage room should be concrete slab, pitched toward the center for cleaning and drainage.

8. Clean and sanitize the staff washroom regularly.

Whereas health standards are becoming more stringent, the Food and Drug Administration, state and local health inspectors, and camping association visitors cannot prevent a foodborne illness outbreak. In the final analysis, the food service personnel of each camp who must provide a complete sanitation program to prevent foodborne illness. Only management can see that the staff makes this happen. Table 8-9 provides a summary of guidelines for the coordinator and food service personnel.

FOOD SERVICE ECONOMY

With the continually escalating cost of food and labor, camp owner/directors are investigating every possible means of effecting savings on the food service budget without sacrificing the quality of meals. In recent years, increasing members of camps have turned to disposable dishes and convenience foods. Others are exploring food catering or contract service among other alternatives.

Disposable tableware

Recently, an increasing number of articles have appeared in camping journals extolling the advantages and economy of disposable paper tableware and plastic flatware. At the same time, there has been much resistance to disposable ware on the basis of conservation of the environment and the desirability of reducing environmental pollution.

On the question of conservation, it is argued that trees—the raw product from which single-service paper products are manufactured—are one of man's greatest natural resources, and forests are being used up faster than they can be replenished. Authorities point out, however, that disposable paper products are made from pulp woods and that these particular trees are being grown at a greater rate than they are being cut. It may, in fact, be argued that the environment is actually gaining by this thinning process.

Critics of the use of disposables protest

that plastic wares are not biodegradable and therefore are a source of needless pollution. There are three different types of plastic materials that are used in making disposables. Two are not biodegradable, whereas the third is. In the case of all three, however, none poses any problem if incinerated. One is recyclable and two are beneficial as inert soil conditioners when composted.

Following are some of the arguments of the protagonists of disposable tableware: (1) improved sanitation—the danger of food-borne illness as a result of improper dishwashing techniques is largely eliminated, (2) easier handling—young children can cope with lightweight disposables, and (3) noise pollution is reduced during clean up.

As regards the relative costs of paper food service versus conventional tableware, more precise information is required. At this time there is agreement that the added cost of disposable products is about the same as the savings in: (1) staff salary budget because of reduced dishwashing requirements, (2) detergents, sanitizing agents, and so forth, (3) conventional tableware replacement, (4) utility costs for heating water, and (5) equipment maintenance.

Camp management staff will need to keep a very close watch on the comparative cost of paper products and each of the five items listed above before they determine the fiscal efficiency of converting to disposable tableware.

Convenience foods

Convenience foods refer to those items that are fully prepared and need only to be heated before serving. They are sometimes referred to as "prepared" or "ready" foods. Convenience foods have been on the market for many years in one form or another. The frozen entree first appeared in the form of the now familiar T.V. dinner. Today frozen entrees are widely used in the commercial field, and the variety of dishes available numbers in the hundreds. One camp reports planning a menu cycle extending for 14 days made up entirely from convenience foods.

Convenience foods are available to camps today in tray packs with as few as eight servings or as many as 40 portions. The pack comes in frozen form and must be stored in the freezer until ready for use. The container is placed in a conventional or convection oven for up to 1 hour. It is then ready for serving directly from the container. When serving is completed, the container is discarded.

Initially, there was considerable reluctance among camp directors and food service coordinators to try convenience foods. They believed that the meals were too repetitive and too institutional. Today's modern food technology has largely dispelled this concern providing great advances in the variety as well as the quality of items available. The arguments favoring frozen prepared foods include the following:

1. No guesswork is required in preparing recipes; there are never any failures.
2. It is easy to predetermine the exact cost of the menu.
3. Receiving is simple since there is no quality assessment required.
4. Food waste is minimal.
5. Cleaning and storage of most pots and serving containers is eliminated; trays are simply discarded.
6. The difficulty of hiring quality staff with experienced food preparation and cooking skills is virtually eliminated.
7. Food service personnel may be significantly reduced.

The disadvantages would appear to be minimal:

1. Convenience foods may only be used when the camp can avail itself of this

service by means of refrigerated trucks.

2. Large freezer space is required for storage.

3. Some suppliers only have convenience foods available in large, 40-portion packs that may present problems for smaller camps.

Concerning the question of economy, the debate resolves itself down to whether the added cost of convenience foods is offset by the combined cost of raw food plus labor costs in the conventional food service operation. The preponderance of evidence suggests that when all cost factors are considered, there is some saving with the use of convenience foods. A number of camp directors argue that even if the cost of ready foods is slightly higher, they can still be justified because they free the food service coordinator of many hiring and replacement problems each season.

Catering services

Up to the present time, very few camps have been able to justify a food service contract on the basis of a reduced food service budget. Most camps that use a catering service to provide all meals admit that the cost over the season is somewhat greater. However, they defend the practice because of the problems that are eliminated during the summer: hiring and replacing qualified staff, purchasing food supplies from a variety of vendors, and maintaining detailed bookkeeping accounts.

Camp directors and food service coordinators should not discount the possibilities of providing some savings through contracting with a food catering company. These companies are in business to provide a viable service, and as more caterers attempt to retain their staff through the slack summer months, the cost of such services to camps should become more attractive.

Government surplus foods

Nonprofit agencies that operate tax-exempt camps are eligible for government surplus foods. The types of food vary from year to year depending on productivity. Substantial savings can be realized by taking advantage of this source of food supplies. Application should be made early in the year to the state distributing agency or the Regional Food Division Office of the Agricultural Marketing Service.

Tips on food service control

Throughout this chapter, many suggestions have been made relating to efficient food service management. The following checklists focus on additional points concerning food service economy.

PURCHASING

1. Is advantage taken of lower prices when a food item is in season?

2. Are orders placed efficiently? Extra deliveries cost money.

3. Is one person responsible for receiving and checking the food order? Surveys show that camps are more lax than resorts and hotels in this regard.

4. Is full advantage taken of the expertise of food supplier salespersons? Are they expected to advise on what items provide the best yield per package?

5. Is purchase made primarily on the basis of planned need?

PREPARATION AND STORAGE

1. Are standard recipes used? Their use can realize valuable food savings.

2. Is training and supervision of staff provided to avoid needless waste?

3. Is it realized that meat shrinkage is proportional to oven cooking time? It is possible to save up to 20% in shrinkage when roasting at low temperature. The meat is also juicier and more flavorful.

4. Is overcooking of fresh fruits and vegetables avoided to preserve the nutritional value?

5. Are menus planned so that leftovers can be used in an attractive appetizing manner?
6. Is care taken to store food properly and thus avoid waste through spoilage?

SERVING

1. Is portion control practiced?
2. Is food pre-portioned before it leaves the kitchen (meat loaf, casseroles)?
3. Are seconds offered in a substantial main course, but not in desserts?
4. Is only one snack served, and that in the evening?
5. Are non–food service staff required to stay out of the kitchen? Camp should not be a short-order restaurant.

EQUIPMENT

1. Are food storage facilities sufficient to take advantage of preseason purchasing?
2. Are regular maintenance checks made on all food service equipment to prevent food loss?
3. Has the cost of renting food service equipment been carefully investigated? This may be cheaper than purchasing outright in a seasonal operation.

ADMINISTRATIVE GUIDELINES

1. One person should be assigned administrative responsibility for the entire food service operation regardless of the size of the camp and its kitchen staff.
2. The food service coordinator should play a key role in the recruitment and hiring of all kitchen personnel.
3. Kitchen staff should be made to feel an integral part of the total camp staff.
4. Effective menu planning is a complex process and requires adherence to a number of important principles including the need to plan early, use of standard recipes, understanding nutritional value of foods, development of a menu form, observing camper food likes and dislikes, and planning for variety.
5. Preparation of the camp food order should be done early and systematically. Specification sheets should be prepared and bids solicited from several vendors.
6. Patronization of local food suppliers should be encouraged whenever quality, price, and service are competitive.
7. The receiving and checking of all incoming food orders should be assigned to one individual.
8. Careful consideration must be given to adequate food storage space and a location close to the food preparation areas.
9. The single most important consideration regarding food storage is proper temperature control for dry, refrigerated, and frozen foods.
10. Special consideration must be given to the storage of leftovers. The danger of food spoilage is high for this category of foods.
11. The physical layout of the kitchen can provide significant savings in energy and time when carefully planned.
12. Careful research should precede the purchases of a major piece of kitchen equipment to determine whether the initial capital outlay can be justified over the expected life of the item.
13. Dishwashing regulations for camps are stringent. Food service coordinators must be familiar with the requirements and adhere to them at all times.
14. The physical environment of the dining hall should contribute to a pleasant and relatively quiet setting for camp meals.
15. There are basically two methods of serving camp meals: family-style and cafeteria-style service. Camp administrators must weigh the advantages and disadvantages of each and choose the one that best meets their needs.
16. The danger of foodborne illness in camps is constantly present. A well-planned program must be implemented to prevent infection from staphylococcus, salmonella, *Clostridium perfringens,* and hepatitis virus A bacteria.
17. Visual cleanliness is not sufficient; pathogenic organisms may still be present. Only the implementation of stringent sanitation practices can eliminate this hazard.
18. The three main causes of food contamination are: the time it takes pathogenic organisms to multiply at a given temperature in food, contamination of the food source, and human contamination. Each of these can be con-

trolled with strict adherence to approved
food service practices.

19. The food service coordinator must be thoroughly familiar with high-risk foods and the conditions that promote foodborne illness.
20. Refuse storage and disposal is an important consideration in the total sanitation program of a camp. All effective means of controlling flies, vermin, and rodents must be followed scrupulously.
21. Because the food budget comprises such a large percentage of the total camp budget, camp administrators must examine every possible means of reducing food service costs while maintaining quality meals for campers.

SELECTED BIBLIOGRAPHY

Detrich, W. B.: Where does the camp food dollar go? Camping Magazine, 47(5):20,25, Mar., 1975.

Editorial: Food purchasing at camp, Canadian Camping, 30(1):1-5, Feb., 1978.

Editorial: Good food service planning requires detailed attention to sanitation, Camping Magazine, 45(3):20-21, Apr., 1973.

Editorial: Should camps use disposable ware? Camping Magazine, 44(6):12-13, June, 1972.

Editorial: When buying for your kitchen, Camping Magazine, 46(5):53, Mar., 1974

Joseph, L.: Designing a camp kitchen with a future in mind, Camping Magazine, 45(1):18,26, Jan., 1973.

Melamed, M.: Most camps need better garbage disposal facilities, Camping Magazine, 43(5):25-26, May, 1971.

Rose, E.: Solving camp food storage problems, Camping Magazine, 41(5):14, May, 1969.

Snyder, O. P.: Preventing foodborne illness. (St. Paul, Minn.: University of Minnesota, Dept. of Food Science and Nutrition and the Agriculture Extension Service, U.S. Department of Agriculture, 1977).

Stevenson, J. L.: Qualities a director looks for in a camp dietitian, Camping Magazine, 45(2):15-16, Mar., 1973.

Strohkorb, A.: How to use 'ready' foods at camp, Camping Magazine, 40(1):22-23, Jan., 1968.

Treadwell, D. D.: Standard recipes can help your food service planning, Camping Magazine, 42(2):12-13, Feb., 1970.

U.S. Department of Agriculture: Summer food service program for children—sponsor handbook for on-site preparation; administrative guide; a menu planning guide for type A school lunches, Food and Nutrition Service, 1977.

West, B. B. et al.: How to improve your food storage, Camping Magazine, 40(2):24-25, Feb., 1968.

West, B. B., et al.: How to save on food costs, Camping Magazine, 40(4):24, Apr., 1968.

Wisconsin Department of Agriculture: Food purchasing specifications for food services. (Madison, Wis.: Marketing Division, Wisconsin Department of Agriculture Trade and Consumer Protection, 1978).

Wolf, I. D., et al.: Meat and meat foods (HS-12). (St. Paul, Minn.: University of Minnesota, U.S. Department of Agriculture and Agricultural Extension Service).

Wolf, I. D., et al.: More for your meat dollars (HS-27). (St. Paul, Minn.: University of Minnesota, U.S. Department of Agriculture and Agriculture Extension Service).

Wolf, I. D., et al.: More for your fruit and vegetable dollars (HS-28). (St. Paul, Minn.: University of Minnesota, U.S. Department of Agriculture and Agricultural Extension Service).

CHAPTER NINE

Business and fiscal management

The Captain of a ship must chart a course across the sea in order to reach his destination and in the same manner a camp director must chart his financial course to guide him through the year. . . . Without a financial path to follow and a goal to reach, the financial aspect of camping is like a ship without a course or destination to reach[1]

Very few camp administrators today, whether in an agency or private, independent organization, have available sufficient financial resources to implement all the long-range improvements they have planned and all the program services they would like to offer. It is therefore, incumbent on those persons responsible for camp fiscal and business management to make judicious use of the limited revenue that is available. This requires the use of sound business methods; anything less reflects badly on the administrator, the camp and, in the case of public or parapublic camps, the sponsoring agency. In the past, many camp directors have tended to apologize for operating their camp in a truly businesslike manner, but today the camping industry is extremely competitive and survival requires the ultimate in efficient business and fiscal management. Administrators of semipublic camps have a further obligation to taxpayers and other supporters of the operation to provide full value for the tax dollar.

The budget may be seen as a clear reflec-tion of the philosophy, goals, and objectives of a camp. The relative importance of various segments of the total camp operation are translated into dollars and cents through the monies allocated to the various camp programs and services. Because program management and business management are inextricably tied to one another, it is important that those persons responsible for preparing fiscal programs recognize the importance of this relationship. Only then will the budget truly reflect the desired program emphasis.

In spite of the importance of sound business and financial practice, it is perhaps the area of management in which camp administrators are least competent. Most men and women who enter the camping profession have had little or no experience in fiscal planning, and as a result, the approach has frequently been one of trial and error. This haphazard conduct of the business side of camp operations has resulted in much inefficiency and, in some cases, gross mishandling of funds.

In the chapter on site and facility development, the need for guidance from architects, engineers, lawyers, and other consultants was stressed. The business and fiscal

---

1. Labbett, C.: Money in the bank—budget or else . . . Camping Magazine, **25**(1):8, Fall, 1972.

management of a camp requires similar aid from experts. Although the directors of many small and intermediate size camps may believe that the services of consultants cannot be afforded, such professional help is invariably a good investment and in most cases can save the camp valuable dollars over the long term. A team of three professionals is usually sufficient to guide the business side of the camp—an accountant, a lawyer, and an insurance agent.

The specific tasks with which an accountant may provide help are:

1. Organizing the internal control and record keeping system
2. Setting up auditing procedures
3. Assisting in long-range planning for the camp as well as estate planning for the owner
4. Assisting in bank and other credit programs
5. Serving as intermediary with government and other agencies with whom the camp must cooperate
6. Advising on a sound tax planning program

In this latter capacity alone, an accountant can save the camp many thousands of dollars, not by avoiding tax regulations, but by deferring or finding means to minimize the burden of heavy taxation. A lawyer and insurance agent can also provide invaluable assistance in their specific areas if they are completely informed about the physical site and total operation of the camp.

OFFICE MANAGEMENT

The administration building or business office is the nerve center for the administrative operation of the camp and as such should epitomize administrative efficiency. It is here that a large number of business functions are carried out, including handling correspondence, preparing reports, filing materials, ordering equipment and supplies, and maintaining countless records. The business office also serves as the reception and communications center for the camp.

Regardless of the size of the camp, these functions are all required. In a small camp, many of these duties are assumed by the camp director, while in a larger organization, the various reponsibilities are delegated to several persons. In large camps, a given task may be assigned to one person who then becomes a specialist within the business office and has exclusive responsibility for that particular duty. For example, one individual might be in charge of ordering equipment, materials, and supplies for the entire camp, another is responsible for filing all materials, while yet another serves as receptionist and telephone operator.

Efficient office management is vital to the smooth operation of the entire camp. Not only is the work of the director made easier, but administrative personnel throughout the camp are relieved of many responsibilities that can better be performed by office personnel who are trained for these duties. The service to campers and parents is enhanced, communications are improved, and the public relations image of the camp is strengthened.

One question that many large camps have to face is whether or not to decentralize some office services. Administrators are often under pressure to provide secretarial assistance in the kitchen for the food service coordinator or to have a stenographer in the health center to handle all medical correspondence, files and reports. Most camps, however, find it more efficient to centralize their office personnel and require the various functional units to bring their clerical work to a central location. There are several advantages to this plan:

1. *Economy.* Fewer employees, equipment, and space are required.

2. *Quality of work.* It is easier to train, supervise, and control personnel.
3. *Efficiency of work.* This results from increased specialization and concentration of work.
4. *Reduced supervisory responsibility.* Department heads are relieved of the supervisory role and have more time for their special responsibility.[2]

A central administrative office is the heart of the entire management operation of any camp. To function effectively it must be well designed, properly staffed, and efficiently managed.

Location and design

The business office should be readily accessible to all who have business there. This requires a fairly central location on the campsite since campers, counsellors, and senior administrators all have occasion to use its services. The business office should be adjacent to the parking lot so that parents, salespersons, and other visitors may have their inquiries handled efficiently. In addition, it should be in close proximity to other administrative offices such as those of the camp director and head of the program.

The actual location and size of the facility usually is a good indication of how much importance the camp director places on office management. Inadequate space and an unattractive facility usually indicates an administrator who does not appreciate the importance of sound office management and the value of its services to the rest of the organization. The facility should be attractive but not pretentious. It should provide sufficient space for all services with special attention given to lighting and ventilation. Above all, it should be functional and free

from noise and distractions. Although space needs depend on the size of the organization, most camp office arrangements should provide the following as minimum requirements.

Reception area. Since campers, counsellors, and visitors come to this office for information, provision should be made to handle their requests expeditiously. Usually some counter space is built in, and chairs are available for those who must wait. Whenever possible, the reception area should be at least partially separated from the main office so as not to disturb the clerical staff.

Main office area. Sufficient space must be provided for members of the clerical staff to carry out their duties. In a small camp, this means a desk for the camp secretary. In a large camp, desks, typewriters, and work space must be provided for several staff members. Regardless of the size of the camp, space is also required for storage of all camp records. Many camps today lease or own duplicating equipment, which requires additional space. If possible, it is desirable to reserve a small separate room for this equipment.

Storage area. Suitable storage space must be available for office materials and supplies. Some camps have their main storeroom, for all types of incoming equipment and supplies, adjacent to the business office. With this arrangement, all shipments can be checked in as they are received.

Private office. In a camp large enough to support a clerical staff, a business manager or accountant usually has responsibility for the supervision of the office complex. In such cases, this person usually has a private office. In small camps, the supervisory role is filled by the camp director, in which case his or her office should be adjacent to the main business office. If other administrative personnel, such as the program director, are

---

2. Leffingwell, W. H., and Robinson, E. M.: Textbook of office management. (New York: McGraw-Hill Book Co., 1950) p. 36

supplied with offices, these should also be located within the administrative complex.

Conference room. Many camps find it useful to have a conference room for pre-camp meetings, program staff conferences, staff and committee meetings, and entertainment of guests.

Equipment

The use of modern equipment is an important consideration not only for office morale but also as a sound business investment. Judicious selection of equipment can mean hundreds of work hours saved during the camp season. Copy machines, electronic calculators, electric typewriters, and a modern intercommunication system are the basis of significant time savings in routine office work. The use of such equipment can mean fewer personnel to do the same volume of work, with the added assurance that it will be done better.

In recent years, some large camps have begun to use data processing equipment to handle some of their major office tasks. When camps are dealing with hundreds of campers and accounts run in the tens of thousands of dollars, the use of the computer as an administrative tool deserves serious consideration.

Small camps that have only one or two office staff members cannot usually afford the luxury of many labor-saving devices. However, camp administrators should examine their office needs very carefully before discounting the possibility of leasing selected pieces of equipment or purchasing them for 9-month use in the city and 3-month use at camp. Some camps have also entered into reciprocal arrangements with boards of education and other urban agencies in which the camp has the use of office equipment during the summer months in exchange for use of camp equipment by the school or agency from September to June.

Personnel

The key to a well-run camp business office is the staff members who work there. The contribution of the office personnel to the smooth operation of the entire camp cannot be underestimated. As with any group enterprise, teamwork is vital. Each member of the office staff must be compatible with the others in the group. In addition, their technical skills should be complimentary.

The number and variety of staff needed depends on the size of the camp. A very large organization requires secretaries, stenographers, typists, filing clerks, and a receptionist–telephone operator. When a large office staff is involved, someone must assume administrative responsibility for the supervision of the group. This person is usually designated as the business administrator or business manager.

Business manager. For the purpose of this chapter, the term *business manager* is used to refer to the person who supervises all phases of business management in a large camp. In addition to managing the business office, it is not uncommon for this person to also assume responsibility for the overall supervision of food service, health center, and property maintenance. In each of these areas, the business manager works closely with the food service coordinator, camp doctor or nurse, and maintenance supervisor.

The scope of the business manager's responsibilities is extensive. It ranges from knowledge of workmen's compensation regulations to the advantages of plastic over galvanized water piping. The business manager is responsible for budget preparation, fiscal accounting, investment possibilities, insurance coverage, long-range planning of facilities, and ordering camp equipment, materials, and supplies. The manager is rarely an expert in all these areas but must be knowledgeable enough to discuss each intelligently with the appropriate specialists throughout the camp.

Because the role of the business manager varies so much from camp to camp, it is not possible to provide a definitive list of duties. However, the job description for the business manager's position usually includes most of the following areas:

1. Budget and financial planning
2. Accounting and reporting procedures
3. Purchase of equipment, materials, and supplies
4. Long-term planning for capital improvements to site and facilities
5. Hiring, training, and supervising business office personnel
6. Coordination of all camp public relations
7. Supervision of transportation arrangements
8. Provision of all forms of insurance coverage
9. Coordination of all legal aspects of the camp operation
10. Supervision of property management and site maintenance
11. Supervision of food service
12. Supervision of health center
13. Regular evaluation of all business practices

Camp secretary. In a very small camp, all the duties listed above become the prime responsibility of the camp director. In this type of operation, the person to whom the director delegates many of these duties is the camp secretary. The secretary supervises the business office and must be familiar with all facets of the camp, as well as its policies and procedures. The secretary is the right hand of the camp director and assumes a quasiadministrative role at times. Because of the vast range of responsibilities involved, the camp secretary must possess a sense of task priorities. During the short camp season, many assignments will occasionally be thrust on the business office at one time, and the secretary must discern between those that require immediate attention and those that can be set aside temporarily. Next to the camp director, perhaps no other staff member has as thorough an understanding of the total camp operation as does the secretary. When viewed in this light, the camp secretary is someone whose expertise goes far beyond the technical skills of typing, shorthand, and filing that are required of most office secretaries in business and industry.

Office efficiency. When a camp employs a business manager, the direct supervision of the office and its management is frequently delegated to the head secretary. Regardless of the size of the staff, it is important that efficient office management be maintained at all times. This requires a clear understanding of job descriptions and a cooperative team effort. Some camps develop a policy manual that serves as a guide for office personnel. This has great merit when turnover of staff is large from one season to the next. Simplifying and streamlining the work of the business office should be the goal of every administrator who has responsibility for this aspect of the camp. Continuous assessment of existing procedures should lead to an increased volume of work without placing increased demands on the office staff.

Responsibilities

Regardless of the size of the camp and the office staff, certain functions are common to almost every camp office. The following section provides a brief description of these tasks.

Receiving visitors. During the season, most camps expect to have many visitors. Each person should be greeted with courtesy and made to feel welcome. Every effort should be made to meet their needs whether they are an apprehensive parent, a salesperson seeking an order, or a camper requesting information.

Telephone. Office personnel must understand the importance of answering the phone promptly and in a cordial, helpful manner. Even when a negative response must be given to a request or question, courtesy should be paramount. Office personnel must also understand that the camp phone is required for professional business; they should be discouraged from making personal calls or prolonging business calls with personal matters.

Correspondence. All incoming correspondence deserves a prompt reply that should be written carefully and with good grammatical construction. A copy of all replies along with the original letter should be placed on file for future reference. Some routine inquiries can be handled by a secretary, while others may be answered with the use of a standard form letter. Care must be taken to see that form letters are not overused. When a form letter is prepared, special attention should be taken to convey a feeling of friendliness and warmth.

Mail. Sorting and delivering mail may be a mammoth task in a large camp and may require much time of one or more staff members. A smooth, efficient system must be devised that ensures accurate, prompt service. The most common practice is to request that parents include the cabin or tent number on each letter sent to campers. All mail is then sorted by living unit. Rather than have several hundred campers pick up mail at a central spot each day, it is more efficient to ask the counsellor or one bunk representative to handle the task.

Filing. An effective filing system is essential to office management. The larger the camp, the more complex the chore. All correspondence, reports, records, and other printed material must be stored in a manner that permits quick, efficient retrieval.

It is recommended that one person be responsible for all filing to ensure greater consistency. However, the particular filing code should be known to other colleagues within the office, otherwise the system may end up in chaos on the filing clerk's day off or the following summer if that individual does not return to camp.

As to the actual method of classifying data for filing, several effective systems are available. Whatever scheme is used, simplicity is the key. One recommended practice is to divide all material into two groups: current (operational) files and permanent files. The former contain records pertaining to the current season, the latter includes all documentation excluding the present season. Within each of these general classifications, all material is filed alphabetically. The data to be filed are then classified according to name, subject, or a combination of these two. A large camp may use both name and subject files, but the majority of camps prefer to use one system combining name and subject. *Name files* are identified by a person or an organization. For example, all vendors with whom the camp deals would be filed in this type of file system. *Subject files* are identified according to the subject matter with which they deal. When giving a title to a subject file, care must be taken to select the best key word, usually a noun. For example, medical supplies would not be filed under "M" for medical but "S" for supplies. The subject "Supplies" could then be broken down into subheadings such as "cleaning and maintenance," "medical," "office," and "program." Program supplies might be further subdivided by activity if this seemed desirable.

The simplest approach for most camps may be to identify broad, general subjects by camp function, which could include business management, campers, food service, health service, maintenance and repair, program, and staff. Many subheadings are included within each of these main classifications. For example, under business management, subheadings might include budget, camp store, contracts, insurance, inventory, invoices, laundry, mail service, public relations, requisitions, taxes, and transportation.

Within each file, all materials should be arranged chronologically with the most recent entries at the beginning of the file. A file should only be started when there are at least five to ten papers under a specific subject heading. For all headings with a lesser amount of material, a miscellaneous folder should be used. A miscellaneous file is used for each letter of the alphabet and is located behind the last file in each alphabetical listing.

Finally, the person primarily responsible for filing material should look through each filing cabinet periodically and discard all obsolete material.

Equipment and supplies. In many camps one staff member in the business office is responsible for ordering all camp equipment, materials, and supplies, which makes it easier to standardize and control the procedure. There will always be a certain quantity of office materials and supplies that must be ordered in sufficient quantity to last for the entire camp season. This order should be placed by someone who is familiar with the business management of the camp.

Duplicating materials. There is a constant need in a large, well-administered camp to produce multiple copies of some materials. These include camper and staff lists, cabin or tent rosters, syllabuses and policy manuals, program instructional materials, camp regulations, minutes of meetings, announcements and instructions to staff, as well as form letters to parents regarding transportation, visitor's day, closing of accounts, and

other matters. Although ditto and mimeographing machines are relatively simple to operate, most camps find it is wise to restrict their use to office staff personnel. In this way, maintenance and service costs are kept to a minimum.

Services to camp staff. One of the main functions of office personnel is providing a variety of services to other staff members. These services include typing such items as: (1) reports or correspondence relating to camp business, (2) menus for the food service coordinator, and (3) program materials and schedules. Other duties involve arranging appointments, setting up committee meetings, or contacting specific groups of campers. When office personnel can assume some of these routine tasks, they free the staff to devote more time to supervisory and advisory functions with campers and colleagues. Sound administrative practice suggests that the time of many intermediate and senior staff members is too valuable to be consumed in tasks that can be effectively performed by junior members of the office staff.

Records and reports

The compilation and efficient filing of camp records and reports is essential to effective business management of any camp regardless of size. The information contained in these records is the factual basis from which public and parapublic camps must report to their sponsoring agency as well as to parents and the public at large. In describing the importance of efficient record keeping in the field of public recreation, Hjelte and Shivers[3] list several purposes of records. The following items are adapted from this material.

1. *To provide valid evidence*. Proper rec-

3. Hjelte, G. and Shiver, J. S.: Public administration of recreational services. (Philadelphia: Lea and Febiger, 1972) pp. 238-239.

ords deal with actual happenings so that fact and not mere opinion or approximation becomes the basis of decision making.

2. *To indicate the present status of the camp.* Records provide information regarding the establishment of the camp and its authority, structure, achievements to date, and projections for the future.

3. *To detect inefficiency, duplication, and other shortcomings.* Records provide the data whereby evaluation of the operation can be made in terms of camp goals.

4. *To afford a basis for compliance with legal requirements.* Records and reports provide written evidence of the extent to which federal, state, and local regulations are met. They also provide essential information in the event of litigation against the camp or its employees.

5. *To assess the camp operation.* Standards should have been established for the conduct of the camp. Records provide a means of comparing not only the program but its total range of services against these established criteria. When they are found wanting, modifications can be made to improve programming and service.

The numbers and complexity of camp records and reports are a reflection of not only the size but also the type of camp. Public and parapublic camps frequently are expected to report in greater detail to their sponsoring authority than are private camps.

End of season reports. Many administrators deplore the need to submit seasonal or annual reports believing that, once submitted to a higher level, they are seldom read, and only rarely are recommendations acted on.

A report should be a compilation of many records. It should be explicit and factual. Reports are an important ingredient of good administration because they supply factual data in a concise form from which camp programs and services are planned and policy decisions made. Problems should be identi-

fied in the report, and recommendations should be made for their amelioration.

Camp directors should require a report from each administrative head at the conclusion of the camp season. The format of the report should be clearly outlined so that each person reporting understands exactly what is required. In a large camp, these reports form one of the best means by which the senior administrator can keep abreast of all facets of the camp.

BUDGET

A budget is fundamental to sound fiscal management in any business endeavor. Camping is a business; it involves revenue, a wide range of expenditures or expenses, and in the case of private independent camps, hopefully, profit. As with any successful enterprise, planning is required and the budget is nothing more than a financial plan. It must be carefully prepared utilizing all available information regarding revenue for the camp and anticipated expenditures. Once prepared and approved, the budget is the financial program for a fixed period, usually 12 months. A budget, then, may be defined as a carefully prepared statement of estimated income and expenditures. It should be the result of the combined efforts of all administrative heads who represent various segments of the camp.

Values of a budget

A carefully prepared budget achieves several important ends:

1. It provides a statement of the financial resources and needs for the camp and thus helps avoid a deficit operation.
2. It informs all concerned parties of the revenue available and how camp goals are to be met with these resources.
3. It provides control of fiscal management and is the best security against misuse of funds.

4. It offers a guarantee of equitable distribution of available funds to all facets of the camp operation.
5. It gives a clear indication of the cost of various programs and services and provides support for future revisions in appropriations.
6. It ensures the most effective use of personnel, facilities, equipment, and supplies in meeting camp objectives.

Guidelines for budget preparation

Invariably, fiscal needs exceed the funds available for a complete camp program. This means that priorities must be established. The following guidelines will assist camp administrators in determining priorities in preparing the camp budget.

Early preparation. A budget is not a document that should be prepared over a weekend in late spring. It should be in the making during the entire year. As soon as the budget for one fiscal year is approved, a file should be started and notes and reminders inserted regarding needs for the following year.

Realistic and accurate. The budget must be based on current needs and be factual in every respect. It should be based on updated inventories and last year's receipts and expenditures. The practice of padding the budget should be discouraged.

Equitable distribution. There should be adequate monies for every program and service offered; none should be ignored or seriously deprived. This does not mean that all activities should receive the same amount of funds. The distribution must be based on rational considerations such as per capita participation and philosophical program emphasis. Some activities require a significantly larger budget than others.

Cooperative preparation. The final budget is the product of consultation with all camp administrative personnel. This is the best guarantee of equitable distribution since each individual consulted is invited to request a reasonable share of the available funds.

Flexibility. The camp budget should provide for unforeseen events. It is impossible to plan for every fiscal emergency that might befall a camp during the season. A special fund provides the necessary flexibility within the budget to cope with such contingencies.

Supportive data. Whenever significant monies are requested for capital expenditures, the request should be supported by explanatory, descriptive material. The supporting documentation attempts to justify the expenditure requested by describing how program objectives will be met.

Centralization versus decentralization

When the budgeting process is totally centralized, the senior camp administrator takes complete responsibility for preparing the camp budget, and little or no consultation with colleagues in involved. Fortunately, this rarely occurs even in extremely small camps.

Decentralization, on the other hand, places the major responsibility for the budget preparation in the hands of each unit head so that the food service coordinator, program director, and other administrative heads have considerable scope in determining how funds are to be allocated. The finance committee, camp director, or business manager allocates lump sums to each unit or division of the camp, and the head of each unit then has freedom in assigning the monies within that department or unit.

Neither of these systems are in use in many camps today. Rather, there is a combination of the two, with variations as to how much consultation and cooperative planning takes place between the centralized authority and the decentralized administrators. Democratic administration speaks loudly for considerable responsbility to rest with those who are closest to the campers. Staff members who actually formulate programs and promote camp services are in the best position to assess needs. They should be given an opportunity to present their case for raising the budget allocation if they can substantiate their proposal.

Types of budgets

Line-item budgets. The line-item budget, though very detailed, is relatively easy to prepare, orderly, and businesslike. Its major weakness is that it focuses primarily on the correct classification of expenditures and makes little attempt to relate these figures to the program or service it is designed to support.

The Planning–programming–budgeting system (PPBS). A relatively new budgeting system, the PPBS has been used extensively by government agencies, private business, and more recently education in an attempt to more closely relate budget to program.

The main features of PPBS are that it places considerable emphasis on planning and programming as essential elements in budget preparation. The first step in this approach is to carefully establish goals and objectives for the camp (planning). These should *not* be stated in theoretical or nebulous terms but in clearly obtainable standards. The second step involves identifying camp activities through which these goals can be reached (programming). The final step requires allocation of resources to the appropriate programs (budgeting). It is recommended that programs be planned over a 5-year period and compared regularly to determine which most effectively meet the objectives established in step one.

Accountability in terms of program objectives is the key to the PPBS system, and program achievement becomes the primary focus rather than program equipment and supplies. Hartley summarizes the values of PPBS over traditional line-item budgets when he states:

1. Information on total system costs is output, or program oriented.
2. Analysis of possible alternative programs and of alternative means of meeting program objectives is more extensive.
3. The planning process is continuous and includes multi-year plans so that future year implications of present decisions are explicitly identified.
4. Policy is an ordered process in a well-defined organization which directs major lines of action toward perceptible program goals.[4]

More detailed supporting documentation is required when developing this type of budget rather than the traditional line-item budget. Perhaps this is the reason PPBS has not been adopted more widely by camp administrators. Nevertheless, the trend must be toward this type of program-oriented budgeting if camp directors are to intelligently direct budget appropriations to areas in which they can be most effectively utilized.

The budget process

Budget making involves the following sequential steps: (1) collection of data, (2) organization or classification of the data, (3) presenting and obtaining approval of the budget, and (4) administering the budget.

Collection of data. The first step in the budget process is to gather all pertinent information. This should begin with a review of the budget of the past few years, not because the present budget will be a carbon copy of previous years, but because it is important to get some indication of the total revenue and expenditures of earlier budgets

4. Hartley, H: Educational planning-programming-budgeting—a system approach (Englewood Cliffs, N.J.: Prentice-Hall Inc., 1968) p. 86.

as well as the detailed breakdown of how money was allocated. All staff members who are to contribute to the final budget should be consulted early regarding their needs so that the collection of data essentially becomes a year-round process. The data itself comprises two main categories: sources of revenue and planned expenditures.

Sources of revenue. The main sources of revenue for nearly all camps is derived from camper tuition fees. In some private, independent camps, tuition fees provide the sole source of income. A recent survey indicates that regardless of the type of camp, at least 80% of income is obtained from tuition fees in the vast majority of camps. This statistic points up the importance of gaining a clear and accurate estimate of camper enrollment well in advance of each camp season. In this respect, returnees are perhaps the best indicator because they are the least expensive campers to enroll, and they should be strong promoters of the camp program since they are returning as satisfied customers. A large percentage of returning campers is the strongest form of advertising a camp can enjoy. Once camp directors have a clear indication of the percentage of returnees for a given season, they should have an excellent index of expected income from camper fees. Secondary sources of revenue include:

1. Capital fund drives initiated by the sponsoring organization
2. Special gifts or donations of money or materials from sources such as service clubs or foundations
3. Complete or partial subsidization of camper tuition by government or other agencies (usually for camps for special populations)
4. Endowment income
5. Appropriation from the sponsoring agency
6. Special fees or charges to campers for selected activites such as horseback riding and tours

7. Camp store sales and other concessions
8. Rental and lease of camp facilities and equipment
9. Interest and dividends from outside investments

Many camps are finding that the best single means of increasing revenue is to winterize at least part of their camp operation. It only stands to reason that valuable camp property and facilities can bring a larger monetary return if they are utilized for more than the traditional 8 to 10 weeks in the summer.*

The camp store goes by a variety of names including tuck-shop, trading post, canteen, and commissary. It is surprising that many camp administrators consider the operation of a camp store a major problem during the camp season and of questionable value as a supplementary source of revenue. Invariably this is because no efficient plan for its operation has been developed.

Some camps use only cash at the camp store, which creates many problems with theft and loss of money. A more practical plan is to request a deposit of five to 25 dollars at the time of precamp registration. The amount varies with the economic means of the clientele as well as the length of stay in camp. Many camps set up an individual sheet for each camper, on which is recorded the item purchased and the amount. This system makes it possible to give the parents a detailed account of how the deposit was spent. Surveys have shown, however, that very few parents ever request such a breakdown and a more efficient system is to use cards such as that shown in Fig. 9-1. Each card is worth five or ten dollars and has small punch squares around the edge. The cards are filed alphabetically by cabin or tent in the camp store, and as campers make

---

*One camp reported in *Camping Magazine* that their total revenue had been increased 43% through off-season rental of camp facilities.

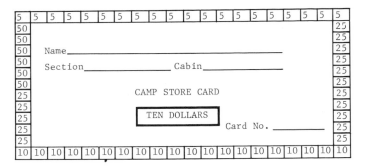

Fig. 9-1. Sample camp store card.

a purchase, their card is punched for the correct amount. If there is a balance at the end of the child's stay at camp, that amount is placed in a sealed envelope and given to the camper on the way home in the camp bus.

Planned expenditures. Expenditures are usually classified as current expenditures or capital expenditures. Current expenditures include regular expenses involved in the daily operation during a given fiscal year. They include all the charges levied against the camp, from staff salaries to postage stamps. Salaries are usually the largest expense in a camp, with food running a close second in resident camps. It is impossible to give any clear indication of relative costs because they vary so much from camp to camp. For example, a church camp may utilize many volunteers on the staff in which food and program costs may exceed the salary budget. Another camp may initiate an activity such as waterskiing, and the cost of a new power boat would greatly inflate the program budget in the year of that capital purchase.

Table 9-1 reflects the tremendous diversity in expenses for different camps. The percentages shown indicate the range of variance among twelve selected residence camps surveyed between 1972 and 1978.

Capital expenses refer to investments in

Table 9-1. Variance in major expenses of twelve selected residence camps*

Expenditure	Percentage of operating budget
Personnel	15 to 54
Food	11 to 41
Program and general administration	9 to 44
Property and facilities	3 to 41

*Adapted from Editorials: The cost of camping, *Camping Magazine*, **45**(4):8-11, May, 1973; **47**(7):5-7, May, 1975; and 51(4):22-26, Mar., 1979.

fixed assets such as land, buildings, or other structures or equipment of a permanent nature. Because capital expenditures usually involve sizable sums of money, they may need to be financed somewhat differently from the general operating budget of the camp. Several of the most common methods are capital fund drive by the sponsoring agency, loans from banks or other sources, and grants from foundations.

Some camp administrators believe that the only way to finance capital improvement is on a "pay-as-you-go" basis. This means that all funding must come from current operating funds, and as a result, additions or improvements must be financed over a period of years. The advantage of this approach is obvious: the plan is less expensive since no large debt service is involved. The great weakness to the "pay-as-you-go" philosophy is that most major improvements never are achieved because the necessary funds cannot be set aside.

The camp administrator, like any good business person, must be prepared to assess realistically the advisability of capital improvement and various methods of financing such a program. It may be that the camp would be wise to take a loan to expand the total operation and realize greater revenue over succeeding years. The advice of a trusted fiscal expert should help resolve this type of dilemma.

A very important area of the expenditure side of the budget is the *depreciation of fixed assets*. Many camp administrators fail to make any provision for depreciation of buildings, land vehicles, watercraft, and other capital holdings. The recommended procedure for determining the annual amount of depreciation is to take the book value or cost of construction and divide it by the life expectancy of the building or equipment, keeping in mind that some adjustment may have to be made to account for inflation. The life expectancy of most equipment is calculated for shorter periods than that of buildings. Government and other agency tables are available to assist the director in determining these amounts. The camp administrator should then pay one twelfth of the total amount into a savings account each month. This account becomes a means of funding capital expenses as they arise.

Classification of data. Once the budget data has been collected from all possible sources, the next step is to organize it into a detailed, logical classification. A wide variety of arrangements is possible in listing the many items that comprise the expenditure aspect of the budget. One system involves classifying all expenditures according to three headings: capital items, repairs, and expendable items. Another method is to select broad classifications such as services (personal)—includes salaries and wages of the staff, services (contractual)—includes all contracts and agreements, communication and transportation—includes telephone, postage, freight, travel, and vehicle maintenance, printing, and advertising—includes cost of brochures, applications, forms, and duplicating, and materials and supplies.

Perhaps the most popular means of classifying expenditures for the camp budget is by department or functional unit. A typical list might include administration, food service, health and safety, maintenance, program, and public relations. Each of these major headings is divided into a number of subheadings, and they, in turn, are further broken down into even more detailed items. The classification shown below has been developed around five main camp functions. "Program" is then further subdivided into nine activities.

CLASSIFICATION BY FUNCTION
    100 Administration
    200 Food service
    300 Health and safety
    400 Maintenance
    500 Program
        510 Archery
        520 Canoeing
        530 Crafts
        540 Mountaineering
        550 Orienteering
        560 Nature study
        570 Sailing
        580 Swimming
        590 Miscellaneous programs

Note that each classification is organized alphabetically, and each item has its own budget code number. Fig. 9-2 provides an example of a detailed budget for one of the activities listed above under "Program."

If the PPBS is adopted, the above itemized breakdown comprises only phase three

```
                        PROGRAM BUDGET

   Activity:  Archery              Activity head:_____

   Budget No.:  500-510            Date:_____

   Budget                          Anticipated      Actual
   number        Item              expenditure    expenditure

   001      Arm guards             _____    _____

   002      Arrows                 _____    _____

   003      Awards                 _____    _____

   004      Bows                   _____    _____

   005      Bow sights             _____    _____

   006      Gloves                 _____    _____

   007      Maintenance, range     _____    _____

   008      Repair, equipment      _____    _____

   009      Targets                _____    _____

   010      Target faces           ===========    ===========

                        Totals:
```

Fig. 9-2. Itemized expenditures for a single activity within the program budget.

of the budget. Phase one consists of developing program objectives for archery, while phase two provides a plan of the anticipated program indicating how these objectives will be met. If any capital expenditures are included, a carefully developed rationale must be presented defending the proposed expenditure.

It should be noted that in the classification examples shown above, staff salaries and wages have not been included. There are two common ways of listing these. The first is to set up a separate classification for salaries and wages with appropriate subheadings:

600 Salaries and wages
610 Administration personnel
620 Food service personnel
630 Maintenance and property management personnel
640 Medical personnel
650 Program personnel

The second possibility involves including salaries and wages of all personnel from a given department in the budget for that department. This latter method makes it possible to more easily show all costs for a given service on the subbudget. In this way, more accurate unit costs may be determined. This is usually done by working out the *cost per camper-week*. Table 9-2 shows comparative costs for four camps.

One final word regarding preparation of the budget data. Some camp administrators pad their budget each year on the assumption that it will be automatically cut anyway.

Table 9-2. Comparative costs per camper-week*

Budget item	Camp A	Camp B	Camp C	Camp D
Facilities	$ 4.63	$ 5.00	$10.46	$ 7.42
Food	14.73	22.00	11.43	13.64
Personnel	9.18	45.00	17.74	25.27
Program, administration, and promotion	7.27	58.00	3.84	14.54
TOTAL	$35.81	$130.00	$43.47	$60.87

*From Editorial: The cost of camping, Camping Magazine, **47**(7):6, May, 1975. p. 6.

The best policy is to submit a budget that is honest and that can be fully defended on the basis of need. The administrator who consistently overloads the budget soon loses credibility.

Budget approval. After all the data has been systematically organized, it usually must be approved by a person or persons on a higher administrative level, such as the camping board, the finance committee, or in the case of a private independent camp, the shareholders or owners. Regardless of the makeup of the approving body, good administrative practice suggests that persons responsible for authorizing the budget should have been informed of its contents before the formal presentation. In this way, problem areas within the budget can be identified and adjustments made so that no insurmountable hurdles are confronted when the budget is finally considered for adoption.

Whoever is responsible for making the presentation must be fully conversant with every facet of the budget and able to justify all figures. Tables using cost per camper-week data or other unit comparisons are also an effective means of justifying the budget. In some cases, it may be expedient to invite administrative assistants to be present to expand or clarify some particular aspect of the budget.

Budget administration. Once the budget has been adopted, it becomes the financial program of the camp for that fiscal year. It is the senior administrator's responsibility to make sure that the camp operates within the budget. How rigidly should the budget be followed? As long as the total budget amount is not exceeded, is it permissible to make readjustments within the total figure? Some administrators follow the budget stringently and allow for little or no variation from it. Others contend that once the budget is approved, the actual expenditures may be revised and monies freely transferred from one department to another. The latter practice negates a basic premise of budget planning. If colleagues are invited to participate in developing a fiscal program, they should expect that program to be followed. The budget, once approved, should be followed fairly closely. At the same time, some flexibility should be provided so that, as emergency situations arise, the budget is pliable enough to provide for them. A common way of meeting some unforeseen eventuality is to transfer funds from less needy areas to the area of unexpected demand. In cases in which the amount involved is appreciable, authorization from the original approving body is usually required.

Accounting procedures

To ensure that camp administrators do not overspend in any budget categories, careful accounting procedures must be es-

```
                              CONTROL SHEET

        Activity:    Archery

        Budget No.:  500-510        Budget amount:  $600.00
```

Date	Purchase order No.	Item	Vendor	Debit	Balance ($600.)
15/1/80	720	6 arm guards	Acme Archery Co.	24.00	576.
		4 doz. fiberglass arrows		95.00	481.
		2 fiberglass bows		70.00	411.
20/1/80	747	24 target faces	National Sporting Goods	74.00	339.
10/3/80	911	48 archery badges	National Archery Association	48.00	291.

Fig. 9-3. Sample control sheet for a single activity within the program budget.

tablished. Strict accountability must be required in every camp operation. Only in very small camps should directors themselves attempt to set up accounting systems that guarantee proper functioning of the budget process. It is much more common to make the camp accountant, bookkeeper, or secretary responsible for establishing efficient fiscal records. Once adopted, however, the camp director should become familiar with the system.

The accounting system must classify all revenue on the income side of the budget and reflect any changes that had not been anticipated when the budget was prepared. The expenditure side is more complex. Regular balance sheets must be provided to indicate exactly where each account stands in relation to its allocation. Fig. 9-3 shows a typical balance or control sheet for archery.

Control sheets should be kept for every budget account so that the budget administrator knows exactly what balance remains in each account. When persons who are responsible for various camp services are authorized to submit requisitions for their own equipment and supplies, they should also have a record of all expenditures to date.

Unlike most business operations, however, the majority of purchases must be made well before the camp season begins, and it is the responsibility of one or two persons to order these items in the early spring.

Another facet of good fiscal accounting is the annual audit. The audit serves to check on how successfully the administrator has managed the camp budget. It should be made by an independent party who is not directly connected with the camp. Careful accounting and auditing procedures provide an important means of maintaining internal control of the entire camp fiscal program so that those who administer the program are above suspicion or reproach.

PURCHASE AND CARE OF EQUIPMENT AND SUPPLIES

Much money is wasted each year by camp administrators who fail to follow good business practices in the purchase and care of camp equipment. Some camp administrators assume that, because camp is a seasonal operation and since many items will be lost or discarded by the end of the summer, the wise procedure is to purchase low-cost equipment, materials, and supplies. This is truly false economy. The purchase of quality equipment, which is well maintained and carefully stored in the off-season, can result in significant savings.

In addition, good equipment promotes greater satisfaction and pride in participation by campers. The camp that features riding as a major program activity but has inferior animals soon loses prestige. Similarly, the camp that promotes waterskiing had better keep its powerboat in good working order if it is to maintain its reputation. Finally, quality equipment is an important consideration when planning a safe, injury-free summer for campers. Poorly maintained mountaineering equipment could prove disastrous.

The inventory

Intelligent purchase of camp equipment, materials, and supplies begins with accurate inventory record keeping. As Walshin says: "Haphazard, off-the-cuff buying procedures cannot provide the margin of control which is so important to an efficient camp operation."[5]

The inventory is the best insurance a camp can have against overbuying or underbuying. If each administrative head has clear accurate records of stock on hand, this information provides the basis for future purchases. An inventory represents an itemized account of each piece of equipment and quantity of supplies on hand, when it was purchased, and its present condition. The inventory should be taken once a year, and in the case of food items for the kitchen, several times during the camp season. When inventory is taken annually, it is best done at the end of the camp season.

The preparation of a standardized inventory form that can be used by all segments of the camp is a highly recommended prac-

tice. An example of a typical program inventory form is shown in Fig. 9-4. All items are listed alphabetically in column 1. Column 2 indicates the numbers of each item that are on hand at the start of the camp season. The number of items that should be ordered on next year's budget is determined by adding columns 3, 4, and 5 and comparing the total with column 2. If insufficient equipment was on hand during the past season, as in the case of bow sights, the number in column 8 must be increased to the desired number. Column 9 lists the number of items actually approved in the budget and purchased. The final column shows the equipment on hand to begin the current camp season.

Guidelines for purchasing equipment, materials, and supplies

Whether all camp purchases are made by the camp director or whether this responsibility is delegated to others, several practices have proven helpful.

1. *Accurate inventories are the basis of all new purchases.* At the conclusion of the camp season, each department and program head should make out a complete inventory report with recommendations for next year's purchases.

2. *Equipment orders should be placed early.* There are a number of advantages to both the camp and the vendor when equipment and supplies are ordered well in advance of the camp season. Early ordering means early delivery so that any corrections can be made and defective equipment returned for replacement. When equipment must be made to specification, the work can be done without the pressure of imminent deadlines, thus ensuring a better product. If a camp receives its equipment well before the camp season, it has ample opportunity to update inventories and mark each item carefully.

Suppliers also appreciate early buying because it enables them to more accurately es-

---

5. Walshin, L.: Planning camp purchasing, Camping Magazine 39(8):10, Nov./Dec., 1967.

EQUIPMENT INVENTORY

Activity: Archery

Recorded by:_____

Date: 28/8/1980

Item	On hand: spring	Condition			Discarded	Lost	Number needed	Number received	Total
		New	Good	Fair					
(1)	(2)	(3)	(4)	(5)	(6)	(7)	(8)	(9)	(10)
Arm guards	22	–	12	6	2	2	6	6	24
Arrows	130	12	55	36	10	17	24	24	148
Bows	26	2	16	8	–	–	1	1	27
Bow sights	14	8	6	–	–	–	10	6	20
Gloves	22	–	12	4	4	2	10	10	26
Targets	6	–	4	1	1	–	1	1	6
Target faces	24	–	–	8	16	–	22	22	30
Target stands	6	–	6	–	–	–	–	–	6

Fig. 9-4. Sample inventory card for a single activity within the camp program.

timate the volume of work to be done and better utilization of staff can be planned. With this in mind, some suppliers offer better prices when orders are placed in the off-season. For this reason, some camps begin to order in September or October after camp closes.

3. *Quality merchandise should be purchased.* Generally speaking, low-cost equipment and supplies mean low-grade material. Whereas selection of quality items means greater initial expense, it has been found to be good economy in the long run. Better grade merchandise invariably lasts longer, has lower maintenance costs, and is more easily repaired. The most expensive deluxe model is not necessarily the best selection for a camp, but purchase of goods in the intermediate or upper price range is recommended.

4. *Purchase only from reputable companies.* Camps should deal only with established firms whose reputation for competitive prices and good service is well known. Camp purchasing agents should be wary of itinerant, fly-by-night salespersons who are able to offer an "exceptional deal." The old axiom, "You get exactly what you pay for," should not be ignored. Reputable dealers also are the best guarantee of the little extras in service. For example, if the camp has a sudden emergency order or is seeking an item that is not normally stocked on the shelves, a reputable firm makes the extra effort to meet this type of request.

It has been estimated by Wellman[6] that a camp normally purchases more than 2000

---

6. Wellman, H.: Principles of purchasing, Camping Magazine, 37(9):13, Nov./Dec., 1965.

different items during the camp season. It must be obvious that no one buyer nor even a group of persons can possibly be knowledgeable enough in all these areas to ensure an intelligent purchase. The camp representative who is responsible for purchasing must therefore rely on the integrity of vendors and their sales staff.

It is not considered a wise practice to limit all purchases in a given area to one company year after year. Although this is a convenient arrangement, it may not be in the best business interest of the camp. Suppliers need to believe that they are in competition for the camp's business but, more important, no one firm necessarily carries the best line of all types of equipment. New items are coming on the market all the time, and a particular supplier may have exclusive rights to one such product. At the same time, it is not wise to "scatter" camp purchases over a large number of vendors. Suppliers must receive enough of the camp's business to warrant providing their top service.

5. *Patronize the local dealer*. Whenever possible, preference should be given to purchasing from local suppliers as long as they can provide comparable goods at competitive prices. The local merchant is usually able to provide better service. Good public relations within the community also make it important to direct as much business as possible to local vendors.

6. *Order standardized equipment and supplies*. Standardization means that fixed styles, models, or types of equipment and supplies are purchased over a period of years, frequently from the same firm. There are several advantages to this practice. Standardization allows ease of ordering and replacement. It also makes possible quantity buying and, in many cases, a better price. For example, if a camp required 100 lanterns to equip the camper tents, one could anticipate a much better quotation if the complete order went to one supplier than if five different firms were asked to provide 20 lanterns each.

7. *Budget for replacements on a regular basis*. This principle is designed to avoid the need for large expenditures of money to replace a given item. For example, if a camp has 20 rowboats that were purchased when the camp first opened, it is reasonable to assume that all 20 boats may require replacement at about the same time. To avoid a major expenditure for 20 new boats, it is necessary to anticipate this eventuality and begin replacing three to five boats per year over a 4- to 6-year period. In this way, the aquatics budget can be maintained at a reasonably constant level. When this practice is adopted, care must be taken to safeguard against some departments or functional units "stockpiling" equipment. All purchases should be based on *planned need,* and only careful scrutiny of annual inventories can prevent overbuying.

8. *Purchases should be within the range of the camp's ability to pay*. Those persons responsible for camp purchasing must continually be on the alert against overbuying or the purchase of sophisticated equipment that the camp does not require. Department heads quite naturally seek the best for their particular area of the camp operation. This is commendable since it indicates a desire to offer an expanding, quality program. However, someone must keep things in proper perspective, for overpurchase in one area means curtailment of spending in another area. Sometimes a camp is inclined to purchase recklessly after a financially successful season. Good purchasing policy implies consistent, regular buying over the long term.

9. *Take advantage of legitimate discounts*. Purchasers must be aware of false bargains. Many apparent discounts are, in reality, no discount at all. In many cases, the

amount of the discount has been added to the retail price and then taken off to solicit the business of the buyer. There are several legitimate discounts of which the purchaser should be aware including: a discount is given by many companies if the bill is paid within 10 days, quantity buying can provide discounts of varying amounts, and goods purchased at the end of season provide significant savings in some cases when suppliers want to clear their shelves of off-season merchandise.

10. *Check all deliveries and establish procedures for immediate payment.* As goods are received, they must be checked against the invoice for number, type, and condition. Any missing or damaged goods should be reported immediately. Once the accuracy of the shipment has been verified, all items should be stored appropriately.

Specifications and bid buying

When a camp purchases merchandise in quantity, detailed specifications should be prepared regarding the type, color, model, size, and so forth of goods desired. If minimal information is provided, the supplier has little guidance regarding how the order should be filled. The more detailed the description, the more precisely the vendor can fulfill the request.

Once specifications have been drawn up, they are sent to several reputable suppliers, usually a minimum of three. Because the preparation of specification is time consuming, bids are not usually prepared for orders under $100. Some camp purchasing agents only submit bids for orders exceeding $500, and these are required every second or third year.

Competitive bidding is one of the best ways of ensuring the lowest price for the goods required. Once the various bids come in, the lowest figure is usually selected. However, occasionally factors such as speed and quality of service as well as ability to supply the exact items requested, may cause the camp to consider one of the higher bids.

Ordering procedure

Camp administrators should refrain from ordering equipment and supplies verbally. Because of the rush involved in a seasonal camp operation, purchases are often made by phone and requests from staff to the camp purchasing agent are given verbally. These practices should be discouraged since they invariably lead to misunderstanding for which there is no solution in the absence of written documentation. All transactions should be conducted in a businesslike manner with accurate records kept on file. These involve the use of three types of forms: requisitions, purchase orders, and vouchers.

Requisitions. In large camps in which the various functional units or departments are expected to funnel all purchases through the central office, requisition forms should be used. They are used by subadministrators throughout the camp to order items needed and should provide space for the name of the item, number or amount, description, and cost. All requisitions should be submitted on a standard form, usually $8\frac{1}{2} \times 11$ inches, for ease of filing. The original requisition is sent to the person responsible for approving and ordering all goods, and a duplicate remains with the person ordering the item.

Purchase orders. The purchase order should also be submitted on a standard form and is usually filled out in triplicate. The original is sent to the supplier, the second copy goes to the department or program head for whom the equipment has been ordered, and the third copy remains with the camp purchasing agent. All purchase orders should be consecutively numbered to provide easy reference. Fig. 9-5 shows a sample purchase order form.

```
┌─────────────────────────────────────────────────────────────────────┐
│  PURCHASE  ORDER                    Purchase order No._____  │
│                                                                       │
│                                     Date_____   │
│  _____                                             │
│  Name of camp                       Delivery deadline_____   │
├──────────────────────────────────┬──────────────────────────────────┤
│  Deliver to:                      │  Billing instructions:           │
│                                   │  Please bill camp on the attached│
│                                   │  voucher forms.  Return both white│
│                                   │  and pink copy with goods.  Include│
│                                   │  our purchase order No. on all   │
│                                   │  vouchers.                       │
├───────────┬──────────────────────┼──────────────┬──────────────────┤
│ Quantity  │     Description       │  Unit cost   │    Total         │
├───────────┼──────────────────────┼──────────────┼──────────────────┤
│           │                      │              │                  │
│           │                      │              │                  │
│           │                      │              │                  │
├───────────┴──────────────────────┴──────────────┴──────────────────┤
│                              Subtotal                               │
│                              Discount                               │
│                              Total                                  │
├──────────────────────────────────┬──────────────────────────────────┤
│                                   │                                  │
│                                   │  _____  │
│  Quotation bid No._____    │      Purchasing agent            │
│                                   │                                  │
│  Requisition No. _____     │  _____  │
│                                   │        Name of camp              │
└───────────────────────────────────┴─────────────────────────────────┘
```

Fig. 9-5. Sample purchase order form.

Vouchers. When the purchase order is sent to the vendor, it is accompanied by duplicate copies of the camp's voucher form. The original voucher is filed with the purchase order to show payment, and the duplicate is returned with payment to the supplier to indicate that the bill has been paid. Some firms prefer to return their own voucher form at the time of delivery.

Whenever possible, responsibility for all camp purchases should rest with one person, and careful records of requisitions, purchase orders and vouchers should be filed in the camp office for quick and easy reference.

Equipment storage

Most camps have a very sizable investment in equipment materials and supplies.

Good management requires that this investment be protected through proper cleaning, maintentance, and storage. Storage during the camp season, while important, is not nearly as critical as storage during the off-season. The deterioration that results from careless storage during the winter months may take a greater toll on equipment than the use during the camping season. During the off-season, as much equipment as possible should be moved indoors to protect it from rust, weather, and vandalism. Temperature, humidity, and ventilation are all important factors to control when considering storage. For example, some items need to be greased or oiled at the end of the camp season to protect them from excessive moisture. This should be part of a regu-

```
┌─────────────────────────────────────────────────────────────────────────────┐
│                          EQUIPMENT SIGN-OUT SHEET                             │
│                                           Date:_____            │
├──────────────────┬──────────────┬──────────┬──────────┬─────────────────────┤
│                  │              │   Time   │   Time   │                     │
│      Item        │     Name     │  issued  │ returned │     Signature       │
├──────────────────┼──────────────┼──────────┼──────────┼─────────────────────┤
│ 2 tennis racquets│ Bobby Smith  │3:10 p.m. │4:30 p.m. │       B.S.          │
│ 3 tennis balls   │              │          │          │                     │
│ 4 horseshoes     │ Jim Brown    │3:12 p.m. │7:50 p.m. │       J.B.          │
│                                                                             │
```

Fig. 9-6. Sample program equipment sign-out sheet.

lar, planned maintenance service program. Other items are susceptible to extremes in temperature change. Unless several camp buildings are winterized and kept partially heated during the coldest months, it may be necessary to transport some items to the city where storage temperature can be regulated.

Equipment issue and marking

Some camps locate all equipment in one central storage area. Other camps set up a number of separate equipment facilities. The advantage of the central area is that it enables one person to easily supervise the entire operation providing improved accountability. Regardless of the physical layout, the system of storage, issue, and retrieval should be simple but accurate and, whenever possible, the responsibility of one person.

The most common practice is to prepare equipment sign-out sheets (Fig. 9-6). The times at which each item is issued and returned are recorded, and the user initials the sheet when the equipment is returned. Another method is to list items of equipment that would be needed for an activity on equipment issue cards. For example, all equipment items that might be needed for an over-night sleepout are listed on a card. The actual items taken are checked off, and the card is signed by the counsellor in charge. When the equipment is returned, the storeroom manager signs it to indicate that everything has been returned in good repair.

A practice that helps safeguard against loss or theft of equipment is the marking of each item so that it can be easily identified. Several ways of marking camp equipment include the use of India ink stencils or stamps on cloth and canvas items, paint on wood or metal articles, and a burning tool or electric drill for leather, wooden, plastic, and metal equipment. Identification labels may also be sewn into some articles. It is important that equipment be marked as soon as it is received. Some storeroom managers place the year of purchase on the item as a check on the expected life of that equipment.

CAMP INSURANCE

Because of the dramatic rise in the number and size of lawsuits involving camps in the past decade, insurance premiums have risen to the point where they represent a substantial item among camp expenses. This fact should not deter those persons responsible for fiscal management from seeking complete coverage. Although the cost of insurance premiums is high, no camp today can afford not be be adequately insured. Failure to cover every contingency could wipe out a camp operation that has taken years of hard work and sacrifice to develop.

The cost of an adequate insurance program varies from camp to camp depending on the size of the organization, the condition of the buildings, the actual scope of the coverage, and other factors. However, regardless of the cost, insurance should be considered part of the general operating budget of the camp and as such may be a factor in adjusting tuition fees upward as premium costs rise.

It is possible today to be insured against a vast number of risks. Generally speaking, however, coverage falls into two broad categories: (1) protection in case of litigation against the camp or the staff and (2) coverage to protect the physical property including the site, facilities, and equipment.

In recent years, more companies have begun to specialize in coverage for camps. The importance of seeking the services of specialists in camp insurance is emphasized in an editorial in *Camping Magazine* that stated,

It is to a camp director's distinct advantage to obtain the services of such a company, whose broad working knowledge of the ever changing problems in the field and a continued dependence upon its reputation with the camp fraternity guarantee outstanding service.[7]

It stands to reason that agencies that specialize in camp insurance should be capable of delivering the most attractive programs both with regard to service and cost. The value of dealing with a company whose personnel are familiar with the unique prob-

7. Editorial: Pointers on camp insurance, Camping Magazine, 38(2):15, Feb., 1966.

lems and complexities of the camp operation cannot be underestimated. One must also assume that those companies that specialize in insuring camp program can offer the most economical service. A number of insurance companies now offer, as part of their service, regular inspections of the camp to detect any hazardous condition. These include inspection of the physical site, buildings, and equipment as well as an examination of the camp program itself. Such a service is invaluable in helping to reduce injuries and can save a camp valuable premium dollars.

The following pages provide a brief description of forms of coverage that are available to camps and the relative importance of each.

Comprehensive liability

Some administrators believe that fire insurance is the most critical type of coverage in any camp insurance package. This is not true; comprehensive liability is widely accepted today as the most vital area of a well-planned insurance program. In the case of a fire, camp authorities can determine the maximum loss that can be anticipated, but with liability, the amount that may be awarded by the court can vary greatly. In recent years, settlements involving camps have increased in both number and size at a truly alarming rate, and decisions against camps have run as high as a million dollars.

For many years, many nonprofit agency camps, and particularly church-affiliated camps, enjoyed considerable immunity from legal action. More recently, however, these exemptions have been waived in most states and provinces so that virtually all camps are vulnerable to legal liability suits.

Liability insurance is basically designed to protect the camp and its staff against a charge of negligence. Such negligence may result in two types of damage: bodily injury and property damage. In the case of bodily injury, insurance specialists now recommend coverage of not less than $100,000 and in most cases $300,000 to $500,000. The increased cost of the higher protection is surprisingly small and should be carefully examined. Property damage can normally be expected to run from a minimum coverage of $10,000 up to as much as $50,000.

In recent years, there has been a trend toward purchase of a third type of liability insurance, namely *personal injury liability*. This form of injury is distinct from physical or bodily damage and involves such conditions as libel, slander, defamation of character, and invasion of privacy.

Some insurance companies are not prepared to write liability coverage for camps. Those that do specialize in this field are very sensitive to the entire area and keep close scrutiny on the camping industry. Recently, day camps have found it increasingly difficult to get liability coverage and travel camps receive even less attractive rates. Premiums generally run so high for these two types of camps that camp tuition fees should not be set until insurance rates are established.

Many American companies refuse to write camp liability insurance unless evidence can be provided that medical insurance (or at least accident benefit) is carried on all campers. The reason for this is that when medical expenses are not covered for an accident, the family of a camper is far more likely to sue for compensation to cover the medical costs.

Special risks. When selecting liability insurance, it is essential that the camp administrator determine exactly what is covered and what is excluded in the policy. For example, there is a standard form called the Owners', Landlords,' and Tenants' that excludes certain conditions unless specific notification is made in the policy. Broad comprehensive policies are recommended today because they automatically pick up most known risks as well as new risks.

Regardless of the type of policy contemplated, the person responsible for insurance coverage must check carefully to be sure that all risks are included. Certain specific items should be covered on every camp policy. The most important are described below.

Products coverage. This special risk relates to food product liability and protects the camp against the possibility of food poisoning.

Malpractice coverage. Another important special risk is threat of a malpractice suit because of professional services rendered on behalf of the camp. This usually involves treatment rendered by the camp doctor or nurse. *Contingent malpractice* is coverage that protects the camp against treatment rendered by medical personnel who are not directly employed by the camp. A fully comprehensive policy should include a statement to the affect that "Coverage is afforded for an occurrence arising out of any professional services or the omission thereof." Such a statement includes services of an osteopath, chiropractor, dentist, or druggist.

Independent contractor coverage. A clause should also be included within the policy to protect the camp in the event that an accident occurs as a result of the negligence of an outside contractor.

Independent program services coverage. If a camp makes use of an outside riding stable, mountaineering school, or waterskiing agency, care must be taken to ensure that the camp liability policy covers these activities even though they occur away from the campsite and under the supervision of another party. It is frequently assumed that if a riding accident occurs at an independent school, the proprietor of the riding school will be held responsible. The possibility is great, however, that the camp will also be named in a suit of this kind.

High-risk activities. Insurance companies usually require that activities such as the use of trampolines or minibikes, horseback riding, and all boating activities be added to any basic policy, thus requiring an additional premium.

Staff coverage. A basic liability policy usually covers officers and senior directors when they are acting on behalf of the camp or within the scope of their job description. Regular employees, however, are excluded from this coverage. Many policies refer to "named insured," but an additional clause covering the "additionally insured" should be included. Individual staff members cannot easily secure this type of coverage, and the cost of including them in the camp's comprehensive policy is small.

Comprehensive automobile coverage. Automobile insurance may or may not be written in conjunction with a comprehensive liability policy. This is a critical area in a camp's total insurance program and limits, of necessity, must be high. Many insurance companies are hedging when it comes to camp-owned vehicles. They contend that, too often, vehicles are old, poorly maintained, and placed in the hands of inexperienced drivers, making them a very poor risk for the insurer.

An increasingly popular solution to the problem of auto insurance is the rental or leasing of passenger cars, pickups, station wagons, or passenger vans for the camp season. Automobile nonownership and leased vehicle coverage should be included in every camp liability policy: If staff members use their own cars on camp business and become involved in an accident, the camp may be named as a codefendant. The employee often has only minimal liability coverage, and therefore the party initiating legal action can be expected to seek redress from the camp.

Any vehicle that is used to transport campers has excessive exposure. If an accident occurs in which negligence is proved, the settlement may run into the millions of dollars. When leasing or hiring vehicles for transport of campers or staff, it is strongly recommended that a photocopy of the certificate of insurance be requested from the firm leasing the vehicle or providing the transportation.

Property insurance

Camp property insurance can be covered by individual policies for fire, vandalism, ice and snow damage, and the like. However, the more popular practice today is to carry an "all risk" property protection plan. This type of plan covers any risks of direct physical loss or damage by external causes. It may include: fire and lightning, windstorm and hail, explosion (other than steam boiler), riot and civil commotion, vandalism and malicious mischief, damage by automobile or aircraft, smoke or water damage, falling tree limbs, building and structure collapse, landslide, glass breakage, power failure, falling objects, theft and burglary, and ice and snow damage.

Fire. The greatest hazard to property is that of fire, and some camps seek financial protection against loss from this source only. Many insurance companies are hesitant to write fire insurance policies for camps. This apprehension is understandable since camps are usually located in fairly remote areas, and service from the nearest fire department may be of little or no value. In some cases, water supplies are unreliable when large quantities are required in a hurry. In addition, camp buildings are usually of frame construction and can burn to the ground in a matter of minutes. Insurance firms are even less disposed to write a policy for only one or two buildings such as the kitchen, dining hall, or main lodge. For this reason, it is easier to get coverage when all buildings are included in the policy.

Camp adminstrators should be aware that several factors contribute to reduced fire insurance premiums. A knowledge of these factors when constructing new facilities can save valuable dollars over an extended period. These factors include sufficient space between buildings, use of approved fire-resistant building materials (especially for the roof), location of fire extinguishers at each building, presence of a full-time custodian on the camp property, and location of the camp in close proximity to a local fire department.

It is important that insurance coverage reflects current property values so that replacement costs or actual cash values are substantially met by the existing contract. One means of estimating the replacement value of camp buildings is to have the insurance company inspect all camp buildings and structures at least every 3 years.

Other hazards to property. As pointed out early in this section, property insurance may include protection against several other hazards. Camp administrators must examine their particular situation carefully before determining which risks warrant inclusion in their policy. Most camps today do include coverage for vandalism and malicious mischief.

Medical insurance

Almost all camps in the United States have some type of camp accident and sickness insurance. In Canada, the number is very small because of the national medicare program.

Most medical insurance programs require 100% participation by campers. Many camps erroneously exclude the staff from these policies on the assumption that they are adequately covered by workmen's compensation. Occasionally workmen's compensation does not provide sufficient coverage, and for these occasions, it is desirable to have all personnel included in the camp medical program. Some camps invite the staff to participate on a voluntary basis in the camp medical program.

Medical insurance rates are usually written on the basis of the cost per person per day, week, or season. Essentially all policies include coverage for accident medical expenses, sickness medical expenses, accidental death benefits, and dismemberment benefits. Insurance is also available to cover specific high-risk activities within the camp program under a special rider. For example, camp trips and tours may be insured separately if desired.

It is important to note that those camps that have a strong and carefully formulated safety program, with a correspondingly good accident record, qualify for special rates by most insurers.

Workmen's compensation

Workmen's compensation is a form of accident and sickness coverage for camp staff and as such could have been included in the section on medical insurance. However the complexities of the Workmen's Compensation Act are such that it deserves separate consideration.

Some camp administrators, even today, are not aware that this is a compulsory requirement and must be paid by the majority of camps. Because it is administered by the state, the requirements, benefits, limits of payment, and rates of coverage vary widely from state to state. This is the cause of much of the confusion that surrounds workmen's compensation among camp directors. It is the responsibility of camp administrators to determine what requirements pertain to their camp. Ignorance of the law is not a valid defense in the event that a camp employee is injured or becomes sick.

Because the regulations governing the act vary from one state to the next, it is not possible to discuss all its ramifications. However, several common areas require some clarification, including the status of the volunteer staff, outside contractors, and the importance of a good safety record.

Status of volunteer staff. Some camps that employ large numbers of volunteers have difficulty finding insurance companies willing to provide protection because the status of volunteer help in camps has not been at all clear. Some states have held that volunteers are eligible for workmen's compensation benefits, while others have not. It is incumbent on camps that use a volunteer staff to determine exactly what regulations govern their operation.

Outside contractors. If a camp hires a subcontractor to construct a new building or make renovations to an existing facility, who is responsible if an injury occurs to a workman hired by the subcontractor, but working on the campsite? The majority of states require the contractor or subcontractor to guarantee this protection, but the responsibility may be imposed on the camp in certain cases if the contractor has not provided insurance. Few camp leaders realize this and so make no effort to determine whether outside firms have satisfactory coverage. Before any work is done in the name of the camp, a certificate of insurance should be requested to confirm that sufficient protection is afforded.

Camp safety record. Some states recognize what are called *experience credits*. This means that a camp that has enjoyed a good safety record over a period of years is given preferred rates in recognition of this accident-free performance. A minimum premium is usually required before a camp is eligible for the reduced rate. It must, of course, be realized that a poor accident and sickness record may result in a surcharge.

Additional special coverage

The types of insurance described up to this point may be considered basic coverage and should be considered mandatory by all camps. In addition, other types of specific protection can be procured as a particular need is identified.

Umbrella liability. Recently, increasing numbers of camps have taken out umbrella liability insurance to protect themselves against a catastrophic loss. Whereas most ordinary hazards are covered by the primary liability policy, an umbrella policy provides additional coverage beyond that offered by the basic policy. Because it is a form of "blanket" coverage that is designed to take care of all eventualities, it can be purchased only in multiples of one million dollars. The cost of this extra policy is surprisingly low for the type of protection it offers.

Ice and snow collapse. For those camps that are located in heavy snow belts, insurance against the hazards of building collapse resulting from ice and snow is strongly recommended. Before a company will insure camp buildings against this hazard, a complete engineering inspection is usually required to guarantee that all roofs are capable of withstanding a given weight.

Tuition fee and tuition refund. These two plans are designed to protect the camp against loss of tuition fees. If a major catastrophe strikes and makes it impossible for a camp to open or the camp faces premature closing, it is possible to protect the owner against loss of income. For example, in the event of a forest fire or any other insured peril interrupting camp operation, the camp can be protected under special tuition fee insurance.

Tuition refund insurance, on the other hand, is designed to cover camp interruption resulting from accident or contagious illness. Table 9-3 lists the basis on which refunds may be awarded and the percentages of refund that might be provided under such

Table 9-3. Conditions covered under a typical tuition refund insurance policy

Occurrence	Percentage of refund
Accident or illness withdrawal	100
Failure to open	90
Late arrival	50
Flood withdrawal	75
Fear of epidemic	100
Individual quarantine	100
Quarantine extension	90

a policy. The premium for tuition refund policies is usually about $2\frac{1}{2}\%$ of the total tuition fee. Such contingency plans avert the possibility of a potentially ruinous summer resulting from loss of tuition.

Theft insurance. Theft insurance is generally regarded as more suitable for camps than burglary insurance. In the case of theft insurance, proof of forcible entry is not a necessary condition for reimbursement.

In summary, camp administrators must make sure that the camp insurance program is completely in order so that nothing is left to chance. It only takes one careless accident caused by negligence for an entire camp operation that has taken years to build to be wiped out. No administrator should approach camp insurance on the premise that "We have known our parents for years . . . they would never sue us," or "No one will sue us . . . we are a nonprofit organization."

ADMINISTRATIVE GUIDELINES

1. Efficient business and fiscal management is an essential requirement of the camping industry. Camps cannot hope to compete for the public's recreational dollar without it.
2. The professional expertise of accountants, lawyers, and insurance agents or brokers should be sought. Their professional advice will prove to be a good financial investment.
3. The camp business office should serve as a model of good management practice and ef-

ficiency. Most camps can be best served by centralizing office services in one pool.
4. Each camp, regardless of size, should assign one person (such as the camp secretary or business manager) to assume responsibility for the business and fiscal management of the camp.
5. The responsibilities of the camp office personnel include receiving visitors, answering the telephone, preparing camp correspondence, picking up and distributing mail, filing, ordering and receiving equipment and supplies, duplicating materials, and providing additional services for the camp staff.
6. An important component of camp business management is the accurate compilation and filing of camp records and reports.
7. As a business, camping must utilize good budgetary practice to be accountable. The budget is the financial program for the camp season.
8. Budget preparation involves a number of important principles:
   a. It should take place over many months.
   b. It should be realistic and accurate.
   c. It should provide for equitable distribution of available funds.
   d. It should involve cooperative preparation on the part of all camp administrative personnel.
   e. It must be flexible.
   f. Supportive data should accompany all requests for increased appropriations.
9. Many sound arguments exist to support the practice of decentralizing budget preparations.
10. Camp administrators should familiarize themselves with PPBS and consider adoption of this type of budget preparation as it is particularly well suited to the camp setting.
11. The budget process involves four main steps: (a) collection of data, (b) classification of data, (c) budget approval, and (d) budget implementation.
12. Alternate sources of revenue besides camper fees must be found if camps are to remain financially viable. Perhaps the best potential source is to extend the use of sites over a longer period by winterizing at least some camp facilities.

13. Those persons responsible for administration of the camp budget must make sure that the camp operates within the approved amounts. Some transfer of funds within the budget may be acceptable, but the fiscal program should normally be followed.

14. Accurate accounting procedures are the best insurance against overspending the camp budget.

15. One of the most important accounting devices is the inventory, which protects the camp against over or underbuying.

16. Those persons responsible for camp purchases should follow established guidelines for buying.

17. The practice of preparing specifications and calling for bids should be followed with all orders of significant volume.

18. Recognized ordering procedures involve the use of requisitions, purchase orders, and vouchers.

19. Equipment storage and issuing should be routinized so that equipment is not only well maintained but can be accounted for at all times.

20. In spite of the steady increase in the cost of all types of insurance, it is mandatory that every camp have sufficient protection against the most common risks.

21. Comprehensive liability insurance is the most critical area of a well-planned insurance program. No camp can afford to be underinsured in this vital area.

22. Camp administrators should examine very carefully special risks that may not be covered adequately in a comprehensive policy.

23. Liability and medical coverage for the staff is a special consideration and should not be overlooked. Workmen's compensation may not provide sufficient coverage in some parts of the country.

24. Comprehensive automobile insurance may not be part of the comprehensive liability policy. In such cases, it is important to secure sufficient coverage against all eventualities. Camps should consider the leasing of vehicles for the camp season.

25. There are many forms of property insurance. Each camp must select those forms of coverage that meet their particular needs. These invariably include fire, vandalism, and malicious mischief, as well as other forms of selected protection.

SELECTED BIBLIOGRAPHY

Avedisian, C.: PPBS—its implications for physical education, Journal of Health, Physical Education and Recreation, 43:111-118, Oct., 1972.

Boy Scouts of America: Camp business management and commissary operation (No. 12005). (North Brunswick, N.J.; Supply Division, Boy Scouts of America.)

Caden, C.: Risk management insurance, Camping Magazine, 50(6):15-16, 19, May, 1978.

Deam, W. B.: Insurance coverage for your staff, Camping Magazine, 39(8):14-15, Nov./Dec., 1967.

Detrick, W. B.: Money care: guidelines for camp budgeting, Camping Magazine, 46(6):11, 17, Apr., 1974.

Editorial: Cost of camping survey, Camping Magazine, 51(4):22-26, Mar., 1979.

Editorial: How much is enough in terms of today's economy and camp's liability coverage? Camping Magazine, 45(1):16-17, Jan., 1973. Adapted from "An owner's and director's Guide to Camp Insurance" by Higham, Neilson, Whitridge and Reid, Inc.

Editorial: Workmen's compensation guidelines explained, Camping Magazine, 46(6):7, Apr., 1974

Eustis, W.: Legal advice helps lessen directors' worries, Camping Magazine, 49(2):10-12, 38, Jan., 1977.

Farrow, J. M., and Pinney, B. M.: Comprehensive liability insurance—the cornerstone of camp insurance, Camping Magazine, 41(5):24-25, May, 1969.

Fine, B.: Further sources of income, Report of Ontario Camping Association Convention, 1971, pp. 26-27.

Jewson, D.: The promotional aspect of camp marketing, Camping Magazine, 50(6):17, 21, May, 1978.

Johnson, H. W.: Selection, training and supervising office personnel. Reading, Mass.: Addison-Wesley Publishing Co., Inc., 1969.

Labbett, C.: Money in the bank—budget, or else, Canadian Camping, 25(1):8-9, Fall, 1972.

Loheed, P. S.: Redesigning multiple camp facilities for year-round programs, Camping Magazine, 51(5):17-19, Apr., 1979.

Mill, G., and Standingford, O.: Office administration and method. (New York: Pitman Publishing Corp., 1972).

Moore, H. E.: Camp finance: and accounting concept in support of a "systems" approach to camp management, Camping Magazine, 46(7):7-8, May, 1974.

Rolfe, S.: Computers in camp management, Camping Magazine, 51(4):12-13, 39, Mar., 1979.

Wellman, H.: Principles of purchasing, Camping Magazine, 37(9):12-13, Nov./Dec., 1965.

CHAPTER TEN

Public relations

I know that you believe you understand what you think I said. But I am not
sure you realize that what you heard is not what I meant.
ANONYMOUS

While business and industry have long recognized the importance of a comprehensive, planned program that effectively interprets their product or service to the public, camp directors have been loathe to take aggressive steps in this direction. It was as though advertising, publicity, and competition were dirty words that smacked of high-powered salesmanship and were inimical to the high ideals of camping. Many persons associated with camping believed that public relations was some tainted process borrowed from high pressure business.

The private camps first followed the lead of successful business enterprises and placed their "product" before the public. Today each camp, whether private, public, or agency, recognizes the need for an active public relations program. In a world in which so many other forces are competing for the public's recreation dollar and in which changing summer holiday patterns make organized camping only one of many choices for families, it becomes imperative that camp directors pursue a sound, aggressive program of public relations if they are to maintain viable enrollment figures.

It is important that a distinction be made between the terms *publicity* and *public relations*. The latter has no doubt evolved from the former, but today the two are recognized as having very different meanings. Publicity is but one aspect of a much broader program of public relations. Publicity seeks to initiate interest in the product or service, while public relations strives to promote and maintain a continuing relationship. Herein lies the fundamental characteristic of public relations as distinguished from publicity. Publicity implies promotion of camping to the public in what is strictly a one-way communication. Public relations on the other hand, is a cooperative endeavor involving a two-way process of interaction.

Another way in which public relations differs from publicity is that while publicity is usually handled by one person or a small committee, public relations is the responsibility of every individual associated with the organization. Even though the ultimate responsibility for public relations rests with the director, every member of the camp staff—office secretary, camp custodian, cook, and every counsellor—actually becomes an ambassador of the camp whenever they deal with the public. The way counsellors and campers conduct themselves in the village store may profoundly affect the camp's image in the local community. Counsellors who are abusive and condescending create one impression; counsellors who are polite and conscious of the conduct of the campers create an entirely different impression. Similarly, the camp custodian may totally alienate parents on their arrival at camp if he fails to take a few minutes to assist them in parking their car and directing them to the business office in a congenial manner. Even if the custodian has done his job and created a favorable first impression, this goodwill can all be undone in a matter of seconds by an ill-mannered secretary in the office.

It must be impressed on all staff members that public relations is the responsibility of every one of them whenever they are before the public; it is a total team effort. Directors must understand that it is not an easy task to impress on a youthful staff the critical importance of their deportment before the public. A strong esprit de corps and pride in "our camp" on the part of all staff members must be a fundamental objective of good public relations.

Since every staff member is a potential public relations agent, it is important to ensure that *all* staff members attend precamp training meetings when public relations is a central topic of discussion. To excuse the administrative or paramedical staff from these meetings may be to leave the way open for the very breakdown in communication the director seeks to avoid.

It should now be possible to define a little more precisely the meaning of public relations as it relates to camping. *Public relations is a planned process in which all staff members endeavor to develop a favorable relationship between the camp and the community it serves.* To bring about this type of relationship, camp personnel at all levels must have a clear appreciation of the philosophy and the objectives the camp seeks to realize.

PURPOSE OF PUBLIC RELATIONS

As was pointed out in the opening chapter of this book, there are many types of camps, and individual camps are different within each classification. Each has its own physical attributes, its own particular organization, and its own special program emphasis and appeal. Even when the basic characteristics of a given camp operation are not that uniquely different from other camps, the one factor that is likely to set it apart from others is its program philosophy. That is to say, two organizations may be similar in almost all respects, but because each has established its own set of program objectives and anticipated outcomes for its clientele, the two camps may appear as different as night and day.

Because of this great variance between camps, it may seem unrealistic to attempt to generalize a public relations approach that will be applicable to all situations. However, regardless of the unique character of a given operation, it is possible to list some basic guidelines for all camps. The following guidelines were adapted from the American Association of School Administrators. They may also serve as a declaration of purpose of public relations for camps.

1. To inform the public about the work of the camps.
2. To establish confidence in the camps.
3. To rally support for proper maintenance of the camping movement.
4. To develop awareness of the role of camping in a democracy.
5. To unite parents and camp personnel in meeting the developmental needs of children.
6. To integrate the home, the camp, and the community at large in improving camp experiences for all campers.
7. To evaluate the extent to which camps are meeting the needs of their clientele.

8. To correct misunderstanding as to the aims and objectives of camps.[1]

THE CAMP'S MULTIPLE PUBLICS

Up to this point, reference has been made to "the public" as though there was one general public with whom the camp must interrelate. In fact there are many publics, and one of the most critical aspects of good public relations is the identification of each. The next step is to recognize that publics differ in size, method of communication, and most important of all, in social, economic, and political interests. It is important also to remember that a given individual may be a member of several publics.

Since the interests of each public may be different, it is important that the public relations approach be appropriate to that particular group. An effective appeal to one group may be totally unproductive to another. The public relations expert has long recognized that not only must the media of communication be suited to the particular public, but the message itself must frequently be modified.

In camping, there are two obvious publics: campers and parents. Additional groups that may need to be considered are the camp staff, camp committee or board, former campers, other camp directors, members of the media, and local general public.

Campers

The primacy of campers as a public must be apparent to every camp administrator. Unless the individual camper is a happy and satisfied customer, all efforts to influence other publics will eventually fail. Camper interests center basically around the pro-

gram and the extent to which camp experiences provide personal fulfillment. In effect, all campers become ambassadors for the camp. It is essential, therefore, that the message they convey be a positive one. The fact that the vast majority of persons attending organized camps in North America are children between 6 and 15 years of age demonstrates the powerful impact the attitudes of these children will have on their parents, other members of their family, and their peers. If they attend a day camp, the potential influence is even greater since, 5 days a week, they bring home reports that become the main topic of conversation at the evening meal. It is imperative that they be strong supporters of the camp and its staff. Research in the field of education concerning pupil and parental approval of school programs indicates that the correlation between the two groups is very high. There is every reason to believe that a similar relationship exists between child and parental attitudes toward camp. Parents who have never had a camp experience themselves and have some misgivings about the value of such an experience will become ardent supporters of camping purely on the basis of the child's enthusiastic reports.

It must also be remembered that today's campers will be tomorrow's parents. It is axiomatic that parents who have had happy and satisfying camp experiences as children will aspire to provide the same opportunities for their children. Conversely, parents who had unfavorable recollections of camp will be unlikely to send their children to camp.

Parents

Satisfied campers are the key to continued parental support. Most camp administrators realize that successful recruitment of new campers is most effectively achieved through the recommendation of one parent

---

1. Adapted from American Association of School Administrators: Public relations for America's schools. (Washington, D.C.: The Association, 1950), p. 14.

to another. The majority of new campers come as referrals from other camp families. As families discuss summer plans over the bridge table, at coffee parties, and over the garden fence, satisfied parents relate the happy experiences that their children have had at a particular camp.

Different publics require different approaches. This is certainly true of campers and parents. From time to time, various surveys have been conducted by persons in the camping profession in an attempt to determine what parents consider to be the important values of camping. Although the results of such studies have not provided complete unanimity, most parents would place the following close to the top of their list:

1. Development of the ability to live, work, and play cooperatively with others
2. Development of self-confidence
3. Provision of a healthy and safe camp environment
4. Development of lasting friendships
5. Development of a love for the outdoors
6. Development of character including self-respect, honesty, and tolerance of others

If, on the other hand, children are asked why they attend camp, their interests centers mainly around program and camp activities. A list of camper values might include:

1. Learning to waterski
2. Making my own paddle in the craftshop
3. Beating my counsellor in tennis
4. Passing my intermediate swimming test
5. Surviving my first overnight sleep-out

It is apparent that parents and children who are contemplating camp for the first time view the summer experience in very different ways. It is important for camp representatives who visit the home to realize that what they say regarding health, safety, and the opportunities for social interaction

within the tent or bunk may make little impression on the potential camper. If the representative plans a short slide presentation to "sell" the camp, the selection of slides will vary depending on whether it is made only to parents or whether the child is also present.

Camp staff

It was pointed out earlier in this chapter that every member of the camp staff is a public relations agent of the camp. Each member must not only be fully conversant with the objectives of the camp, but must be familiar with, and in support of, the camp philosophy. Staff members have many occasions when they will be required to interpret the camp and its objectives to campers, parents, and the general public. Wholesome camper-counsellor relationships have an important bearing on sound public relations. Just as the camper's attitudes profoundly influence those of the parent, so those of the camper are shaped by the counsellor. While the camper serves unconsciously as an agent of public relations for the camp, counsellors must be consciously aware of their role as promoters of the camp and its program.

If public relations is to be effective, it must be a total, cooperative effort. Internal frictions between various segments of the staff are not uncommon in the camp setting. This is generally attributed to the fact that people live and work in such close proximity to each other during almost every waking hour of the day for an entire summer. Recognizing this danger, the camp administrator must consciously strive to strengthen morale among the various segments of the staff. The counselling staff must appreciate the problems that confront the kitchen staff. Similarly, each member of the program staff must have a clear understanding of all policies that relate to the health center and the medical and paramedical staff. Clear lines of communication and understanding must exist between the in-camp program staff and the out-tripping staff to ensure that these two program groups are not in competition with each other. This can only be achieved when the camp administrator successfully interprets the total camp operation to all staff members and solicits their full cooperation toward common objectives.

Camp committee or board

Many camp administrators are responsible to an advisory camp committee or board of directors. When such policy-making groups exist, their members are usually people from the community, such as representatives from business, education, social agencies, and other professions, who bring some special expertise to the group. As such, the camp committee or board represents a very special public and requires a very particular approach. As members of the business community, they are usually more receptive to hard statistical data and objective evidence rather than an emotional appeal that might be effective with a group of parents. Since this group makes decisions that deal with the fiscal aspects of the camp, graphs and charts are often effective with them while these same graphs and charts would be totally unacceptable for another public.

Former campers

Former campers may be quite responsive to an emotional appeal. They are normally filled with nostalgia and happy memories of enjoyable days at camp. They should not be overlooked as a potential public. Some campers may be unable to return each summer for any number of reasons, but just because they do not return for a summer, their names should not be dropped from the mailing list. They may be anxious to re-register after a season or more away from camp or may have younger brothers or sisters who are potential campers. The former

camper is also a potential candidate for a staff position.

Camp directors

Good public relations should exist between camps. Too often, camp directors see themselves in competition with other camps rather than working harmoniously to further organized camping. It is mutually advantageous to work in a spirit of cooperation since experience shows that camps that do work together find that many referrals come from camp colleagues. Parents who send their girls to one camp often seek the advice of another director in selecting a boy's camp for their son. An inquiry from parents reveals that they wish to send their child to a camp that has a strong out-tripping program. Because the first camp does not offer this program, the director will recommend another camp that does stress this aspect of camp programming. Perhaps most important is the need for camps to assist and support one another at times when camping is under attack. It is important that camp executives seek membership in their professional organization at the state, provincial, and national level to further camping with the strength that collectivity provides.

Mass media representatives

Members of the press, radio, and television are a very special public, that requires carefully planned, cooperative action. The surest way to endanger public relations with this public is to show favoritism to one representative at the expense of another. Each must be treated honestly and impartially if the camp hopes to maintain support of the communication media.

Local community

The local community includes the neighbors that are adjacent to the camp property. It is also a very unique public requiring special public relations. More often than not, contacts with this public will be personal encounters. They may be made through campers, counsellors, or other staff members including the business manager, camp driver, camp nurse, or camp doctor. In each case, the need for warm, cooperative relationships is important, and although these relationships should be beneficial to both parties, the camp usually stands to lose more if this partnership is threatened.

General public

This public refers to more than just the parents; it also refers to all groups outside the camp including other social agencies, schools, and representatives of government. It is vital that camps maintain the goodwill of the public-at-large for one never knows when a camp will need to rely on the support of some segment of the community to continue offering its service. Camping is not conducted in a vacuum. It is but one organization among many that touches a given clientele, and each camp administrator must recognize the interdependency of the many public service organizations as it seeks the support of the general public.

PRINCIPLES OF PUBLIC RELATIONS

Because there are many types of camps, each with its own particular philosophy or program emphasis, it is impossible to provide a model of an ideal public relations program that would be suitable for all camps. It is possible, however, to provide some guidelines that can serve as the basis for developing a strong public relations program for any camp.

1. *Public relations is founded on a quality camp.* There is no substitute for a strong, well-organized camp. No amount of skillful and carefully devised public relations can make up for an inferior product. It is possible that a poor camp may be "masked" by an outstanding publicity campaign for a short time, but no matter how strong the salesmanship, the camp will soon flounder without a marketable product. On the other hand, a solid well-planned camp organization with a quality program should quickly win the support of satisfied campers. This enthusiasm soon spreads to parents and friends because news of a successful camp travels quickly. Only a first-rate product will be able to withstand ill-founded criticism that may be directed toward a camp.

2. *Public relations is based on truth.* All information disseminated by the camp must be comprehensive and accurate. Misrepresentation in any form ultimately will create negative public opinion. Parents have every right to expect factual information about a camp. Half truths or failure to fully describe a given situation is unacceptable. For example, a day camp brochure advertised that the camp was located within 10 miles of the city. This statement, as far as it went, was true. What the brochure failed to point out was the residential part of the city from which the camp drew most of its clientele was over twice that distance from the camp. Another day camp advertised it was only "a short 15 to 20-minute drive" to camp each day. This again was a true statement as far as it went. The brochure did not tell the parents that, including pickup time, the majority of children were on the bus longer than 1 hour each way.

3. *Public relations is a two-way process.* At the beginning of this chapter it was pointed out that a basic difference between publicity and public relations is that the latter is predicated on two-way communication. To suggest that the flow of information is only from the camp to its publics is to place tremendous limitations on the potential value of any public relations endeavor. Each of the camp's publics should have much of value to communicate to the camp, and unless the camp consciously strives to

keep these avenues open, it cannot hope to be sensitive to the changing needs and concerns of the group it serves. The establishment of an advisory camp committee is a useful means of gaining better insight into how parents and members of the general public feel about a camp.

4. *Public relations involves all camp personnel.* Good public relations does not just happen. It is successful only to the extent that it is carefully and intelligently planned. This means that staff members must be alerted to their role in providing the best possible image of the camp.

5. *Public relations is continuous.* One of the shortcomings of many camp public relations programs is that the major thrust is made only as enrollment time draws near each spring. Such an approach is similar to a recruitment campaign in which the public, and parents in particular, are propagandized for a short, intensive period. Experience in the world of business has proven such a tactic to be generally unsuccessful. The tendency is for the parents and the public to develop a somewhat apprehensive attitude toward the camp if they are only approached when a new fund-raising campaign is planned or when enrollment dates approach. Good public relations, means continuous contact and interpretation of the camp to its publics. The program must be carefully planned so that regular communication is maintained and confidence sustained throughout the entire year.

6. *Public relations is based on complete knowledge of the community.* It is important that the camp make an early and accurate assessment of the various publics it serves and that careful consideration be given to the most effective approach for each of these publics.

7. *Public relations makes use of many media.* Because the camp must reach several publics, a variety of techniques and approaches must be used. One of the problems faced by those who are responsible for planning an effective camp public relations program is to determine what is the best approach for a particular public. Since it has been stated that the program should be ongoing throughout the year, this in itself suggests the need for a variety of techniques to maintain the interest of the client.

PUBLIC RELATIONS MEDIA

Public relations is more than a set of rules—it is a broad concept. It is the entire body of relationships that make up one's impressions of a camp and those who operate it. Every individual act and every word spoken has the potential to influence public opinion positively or negatively. Those persons responsible for administering public relations must continually remind all persons associated with the camp of this fact.

Another general assumption, supported by most camp administrators, is that person-to-person contacts are by far the most effective means of communication. Such face-to-face discourse will take place at many levels—camper to counselor, camper to parent, camper to friend, counsellor to parent, administration to parent, parent to parent. The word spreads, and public opinion is formed. Whether the opinions formed are favorable toward the camp will, in large measure, depend on the attitudes of campers.

Camp brochure

Perhaps the most widely used form of printed material is the brochure. This may take the form of a fairly comprehensive booklet, a smaller pamphlet, or a simple folder. The size of the brochure depends on how the camp plans to use it and the financial resources available to produce it. Frequently, the first contact a camp will have with a potential camper or parent is a request by mail or phone for some printed material regarding the camp. Almost all camps have developed a brochure for this purpose. Discounting the initial inquiry, the brochure becomes the first formal communication with the interested family, and it is vital that this impression be a favorable one. The first step is to ensure that the material is received promptly; it should be mailed on the day the request is received. The brochure should be accompanied by a personal letter from the director, but when the size of the camp is too large for this to be considered practical, a short personal note should be added to a carefully prepared form letter.

Purpose. What is the brochure designed to do? For many camps it is considered the single most important recruitment instrument; for others, it serves as little more than a reminder of camp dates and fees. Some camp brochures are planned to appeal to parents and the content reflects this emphasis; others are aimed at the potential camper and are "child oriented." This raises a fundamental question as to which is the more strategic approach. The consensus among most camp directors and those assisting in the preparation of brochures is that the brochure should attempt to appeal to both parent and child. To do so means careful selection of content, both text and pictures. Another early consideration is its distribution. If the brochure is to serve as a primary public relations medium, it will require wide circulation. If, on the other hand, it is to be used in conjunction with many other techniques, more limited mailing may be all that is needed.

Cost. Having answered some of the questions as to how the brochure is to be used, the administrator must now determine how much money will be spent on this type of promotion. Regardless of the financial resources available, if a brochure is to be used, it should be a quality product. If there is

limited funding, it is better to settle for an excellent 4-page brochure than a poor quality 8 to 12-page booklet. An inferior brochure implies that other facets of the camp operation may be substandard. It will pay to get quotations from a number of printers. As with all purchases, deal only with a reputable firm that does quality work. It may be false economy to accept the lowest bid when that quotation comes from an unknown printer.

Design. Some camp directors believe that the only way to provide a brochure that reflects the unique aspects of their camp is to have the camp staff undertake the photography, selection of pictures, and preparation of the text. These directors are in the minority. Preparation of a truly creative brochure should be in the hands of professionals who are specialists in this field. Most printing firms are able to provide the kind of expertise required, and failure to utilize a professional photographer, artist, or script writer will usually prove to be false economy.

The printer is also the best person to advise on the type and weight of paper, ratio of words to pictures, and use of color. Color is expensive, but there are different ways of utilizing it, and some productions are much less expensive than others. For example, brown ink on beige paper can be very attractive. Regarding size and shape, a factor to remember is ease of handling, filing, and mailing. Careful selection of size and weight may mean valuable savings in mailing costs. Folders that need to be opened out on a table to read are good for posting on bulletin boards but are not very practical for family perusal.

Content. If the brochure is to be a primary source of publicity, it should tell the parents and the child as much as possible about the camp. This implies a careful selection and balance between text and pictures. The content, both words and pictures, must be completely accurate and honest. Administrators should strive to describe their camp in its best possible light, but this cannot include inaccurate or deliberately misleading information. A muddy pond should not be called a lake, a small clearing in the woods is not a "spacious playing field" and a four-to-one camper-staff ratio should not include kitchen maintenance, and clerical staff members. The following list is suggested as a guide to information that should be included in a camp brochure:

1. Camp location
2. Description of site and facilities
3. Experience and qualifications of management team
4. Number and qualifications of staff members (including camper-staff ratio)
5. Number, sex, and age of campers
6. Scope of program and special program emphases
7. Information regarding transportation and communication
8. Camper health and safety (including such items as camp menu, health services, and water safety)

The presentation of this information should develop a feeling of trust and confidence in the parents and excitement and anticipation in the child.

The cost of producing an attractive brochure is such that it is recommended that the camp print enough to last several years. This has implications for the content. Information such as camp fees and schedule of camp dates cannot be included. This information is usually provided in an insert that may be stapled into the center leaf of the brochure. Other information such as visitor's days, nearby lodging accommodations, clothing guides, and transportation and baggage details, is usually mailed out separately or included with the registration mailing. Some camps include a list of the names and addresses of all last season's campers with

the brochure in the belief that this is another effective form of public relations.

"A picture is worth a thousand words." This platitude was never more true than in the case of the camp brochure. But each picture must say something to the viewer. To children they express excitement, fun, and action; this means candid pictures, not posed shots of staff and tent or cabin groups. At the same time, the pictures must convey safety and social compatibility. To achieve these objectives, the camp should hire a professional photographer.

From what has been said thus far, it may appear that preparation of the brochure should be placed entirely in the hands of professionals, thus devoiding it of any distinctive image or style. Such should not be the case. Each brochure must reflect a unique quality that sets that camp apart from other camps. To achieve this, there must be a cooperative effort between the camp representative and the professional. It is up to the camp director or person in charge of public relations for the camp to communicate clearly to the photographer, design artist, script writer, or printer the distinctive quality that is to be conveyed. For one camp, this may mean an emphasis on the rustic, survival-type atmosphere of the camp. Another camp may wish to convey an intimate hominess. In short, the professionals who are working on the brochure must clearly understand the underlying philosophy of the camp to be able to reflect that philosophy in the brochure.

Other printed material

Some form of printed material should go to the camper's family regularly throughout the year. This material may include regular correspondence, enrollment forms, camp bulletin or newsletter, or other business notices regarding visitor's day, baggage and transportation arrangements, and camper accounts.

With regard to regular correspondence between the camp and home, replies should be prompt, courteous, and carefully written. Whenever possible, avoid form letters that create an impersonal atmosphere. During the camp season, a few camps ask all counsellors to write a short personal note to the parents of the campers in their tent or cabin. This letter should be short and positive in content. Invariably this practice is favorably received by parents.

Periodic newsletters or bulletins are designed to keep parents and campers apprised of changes for the coming season, program innovations, news of returning staff, and so on. If the mailing of these can be timed so that they accompany standard business items, such as the enrollment package and the billing statement, it lends an informality to the contact whereas the business notice alone tends to be cold and impersonal.

Another practice that contributes to the personal touch is to send Christmas greetings on a specially designed camp card to both campers and staff. Again, a few camps personalize this practice even further by having counsellors of the previous season sign the card. The same practice is followed regarding camper birthdays that occur in the off-season.

Parent interviews

If it is assumed that the initial contact with a prospective camp family has been made by means of the brochure, most camp directors like to follow up with a phone call in which a personal meeting between the family and recruitment personnel is suggested. One camp owner reports that he travels 40,000 miles annually, over a 4-month period in the off-season, to make personal family visits. While few persons in

charge of recruitment are able to devote that amount of time and expense, this type of personal contact with prospective campers and parents is invaluable.

Some directors invite the interested parents and potential camper to their home, but it is strongly recommended that camp personnel offer to visit the home of the family. This has several advantages. Besides placing the initiative where it properly belongs, it places the family more at ease to have the meeting in familiar surroundings. In addition, the camp representative is likely to learn far more about the family and the personal traits and interests of the prospective camper. For example, if an alert camp director observes a swimming trophy that has been won by the child, this information will provide a talking point when the youngster arrives at camp.

The question again arises as to whether the home visitation should be directed primarily toward the camper or parents since, in each case, the presentation will be different. Most parents assume that their child should be present, and the majority of camp directors accept this idea. The success, therefore, lies in making an initial presentation to both parents and child at which time the youngster will be encouraged to raise any questions he or she may have. It may then be advisable to excuse the child so that the parents questions can be answered.

The purpose of the home visit should be to provide an opportunity to tell more of the camp story and at the same time give anxious parents an opportunity to ask any question they may have regarding the camp. Another important reason for the home visit is that it enables children to meet a potential parent-substitute with whom they will be comfortable once they arrive in the unfamiliar setting of the camp. Many children attending camp for the first time experience much apprehension and trepidation. To recognize a familiar adult face on arrival can do much to allay these concerns.

Some large camps prefer several promotional meetings to which a group of parents and their children are invited. These meetings are usually held at a hotel, church hall, or other public meeting place. When group meetings are scheduled, the number of persons attending should be small enough so that parents have ample opportunity to speak to the camp representatives and express any concerns they may have. The camp director must make a conscious effort to spend sufficient time with every family to provide this opportunity.

To determine the number and location of recruitment meetings, the director must carefully assess the geographic areas from which the camp clientele is drawn. Having done this, it may be necessary to plan two or three such meetings in different parts of the major city near which the camp is located. The director may also wish to visit neighboring cities from which the camp has received inquiries. Group meetings may be advertised in local papers but when applicable, the weekly neighborhood papers have been found to be more effective. Another possibility is to invite parents of former campers to suggest names of families to be contacted. Each of these referrals should then receive a phone call or personal letter of invitation to the group meeting.

Visual presentation

For many years, industries have recognized the advantage of a carefully planned audiovisual presentation as a sales technique. Since it is not always possible for the camper and parent to visit the camp while it is in operation, the next best thing is to bring the camp into the home through the use of a slide or movie presentation. A verbal presentation is enhanced if the family can see the story as they hear it. Printed material in the hands of the parent or camper sometimes detracts from the presentation.

The choice between movies and colored slides is a personal one. Although motion pictures add another dimension to some aspects of the presentation, they have the very real disadvantage of not being as flexible. With slides it is a relatively simple matter to lengthen or shorten the presentation and to update or vary the theme according to the audience. Although it is possible to achieve the same objective with movies, this type of editing is more complicated.

If it is decided to prepare a slide presentation, much care must be taken to put a professional showing together. Research indicates that the viewer's attention will begin to wane after 12 to 18 minutes. As a rule of thumb, the visual presentation should not exceed 20 minutes. Too many pictures may be worse than none at all. The average viewing time per slide should be a maximum of 10 seconds. If you wish to dwell on a particular aspect of camp life, it is better to show several slides rather than attempt to hold the viewer's attention on a single picture.

An interesting question now arises as to whether the selection of pictures complements the commentary or whether you choose the best slides and develop the verbal presentation around them. The decision as to which approach is used should depend on whether one considers the visual or the verbal presentation to be the more important in conveying the message. Regardless of the method selected, a carefully planned presentation must be achieved so that the story is told in the most compelling way. When preparing the narration, it may be wise to write it out in detail. However, the actual presentation should be made in an easy, relaxed manner. Some public relations representatives recommend putting the talk on tape. It is a fairly simple matter to program slides to synchronize with the commentary, and most large photography suppliers can advise the camp director on this matter. Keep in mind that when a tape is used, it precludes any questions or comments by the viewer during the showing. The use of titles may also enhance the presentation and give it a more professional touch.

Careful attention should be given to the mechanics of the presentation itself, including use of a well-darkened room, comfortable location of the audience, and strategic placement of the person making the presentation so that he or she is partly facing the audience as well as the screen.

A few camp directors do not favor a slide or movie presentation. They maintain that it is too high-powered and prefer a more informal relaxed meeting with the potential camp family. They prefer to carry with them a selection of colored photographs of the camp in an album that is designed to tell much the same story as slides.

Camp reunion

It is traditional for the vast majority of camps to hold a camp reunion during the off-season. Originally, the reunion was, as the name implies, an opportunity for campers and staff to come together and reminisce about the wonderful experiences they shared the previous summer. As such, the reunion was often scheduled in the late fall. Gradually camp directors realized that if the reunion was moved to the beginning of the recruitment season, in early spring, it could serve to stimulate both campers and staff to return for the forthcoming summer.

Today, the camp reunion fulfills a number of different purposes; it (1) recaptures the spirit of the previous season, (2) stimulates enrollment of former campers, (3) augments recruitment of new campers, and (4) satisfies a combination of the above. The first step in planning a reunion is to clearly establish its purpose. If, for example, it is decided that the reunion should promote enrollment of former campers, as well as recruitment of new ones, this decision has clear implications for the time of year it is held as well as those who will be invited. For recruitment purposes, the reunion is perhaps best held in early spring as parents consider plans for the coming summer.

If only former campers are to attend, the mood to be developed should be one of nostalgia with program emphasis on reliving the happenings of the previous summer. However, such a program would be in poor taste if many of those attending were coming to the camp for the first time. New campers and their parents will be primarily concerned with meeting the staff and having an opportunity to ask questions regarding the pending camp season. Regardless of the purpose of the reunion, sincere effort should be made to have as many staff members as possible attend. For many campers, the highlight of the reunion is the opportunity to renew friendships with counsellors of the previous summer.

Most camps plan one major reunion per year in the city from which the largest number of campers and staff are drawn. If substantial numbers of camper families are located in other large centers, more than one reunion may be warranted.

A variety of facilities may be considered when planning the reunion, ranging from community, school, and church halls to hotel salons, ballrooms, and banquet rooms. Important considerations are central location, convenience of parking, public transportation, and suitability of the facility for the camp clientele and the program planned.

The program itself may take many forms, but three components are invariably present: (1) a brief word of welcome by a senior representative of the camp, (2) plenty of op-portunity for informal talk and camaraderie, and (3) some form of refreshments. The lat-ter may be as simple as soft drinks or as elaborate as a formal banquet. Ideas for pro-gram content are limitless. The object is to select a format that generates much enthu-siasm among both returning and potential campers. The following are some reunion programs that have proved successful: camp slides or movies taken the previous sum-mer, special activity such as swimming, bowling, or skating, Father and son or mother and daughter competitions, Indian challenge competition, novelty relays, car-nival, outdoor picnic, sit-down dinner with award presentation, and staff entertainment.

Visitor's day

There is wide variance among camps re-garding the practice of inviting parents to visit the camp during the season. Many agency camps have groups of campers for only 5 to 14 days and believe that it is in the best interests of the camper if the parents do not visit during that time. Some private camps, on the other hand, set aside as many as four separate days each month as "offi-cial" visiting days. Some small camps en-courage parents to drop in at any time dur-ing the camp season on the assumption that there will never be more than one or two families on any given day, and this should present no hardship for the staff. Regardless of the number of days reserved for visitors, nearly all camp directors agree that visiting camp during the first 2 weeks of any session should be discouraged since this is the pe-riod when campers are settling in to the new surroundings and may therefore be ex-periencing some degree of homesickness. Parental visits at this time frequently mag-nify any problems of adjustment to the camp setting. As a result, the most common prac-tice is to set aside between 1 and 4 days

during the second and third weekend of each month as the recommended time for visitors.

The purpose of visitor's day is to allay any anxiety parents may have regarding their child's stay at camp. It also provides an ex-cellent opportunity to see the entire camp in normal operation. As such, it becomes an important public relations vehicle, and all staff members should be alerted to put forth a little extra effort on these days. For exam-ple, several staff members may be assigned to greet parents as they arrive and assist them with parking and then locating their child. If a special picnic and swim area is set aside for visitors, it will be necessary to have staff members on duty to patrol the water-front and to assist parents with any requests they may have.

Campers should be encouraged to take their parents on a tour of the camp, and it is usually wise to set aside a specific time for this. Parents may be invited to join the campers in the dining hall for the noon or evening meal; they may bring a picnic lunch; or they may wish to take their child away from the camp for a meal. In the latter case, campers should be advised to always "check out" with their counsellor or section head and inform the staff as to when they will return. Much of the day should be spent following the normal program routine in which campers, who have visitors, are en-couraged to participate. Parents and other visitors should expect to observe a typical camp day with regular camp programs. The purpose is to inform, not to entertain.

Ample time must be provided for visitors to meet and chat informally with their child's counsellor. It would be highly desir-able for all visitors to have an opportunity to also meet with the director, but in a large camp, time may preclude this possibility. In this case, senior staff members should be readily available to discuss any concerns that parents may have regarding their child's stay at camp.

An extension of visitor's day that may prove very successful is a mother and daughter or father and son weekend at the camp before or after the camp season. When held in the fall, the weekend becomes a form of reunion. If scheduled in June, it serves as an excellent means of orientation for new campers and their parents. The weekend involves the parent and child sharing living accommodations and participating in programs together. Expenses may be kept to a minimum by having only a skeleton staff on hand. All meals should be jointly prepared by parents and campers. Informality and fun should be the keynote. However, all camp safety rules regarding the waterfront and activities such as archery and horseback riding must be observed by all concerned.

Mass media

Camps have rarely taken full advantage of publicity through the mass media. It may have been assumed that what goes on at camp is not that newsworthy, and as a result, camp directors have waited for the media representatives to come to them. There are essentially two ways in which the mass media may be utilized. The first is through paid advertising whereby the camp is charged for a short newspaper, radio, or television advertisement. These must be eye- or ear-catching and must briefly answer the five questions—who, what, when, where, and why. The second method of using mass media is through human interest stories. Newspapers, radio, and television will accept special features about camp if they are presented in an imaginative manner or deal with a novel topic. Such news items usually have far greater value than any amount of paid advertising. The secret is to come up with some unique idea that contains high reader, listener, or viewer appeal.

Newspapers. Experience has shown that camps usually have greater success if human interest articles are submitted to the local weekly newspapers. When dealing with the local newspaper, two things must be remembered: these papers usually have a 2- or even 3-day deadline, and they rarely have sufficient staff for personal coverage. As a result, an article is far more likely to be published if it is prepared in a form that is ready for printing. Several rules should be followed when preparing a feature story:

1. Use plain white $8^{1}/_{2} \times 11$ inch paper
2. Use only one side of the paper
3. Type all copy and double space
4. Start the copy one third of the way down the first page (Do not prepare a headline.)
5. End each page with a complete paragraph
6. Leave ample margins on the sides and bottom of each page
7. Tell the story briefly, in accurate, simple language
8. Answer the questions, who, what, when, where, and why, early
9. Punctuate and paragraph accurately
10. Avoid abbreviations and slang
11. Get the story in on time

Radio and television. The advantage of coverage by these media is that they reach a large audience. It is generally assumed that radio and television time is very costly and therefore beyond the means of most camps. This is not the case. Virtually all stations are required, by law, to devote a percentage of time, free of charge, to public service programs. The challenge is for camp public relations staff to develop a story that is newsworthy and has enough human interest value to compete with other agencies and groups who are vying for valuable air and viewing time.

Public speaking

This is another avenue through which the camp director can cultivate public relations.

Many service organizations and other groups welcome an interesting and carefully prepared presentation on the general topic of camping or on some unique aspect of the profession. Such presentations are usually enhanced by a first-class visual presentation of slides or movies.

Official reports

Agency camps are usually required to submit an annual report to the camp committee or the board of directors of the organization at the end of the camp season. Such a presentation should contain factual information rather than personal opinion. Photographs, diagrams, charts, and graphs provide pictorial material that should clarify and increase interest in the report.

ADMINISTRATIVE GUIDELINES

1. A comprehensive public relations program is the responsibility of every person connected with the camp. It involves not only management but all counsellors, as well as kitchen, health center, maintenance, and administrative personnel.
2. Camps must interrelate with several publics, including campers, parents, staff, members of the camp committee or board, former campers, other camp administrators, representatives of the media, local community, and general public.
3. Of all the publics with which the camp must deal, campers comprise the most critical group. Happy, contented campers can influence most of the other publics in a positive manner.
4. Successful public relations begins with a quality camp program. Unless the product itself is seen as having real worth, no amount of "window dressing" can improve the image of the camp.
5. Camp public relations should be based on those principles that have been successfully used in the field of business. These principles confirm that public relations is predicated on a quality product, it is truthful, it is a two-way process, it involves all personnel, it is continuous, and it is based on thorough knowledge of the community it serves.
6. Camps utilize a variety of media to promote the camping industry, including brochures and other forms of printed material, parent and camper interviews, visual presentations, reunions, visitor days, mass media, public talks, official reports, and others.
7. Camp public relations, to be fully effective, must involve two-way communication. Camp should welcome constructive feedback from campers, parents, and other publics.

SELECTED BIBLIOGRAPHY

Attfield, R. P.: Things go better with . . . good public relations, Canadian Camping, **27**(1):15-17, Nov., 1974.

Baer, J.: Parents—your best camp promoters, Camping Magazine, **47**(5):10-12, Mar., 1975.

Baer, J.: Proven techniques for camper enrollment, Camping Magazine, **47**(6):10-13, Apr., 1975.

Camp Fire Girls: Camp promotion and publicity. (New York: Publications of Camp Fire Girls, Inc.).

Dickhaus, S. M.: Camp promotion, Camping Magazine, **49**(1):18-19, Sept./Oct., 1976.

Gabel, P. S.: Creative and innovative camp brochures, Camping Magazine, **44**(8):8-10, Nov., 1972.

Handler, L.: Reunions—how, when and why, Camping Magazine, **39**(7):30, Sept./Oct., 1967.

Heller, J. H., et al.: Camping with a purpose . . . a 4-H handbook. (Washington, D.C.: U.S. Government Printing Office, 1972).

Kraus, R. G., and Curtis, J. E.: Creative administration in recreation and parks. (St. Louis: The C. V. Mosby Co., 1977).

Levine, C., and Levine, H.: Effective public relations for community groups. (New York: Associated Press, 1969).

Loren, H.: The camp drop-out, Camping Magazine, **41**(8):14,20, Nov./Dec., 1969.

Morawetz, B., Flynn, E., and Powter, C. B.: visitors at camp, Canadian Camping, **23**(4):21,25, Summer, 1971.

Publicity Handbook, Booklet No. 79. (Washington, D.C.: National Recreation and Park Association).

Shivers, J. S.: Camping, administration, counseling, programming. (Englewood Cliffs, N.J.: Prentice-Hall Inc., 1971).

Speak out: a public relations guide for professionals in recreation, health, physical education and sports, Journal of Health, Physical Education and Recreation, **43:**41-56, Oct. 1972.

Tisdall, C. W.: New brochures, Convention report of the Ontario Camping Association, 1977.

Wasserman, R.: Can good P.R. sell your camp? It sure can help! Canadian Camping, **43**(8):12-13, Nov./Dec., 1971.

CHAPTER ELEVEN

Evaluation

The unexamined life is not worth living by any man.
SOCRATES

A final, but major, responsibility of camp administration is evaluation. Just as in any successful business, the need for regular evaluation is an essential part of good camp administrative practice. This evaluation involves answering myriad questions such as: How successful was the camp season? Was it a financial success? How did the staff compare with that of previous seasons? Who should be invited back next year? Which were the most successful programs? Why was senior camp enrollment down? Are there ways to strengthen camp public relations? Can the food menu be improved without increasing costs? What was the camp's health and safety record? What percentage of returnees can be anticipated next summer?

Evaluation can be defined as *the process that is concerned with determining the worth and effectiveness of the total camp experience*. It includes assessment of the camper experience, the program, the staff who conduct it, as well as the administrative services and facilities that support the program.

FACTORS LIMITING EVALUATION

In spite of the obvious importance of conducting a complete camp evaluation, many camp administrators either ignore it or do such a superficial job that it has little value. There are several reasons why camp directors have avoided this important task. Undoubtedly, a few administrators take a rather self-righteous position regarding evaluation: "I don't need to evaluate; I know what's going on in my camp." These directors *should* know what is going on in their camp—that is an important function of any administrator. But *do* they know everything that is going on? Should it not be possible to gain much valuable knowledge from the insights of others? After all, different people view the same operation from entirely different perspectives and these other viewpoints may be invaluable in ensuring an improved experience for campers.

More than one camp administrator has been heard to remark, "Tom knows that he is one of our best counsellors. He doesn't need me to tell him how well he is doing." But the fact is that, in most cases, he does require this type of reinforcement. Research confirms that many employees do not accurately perceive their own strengths and weaknesses. Even if they do, it is great for one's self-esteem and morale to be complimented on a job well done.

For many camp directors, the pace of the camp season is so hectic that they tell themselves they are too busy to find time for a systematic and well-planned evaluation. This position is strengthened if they are not persuaded as to the real values of such an assessment in the first place. After all, if a comprehensive, thorough evaluation is to be done in which staff, campers, and other administrators are invited to participate, it is entirely probable that some of the comments will be negative and directors will hear some criticisms of themselves and their administrative style. It is not surprising, therefore, that administrators should avoid an exercise that can lead to loss of self-esteem.

Some camp directors fail to conduct an evaluation because many of the variables to be measured are qualitative and objective measuring instruments are not available. It is true that some of the anticipated outcomes are intangible, but this does not relieve the administrator from seeking the best available techniques and applying them.

A few administrators shy away from use of available techniques arguing that such instruments are useless except in the hands of an "expert." They believe that most camp personnel do not possess the technical knowledge necessary to develop a survey, checklist, or questionnaire or conduct a reliable interview. As the rest of this chapter confirms, this is an erroneous assumption.

Perhaps the most valid reason for neglect of camp evaluation is lack of time. Once a program is completed in an 8- or 10- week camp season, there is little inclination to look back. Too many other pressing matters lie ahead. The logical solution to this problem seems to be to postpone the evaluation process until camp closes and then to sit down and quietly assess what has transpired in the season just concluded. Time, however, makes this impossible for many camp personnel who should actively share in camp evaluation. For the majority of the staff, the end of camp signals their return to school or their regular job. Under these circumstances, it is not surprising that camp evaluation suffers so that one season's mistakes and shortcomings are perpetuated the following summer.

PURPOSES OF EVALUATION

In spite of the many obstacles that impede good camp evaluation, the necessity for this culminating administrative function cannot be questioned. What is the good of spending hundreds of hours planning a camp program, preparing a staff to implement it, and finally carrying out the program, if its success or failure is not effectively evaluated? Unless existing practices and outcomes are carefully examined, how is it possible to chart new and better paths and directions? Without evaluation, a camp is doomed to perpetuate yesterday's errors, and these mistakes can no longer be tolerated in today's society in which so many other viable agencies are competing for the recreational dollar.

It seems to be a characteristic of the times in which we live that the public is demanding a greater degree of accountability from government, public leaders and servants, industry, public education—virtually all segments of society. Leaders in the camping profession should not be surprised, therefore, that camps are now being required to account more accurately regarding the value of their service. Perhaps this factor, more than any other, has pushed camp administrators to increasingly accept responsibility for implementing an effective evaluation process in camps today.

The following list is a summary of the reason why camps, both private and public, should evaluate:

1. To determine the extent to which the objectives of the camp program are being met

2. To provide evidence (both subjective and objective) of the worth of camp programs
3. To identify and rectify shortcomings in the total camp operation
4. To compare the total camp program with recommended standards (for example, A.C.A. accreditation standards)
5. To assist the camp staff in performing their jobs more effectively
6. To assess the effectiveness of staff performance for purposes of rehiring, promotion, or dismissal
7. To provide a check on the administrative effectiveness of senior personnel, including the camp director
8. To determine the economic efficiency of the entire camp operation
9. To discover whether campers really enjoy camp

SCOPE OF EVALUATION

A comprehensive camp evaluation program is far-reaching. To understand the full implications of its scope, several questions need to be answered.

Who evaluates?

Everyone who is directly associated with the camp operation should be given an opportunity to evaluate. Campers and parents, as consumers, have a right to evaluate not only the program but those who conduct it. Counsellors are perhaps in the best position to assess the campers. They can also provide valuable contributions regarding senior personnel as well as the programs they conduct. Administrators should evaluate all facets of the operation, including self-assessment. In addition, food service personnel, medical personnel, and maintenance staff should be expected to provide insights into their own areas of concern.

Evaluation should not be limited to those who actually operate the camp. Those camps that have an advisory board or council frequently find that this advisory group sets up an evaluation subcommittee to examine the total camp operation on a continuing basis. Outside agencies also play a prominent role in the assessment process. Many camps are part of a national organization such as the Boys Clubs of America, Young Men's and Women's Christian Associations, 4-H Camps, and Boy Scouts of America. Each of these agencies develops its own guidelines including, in some cases, a Program Evaluation Manual. The Boys Clubs of America has such a manual in which over 50 recommended practices are listed as standards against which local programs can be measured. In another piece of literature prepared by the Boys Clubs, the organization points out that "Evaluation, is a regular, integral part of Boys Club operation, not just a procedure which is done because of pressure from an outside group or because of some crisis."[1]

One of the most valuable resources available for camp appraisal is the accreditation program for organized camps that is conducted by the American Camping Association.[2] This program requires that two trained consultants visit camps seeking accreditation to determine if standards of desirable practice are being maintained in the camp under study. The standards are designed to serve not only as an instrument by which accreditation can be measured, but also as a tool for self-education and self-evaluation by camp directors.

Members of the ACA have worked for nearly 50 years to develop these standards.

---

1. Boys Clubs of America: Program evaluation in a Boys Club. (New York: National Manual of Boys Clubs of America, 1967).
2. American Camping Association: Camp standards with interpretations for accreditation of organized camps. (Bradford Woods, Martinsville, Ind.: American Camping Association, 1976).

The camp standards manual itself has been revised many times, most recently in 1976. It includes 14 mandatory requirements plus 149 other standards covering the following categories.

Part 1-A Site Standards

Part 1-C Administration Standards

Part 1-C Personnel Standards

Part 1-D Program Standards

Part 11-A Basic Standards for Specific Programs

Part 11-B Standards for Selected Programs

Part 11-C Standards for Special Situations

Part 11-D Standards for Campers with Special Needs

In addition to the standards themselves, a detailed interpretation is provided for each standard. In Canada, camp accreditation is under provincial jurisdiction, and most provinces have an accreditation program similar to the national program in the United States.

When does evaluation take place?

The well-organized administrator recognizes that evaluation is a continuous process. It is true that some decisions regarding hiring of personnel and submission of budgets must be made annually to meet predetermined deadlines, but the information and evaluation on which such decisions are made extend throughout the year. All staff members who participate in evaluation should be encouraged to do so continously during the camp season. Those persons with major administrative responsibility should be expected to carry on such assessment in the weeks and months after the camp season ends, and as the pace of camp activity quickens in the spring, the process of evaluation is renewed once again.

When evaluation is seen as a continuous process, it becomes somewhat more leisurely and relaxed. It is based on many impressions and sources of information gleaned over a long period, which invariably results in more rational appraisal and more intelligent choices. Hectic, hit-or-miss evaluation that is limited to a week or 10 days at the end of the camp season usually leads to careless, nonobjective decision making.

How do we evaluate?

In attempting to evaluate their camps, some directors rely almost entirely on their own insights and observations during the course of the camp season. Others maintain that the real index for evaluating a camp's successes and failures is the percentage of returning campers each year. These administrators look only at the "bottom line" and make no attempt to analyze why the number of returnees is either up or down. Still other directors are guided by the informal comments of campers, parents, and staff members but make little effort to tabulate these in any systematic manner. Fortunately, many camp administrators are now realizing that a much more systematic approach needs to be taken if the evaluative process is to have any real worth.

Camp evaluation is of two general types: *informal* and *formal*. *Informal evaluation* occurs continuously whether the camp administrator likes it or not and takes place at many levels. Campers compare programs throughout the season and have no hesitation in making their likes and dislikes known. Parents assess the effects of the camp experience on their children, but rarely do these concerns or accolades get back to those who are in a position to make use of this information. Comparisons of counsellors and their performance is a favorite pastime of campers whenever they get together, but these random observations could prove of great value if they were tabulated systematically and objectively. It is human nature for counsellors to informally rate their section heads along with all other senior personnel, including the director, but how often are junior staff members invited to rate supervisory personnel formally?

Wise administrators take full advantage of these many forms of casual evaluation. To the extent that administrators possess a high level of self-adequacy, they welcome constructive criticism from all levels and give careful consideration to each suggestion. Unfortunately, criticism is frequently construed to be negative and, as such, places the administrator on the defensive. Constructive criticism can be very healthy and positive and should lead to significant change for the better.

But a sound appraisal process does not stop with the type of random evaluation described above. The conscientious administrator finds ways of organizing this information more systematically so that it may be quantified. For example, annotated records could be kept of parental comments, and they could even be classified by topic so that remarks regarding camper transportation, food services, camp-parent communication, or health and safety of campers could each be recorded separately. Campers should be given the opportunity to come together informally and discuss topics of mutual concern such as program preferences. The program staff needs to listen and record these observations for consideration and possible implementation.

Formal evaluation implies that the camp administration has initiated some form of self-evaluation or an outside body has been invited to conduct a camp appraisal. When the evaluation process is formalized, it invariably involves some form of gathering and recording data. The actual techniques that can be used include questionnaires, checklists, inventories, surveys, evaluation by experts, analysis of existing records, interviews, conferences, and standardized tests. Some of these methods are described more fully later in this chapter.

Another means of classifying evaluative data is to consider the *objective* and *subjective* nature of the fact-finding process. *Objective* instruments attempt to remove the human element so that the chance of error from this source is minimized. *Subjective* evaluation, on the other hand, usually involves the formulation of some ideal concepts against which the campers, staff, or program are measured. Since the person evaluating must interpret these ideal concepts, human variance may be quite significant.

Another way to look at evaluation is to consider the type of data to be gathered. Some information is essentially *quantitative* in nature while other data is *qualitative*. The percentage of campers returning each summer is quantitative data. Information regarding the number of accidents that occur in various activities is another example of quantitative measurement. Quantitative information, is usually associated with a high degree of objectivity.

There are, however, many qualitative elements in the camp setting that do not lend themselves to easy quantification. The counsellor-camper relationship, the counsellor as teacher, and the extent to which campers have gained an appreciation of the outdoors are important outcomes that deserve evaluation, and yet the approach must be largely subjective. In these cases, such instruments as rating scales and inventories must be used by persons who have clear, predetermined criteria in mind regarding the element to be measured. Subjective or qualitative ratings are an essential aspect of a comprehensive evaluation process. When administered with care, subjective testing contributes much to the fact-gathering process. In addition, subjective judgment may play an even more important role when the data that has been assembled is interpreted.

The evaluation process cannot be discussed without some reference to research. Research represents the purest form of data collection and interpretation. It is probably safe to say that camp programs will only make significant improvements as those in the field become more involved in applied research as a means of solving the many problems plaguing camp administration. To date, research in camping has received little attention. The reasons, no doubt, are several: lack of time and money as well as a failure to understand that applied research should provide the basis for the resolution of many questions. Gradually camp administrators are beginning to realize that more accurate answers can only be found through the application of more scientific methods. The American Camping Association is playing a leading role in this matter. As federal and state governments, foundations, national organization, and colleges and universities provide the leadership and funding, more research is sure to be one of the future trends in the camping field.

Against what do we evaluate?

If the evaluation process is to be successful, camp administrators must have a clear knowledge of the standard or outcomes that are sought. There is little point in attempting to assess the worth of camp programs unless the program director has full awareness of what constitutes an excellent program. Appraisal of counsellor teaching effectiveness is only possible if those persons responsible for the evaluation have a clear idea of what comprises superior teaching. Similarly, food service managers cannot aspire to offer a well-balanced, nutritious menu unless they have a full appreciation of scientific menu planning. One of the main reasons that so many mediocre camps have continued to operate is the failure of camp

administrators to realize the high level of standards that have evolved in the camping field. Membership in the ACA and other professional organizations concerned with camping is one of the best means of overcoming this problem.

What is evaluated?

The answer to this last question is, everything that in any way impinges on the quality of the camp experience. To be complete, the camp evaluation program must be organized to deal with five areas of assessment: camper, program, staff, facilities and equipment, and supporting administrative services. It is possible to break down each of these categories still further for analysis of specific areas. For example, within administration, one might isolate such topics as camper recruitment, community relations, finance, or record keeping. The remainder of this chapter provides a detailed discussion of each of the five major areas.

EVALUATION OF CAMPERS

The central focus of all evaluation is the camper. The camp's total existence is designed to provide its clientele with a rich, fulfilling experience. It therefore follows that all evaluation must be structured to measure the extent to which camper objectives have been realized.

In the opening chapter of this book, the following general objectives of camps were described: (1) to provide fun and adventure, (2) to teach safe and healthful living, (3) to promote "at-homeness" in the outdoors, (4) to increase spiritual meanings and values, (5) to develop leisure time skills and knowledge, and (6) to promote democratic living. As one examines each of these general objectives, it becomes apparent that to measure camper change in these six areas is a formidable task. As important and desirable as these objectives may be, the fact remains that much research is still required to develop satisfactory means of measuring shifts in such intangibles as attitudes and values. Social scientists report that many of the expected changes do not always show up immediately so that it may be impossible to credit the camp experience with the ultimate shift in behavior.

Difficult as the job may appear and in spite of the limitations of measuring instruments presently available, this important area of evaluation cannot be ignored. The first and perhaps most constructive step that can be taken is to break down each of the broad general objectives into specific operational objectives. One of the steps in developing the camp program involves setting up general program objectives followed by the listing of very specific operational objectives. If camp administrators are prepared to have the staff work through the identification of these specific objectives and commit them to paper, it will be reassuring to find that they form the basis of a measurable means of evaluating camper growth.

While very few scientifically prepared tests, inventories, and checklists have been designed specifically for the camp situation, many instruments are available that could be adapted to camp use. For example, sociogram techniques and interest and appreciation inventories could be used as pretests at the beginning of camp followed by posttests at the end of the camp season to determine what changes can be attributed to the camp experience. Obviously such results must be interpreted and used judiciously. It may be that some apparent changes are only temporary while others, which are more permanent, should not be attributed to the camp experience alone.

Staff evaluation of campers

A large number of camps keep a progress record file for each camper. This form is used to record all pertinent data that relate to the individual camper's progress during the camp season in such areas as skill development as well as changes that are observed in selected personal traits. A sample progress report is shown in Fig. 11-1 for a camp that features out-tripping for all youngsters.

Many camps also use a special evaluation form for senior campers to determine their readiness for the counsellor-in-training program. Fig. 11-2 provides a typical assessment sheet for this purpose.

The personal file for campers should also contain any other information that would help complete the profile of that individual. This might include a record of program attendance, badges and awards won, projects completed, food likes and dislikes, or any idiosyncrasies about the camper that would assist the staff in doing a more thorough job.

Parental assessment of campers

While much of the information that is placed in the camper's personal progress file is derived from staff observations and assessments, many valuable insights can also be gained from parents of campers. The advantages of seeking parental evaluation include:

1. The parents can better verbalize the thoughts of the young child regarding the camp experience.
2. The parents have a relaxed, unhurried opportunity to observe any changes in attitude, behavior, or skill development.
3. The home provides an opportunity to observe longitudinal changes, not just over the winter months, but over several years during which the child attends camp.

Much evidence indicates that parents generally reflect the attitudes and values of their children. Why then should camp directors avoid parental evaluation? The responses of parents may be solicited through

```
CAMPER PROGRESS RECORD

Name:_____ Date of arrival:_____

Parent or
guardian:_____ Cabin No.:_____
```

A. <u>Skills development</u>: (Record any progress made.)

Activity	Start of camp	End of season
Archery Arts and crafts Campcraft Canoeing Nature lore Sailing Swimming Tennis Woodcraft		

B. <u>Personal characteristics</u>: (Comment briefly giving specific examples wherever possible.)

1. Relationship with peers:

2. Relationship with you and other staff:

3. Acceptance of camp rules:

4. Habits regarding personal cleanliness and hygiene:

5. Changes in personal habits during season:

6. Changes in attitudes or values:

C. <u>Out-tripping</u>:   Number of days out of camp:_____

1. List trip skills developed:

2. List trip skills needing improvement:

3. Acceptance of trip responsibilities:

4. Relationships with others on the trip:

```
_____        _____
         Date                    Counsellor's signature
```

Use reverse side for further comments.

Fig. 11-1. Sample camper personal record to be completed by cabin counsellor.

```
┌─────────────────────────────────────────────────────────────────────────┐
│                   SENIOR CAMPER RATING FORM                               │
│                                                                           │
│                                                                           │
│   Name _____    Age: _____        │
│                                                                           │
│   Cabin No. _____         Grade completed: _____      │
│                                                                           │
│   Camping experience: _____      │
├─────────────────────────────────────────────────────────────────────────┤
│   Scoring:  Outstanding = 5        Place appropriate score opposite       │
│             Excellent   = 4        each characteristic and total          │
│             Good        = 3        at bottom.                             │
│             Fair        = 2                                               │
│             Poor        = 1                                               │
├─────────────────────────────────────────────────────────────────────────┤
│                Characteristic                          Score              │
│                                                                           │
│    1.  Physical skills                                 _____              │
│    2.  Tripping skills                                 _____              │
│    3.  Special skills and talents                      _____              │
│    4.  Sense of humor                                  _____              │
│    5.  Concern for others                              _____              │
│    6.  Acceptance by peers                             _____              │
│    7.  Cooperation                                     _____              │
│    8.  Ability to accept responsibility                _____              │
│    9.  Judgment                                        _____              │
│   10.  Ability to accept criticism                     _____              │
│   11.  Socioemotional maturity                         _____              │
│   12.  Leadership potential                            _____              │
├─────────────────────────────────────────────────────────────────────────┤
│                  Rating out of 60  =                   _____              │
│                                                                           │
│   _____           _____          │
│          Date                        Signature of counsellor             │
│                                                                           │
│   Use reverse side to further amplify your evaluation.  Give specific     │
│   examples to support your observations wherever possible.                │
└─────────────────────────────────────────────────────────────────────────┘
```

Fig. 11-2. Sample senior camper rating form.

PARENTAL QUESTIONNAIRE

Directions:
1. Answer each question only as it applies to your child's stay at camp.
2. Place a checkmark in the appropriate column.
3. Return the form in the enclosed envelope.
                        All replies are confidential

Social
		Yes	No	No change
1.	Have relationships with other children improved?			
2.	Have relationships with adults improved?			
3.	Development of any new good habits?			
4.	Development of any habits of which you do not approve?			
5.	Increased self-confidence and self-reliance?			
6.	Greater tolerance toward others?			
7.	Were camper-counsellor relationships good?			

Health and safety
8. Were the camp meals satisfying?
9. Did child come home rested and in good health?
10. Was there satisfactory balance between rest and activity?
11. Was sufficient attention given to personal hygiene?

Program
12. Were any specific new skills learned?
13. Were any new interests developed?
14. Was adequate progress made in swimming?
15. Was there satisfactory balance between physical and other nonathletic forms of programming?
16. Was there a satisfactory balance between instruction and recreation in camp programming?

Administration
17. Were camp-parent communications satisfactory?
18. Were visiting day arrangements adequate?
19. Were camper transportations arrangements satisfactory?
20. Has the camper progress record been of value?

*Did your child enjoy the camp season? (If yes, what were the highlights? If no, what were the reasons?)

Other comments:

_____   _____
Date   Parent's signature

Fig. 11-3. Sample parental evaluation questionnaire.

informal conversation, formal interview, or prepared questionnaire.

If a parental questionnaire such as that shown in Fig. 11-3 is used, it usually provides a source of information that is characterized by a high degree of sincerity and integrity. The form should be skillfully prepared and accompanied by an explanatory covering letter. The questionnaire itself should be short, clear in its directions, and simple to complete.

It is important to stress at this point that each camp should develop its own questionnaires and checklists that reflect the particular objectives of its operation. The samples included here are designed to assist administrators with developing a workable format and provide examples of types of information that may be useful.

EVALUATION OF THE PROGRAM

Evaluation is an integral part of program development. Whether a new camp program is being planned or an established program is under review, the basis for selection and implementation of activities must be the result of a careful evaluation process. Since the camp program is the medium through which camp objectives are hopefully realized, it should be constantly subjected to careful scrutiny in an attempt to find ways of improving it. The purpose of program evaluation is to determine to what extent the experiences offered lead to fulfillment of the established objectives of ·the camp. Characteristics of good program evaluation include the following:

1. The close relationship between program planning and evaluation must be appreciated by all those involved in program development.
2. Program evaluation should provide for assessment by both campers and counsellors.
3. Systematic procedures for gathering appraisal data must be developed.

4. These procedures should be agreed on by those involved in the assessment process.
5. All changes in camp programming should be based on evaluative evidence.

Methods of evaluating programs

At the present time, there are essentially three ways in which camp programs can be evaluated.

1. *Close observation of campers by qualified staff to determine what, if any, progress is being made in skill development.* The success of this method hinges strongly on the observers' thorough knowledge of the activity and their ability to differentiate between low, intermediate, and high level performance.

2. *Systematic questioning of counsellors and campers involved in the program.* This interrogation may be done verbally or by means of carefully developed questionnaires. Many program administrators ask campers to rate programs at the end of each summer by means of a questionnaire. Such questionnaires can provide much valuable information regarding the qualitative aspects of the program if campers are invited to rate activities on a five-point scale of outstanding, excellent, good, fair, and poor. Another technique is to list all camp programs alphabetically and request that campers place them in rank order with the most popular at the top, down to the least popular. These rankings should play an important role in any program revision that is considered for the following season. Fig. 11-4 provides an example of an evaluation card that might be completed by the counsellor in charge after each camp program is completed.

3. *Testing campers periodically to determine progress.* The most objective means of determining whether campers have made progress toward the stated operational objectives of a given program is to administer

```
                          PROGRAM EVALUATION CARD

     Activity:_____  Number of participants:_____
     Description of group:


     Camper interest (circle one)

          Extremely high        High        Moderate        Low

     Comments:




              _____              _____
                   Date                       Counsellor in charge
```

Fig. 11-4. Sample program assessment card.

some form of pretest and posttest. If a camper elects to take canoeing instruction, the counsellors responsible for canoeing conduct a performance test before instruction begins to determine the camper's paddling ability. Then at the end of the instruction, the same test, or a similar one, is administered to measure how much progress has been made. When tests of this type are developed, it is very important that they be valid; that is, that they actually measure what they purport to test. It is not possible to measure paddling competency by keeping accurate attendance records of lates and absences. While attendance may be a reasonable index of camper interest in canoeing, it tells nothing about performance of the actual skills to be learned.

It is not meant to imply that examination of attendance records is not a useful form of program appraisal. On the contrary, perusal of attendance statistics is often an excellent means of assessing the effectiveness of program planning, organization, and staff leadership. In many cases, it is not the inherent nature of the activity itself that provides strong camper interest and satisfaction, but rather the excitement that a highly motivated and well-organized staff bring to the activity. In the case of elective programs, attendance may be one of the best criteria for assessing the relative value of different activities.

Evaluating program methodology

While it is of paramount importance to examine the program itself and its effect on the recipients, it is also vital that the manner of presentation be given careful consideration. Factors such as: control of the physical setting in which the activity is offered, planning for maximum participation, careful grouping of participants, and the manner in which the program staff are utilized, can profoundly influence the success or failure of the program, as perceived by the camper. All those factors that affect the manner of presentation should be carefully examined as part of a total program evaluation plan.

Before leaving this section on program evaluation, it may be helpful to postulate a number of questions regarding the overall camp program. These questions should serve as a simple, but efficient instrument for the initial examination of program in almost any camp. If the answer to any of these questions is negative, it is a clear indication of a problem area that requires further deliberation.

ADMINISTRATION

1. Is the total camp program coordinated under a single administrative head?
2. Is the primacy of program recognized by all administrative personnel in the camp?
3. Is program budget distributed on the basis of planned need?
4. Are facilities and equipment sufficient to meet the goals of the camp program?
5. Is the program supported by a comprehensive insurance program?

STAFF

6. Is the in-service training of program staff adequate?
7. Are all those associated with program (campers, staff, program administrators) encouraged to provide continuous evaluation of the program, and do recommendations lead to change?
8. Are seasonal written reports required of all program heads and specialists?

PROGRAM

9. Have clearly stated operational objectives been formulated for all facets of the program?
10. Does the program take into consideration the needs and interests of the campers it is intended to serve?
11. Are all human, physical, and fiscal resources utilized to their maximum potential?
12. Does the program provide for individual differences in skill, aptitude, maturity, and intellect?
13. Does the program offer sufficient emphasis on the "carry-over" value of leisure time pursuits?
14. Is careful consideration given to selecting the optimal size and makeup of program groups?

15. Is full consideration given to maximizing the method of program presentation?
16. Has special consideration been given to the planning of rainy day programs?
17. Are campers able to realize a sense of achievement through program participation?
18. Are the social values of participation stressed, including such factors as tolerance, group loyalty, and concern for others?
19. Is there ample opportunity for creative self-expression?
20. Does the program promote development of leadership skills?

EVALUATION OF THE STAFF

As was stated earlier, the success of any camp program depends largely on the quality of the leaders conducting that program. It is therefore paramount that camp administrators do everything possible to assist camp personnel in carrying out this important role. Ongoing evaluation of the staff is an important step in assisting counsellors and other staff members to perform effectively. Staff evaluation begins with recruitment of personnel. When careful evaluation of all prospective staff members is done at the time of hiring, the task of future evaluation is greatly simplified.

Problems of staff evaluation

Innumerable difficulties that are associated with staff evaluation complicate the process. The two most basic problems center around lack of agreement as to what criteria are important in assessing camp staff and the development of effective instruments to measure these criteria.

If it is accepted that the role of the camp counsellor is in many ways compatible with that of the school teacher and that similar qualities are required in the two roles, examination of studies on teacher effectiveness should help shed some light on how camp staff can be evaluated. The National Education Association reports that more time and research money has been directed toward studies of teacher evaluation than any other area of education, and in spite of this investment of time and money, much disagreement still exists regarding this controversial subject. Berry, in discussing teacher effectiveness, states: "One of the major barriers to experimental research in the field of teacher education has been the lack of satisfactory criteria of teaching success."[3] Berry also points out that human traits are so elusive and teaching and learning processes so complex that simple and objective measures of teaching effectiveness have not yet been developed. The human traits and the teaching-learning process to which Berry refers are equally applicable to the camp setting in which very little research has been conducted to determine counsellor effectiveness.

In addition to the fundamental problems of selecting valid criteria, as well as instruments for their measurement, other problems confront camp administrators as they tackle staff evaluation. Some of the more important include the following:

1. Evaluation may be seen as threatening, punitive, and of little help to the staff. Additionally, those persons responsible for staff appraisal often consider it a distasteful assignment.
2. Staff frequently complain that they are not involved to any significant degree in the evaluation process, particularly as it relates to selection of criteria and evaluation procedures.
3. Too little attention is given to self-evaluation and its potential for professional growth.
4. Staff contend that the criteria for selection are based more on the personal

bias of camp administrators than on good research or theory.
5. Poor communication exists between those being evaluated and the evaluators. Staff complain that frequently they have no knowledge of the criteria on which the evaluation is based. The result is anxiety and uncertainty on the part of the staff.
6. Staff lack confidence in the ability of those evaluating to do it accurately and objectively. In many cases, they complain that evaluation is limited to a single report, which may lead to accusations of personal bias.
7. Too often, staff are informed of their limitations but given little or no help in overcoming these weaknesses. To inform a counsellor that he or she needs "better control of campers" pinpoints the shortcoming, but unless specific suggestions are made as to how camper control can be achieved, little improvement can be expected.
8. Staff are given insufficient time to remedy weaknesses. Counsellors report that they are given a weak assessment the last week of camp and then are not hired the following season. When counsellors receive a critical report, they must have sufficient opportunity to correct the shortcomings accompanied by adequate supervision to assist them to do so.
9. Staff evaluation is too haphazard and sporadic to be truly effective. A good assessment program must be ongoing and include all those involved in program.

Recommended program of staff evaluation

In light of the numerous problems associated with staff assessment, it is not surprising that some camp administrators choose to discard it completely. The purpose of listing

---

3. Berry, J. R.: Does professional preparation make a difference? The Journal of Teacher Education, 13:386, Dec., 1962.

these potential weaknesses is not to discourage camp directors from adopting a program of staff evaluation, but rather to alert them to potential trouble areas so that weaknesses can be avoided. Evaluation of camp personnel is too important to be ignored, but much effort must be made to improve some existing practices. The increased professional growth of the staff will more than justify the effort required. The following guidelines should help camp administrators set up a staff evaluation program that overcomes the weaknesses described above and leads to a much improved program.

1. The staff evaluation process should be administered in a systematic, well-organized manner.
2. Evaluation should seek as its fundamental outcome the professional growth of each staff member. Strengths should be reinforced and weaknesses overcome.
3. Staff evaluation should be based primarily on research into staff effectiveness rather than the personal bias of those administering the program.
4. Staff should be made fully aware of the complete evaluation program before the process begins.
5. Staff should actively participate in the formulation of evaluative criteria and procedures to be followed.
6. Evaluation criteria should focus on relevant performance and avoid extraneous factors.
7. Staff evaluation should emphasize self-evaluation as well as assessment by others.
8. Evaluation must be followed by constructive supervision to assist the staff in overcoming performance shortcomings.
9. The staff evaluation process itself should be assessed regularly for purposes of identifying possible improvements.

Criteria for evaluation

Because little experimental data is available on the qualities and characteristics that make an effective camp counsellor, it is not surprising to find considerable variance among the lists of criteria that are presently used. The following observations are the result of the examination of many staff assessment forms, including some drawn from outside the camping profession.

Some camps attempt to keep their staff assessment as simple as possible and identify as few as three areas of concern: personal characteristics, quality of teaching, and special contributions to camp life. Pestolesi and Sinclair,[4] on the other hand, have developed a self-appraisal form for physical education teachers including 92 items that the teacher must check as needing none, some, or much improvement. A recreation department in New York state rates its employees under eight major headings: knowledge of duties, performance of duties, effectiveness in working with others, leadership characteristics, judgment, adaptability, use of resources, and written and oral expression.

In attempting to establish those criteria that are seen as the key elements for staff in a given camp, one effective approach is to identify the performance areas that a staff member is expected to fulfill. For example, most camp directors agree that cabin counsellors have three basic assignments: (1) supervising their cabin, (2) program and instruction duties, and (3) dining hall supervision. Some camps might add other performance areas such as special camp assignments or out-tripping if the latter was

---

4. Pestolesi, R. A., and Sinclair, W. A.: Creative administration in physical education and athletics. (Englewood Cliffs, N.J.: Prentice-Hall Inc., 1978), pp. 254-258.

featured at a given camp and was required of many counsellors.

Another approach to the evaluation counsellor performance involves listing the various groups with whom they have association and attempting to evaluate each of these realtionships. Using this approach, staff evaluation is based on counsellor-camper relationships, counsellor-parent relationships, counsellor-counsellor relationships, counsellor-administrator relationships, and counsellor-community relationships.

Because of the unique nature of performance expectations within some camps, those persons responsible for staff evaluation should, in consultation with the staff, develop specific criteria for each individual camp.

The evaluation process

There are several recognized methods of evaluating staff including personal observation, camper progress, and staff ratings.

Personal observation. Perhaps the most obvious form of staff evaluation is the continuous observation that counsellors undergo at the hands of their immediate supervisors. Early in the season, counsellors should be under almost constant supervision as they handle their daily assignments, whether it be controlling their campers around the cabin and in the dining hall, conducting instruction or camp program, or lifeguarding in the swimming area.

Staff observation can also be formalized to the extent that counsellors are forewarned by their supervisor that they will be observed as they handle a particular program. Under these conditions, the supervisor actually prepares a written evaluation and uses this as the basis for a follow-up conference.

Camper progress. The ultimate method of appraising counsellor competence is to assess what camper progress has taken place as a result of exposure to a given staff member. This technique is most effective if cabin counsellors are responsible for their campers the entire camp day. When campers are exposed to several staff members, in addition to their cabin counsellor, it is virtually impossible to determine what effect a given staff member has played when progress is measured.

Camper progress is most easily measured when individuals participate in regular instruction over a significant period. If, for example, a group of youngsters has 12 tennis lessons in a 2-week period, the progress that campers make under different counsellors may be a valid measure of the relative teaching ability of those instructors.

Staff ratings. Ratings may be done by campers, peers, supervisory personnel, or by the staff members themselves. Camper ratings are strongly affected by the maturity of the camper; ratings by 6 year olds cannot be taken as seriously as those of senior campers. When it is remembered that campers are consumers and are rating their counsellors informally all the time anyway, camp administrators should not hesitate to formalize this method of staff evaluation. Students in universities and high schools have been effectively evaluating their professors and teachers for some years, so camp administrators should be encouraged to use this technique with older campers.

When staff members are invited to evaluate each other, experience has shown that a minimum of three ratings is desirable to prevent personal friendship or bias from interfering with the objectivity of these assessments. When a peer evaluation is used, it is frequently combined with an interview or conference to which raters are invited.

Self-evaluation can be a very effective form of appraisal if staff members do not feel threatened by the entire process but consider it as an ongoing means of gaining insights into better staff performance. As long as staff members feel anxious and see evaluation as negative criticism, self-rating will have little value. But when evaluation is conducted in an atmosphere of mutual trust between staff and administration, it has the potential to become the highest level of appraisal since it comes from within and does not rely on some external agent to point out strengths and weaknesses.

The most common form of staff rating is that which is done by a supervisor or administrative head. To be effective, this type of evaluation depends on confidence and respect between the two parties. This relationship requires a rapport that can best be achieved in an equal partnership type of arrangement rather than the traditional boss-worker association. Counsellors must believe that they are free to talk openly about their performance and ask questions regarding problems they are experiencing. It is not a time for negative criticism by the supervisor, but rather an opportunity to let counsellors know how well they are doing. Evaluation conferences should not be called only when a problem arises, but should be marked by ongoing relationship between two persons in which both are striving to help the counsellor gain better insight regarding strengths and weaknesses.

From the above, it should be clear that staff evaluation and supervision are interdependent: one cannot be effective without the other. Staff evaluation that is not supported through supervisory conferences marked by open exchange, can lead to frustration and resistance to the entire evaluative process. Conversely, staff supervision that is not based on prior evaluation, frequently lacks direction and therefore is seen as an aimless exercise by the counsellor.

It is suggested that scheduled evaluation conferences between a staff member and supervisor be held at least three times during the normal 8-week camp season. These should be scheduled a few days after camp opens, at midseason, and at the end of camp. It is assumed that many informal meetings will take place between these scheduled sessions.

A written rating scale can take many forms, ranging from an open-ended evaluation form on which the rater is asked to list strengths and shortcomings and comment fully on these to a formalized checklist on which the evaluator rates a number of characteristics on a four- or five-point scale. Some rating forms are comprised of a number of questions to which the respondent answers either "yes" or "no." Regardless of the format, the form should provide for identification of areas of concern and suggestions as to how these shortcomings may be ameliorated. These recommendations should form the basis for at least part of the follow-up conference.

EVALUATION OF THE ADMINISTRATION
Administrators

The importance of the administrative role has been the theme of this entire book. No single force exerts more influence on the entire camp operation than the quality of the administration. The development and implementation of camp policies and programs, recruitment and selection of camp staff, disposition of fiscal resources, and all other matters of consequence are under the administrator's jurisdiction. Because of the profound influence that administration has on the quality of the camp experience, it is essential that those in administration be exposed to the scrutiny of the evaluative process.

Camp administrators who possess a positive self-image and feel secure in the conduct of their duties should welcome constructive criticism and suggestions from

```
                        ADMINISTRATOR EVALUATION FORM

Administrator's name_____ Date_____

Note:  In order to assist administrative personnel
       to improve their effectiveness, you are
       asked to assess the person whose name
       appears above.
```

A list of 20 traits that are considered to be important for camp administrators is found below. Place a check (✔) in the appropriate column on the right. Additional comments are welcomed regarding the individual or the camp administration generally.

	Outstanding	Above average	Average	Needs improvement	Poor
1. Demonstrates insight and vision regarding camp objectives and long-range plans	—	—	—	—	—
2. Sets high standards for the staff and camp	—	—	—	—	—
3. Possesses the physical stamina and drive to handle the rigors of the position	—	—	—	—	—
4. Demonstrates pleasant personality and good communication skills	—	—	—	—	—
5. Is consistent and fair: does not play favorites	—	—	—	—	—
6. Solves problems rationally: can come right to the heart of things	—	—	—	—	—
7. Gets along well with other people	—	—	—	—	—
8. Demonstrates ability to get staff to work to-gether as a team	—	—	—	—	—
9. Recognizes staff contributions and a job well done	—	—	—	—	—
10. Is approachable and a good listener	—	—	—	—	—
11. Takes personal interest in each staff member	—	—	—	—	—
12. Welcomes and respects the opinions of others	—	—	—	—	—
13. Instills confidence and trust	—	—	—	—	—
14. Criticizes constructively	—	—	—	—	—
15. Is continuously alert to new ideas	—	—	—	—	—
16. Has ability to recruit competent staff and place the right person in the right position	—	—	—	—	—
17. Encourages the professional growth of staff	—	—	—	—	—
18. Is well informed at all times regarding the total camp operation	—	—	—	—	—
19. Delegates responsibility and authority effectively	—	—	—	—	—
20. Encourages effective, continuous evaluation	—	—	—	—	—

Comments:

Fig. 11-5. Sample form for evaluation of administrators.

colleagues, campers, parents, and camp committee members. Much can be learned from each of these sources that could help administrators fulfill their roles more effectively.

Boles and Davenport[5] suggest that leaders are made up of five different "selves": (1) the way they would like to be, (2) the way they see themselves, (3) the way they act, (4) the way others would like them to be, and (5) the way others see them. The degree of congruence that exists between these various "selves" says a great deal about their effectiveness in an administrative role. Self-examination can tell the leader much about selves 1, 2, and 5 and is therefore an important component of administrator evaluation. The purpose of self-assessment is aptly summarized in the following statement by Brouwer:

The function of self-examination is to lay the groundwork for insight, without which no growth can occur, Insight is the "oh I see now" feeling which must, consciously or unconsciously, precede change in behavior. Insights—real, genuine glimpses of ourselves as we really are—are reached only with difficulty and sometimes with real psychic pain.[6]

Many evaluation instruments have been developed to assess administrators in business, industry, and education, but few appear to have been constructed for specific use with camp personnel. Fig. 11-5 provides a sample instrument that should assist directors in preparing such a form for their own camp.

Administrative services

Not only should those who manage the various camp services be part of the evaluation process, but the services themselves should be subject to the same careful assessment. No area of the camp should be exempt from appraisal.

Camp property, facilities, and equipment must be inspected regularly not only for purposes of safety and good maintenance, but also with a view to possible improvements. The suggestions of campers, parents, and staff regarding additions or changes should also receive careful consideration.

The health and safety program of the camp should come under continuous examination. Are there some activities that have an unduly high accident rate? If so, what are they, and how can the injuries be reduced? Have cabin counsellors received sufficient instruction in identifying minor health problems among campers? Have all possible precautions been taken to minimize the danger of accidents on out-trips? Can the daily routine for treating campers at the health center be improved? These and many other questions should form the basis of evaluation in this important area.

Similarly, the food service operation must be assessed regarding such matters as the cost efficiency of camper meals, quality of the menu, effectiveness of the sanitation program, and efficiency of dining hall management. Because of the technical nature of some of these considerations, appraisal be outside experts may be required to ensure that all possible steps are being taken to provide safe, efficient service.

Regular review should be made of camper recruitment practices, the public relations program of the camp, and the record keeping system, as well as the manner in which the budget is prepared. In short, just as campers, CITs, junior counsellors, section heads, food service, maintenance, medical staff, and all management staff, including the camp director, should be evaluated, so too every facet of program and camp ser-

5. Boles, H. W., and Davenport, J. A.: Introduction to educational leadership. (New York: Harper & Row Publishers, 1975) pp. 305-307.
6. Brouwer, P. J.: The power to see ourselves, Harvard Business Review, 42. 166-182, 1964.

vices should be submitted to regular appraisal.

AFTER EVALUATION—WHAT?

Evaluation must not simply be a summarizing of those things that the camp did well and those that the camp did not achieve or accomplish. As Jack Pearse, former President of the Canadian Camping Association, has stated: "Evaluation is fruitless exercise if its purpose is to prepare for what was happening yesterday."[7] The heart of the evaluation process lies in the implementation of the recommendations that grow out of the process. Unless careful consideration of the data gathered leads to implementation of new ideas or confirmation that present programs and procedures are the best that can be offered, the entire process has been an exercise in futility. If camp administrators have adopted a thoughtful, comprehensive evaluation process, they can be confident that the results of this program will lead to new ideas and innovations that can only result in a more rewarding camp experience for hundreds of thousands of boys and girls and men and women as each new camp season begins.

ADMINISTRATIVE GUIDELINES

1. Evaluation is the vital culminating phase of the total administrative function in camp.
2. Everyone who is directly involved in shaping the total camp experience should participate in the evaluation process, including campers, parents, counsellors, administrators, as well as those who are responsible for each camp service.
3. Evaluation is a continuous process; it should not be limited to a few busy days at the end of each camp season.
4. Total camp appraisal involves informal as well as formal assessment. It includes subjec-

---

7. Pearce, J.: Evaluation of your operation, Report of the 1971 Ontario Camping Association Convention, Toronto, 1971, p. 33.

tive and objective evaluation and is concerned with quantitative as well as qualitative judgments.
5. For camp administrators to determine what it is they wish to evaluate, they must have a clear understanding of the goals and outcomes sought.
6. Camp evaluation is all-embracive and includes appraisal of camper, program, staff, facilities and equipment, and all supporting administrative services.
7. Whereas counsellors should be expected to play a major role in camper assessment, parents can also shed valuable insight as to the camper's true appreciation of the camp experience.
8. The camp program should be subjected to continuous appraisal by campers, counsellors, and program administrators. Since the program is the primary vehicle through which camp objectives are realized, it should be under constant examination and revision. Program evaluation should also include careful scrutiny of the manner in which programs are organized and conducted.
9. In spite of debate as to whether acceptable criteria exist for evaluation of staff, the best instruments available should be used until further research provides clearer directions as to how staff should be appraised.
10. Camp administrators must be alert to the weaknesses that staff members have identified in present methods of evaluation and every effort should be made to overcome these shortcomings.
11. The staff evaluation process should include personal observations by supervisors, examination of camper progress, and written staff ratings. Consideration should be given to ratings prepared by campers, peers, supervisory personnel, and staff members themselves. Self-appraisal can be an extremely effective evaluation device if carefully planned.
12. Successful staff-supervisor evaluation is contingent on a relationship that is characterized by confidence and mutual respect. This is the essence of the supervisory process.
13. The camp management team should not be

exempt from evaluation, not only by members of the administrative team itself, but by other groups including campers, parents, and junior and intermediate staff members.

14. All administrative services should be continuously appraised, including evaluation of the camp property and facilities and equipment, particularly in reporting any hazardous condition in camp. In addition, food, health, maintenance, business, and general administrative services should all be reviewed not only by those responsible for each service but by others external to each operation.

15. Evaluation should lead to change for the better. Unless the assessment process results in improved programming and camper services, there is little justification for the entire procedure.

SELECTED BIBLIOGRAPHY

Christensen, B.: Staff evaluations, Convention Report of the Ontario Camping Association, 1976, pp. 167-171.

Garton, R. A.: School administration: challenge and opportunity for leadership. (Dubuque, Iowa: Wm. C. Brown Co., Publishers, 1976). Chapter 10.

Hall, J. T. et al.: Administration: principles, theory and practice with applications to physical education. (Pacific Palisades, Calif.: Goodyear Publishing Co., Inc., 1973). Chapter 6.

Lowes, B.: How to evaluate your camp, Canadian Camping, **29**:(5):1-12, Oct., 1977.

Rabinowitz, A.: Ongoing evaluation can help counsellors do a better job, Camping Magazine, **35**(5):14, Apr., 1963.

Rodney, L. S., and Ford, P. M.: Camp administration. (New York, John Wiley & Sons, 1971). pp. 164-168 and 205-215.

Slate, L. M.: How to see yourself as your employees see you, School management, pp. 88-91, June, 1966.

van der Smissen, B.: Evaluation and self study of public recreation and park agencies: a guide with standards and evaluative criteria. (Arlington, Va.; National Recreation and Park Association, 1972).

van der Smissen, B.: Research camping and environmental education. (University Park, Penn.: Penn State HPER Series No. 11, 1976).

Voltmer, E. F., et al.: The organization and administration of physical education. (Englewood Cliffs, N.J.: Prentice-Hall Inc., 1979). Chapter 18.

Index